# THE SCENTED GARDEN

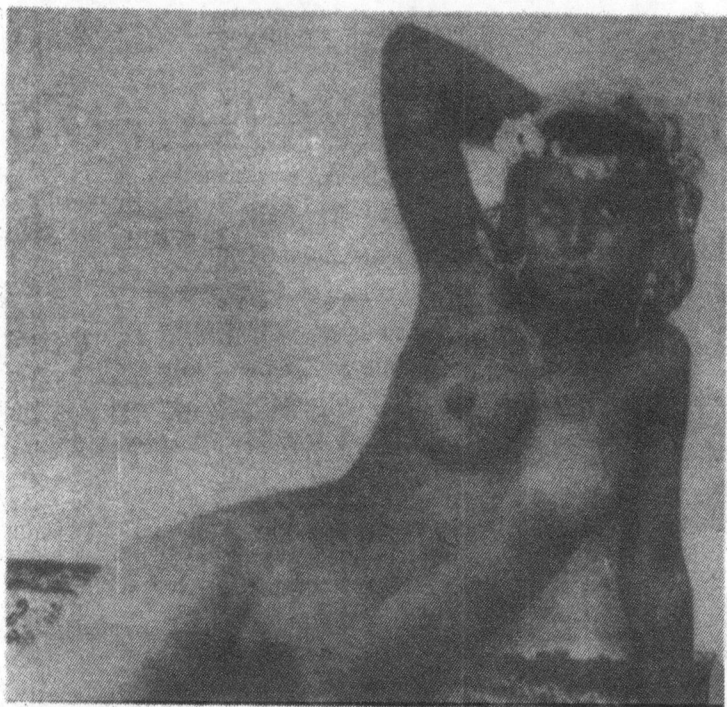

*Sixteen-year-old Girl from Barbary*

*The Scented Garden*

# ANTHROPOLOGY
## OF THE SEX LIFE IN THE LEVANT

## By BERNHARD STERN M.D.
*Translated by DAVID BERGER M.A.*

Fredonia Books
Amsterdam, The Netherlands

The Scented Garden:
Anthropology of the Sex Life
in the Levant

by
Bernhard Stern M.D.
Translated by David Berger M.A.

ISBN 1-58963-088-2

Reprinted from the 1934 edition

Fredonia Books
Amsterdam, The Netherlands
http://www.FredoniaBooks.com

# CONTENTS

vii

x

# LOVE AND LOVE CHARMS

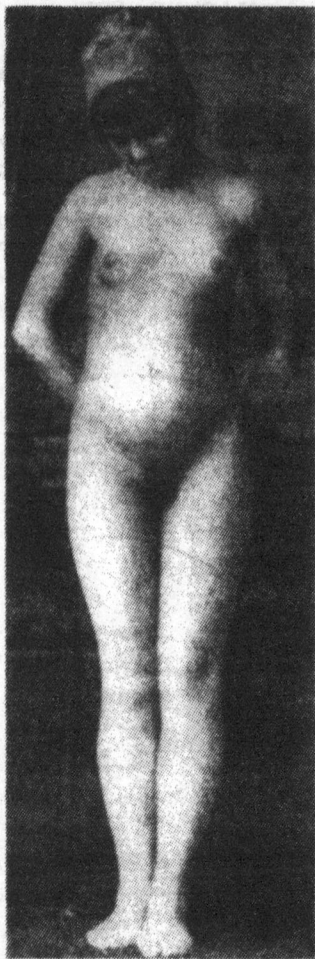

*Fourteen-year-old Bohemian*

Love potions have been used in all times!

Ovid wrote of their power to make persons of both sexes, who at first were quite indifferent to each other, to fall in love. The power of such love potions were often only psychic and harmless; in other cases the drinks consisted of poisonous matter, which, however, worked charms on the libido, the so-called aphrodisiacs; at times a person of the female sex through stupefaction was transported into a deep sleep by strammonium, hyoscyamus or belladonna, so that the debaucher had little difficulty in satisfying his lust.

Older people need such love potions to inoculate, like the virus of small-pox, the object of their offering for mutual love. The Italian Porta relates of the miracles effected by hippomanes, a black skin, the size of a dried fig, which grew on the forehead of a new born foal, which when burnt to a powder by the Greeks was used, with the blood of the beloved, as a love philtre. The Romans knew how to prepare similar love potions. Lucullus is said to have lost his mind, and finally his life through such a drink. A similar misfortune befell the poet Lucretius, who took his life under the spell of love. Apuleius is supposed to have won the heart of the wealthy Pudentilla with the use of such a philtre, composed of asparagus, crabs' tails, fish spawn, pigeon blood, and the tongue of one of Aesop's fabulous birds.

A superstition exists in France that a man can make himself beloved if he carries on his heart the head of a hawk, or if he gives the object of his love the last hair of a fox's tail to swallow. Marx in his researches revealed the ingredients of love potions of former times: a branch of laurel, the brain of a sperling, the bones from the left side of an ant-eaten toad, the blood and heart of a dove, the testicles of an ass, a horse, a hen, and most particularly menstrual blood. More will be said later in this section concerning the last, also in the chapter on menstruation.

In the present day orient the belief in love charms exists among the Moslems as well as among the Christians and Jews of high and low degree.

A southern peasant named Nowak Opalitsch, living in Zabigje, after a communication from Frederich S. Krauss for love anecdotes employed the following *oracle of the coal*: He threw two pieces of coal along the surface of water, one for the boy, the other for the girl. If the fates will it that the boy and girl become mated, then the two pieces of coal immediately come together. If it happens that the girl desires the boy, but he does not care for her, or vice versa, then one coal pursues the other but it cannot overtake it.

In order to win the mutual love of a shy person, superstitious Bosnians gaze upon the beloved object through a charmed ring, and she is thereupon consumed with burning love for the person looking upon her. Such ring—says a Moslem sage—caused a young Turk in Dervent to kill his own father. A pretty woman wished to conquer the son and looked at her beloved through her magic ring; a glance grazed the father, and now father and son were simultaneously inflamed with wild passion for the same girl, so that the jealous youth murdered his father.

A Serbian remedy for love charm, among the Serbians, the Montenegrins and the Herzegowiners, was called *cabbage* by the southern Slavs. According to the report from Leist this

16

*cabbage* is none other than the Doldengrowth, *Liguisticum offi-cinale*, which had been used in Germany for superstitious pur-poses with reference to awakening or averting love, as the German love-tree indicates. In Europe the root of the love-tree is sold even today as a remedy for sicknesses of the domes-tic animals. The plant is seldom found in middle Europe, but it is frequently met with in the warmer mountain regions of European Turkey. The Turks call it: *amus*; the Arabs: *kemun meluki*; the Persians: *nancha*; the Indians: *dschoanni*.

The Roumanian peasant girl knows, as Flachs tells us, the following little methods of drawing to her the love of a given man, who is alone, or to alienate the affections of another girl or woman. The young woman winds a metal violin string, such as the G string, around her finger into a ball. The string then has the power to soften the hardest man's heart, so it manifestly stands in somewhat of a mystic tie with the hearts of men. The ball is then sewn to the seam of her underwear. In the course of the same day the maiden must say the following little speech thrice at different times, "As the string is wound around my finger, so must his senses and thoughts revolve about me!" The maiden kneads a man's figure out of wax, places it before the blazing fire, and says: "As this puppet softens at the fire, so should the heart of my beloved soften for me!"—Older girls desiring marriage may find the following advice. of the Gypsies helpful. The maid must go to a herdsman's cottage, but she must be careful not to awaken the dog which is watch-ing the cottage. From the cattle trough she must take a lump of salt and go home with it. On the following day she must salt her food properly. To that she must add a luck-bringing spice or plant—garlic, basilien leaves, evergreen, or a pine twig. After a comfortable meal she should remain in the sun for the entire day without quenching her thirst. During the next night there will appear in her dreams a man deter-mined by fate who will bring her water and ride home as her

17

husband. This dream will soon become reality. The Roumanian women know many more incantations whose recitation under carefully prepared formulas brings success in love. The following magic love-speech, faithfully translated from Flachs will serve as an example: "On Sunday morning, as the day dawned, I arose, left my house and table and on the way, on the small bridge to the wide street, the people who saw me said, 'That is Marghiola, the beautiful, not Diana, the beautiful, but Marghiola, the kind, about whom the whole world has read!' Just as the Hibiscus is chosen of all flowers, of all scents; just as the Pope cannot go into the church without Hibiscus and without Isope—so shall not the boys be able to dance without her. All other maidens shall look like crows beside her, dirty crows which one throws over the hedge." This magic love-speech must be recited over a water-filled dish, in which there have been placed Hibiscus leaves tied with red silk cord, a coin, and a pine twig.

The Kamasutra says in the section on "Various Practices": "The woman who hears a man blow upon a reed-pipe is afflicted with *Salvinia cucullata, Costus species, Tabernaemontana coronaria, Flacourtia cataphracta, Pinus deodora* and *Asteracantha longifolia*, and becomes subject to him. In the section on "the enchantment of women" an ointment is named from the leaves of *Tabernaemontana coronaria. Costus species (arabicus)* and *Flacourtia cataphracta* bring about enchantment. Another ointment is the oil, composed of the leaves of *Boerhavia procumbens, Sida cordifolia (rhombfolia), Ichnocarpus frutescens* (or *Hemidesmus inducus*), yellow amarynth and blue lotus; garlands are also woven of these. He who uses a powder of dried Nebumbium species, blue lotus and *Mesua roxburghii* with honey and melted butter, will become rapacious. These, tied with the leaves of *Tabernaemontana coronaria, Flacourtia cataphracta* and *Xantochymus pictorius* make another salve. If one carries the eye of a peacock or a hyena streaked with

18

favorite presented to her sister-in-law, the wife of Kaimakam-pascha Redscheb, at her delivery of a female child; such a present and such disturbance over the birth of a girl, the daughter of a Vizier, had never been heard of before.

Under Sultan Mustafa III, the birth of the Princess Hebe-tullah, the first child of the Sultan, was celebrated with the extraordinary seven-day illumination, usually reserved for the birth of a prince. A month before the birth the prominent men of the guilds and the markets were instructed to keep themselves in readiness for an extraordinary decoration and illumination of the city. The whole city, therefore, swam in joy and a flood of light; poetry, laughter, and enthusiasm reigned. On the seventh day, in the name of the Vizier, the minister of the interior brought a golden cradle, set with precious stones. If Mustafa III celebrated the birth of a daughter to such an extent, it is not surprising that at the birth of the crown prince Selimhe he directed that the city be illuminated for seven nights and the sea for three nights with a flood of light. Captives from the Bango were given their freedom, among them several Catholic Armenians. The mother of the prince was a Georgian slave. Their joy was tempered by the death of the first-born daughter, Hebetullah, who had been engaged while yet in her cradle.

In several passages the Koran takes no notice of man's supremacy over woman. Chapter IV, 36: "Unto the men shall be given a portion of what they shall have gained, and to the women shall be given a portion of what they shall have gained."

IV, 38: "We have appointed unto every one kindred, to inherit part of what their parents and relations shall leave at their death." The Koran frequently objects sharply to any failure to give a woman her just due; so in VI, 140: "That which is in the bellies of these cattle is allowed to our males to eat, and is forbidden to our wives: but if it prove abortive, then they are both partakers thereof."

"O maiden, red apple,
The summer shall not pass
Ere I shall climb upon you."

"O, my lover, my Atlas bolster,
The summer shall not pass
Ere I shall lay myself beneath you."

The love of which the Persian poets sing in their poems has also either a symbolic or a highly profane meaning; the word *Ischk*—Love—is always followed by the idea *Was'l*, the sexual intermingling.

In the higher class of superstitions the Persians have many about charms, magic, and lucky stars, especially in matters of love, and they use all kinds of means and amulets of the strangest nature to catch a man or at least to interfere with the fertility of their rivals. Dr. Polak tells of a famous tower near Isjbahan to which girls and widows betake themselves to get their man. They ride in two stages; upon each must be placed a nut which the pilgrim must crack while reciting a certain curse. It is often dangerous to play the part of the magician of love. So it is said that in Turkey about the time of Achmed III, on the report of the Governor of Rakka: that the Persian Shah known by the name Ebubekr and by the nicknames *Seijah*, the Rapacious, through the art of magic fooled the people and betrayed the women—he was executed. History tells us of an instance in the regime of the same nobleman, that the mere thought of arousing love was penalized with death, because this thought secretly involved a woman of the Sultan's harem; the unlucky thinker was the nephew of the mighty Grandvizier Koprili, the master of the stable, Kiblelisade Alibeg; neither his own position nor his uncle's protection could save him.

In Volume IV of his history, Hammer mentions this noteworthy incident "one of the historians of the kingdom of

Raschid, given to the most authentic reports, says delicately yet clearly that nothing in Osman history surpasses the capital offense of profaning the emperor's harem." The penalty is fixed by the Kislaraga, the head eunuch: because "Alibeg was one of those men whose body was preserved in the treasure of chastity, secretly faithful." So not the deed, not the rendezvous, but the mere attachment, the secret desire for either a wife or a slave of the emperor's harem appears here as a crime against the state, which brought a martyr's death to the concealer of that unhappy love.

The dominion of Achmed III was famous for such strange cases. For Hammer reports an other interesting incident. This happened to a rich Persian Armenian, who was known at Constantinople by the name *Gumischmemdase*, silver-mass. Rumor has it that he caroused with an immoral woman during her husband's absence; apprehended in her house, he was brought before the court. Although prejudice existed against him' "because the Persian Armenian was in the habit of pursuing women," yet the evidence of his damnable lewdness was not easily obtainable; so a crowd of zealous Moslems showed the court, "that this cursed unbeliever, with the arch of the devil's restlessness, had spoken to the Moslem women in passing, and for this offense he was sentenced to be hanged and, in the presence of the Vizier, in the Persian-Armenian quarter, the sentence was executed.

According to the laws of Islam, this last reason is sufficient for execution; but besides this no one receives the death sentence even if he is of lovable temperament with a maniacal tendency towards conquest, and has high bushy eyebrows. . . .

Although love-magic in Turkey is not at all free from danger, the Turkish love physiologist prescribes many means of enchantment and recommends especially the *blood oath:* If a man wishes to possess a woman—for the ultimate goal of *love* among the orientals is coitus—and if the woman stands opposite him, then he places all his hopes and his entire desire into his eyes. If he then gazes upon the beloved woman, he must stare into her eyes, press his left arm sufficiently to start the blood in motion; and when the beloved woman is near enough to hear him, he must say: "There is no God besides God! And so it is certain that my blood will dry up before my desire to possess you can be suffocated!" These signs of the desire for love must cleverly infuse the imagination of the woman, so that her fantasy becomes the advocate for the lover and immediately pleads his cause. In the organs of the woman there develops an irritation which makes sensuality the mistress over her body. And of all the organs of the woman the womb is the most impressionable and is the one which has the greatest power over the brain, with the result that the excitement in the womb of the woman compels her to give up her opposition and drives the beloved person into the arms of her lover. If this method does not work the first time, then it must be tried again, and even a third time. One must also send his beloved red roses upon which he has blown his wishes three times with his entire soul. If you can come closer to the woman, infuse her even more with your glances, fascinate her, command her to love you and to belong to you. If you cannot come close to her or if you have no opportunity to speak to her and perhaps to touch her forehead with your index finger, then ride by her window, speeding your horse dauntlessly, or stand hours long before her house and stare upon it continuously. Music and song are also powerful methods of spiritual love-magic."

The enchantment which is born of a glance is called: *Asimah;* the good suggestion: *Ahham;* the bad suggestion: *Rorr.* A twig of *Asimah* is jealousy or fascination. As soon as the charm of the glance begins to take effect and you are near the enchanted person, place your hand upon hear head and command her with authority, but in a sweet tone and gently, to do your bidding. If she is in the midst of a crowd, say to

22

her: Follow me! . . . This fascination works as well with a woman whom one wishes to possess as with an animal which he wishes to tame."

I am beginning to gather the customs and superstitions which fate presents to husbands and wives in marriage, love, and faithfulness.

In Morocco the skin of a bat is smoked with the rosin from the root of an *unbellifere*. If the woman places this remedy in the clothes of her faithless husband, she is certain to win back his love. According to the Syrian, Eijub Abela, the following customs are prevalent in Syria: the number which forms the proportion of subjects does not have to be accurate; but if it is accurate there is the danger that a woman will marry more than one man if she loses her first husband through his death or if he disowns her. If the woman-subject who belongs to her proportion stands or lies inverted, her husband must do mischief to her. If she inadvertently puts on another woman's shoe, she will immediately lose her husband through death. A woman must not give the flowers from her hair to any other woman; that one takes with the flowers the love of her husband. The Christian in Syria believes that her husband does not love her if he awakes with the rising sun, gets up, and leaves the house. The Mohammedan woman becomes melancholy if the sea begins to rise at the moment when she is bathing: that indicates to her that her husband is becoming estranged from her. To recapture an unfaithful husband Christian and Mohammedan women alike must employ the following means if they wish to be perfectly certain of success. The stricken woman secretly places some of her urine in a drink which she gives to her faithless husband. As a result of this he again falls in love with her. The immediate effect which women ascribe to urine encourages young maidens to use a drop of their monthly flow if they wish to awaken love in a certain man. The last mentioned superstition exists not only

23

in the orient but also in central Europe.  On the other hand, if a man in Syria wishes to arouse the love of his wife again, or to prevent her from being unfaithful, he must cut his nails, burn the part cut off and secretly place the ashes into a drink or food for his wife.

In Bosnia if a man is untrue to his wife, the stricken one goes to the abode of the Wise Woman.  She fetches a frog, lays it in a copper pan, and roasts the animal gradually over an open coal fire.  From the painstricken trembling of the martyred animal the Heart-healer evolves the method for recreating the love of the faithless husband.

If the Roumanian girl wants to discover whether her intended husband is rich or poor, so she says—as Flachs reports from Roumanian sources—on St. Vasil's day, which falls on the first of January, beginning at a favored spot, she must count the posts of a fence backwards, beginning with ten and ending with one.  If the last found peg is encrusted her husband will be rich; if the peg is smooth, poverty is the fate of the marriage.  The Roumanian peasant girl can predict whether her marriage will be a happy one: a water filled bucket, in which an over-ripe cabbage, a little branch of an apple tree, and a silver coin have been placed, is permitted to stand throughout New Year's night.  If her intended husband appears in her dream with "greens" such as plants or leaves, that foretells a happy marriage; if she dreams of buffalos, or only of a buffalo, then the sun will not shine upon the happiness of her home.

In the following manner the Roumanian bride determines how she will fare generally in her contemplated marriage: a friendly woman, who is known to have a good, luck-bringing hand, reads the future.  She retires to a small chamber and places four bowls on the table.  In one of the bowls she puts a hog bristle, in the second, flowers, in the third, several of those gold threads which form a part of the bride's headdress, and in the fourth, bread.  The bowls are thereupon covered with

24

cloths. The anxious maiden enters and chooses. She lifts a cloth and knows at once where she is: if she has chosen the bowl with the hog bristle, there is valid cause to anticipate sorrow, for that means that her husband will be old and the marriage unhappy; flowers indicate few but happy days; the gold threads, that she shall know no want, she shall find the world lucky, nevertheless her heart will be nourished on bitterness; the bread indicates untroubled happiness in marriage.

## CHAPTER TWO

# MARRIAGE IN ISLAM: THE KORAN AND POLYGAMY

*The Bible on the holiness of marriage—Indian Conceptions—Mohammedan aspect of the purpose of marriage—God and family—The unmarried status according to the interpretation of the Roumanians—Moses on polygamy—Jewish polygamy at the present time—Moslem polygamy—Introduction of polygamy in the Osman domain—The Turk Omer Haleby makes a point for polygamy—Polygamy of the heathen Arab—The Koran—Forbidden marriages—Exceptional laws for prophets—Marriages in Persia—Rental marriages.*

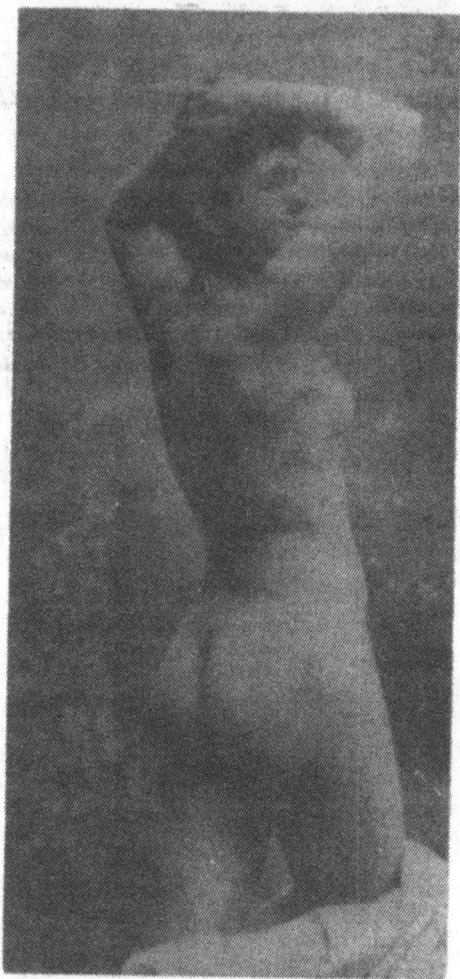

*Twenty-three-year-old Russian*

Prophet Ezekiel, XVI; 1: characterizes the holiness of marriage, as he reproaches Jerusalem with its faithlessness and compares it symbolically with a prostitute. It is pictured as the woman whom he had raised and fostered, made great and charming through his kindness, and how it happened that when her time for love had come: " . . . and I spread my skirt over thee, and covered thy nakedness; yea, I sware unto thee, and entered into a covenant with thee, saith the Lord God, and thou becamest mine. But thou didst trust in thine own beauty, and playedst the harlot because of thy renown, and pourest out thy fornications on every one that passed by. . . ."

Just as the Old Testament—it is only remembered for its lofty poetry—old Indian writers on religion also portray love and marriage. Bhartrihari says: "In this world love is meant to join two hearts in a single thought. If the feeling is not deep, it is like the union of two corpses. Marriage without love is a body without a soul, says Tiruvalluver, the godly outcast." Among the Moslems, however, the sensual is most important: one day Ali, the son-in-law of Mohammed, asked the prophet about marriage and coitus. The prophet answered: "Coitus is one of the reasons for maintaining our health. Each of you who is capable of intermingling should get married; marriage tempers wicked desires and guides one from the road that leads to incest and adultery." The sacredness of the family is essential for piety. The Koran commands, IX 24: "Speak, as if your fathers and your sons and your brothers and your wives are dearer to you than Allah and his messengers, . . . and wait until Allah comes with his commands. . . ." And in 64 sub. 14 it is said: "O, you who believe! You have an enemy in your wives and children!" in other words, providence can take care of those who forget the service of God.

Among the Christian Balkan peoples to remain continually in an unmarried state is considered as inexcusable, yes even— as among the Roumanian peasant folk—as sin, which, except through abundant donations—spending for church purposes— cannot easily be forgiven.

In Deuteronomy XVII, 17: it is said: " . . . Neither shall he multiply wives to himself, that his heart turn not away." But in II, Chronicles XI, 21: it is related: "And Rehoboam loved Maachah the daughter of Absolom above all his wives and his concubines: for he took eighteen wives and three score concubines; and begat twenty and eight sons and three score daughters." In I, Kings XI, 1 and 3: it is made known that King Solomon had 700 wives and 300 concubines.

Even the present day Jews in the orient, especially in Arabia, Syria, and Palestine, are partly polygamists and do not recognize the laws for monogamy set down by Rabbi Gerson in the twelfth century. They take the liberty to marry a second wife if the first one has no children or even if she has failed to bring any boys into the world. As with the Moslems, however, the first wife may demand that the second be given a separate household. As a noteworthy comment, Dr. Polak remarks that polygamy does not flourish among the Jews who live in Persia.

Polygamy is not generally as universal among the Moslems as Europeans think. Vincent relates that in a number of Moorish tribes of the West Sahara he did not find a single man who had more than one wife. The Turks also are mostly satisfied with one life-companion. Only rich and distinguished people marry more than one woman and in addition buy themselves slaves; although open slave trade is forbidden, it nevertheless flourishes secretly. The cost of a slave varies between $20 to $2,000.

Nothing will be said here for or against polygamy. I only wish to report what Hammer has to say in opposition from the historical point of view, and then permit a word to a modern Turkish love physiologist, Omer Haleby, for a characteristic defense of polygamy.

The majority of women who demand domestic peace and who do not have to demand the unity of the family—so Hammer thinks—have for the longest time, among the Asiatics as among the African people, prevailed over the despotism and superiority of man, while there where the urge of a man for more than one wife is prevalent, there exists no such resulting life comradeship and enjoyment of a united destiny, but all are degraded alike. This aspect of barbaric policies is doubly false, according to good sources verified by history; in the first place, particularly there where polygamy is lawful, the preference for a noble manly nature is recognized as the true man rather than the superfluous play of his lust, of which the Osman history in Roxelane, the powerful consort of Sulaimus the Great is a shining example; secondly: those vulgar natures, who are only the slaves of sensual lust, without the predominating will power and purpose in life, laughing among themselves, share in degradation before other deserving favorites the shreds of the torn raiments of the glory of the ruler and the happiness of the people, of which the domain of Sultan Ibrahim is a noteworthy example.

In another place Hammer writes the following on polygamy and the status of the woman in the Orient: the level upon which woman stands as wife, as consort, as courtesan is

31

clearly distinguished in Asia Minor just as in Europe, but the Asiatic language has no word for the housewife, but only for the man of the house; in the other designations of the relationship of woman to man lies the concept of a separate establishment or a chamber for a particular reason. The Arabian word *harem*, erroneously considered a synonym for lottery in Europe, indicates the idea of untouchable holiness. The Persian *schebistan* means night—or sleep-making, and the Turkish *odalik*—which drifted into European languages through the French *odalisque*—comes nearest to the German lady. The eastern countries consider women in their ordinary environment, not as persons, and not as things, but as a private room for lust, inviolable by strangers, as a chamber, as the German little chamber or consort shows. In another it is favored with the name of *the Mother and the Son*; one is called the *walide*; one who brings forth, the other *chasseki*, the innermost; one has supervision over the harem, the other is devoted to the innermost lusts; and now one, and now the other, but often both are taken in as part of the household, so that the Arabic and Persian title, "The lady and mistress of the harem," which should be confined to the particular household, is often in reality extended to the lady of the land and the mistress of the ruler.

As far back as in ancient Persia, the incubator of the most cultured despotism and the most ingenious slavery, examples are not lacking that women were not only the mistresses of the harem but also of the kings, were not only the tyrants of the heart but also of the kingdom, at which it was remarked that four times the number of legitimate wives, according to Islam law, already found themselves among the four consorts of Darius, named Atossa, Artystone, Parmys, and Phaidyme. The Persian Roxelane has thrown light on the Turkish customs through the name "the brilliant"; and even so the Osman desire for power, the Persian imperiousness "born of a Peri";

through the bloody measures of an expiring dominion, was of historical significance. The fighting finish and the valor of Rhodogune, who—conceived to have been attired in curls—sat on her horse with her hair down, as she received the tidings of the attack of the enemy and did not look after herself until she had vanquished the enemy, finds its parallel among the Turks in manly Mute, with whom Kosem, the Greek, served in the army for the maintenance of her rule. In the pre-Osman, Tatter, and Turkish history, stand out the names of great women, who shared the kingdom as mother or favorite of the son or as consort of the ruler; only the history of the Arabic dynasty knows but one or two names of female rulers of noted achievement, but there are therefore more religious and learned women and poetesses, or romantic ideals of beauty and love. The despotism of the Caliph, the king of kings of the Persian domain does not lag behind in iron and bloody force, yet the Arab pays that homage to women which purveys the spirit of Arabian chivalry, and which, filtered through the walls of Europe by the crusades, has tempered the rudeness of European nobility. From these historical facts—thinks Hammer—it is evident that the intermingling of women as rulers in the history of the country is not inconsistent with greatest despotism; on the contrary, that very same respectfulness and homage is not recognized as a right to take part in governmental functions; that the Asiatic despotism is not, as some writers think, derived from the compulsion of the harem, nor vice versa, for even among the liberty loving Greeks, women were in no better position than in the eastern harem, and even under the despot Joche, the Arabian caliph, the blossoming of noble women-homage was displayed by song and sword.

According to the Arabs, the custom of reverencing women gives rise to all of the nobler feelings in man, the subjugation of all passion under the same ennobling sceptre of love, the loftiest attire for honor and speech, the disclosed mastery over rivals, but not in the command of the kingdom, which has descended to man legitimately and through the right of the mighty. Of this delicacy of Arabian emotion the Turkish nature has no inkling, and yet Osman history shows us that the despots were often commanded by their slaves, and the potentates by their harems.

The Russian Roxelane, the Venetian Baffa, the Greek Kosem, and other women, so Hammer closes his remarks, have finally taken command of the Sultan, and through him a part of the kingdom; and this commanding mastery of one was a blessing compared with the demoralization which resulted for example under Sultan Ibrahim through the many headed command of the women; the Russian, the Venetian, the Greek ruled over Suleimus, Murad III, and Achmed I, but the unnerved Ibrahim was trod upon by the entire harem.

In opposition to Hammer, filled with the morals of the occident, and guided by the experiences of the historians of the orient, the Turk Omer Haleby says, after consideration and judgment of the dictates of oriental sensuality, that polygamy is to be preferred over monogamy for the following reasons. With a number of wives man is more certain to have a definite number of children; he need not fear sterility, discord, and incompatability, which marriage with a single woman so easily brings about—marriage with a single woman who so often becomes all powerful. Monogamy is only sensible if one is not in a financial position to maintain more than one woman. In that case, however, he should be true to this one woman and under no circumstances commit adultery.

If the wife remains childless, then he should take a slave for the single purpose of making her pregnant; if she gives birth to a child, he should treat her well, but without forgetting what he owes to his legitimate wife; for this woman, through the will of Allah may yet become fruitful. One remembers the story of Abraham and Hagar, and that God made a mother of a woman like Sarah who was old and had lost her prestige. But with the exception of this last mentioned instance—namely in the case of material impossibility—monogamy is, according to Omer Haleby, contrary to the commands of Allah; and to be sure, because he is first driven to adultery through weariness, the monotony through the petty attentiveness which a woman lavishes on her husband if she remains the only wife, if she rules him so that he becomes her slave; secondly: because monogamy does not sufficiently favor the birth and multiplication of believers; thirdly: because monogamy demands phallic foolishness exactly in the same measure as absolute abstemiousness; fourthly: the laws of nature are against it, for it has created all male creatures as polygamists, as for example: the hen, the horse, the dog, the bull. . . .

"These"—so continues Omer Haleby—"these are the principles. In practice, however, one has regard for his constitution, his temperament, his occupation, and the limitations which the functions of his brain demand. True, you are free to have but one wife, if one is enough for you and if she is fertile; but you should have four wives if your fortune warrants it, and if you can give each one of the four the same attention, the same care, a like sum for her necessaries, and a separate household. Thanks to polygamy you need not seek outside of the house that which you have at home. You find in your own home all joys which you desire, all bodily pleasures and passions."

"Monogamy often leads to adultery, to onanism, to pederasty; for vice, like misfortune, always comes in groups and chains, one leads to another. O, you believers, do not follow the advice of those idolaters who falsely call themselves worshippers of Jesus, for they pretend to recognize him as the teacher, but create of his teachings temples of Satan and Polytheism!"

The heathen Arabs had eight to ten wives, which gave rise to disordered home life. Mohammed therefore advised the Arabs to marry at most four wives, and then only if their circumstances permitted. This advice is given in the fourth chapter of the Koran: "If you have no fear of being unable to provide for your orphans, then take, after deep consideration, one, two, three, or at most four wives. But if you do fear that you will not be able to provide for them, then take only one wife or live with such slaves as you can acquire." The following marriages are forbidden: "You must not marry a woman whom your father has married—it had often happened (namely: what had happened before the revelation of the Koran had been permitted). For that is shameful and abominable and an evil way. It is further forbidden for you to marry: your mother, your daughter, and your sister, your aunt on your mother's and father's side; your brother's daughters; your sister's daughters; the nurse who suckled you; your half-sister; the mothers of your wives and your step-daughters whom you have taken under your protection, and those who are born of women with whom you have lived; but if you have not yet lived with them, then it is no sin to take them. Further; the wives of your sons who are descended from you; two sisters at the same time, this had been done for a long time. You must also take no free married woman; only your slaves are an exception. So God writes it for you. Everything else which is not here forbidden is permitted. You may take women according to the circumstances of your fortune, but no bad or dissolute ones." In a further place in Koran V it is said: "You are also permitted to marry free women who believe, and also free women of those who have received a writing in your presence, if you say your morning prayers with them and live chastely with them, that they will not become adulteresses and prostitutes. . . ." Mohammed naturally provided the exception here for himself, for he modelled all of his writing after his own desires. In the Koran XXXIII he lets God say: "You, O Prophet, we permit your wives which you have bought through morning prayers, and even your slaves whom God has given you (although these were taken as booty in war rather than bought), and the daughters of your uncles and aunts on your mother's and father's sides, who were saved with you from Mecca, and every believing woman who has committed herself to the prophet and whom he wishes to marry. This freedom you shall have above all other believers. We know quite well what we have commanded your wives and slaves in this respect; therefore you will commit no wrong if you make use of this freedom. You may turn back, if you wish, and take her whom you have heretofore abandoned, if you now have a desire for her; all this shall be no crime for you." Doubt may have assailed the prophet, if he was capable, if he took such freedom, to satisfy all the women whom his heart desired. For he permits God to comfort him again: "It shall be easy for them to be satisfied, that they shall not be troubled and shall content themselves with the fact that you endure each of them." A somewhat dark passage forbids one of all things even for the prophet: "You are not permitted to have other women (kept women and concubines, so the interpreters think), not to barter your wives with others, if their beauty no longer pleases you, but your slaves shall be an exception to this." The Koran IV touches upon bartering: "If you wish to exchange one woman for another, and you have already given the one an endowment, then you must not take anything from it. Is it proper for you to deprive her of anything? That would be a shameful act and a manifest sin. Would you retract if you were with another and had entered into a solemn covenant?"

Among the present day Persians there is a custom that one does not take along his wife on trips, expeditions, or service in the province, but at any station where he lingers for any length of time, he marries a *sighe*—hires a wife. In the city

Kirman, the Mullas used to offer every person who came to spend only a few days there a wife as a *sighe*. In Persia, according to Dr. Polak, it is also customary, if one does not marry within the family, at least to marry within the tribe; the Affchare takes a wife from the Affchare tribe, the Kaschkai from the Kaschkai. A nomad maiden disdains the brilliant proposals from the cities and marries only within her own tribe.

CHAPTER THREE

# THE WIVES OF THE PROPHET MOHAMMED

*Mohammed's eleven wives—The first wife Chadidschah—The faithfulness of the prophet—Sauda—Oischah—Hafsa—Sainab—Omm Salama—Sainab II —The first schism in Islam—Daschauairia, the eighth consort of the prophet —Cafia—Omm Habıba—The affair of the prophet with the Koptin Mariam —The wrath of Hafsa—Allah's help `for the prophet—Maimanna, the eleventh wife of Mohammed—The memory of the wives of the prophet— How Mohammed converted his wives to unpretentiousness—The imitator of the example of the Mohammed: the Sultan with more than four wives.*

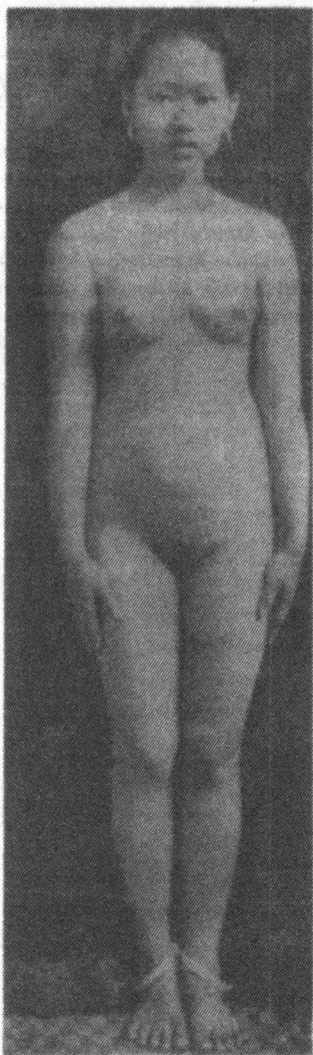

*Eighteen-year-old Chinese*

Mohammed's first wife was called Chadidschah. Although she was ten years older than the prophet, she remained until her death constantly in his favor. When she died at the age of sixty-five, the prophet mourned bitterly and never recovered from his grief. For a long time thereafter he clung to her memory in love and fidelity. Aischah, the next favorite wife of Mohammed, asked him one day: O Apostle of God! Chadidschah was already old; did not Allah give you a younger and better wife to replace her?" But the prophet answered: "No, of course not! Allah has given me no better one. Chadidschah loved me when I was alone and without support. She believed my words when the world still gave me the fig. She was generous and kind to me when all men were my enemies. She gave me all that she had; offered me her goodness and her blood."

Chadidschah was followed by Sauda, daughter of Semaa, widow of Sokran, one of the first followers of Islam. She survived Mohammed and died under the Caliphate of Omar.

The above mentioned favorite Aischah was married by the prophet when she was seven years old. But the marriage began two years later. In the meantime Mohammed married Hafsa, the daughter of Omar, the widow of Hobeisch. She lived eight years with the prophet and died many years after his death in the forty-fifth year of Hidschret, under the Caliphate of Moawijes. In the hands of Hafsa was placed the first copy of the Koran, which was assembled at the behest of Abu Bekr, the father-in-law and first follower of Mohammed, the first Caliph.

The fifth wife of Mohammed was Sainab. Besides Chadidschah, she was the only wife of the prophet who died during his lifetime; all the other—nine in number—survived him.

Sainab and his sixth wife, Omm Salama, Mohammed married after his second expedition to Nedschd, and after the injunction against wine drinking and gambling. Sainab gave Mohammed—for one pays to be a wife in the Orient—a dowry of 400 pieces of gold. Omm Salama is supposed to have been extraordinarily beautiful.

After the expedition against Beni Koraische, the massacre under him, the capture and death of his old enemy, the Jew Salam, Mohammed married his seventh wife, another Sainab, whom his adopted son Sid ceded to him. The separation of Sid and Sainab was the first divorce in Islam, and resulted in a scandal for Mohammed, much to his regret, as I will relate in greater detail in the chapter on divorce.

Mohammed was at that time fifty-seven years old. A new fortunate expedition against Beni Mostalak was celebrated with a new marriage for the prophet: Mohammed married as his eighth legitimate wife the beautiful Dschauairia, who was famous "for her nobility of character and the charm of her entire person." She remained with the prophet for about five years and survived him by about thirty-five years.

After the expedition of Chaibar against the Jews, Mohammed conceived the idea of associating himself with a ninth wife. His favor fell upon a daughter of the tribe of Aaron, called Safia. The marriage was celebrated with great pomp in El Sahba, on the march of the army to Medina. Safia lived with Mohammed three years and several months; she did not die until the fiftieth year of Hidschret.

After his return from Medina, Mohammed married Omm Habiba, the daughter of the sheriff of Mecca, the widow of Abdallah. The marriage was supposed to have been arranged before then, when the widow had still been in Abyssinia. Omm Habiba was the tenth legitimate wife of Mohammed.

About that time—Mohammed numbered fifty-nine years—an incident arose which critically disturbed the peace in the house of the prophet.

At that time there came into Medina several Mokaukas, princes from Alexandria and Egypt, bringing gifts for Mohammed: a eunuch named Maiudh, and four young girls. One of the latter, the Koptin Mariam, cast such an evil spell over the prophet that he determined to sleep with her; he would have liked to make her his wife, but he could not because she was a slave. In order to avoid scandal—for he had himself declared adultery to be such—he wanted to commit the sweet sin in secret.

This act took place at the home of his absent wife Hafsa, and even upon her own bed, and in addition on a day on which the prophet had promised to act to Hafsa or to Aischa. When Hafsa heard of this and took Mohammed to account, he became greatly terrified—in spite of his many wives and the tyranny in his family life—he was a hero of the slipper—and promised Hafsa that he would not touch the Koptin Mariam again, if she would keep the occurrence secret; but Hafsa first satisfied herself, and the prophet also promised her that as a reward for her silence her father Omar and Aischa's father Abubekr should become his successors in the government. In spite of all this, Hafsa related the incident to Aischa. Now Mohammed became very angry and as a penalty for the prattling

43

he left his wives for a whole month and spent this time in the rooms of Mariam, until, upon the intercession of the Angel Gabriel, he took Hafsa back into favor. He nevertheless kept Mariam together with her sister Schirina with him until his death; Mariam survived him by about five years and lies buried at Medina.

Mohammed used this incident as the theme of the 66th chapter of the Koran, entitled "The Forbidden," where he permits God to sanction the foregoing. It says there: "O prophet, why do you wish, for the sake of pleasing your wives, forego that which God has permitted you?" (In the 5th chapter runs the verse: "O you believers, deprive yourselves not of those good things which God has permitted you." This verse was written against the ascetic life of the monks.) If the prophet entrusted an adventure of his to one of his wives in secret, but if she babbled about it, of which God gave him knowledge, he partly berated her for her prattling and partly ignored her for her indulgence. And as he berated her, she asked: "Who could have told you of this?" And he answered: "He who knows all has pointed it out to me. If you both (Hafsa and Aischa) will now turn again to God, for your hearts to be cleansed, then it is good; but if you unite against him (Mohammed) . . . he leaves you, then it can very easily happen that his Master will give him other wives in exchange, who are better than you, namely: God loving, true believing, full of humility, repentent, religious, and temperate, some of whom have already known men, others who are yet virgins."

This threat helped, as we have seen. While every Moslem must obey the law that he must not deceive his wives on the nights sets aside for them, Mohammed here, for his own pleasure and protection, circumvented the law with the help and favor of God, in that he let everything be permitted to him.

A short time after this excitement he began to die. But already marked by death, in Schorf, six miles south of Mecca, dressed in the Ihram, the pilgrim dress, evading the law which forbids coitus on a pilgrim journey and in pilgrim dress, Mohammed married another wife, the eleventh; that was Maimanna, the daughter of El Harrith, the last of his legitimate wives. Soon thereafter the prophet died. Four years later in Mecca, as Maimanna lay dying, she said: "Carry me out of Mecca; for the Apostle of Allah has promised me that I shall not die in this city." She let herself be brought to Schorf and placed in a tent near the tree under which she had celebrated her wedding night with Mohammed.

Altogether Mohammed had eleven wives; Mariam remained only his concubine. Since the death of Chadidschah, who had been the only one during her lifetime, Mohammed always lived with more wives than had been sanctioned in Islam, at the end with nine at a time; for Sainab I had died before Mohammed's death.

The memory of these women is highly venerated. All bear the title: "Mother of believers." Even Timus, who raved against the believers and unbelievers alike, during the siege of Damascus, visited the graves of Omm Selmaor Salama and Omm Habiba—the sixth and tenth wives of the prophet—to bring to their remains every inch of his respect.

Mohammed's favorite wife was Aischa. There is a tradition that she was present at the time when the Angel of Death, Israel, on the twelfth day of the month of Rebi el Auel at noon in the eleventh year of the Hegira, asked the prophet's special permission to come in and to be permitted to take his soul.

The prophet did not get along very easily with all of his wives. Outside of the example which has previously been related, the following was also confirmed, and which is known above all things, that Allah's help never failed him.

When Mohammed's wives demanded greater luxury of him, he gave them the choice of remaining with him or leaving him. This is mentioned in a passage in the 33rd chapter of the

Koran: "Say, O prophet, to your wives: If you desire the joy of earthly life with its splendor, well, then I will provide substantially for you and leave you in an honorable manner. But if you desire God and the messenger of God and a home in the future life, then God has provided a great reward for the righteous among you. O you wives of the prophet, whichever one of you commits an obviously shameful deed shall be punished twofold. . . . She, however, who devotes herself to God and his messenger and conducts herself righteously, shall be doubly rewarded, and we shall make honorable provision for her. O you wives of the prophet, you are not like other women. If you fear God, do not be too friendly in your speech, lest you arouse lust in the heart of the lovesick; but speak as is proper." Mohammed provided for his person all things according to his taste and wish: "O you wives of the prophet," says he, "remain pretty at home . . . , for God wants of you, because you belong to the house of the prophet, that you avoid all sicknesses and see that you care for yourselves with an exceptional cleanliness."

The example of the transgression which Mohammed gave in marrying more than four wives did not remain without initiation among the Caliphs and Sultans. As the insatiable caprice and lust of the Sultan Ibrahim was not satisfied with a horde of slaves and also a menage of seven sultanesses, seven favored wives, he married an eight as a legitimate consort, against the canon which prohibits this for Osman rulers; a canon which had already been violated before Ibrahim by Sultan Suleimus through the marriage with Roxelane, by Osman II through the marriage with the daughter of commander of his army. The Kislaraga and the Grand Vizier were the authorities of the Sultan Ibrahim who sanctioned the marriage. The marriage feast was celebrated at Daudpascha, and the viziers brought as wedding presents, in addition to ornaments and jewels, a beautiful slave for each,. so that the wedding presents tended to satisfy the taste of both the bride and the bridegroom.

CHAPTER FOUR

# RIGHTS AND DUTIES OF THE MARRIED MUSSULMEN

*The wife's rights—The separate establishment of every single wife—The apportioning of nights—The Koran on the obedience of wives—Omer Haleby on duties and rights—The slave as a wife—Moslem-Christian marriages—The Koran on this question—A fetish of the Mufti Abdullah—The cunning of the patriarch Parthentus—Osman-Byzantian prince-marriages.*

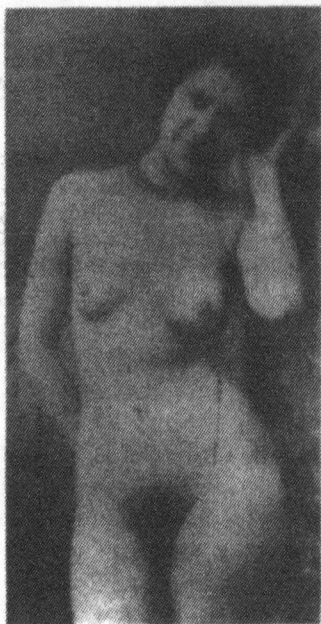

*Nineteen-year-old Magyar*

On the duties of married mussulmen to each other it is said in the Koran IV: "If you treat your wives well and fear to do them harm, then God will know well what you are doing." Further in the same chapter: "It is not possible that you should love all of your wives alike even if you want to. Do not turn from one of your wives with apparent aversion, leave her in uncertainty."

If one is already married and takes another wife, he must devote three successive nights to her; if she is a virgin, then he must give her seven successive nights. Without the consent of his wife, a husband must not permit a child whom he has had with another house to tarry in her house; this likewise pertains to children which the wives previously had by other men. Every wife is entitled to a separate house, be it a house for herself or a row of rooms separate and distinct on all sides.

The first wife is entitled to particular care and advantages. If a man takes a second, third or fourth wife, a widow, or takes back one whom he had previously abandoned, he is obligated to devote three successive nights to her.

"Can you," asks Omer Haleby of his first wife, "be jealous of your privileges? Will you be jealous if on the seven nights which your husband must devote to a virgin, he decorates his house with her flower? Are these not things which you have yourself also enjoyed? Then do not guard so rigidly your prerogatives! Do not be impatient in relation to the tenderness which you must expect of your husband. You will get your share without that. For although the husband has the right to apportion the quality of his tenderness according to those he loves, according to the fire of his heart, he at least has the duty in a quantitative sense, to spend his nights with his wives in turn, and he must not favor one with the night portion of another, unless she does not give him her permission willingly, as Sauda did, for she—abandoned and again married by the prophet—yielded her first night and the right to the bed of their joint husband to Aischa. If Sauda dealt in this manner in order to come back into the favor of the prophet, that was what happened, for she had no thought other than to see herself in the day of the great and highest law of the land as the cleanest and most chaste wife of our holy prophet. So wherefore shall you, O daughters of Islam, be jealous and impatient, since your husband, unless he is afflicted with sickness, must divide his nights among his various wives, unless you do not desire him, until he remains for his pleasure with only one of his life's companions! Even in this matter there is a notable exception: Mohammed, during a severe illness, called all his wives around his bed and asked their permission to remain with Aischa until he had fully recovered."

Omer Haleby does not, however, report whether the wives acceded to this request. He merely adds thereto, in order to warn against obstinacy: "Never forget: even if you have the legal right to punish your husband should he depart from the equality which he owes all his wives—never forget that he also has the power of playing the schoolmaster and of chastising you with strokes of the stick, if you do not obey his commands!"

Concerning these duties of the wife towards her husband, it is said in the Koran IV: "Righteous women should be dutiful and silent. . . . Those women who you fear will provoke you through their behavior, give rebukes, stay away from her, lock her in her chamber and chastise her. But if she obeys you, seek no opportunity to be provoked with her."

And in the passage on the "Duty of humility" of wives, chapter 66, 10-12 reads: "Allah sets a parallel for the unbelievers: The wife of Noah and the wife of Lot. Both stood under two of our righteous servants, yet both betrayed them, and both earned nothing for them from Allah. And it was said: "Go into the fire together with those who are going!" . . . And Allah sets a parallel for the believers: The wife of Pharaoh, who said: "My master, build me a house in Paradise and save me for Pharaoh and his deeds." And Miriam, the daughter of Imran, who hid her shame: We therefore breathe our spirit in them, they were of the humble."

"Do not forget," adds Omer Haleby to the moslem women, "that the husband is the worker; that from his works rise the ornaments which enhance your beauty; that the strength of his arms protects you, your children, your servants, your home! That from his member flow your loftiest pleasures, your greatest happiness. Mimic in each and every respect the conduct of the venerated wives of the prophet: even just as they, seek to satisfy the desires and needs of your husband. If you are having intercourse, do it with that deep emotion which fully bespeaks the grandness of the act which you feel. Give yourself up entirely to the act, put into it your soul, your spirit, your body! Think, that in this significant moment you are a co-worker of your husband, like the universal spirit of love, which all nature awakens in the time of the beautiful and fragrant month of May. If, however, the embraces of your husband are too hasty to arouse joy in your bosom, if you do not partake wholly of his emotions, if you cannot increase his pleasure with your own—at least let him think otherwise. Allah who sees all and is charitable, will forgive you this guiltless deceit, and in this manner you will retain the tenderness of your husband, his care and high estimation. O women, do not seek your true joy in irregular or violent coitus; seek it neither in onanism of any kind nor in pederasty, neither in the practices of Sappho nor in hashish dreams or love potions! Seek it only in the fulfillment of your duties as wife, as mistress of the hearth, as mother of the family. These three things together with a religious faith in coitus are the only ones which give you the right to a place in Paradise and make houris out of you, so that you will remain ever potent and ever virginal. Be good Mohammedans, in that you do not have intercourse simply for pleasure, but adhere to the great universal law that your features may light up with the fire of a mother's joy, that you may thus insure your sacred happiness on earth and in the everlasting hereafter. Has not Mohammed said that God cursed him who abandons his wife merely because she can no longer satisfy his lusts! And did not Mohammed say to his pupils: "Respect marriage as an institution whose aim is the propagation of the human race!" And has this not been given to you, O women, as the ground for the possibility of divorcing your husband if he is impotent?"

A passage of the Koran, chapter IV, reads: "He who does not possess sufficient fortune to be able to marry a free believing woman, shall take a converted slave; but marry her only with the consent of her master. They must be chaste and not loose, and they must not have strange lovers." But the Koran adds later: "Slaves are only permitted to him who fears free women because of the sin into which they may easily fall. Yet it is better not to take any slaves."

Cohabitation with their masters existed even among the Hebrews as a definite right of the slaves. The second book of Moses XXI 10 relates as law: "If he take him another wife, her food, her raiment, and her duty of marriage, shall he not diminish. And if he do not these three unto her, then shall she go out free without money." The Moslem law commands the

52

following with respect to the enjoyment of slaves in marriage and in love: If one purchases a slave, unless she is no longer a virgin, he must not sleep with her for a month; with the slaves who are still virgins he must wait for her menstruation before he touches her; and if she is sick he must wait three months. To do otherwise is a sin. If one wishes to sell a slave, he must cease having intercourse with her at least a month before the time set for her transfer."

In Persia the children of a slave are recognized as legitimate. They enjoy fully the same rights as those of the wives. In addition, the slave, at the moment of her delivery, ceases to be a slave.

Omer Haleby gives a detailed explanation of the Turkish laws and customs which govern the slave and her relation to the master with whom she has sexual intercourse: The right which a master has over his slave, legitimatizes the children which descend from their reciprocal relationship; yet the first born of each slave must first be expressly recognized. If the master does not recognize any one but himself as the father of the child which she is carrying in her womb, he has the right to consider as his own the child which the slave conceals in her womb. The legitimacy of the child depends on the free recognition of the father, and the latter can exercise the right of recognition even if he has already disposed of the fate of the child, given it away or sold it. He can likewise recognize the child after he has sold the mother-slave and she has then given birth, in case the delivery takes place during the first six months after the sale. In this case, from the legitimacy of the child there results a simultaneous freeing of the mother-slave and a recision of the contract of sale. The master is at liberty to marry the slave after her freedom. But if the freed-one refuses the marriage, he can not bring her back under his power again, nor can he compel her to accept his hand. Only the children who descend from the illegitimate intercourse of a man with the slave of another can be termed bastards.

The lot of the slave is not in the least as sorry as one may believe; many slaves were the mothers of great rulers, and then themselves became rulers of the harem, often also of the kingdom; the mother of Abdul Asis was a serf, the mother of the present Sultan Abdul Hamid II, an Armenian slave. It is only bad for the slaves so long as they remain with the slave dealer. So it happened at the time of Mustafas III, that a slave of the Constantinople slave market was driven by vindictiveness for her bad treatment to murder the children of the slave dealer; as punishment she was finally hanged in the slave market.

At the Sultan's home conflicts often arise between sons of the Sultan who descended from a marriage with an honorable lady and sons who sprang from slaves. As a famous incident, this story of Hammer's is related: "The first thought of Mohammed II after his elevation to the throne, was to send his brother Achmed to the grave of his father Murad. Achmed was, to use an expression of the Byzantians, born in purple of the Princess of Sinope, the daughter of Iscfendiaroghlis, while Mohammed was born of a slave; and the death of his born-in-purple brother seemed indispensable to the son of the slave to make certain of the throne. While the Princess of Sinope appéared in the palace hall to show the stepson of the Sultan her grief over the death of his father and her husband, he sent Ali, the son of Ewrenos into the harem to choke her son, his brother, in his bath. On the following day the son of Ewrenos, the murderer himself was cleared out of the way, and the mother of the victim, the Princess of Sinope was given as a wife to a slave called Ishak. Mohammed, the son of a slave, would have liked to have arranged for a like fate for his second stepmother, because she was also a princess—a Serbian—but out of fear that her father, George the Dishonorable, might take vengeance through war, he sent this wife of his dead father back to her father in an honorable manner with gifts, with considerable

54

tokens of widowhood and with a renewal of the subsisting peace."

An important question in Islam was always the relationship which one must have with an unbelieving woman. In the Koran II 220 it says: "Take no idol worshipper for a wife until she has been converted. To be sure, a believing slave is better than a free idolatress, even if she does not please you as much. Also marry no idolator until he becomes converted."

The Koran LX verses 10-12 decrees in this respect as follows: "O true believers, when believing women come unto you as refugees, try them: God well knoweth their faith. And if ye know them to be true believers, send them not back to the infidels: they are not lawful for the unbelievers to have in marriage; neither are the unbelievers lawful for them. But give their unbelieving husbands what they shall have expended for their dowers. Nor shall it be any crime in you if ye marry them, provided ye give them their dowries. And retain not the patronage of the unbelieving women: but demand back that which ye have expended for the dowry of such of your wives as go over to the unbelievers; and let them demand back that which they have expended for the dowry of those who come over to you. . . . If any of your wives escape from you to the unbelievers, and ye have your turn by the coming over of any of the unbelievers' wives to you, give unto those believers whose wives shall have gone away, out of the dowries of the latter, so much as they shall have expended for the dowries of the former. . . . O prophet, when believing women come unto thee and plight their faith unto thee, that they will not associate anything with God, nor steal, nor commit fornication, nor kill their children . . . then do thou plight thy faith unto them and ask pardon for them of God." The matter has in this respect remained somewhat obscured to this day.

In the year 1723 the Mufti Abdullah at Stambul issued an interesting and characteristic edict. Following in full, this determination purports to concern marriage with non-moslem women: "Whatever rubbish happens to the heretic, so are men exterminated through war, boys and women made slaves, possessions rendered booty. Women and boys are compelled to accept Islam through means other than war, yet it is not permitted to lie with woman before they have been converted. With regard to the original unbelievers, the Christians, so are their boys and women slaves, their goods booty, their boys and women can not be compelled to accept Islam; yet it is not permitted to lie with their women either unless they become moslems."

Hammer, who relates this edict, continues: That is above all a fine distinction of Moslem war laws, by virtue of which the heretic, but not the believer, is forced to Islam, that one is given to Moslem only as a convert, this one, however, also unconverted. This contradiction by which the Mohammedan heretic fares worse than the Christian, in that the first can be forced to change their belief, and not the second, in that the Christian is given a lawful price for violence, is made clear from a dogmatic-juristic point of view, by virtue of which the original unbeliever can be guilty of no breach of faith, because he has not been acquainted with the teachings of Islam, the heretic on the other hand, as a revolting offender against the true teachings, may be compelled to return; but although they are much nearer to Islam through prior revolt and subsequent compulsion, to save their skins, they must change their teachings of faith, and will not be forced to divest themselves of their reputations, while the Christians are free in their choice of religion, they are however enjoined in their lust. To this is added the political consideration that the transition from orthodox teachings to heresy is much easier to presuppose than the revolt from Islam to Christianity, and that corruption in religious matters is much more remote in the hands of the Christians than in those of the heretics.

56

At the time of the Sultan Mohammed IV the Greek patriarch Parthenius brought about the abolition of the multiple evil rental marriages of the Turks and the Greeks, which gave him the name *the Virginal*. These marriages, consummated at a definite time, were called *Kabin*, concubinage. The patriarch, "as cunning as he was virginal," went to the Mufti and requested a decision: "Is it permitted for a Moslem to know carnally a woman who eats hog's meat and drinks wine, and if children of such an unclean union are not undeserving of the mother love of Islam?" The Mufti answered after mature consideration that such marriage was not permitted by law. "Then you must forbid it in Rumili," replied the patriarch, "where it is only too common." The Mufti consulted with his Grandvizier, and it resulted in a command which forbade marriages between Moslems and Christians who had not yet been converted to Islam. The English Consul Rycaut is the authority of Hammer for this reported decision. The Osman Sultans have none the less frequently married Christian women.

Sarische Pascha, the commander of the fleet, stole from a Frankish ship in the entrance of the Dardanells, a Frankish princess meant for the Kaiser of Byzantium, for the harem of the Sultan Bajesid, who was already married to two Christians —two princesses—a Serbian and a European.

In the year 1346, Emperor Cantacuzen sent to the Sultan Urchan thirty ships, a multitude of cavalry, and the most creditable of his manor to fetch the imperial bride. The emperor forsook the army, the court, and the family for Selymbria, where, in the plain before the city there had been erected a cloth covered stage upon which, according to ancient custom, at the marriage of a princess at a ceremony foreign to the Byzantian court, the bride must be shown to the people before her departure. Next to it was the royal tent in which the empress and her three daughters found themselves; on the evening set for the delivery, the empress remained in the tent

57

with the other two daughters, the emperor sat on his horse, all others stood around in expectation; on a given signal, the silk, gold-embroidered curtain of the stage fell simultaneously on all sides, and the bride of the Sultan stood in the midst of kneeling eunuchs, illuminated by torches, for the inspection of the people. The clamor of trumpets, fifes, reed-pipes, and other musical instruments sounded, and as this died away, the singers sang wedding pieces which they had composed in praise of the bride. After other surrender-ceremonies of a Byzantian princess-bride,. soldiers, state officials, Greeks and Turks were feasted for many days; thereupon, midst great jubilation, the Greek princess was led away to the marriage bed of the sixty year old Osman barbarian, for whom, as a twelve year old boy, his father Osman had stolen as his first bride, a Greek castle-maiden. Between the first and second marriages lay a half century of conquests; instead of the stolen Greek bride, a willingly surrendered Greek daughter of an Emperor was now married to the Sultan with great pomp.

The relationship between the royal houses of Osman and Byzantium as a result of this marriage showed a marked friendliness. In 1348, Urchan with his entire family visited the court of his father-in-law at Skutari at his residence in the suburb of the Asiatic coast, and spent many days in hunting and dining. The emperor sat at a table with Urchan, his son-in-law, at another table nearby sat the four sons of the Sultan by prior consorts, and around them the most respectable Greeks and Turks sat on tapestries which were spread on the ground. Then Urchan remained in camp with the fleet, but the emperor with his daughter, Theodora, the royal consort, and her four stepsons left for Constantinople, where they spent three days with the empress-mother and the princess-sisters, and then presented with riches, they returned to Bithynia.

At the court of Suleimus the Great, a Russian was the all powerful consort of the ruler. Through charm and talent she had elevated herself from slave not only to consort of Suleimus, but as the only one to enjoy his bed, and she controlled the sovereign even long after her beauty must have waned, through the superiority of her spirit and character of her mind.

It was not a gentle mind, for this Russian, Churen-Roxelane, was accused of causing the execution of two grandviziers —Ibrahim and Achmed—and the murder of his son Mustafa, which Suleimus committed. She is also blamed for sowing the seeds of civil war in the brotherly discord which followed the discovery of the prince in the sanctity of the harem, and which is said to have brought about the enervation of the ruler; her monument in the cemetery of Suleimus commands absolutely as he does the kingdom, at the side of the greatest Osman emperor. This Russian monument, says Hammer, stands in the middle of the empire, on the third of the seven hills of Istambul, as deeply significant a memento as that statue of a horseman on the hippodrome of the Greek Constantinople, whose inscription foretells the Russian conquest of the state.

Other instances of the command of foreign women over Osman rulers and through them over the Osman domain are pictured later in detail in the chapter on the influence of the harem.

## CHAPTER FIVE

# DIVORCE AND WIDOWS

*Writing on attempts to reconciliate—Family-divorce-judges—Time for con-sideration—Alimony for the divorced wife—Summons to the husbands for mildness—Divorce in Persia—Ancient Arabic divorce from bed but not from board—Mohammed's phillipic against divorce—Mohammed's violation of his own law—Allah's help for Mohammed—The Koran on widows.*

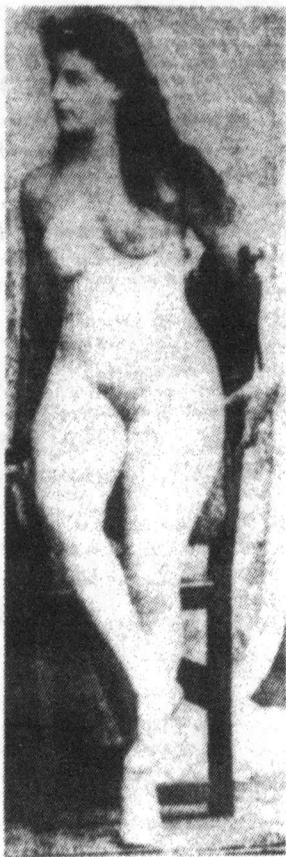

*Seventeen-year-old Slav*

The Koran does not give a rash opinion on divorce and says in Chapter IV: "If a woman has feared the anger or aversion of her husband, they should consider the thing amicably; for reunion is better than divorce." IV, 39 continues: "If ye fear a breach between the husband and wife, send a judge out of his family and a judge out of her family: if they shall desire a reconciliation, God will cause them to agree. . . . If, however, they separate, God will suckle both with his bounty" —namely, peace and rest.

More is said of divorce in the Koran in chapter II, 226-230: "They who vow to abstain from their wives, are allowed to wait four months, but if they go back from their vow, verily God is gracious and merciful; and if they resolve on a divorce, good is he who heareth and knoweth. The women who are divorced shall wait concerning themselves until they have had their courses thrice, and it shall not be lawful for them to conceal that which God hath created in their wombs. Their husbands will act more justly to bring them back at this time, if they desire a reconciliation; but the men ought to have a superiority over them. . . . Ye may divorce your wives twice; and then either retain them with humanity, or dismiss them with kindness. But it is not lawful for you to take away anything of what ye have given them. . . . But if the husband divorces her a third time, she shall not be lawful for him again, until she marry another husband. But if he also divorce her, it shall be no crime in them if they return to each other."

To become separated from women with whom one has already lain demands four months of consideration. The direction that a divorced woman wait three months before she marries again, is also found in Jewish customs, as Ullman and Geiger relate. To divorce a still virgin wife, the Moslem requires no time for consideration. For it says in the Koran II, 237-237: It shall be no crime in you, if ye divorce your wives, so long as ye have not touched them, nor settled any dowry on them. And provide for them necessaries, according to what shall be reasonable. But if ye divorce them before ye have touched them, and have already settled a dowry upon them, ye shall give them half of what ye have settled, unless they release any part, or he release part in whose hand the knot of marriage is . . ."

Koran XXXIII, 43: "O true believers, when ye marry women who are believers, and afterward put them away, before ye have touched them, there is no term prescribed you to fulfill towards them; but make them a present and dismiss them freely with an honorable dismission."

Koran, chapter 65: "O prophet, when ye divorce women, put them away at their appointed term; and compute the term exactly. . . . Oblige them not to go out of their apartments, neither let them go out, until the terms be expired, unless they be guilty of manifest uncleanliness. . . . Thou knowest not whether God will bring something new to pass which may reconcile them after this. And when they shall have fulfilled their term, either retain them with kindness, or part from them honorably: and take witnesses from among you, men of integrity; and give your testimony in the presence of God. . . ."

Koran, chapter 65, 6: 'Suffer the women whom ye divorce to dwell in some part of the houses wherein ye dwell; according to the room and conveniences of the habitations which ye possess: and make them not uneasy that ye may reduce them to straits. And if they be with child, expend on them what shall be needful, until they be delivered of their burden."

Koran II, 242: "And unto those who are divorced, a reasonable provision is also due; this is a duty incumbent on those who fear God."

In Persia, the divorce, *Tekal*, may be had on the ground that the wife remain childless; secondly, if she be dissolute and is suspected of being unfaithful; thirdly, if the husband believes her to be, *bed khadem*, of evil pace, that is, if soon after her entrance into the house some misfortune occurs; one considers her then as a bad omen and seeks to be rid of her. Only in the rarest case does a divorce result from the complaint of the wife that the husband neglects his marital duties. Outside of these grounds the husband cannot obtain a bill of divorce legally in Persia.

The Arabians had a custom, says Ullman in his remarks on the Koran, that if one divorces himself from a wife, but later wishes to take her back into his house, he must do it with this statement, "You will henceforth be regarded as my mother," from which the wife steps into the relationship of a mother to the husband. A wife by the name of Chaulah Bint Thalabah was divorced by her husband under the formula: "You will henceforth be regarded as my mother." Thereupon Moham-med announced in the 58th chapter entitled, "She who disputed" in verses 1-4: "Now hath God heard the speech of her who disputed with thee concerning her husband, and made her complaint unto God; and God hath heard your mutual discourse: for God both heareth and seeth. As to those among you who divorce their wives, by declaring that they will there-after regard them as their mothers; let them know that they are not their mothers. They only are their mothers who brought them forth; and they certainly utter an unjustifiable saying and a falsehood. . . . Those who divorce their wives by saying such words and afterwards would repair what they have said, shall be obliged to free a captive before they touch one another."

Furthermore, adopted sons were considered as natural sons, and the obstacles in marriage which stood in the way of the latter through the relationship of kinship, pertained also to the former. Mohammed wished to abolish both of these customs and said in chapter 33, 4: "God hath not given a man two hearts within him," namely: artificial kinship cannot live like a natural one; further, concerning the other custom: "neither hath he made your wives, some of whom ye divorce, regarding them thereafter as your mothers, your true mothers, nor hath he made your adopted sons your true sons." Chapter 33, verse 40: "Mohammed is not the father of any man among you; but the apostle of God and the seal of the prophets."

Mohammed commanded the foregoing for personal reasons, because he himself married the wife of his freed Sid, whom he had adopted as a son, and which, according to the custom, he should not have done. Ullman remarks, in his commentaries on Chapter 33 of the Koran: Sid Eby Haretha, formerly a slave of Mohammed, then freed by him and adopted as his son, received from him as a wife Sainab, daughter of Dschahasch and Amima, who was Mohammed's aunt. Later, however, Mohammed himself fell in love with Sainab, and he wanted Sid to divorce her so that he could marry her. Sainab and her brother Abdullah were opposed to this, whereupon Mohammed apparently relinquished his desire, until he had an opportunity to win them both as well as Sid, so that Sid divorced Sainab and Mohammed finally married her.

The prophet had this act sanctioned in the 33rd chapter of the Koran in which he takes help of Allah for his passion and his egotism in the following language: "It is not fit for a true believer of either sex, when God and his apostle have decreed a thing, that they should have the liberty of choosing a different matter of their own. . . ." Mohammed considered his love for Sainab as approved and predetermined by God. For he lets himself be apostrophized by God: "And remember when thou saidst to him unto whom God had been gracious, and on whom thou also hadst conferred favors, Keep thy wife to thyself and fear God: and thou didst conceal that in thy mind which God had determined to discover. . . . But when Sid had determined the matter concerning her, and had resolved to divorce her, we joined her in marriage unto thee; lest a crime should be charged on the true believers, in marrying the wives of their adopted sons, when they have determined the matter concerning them; and the command of God is to be performed. No crime is to be charged on the prophet as to what God hath allowed him." Everything seems to have been allowed for the prophet.

Mohammed was troubled lest his divorced wives and the widows who would remain after his death marry again, for he admonished the believers: "The wives of the prophet are your mothers." And in a later passage in the same chapter he says: "Neither is it fit for you to give any uneasiness to the apostle of God, or to marry his wives after him forever; for this would be a grievous thing in the sight of God."

Concerning widows the Koran decrees as follows in II, 241-242: "And as such of you as shall die and leave wives ought to bequeath their wives a year's maintenance, without putting them out of their houses; but if they go out voluntarily, it shall be no crime in you for that which they shall do with themselves."

Upon remarriage of widows it is said in chapter II, 234-236: "Such of you as die and leave wives, the wives must wait concerning themselves four months and ten days, and when they shall have fulfilled their term, it shall be no crime in you for that which they shall do with themselves, according to what is reasonable. And it shall be no crime in you, whether ye make public overtures of marriage unto such women within the said four months and ten days, or whether ye conceal such your designs in your minds. But make no promises unto them privately, unless ye speak honorable words; and resolve not on the knot of marriage until the prescribed time be accomplished."

Before Mohammed the custom existed that if a man died, his wife devolved upon his kin together with all her possessions. The prophet forbade this in the Koran IV: "O true believers, it is not lawful for you to be heirs of women against their will, nor to hinder them from marrying others, that ye may take away part of what ye have given them in dowry; unless they have been guilty of a manifest crime; but converse kindly with them. And if ye hate them, it may happen that ye may hate a thing in which God hath placed much good."

The levirate is very much like a kind of successive polyandry and the rest has been created from the former right of a brother to his brother's wife. Joseph Muller has collected numerous examples in his small treatise on the sexual lives among primitive folk. I mention here only that in Moses 5, book XXV 5, it is referred to as a right of the wife and a burdensome duty for the husband. Heinrich Pottinger tells of the Beludschen: "The engagement is considered so sacred that, if a bridegroom dies before the wedding, his brother feels duty bound, through rules of chivalry and propriety, to marry the bride." Among the Arabs as well as among the Semites the levirate was a recognized custom. The Koran later forbade women to be wed against their will. "Still," says Klemm, "a widow seldom repulses the advances of her brother-in-law, for such a union preserves the unity of the family."

Winckler relates, in an address before the Society for Ethnology, 1898, an Arabian inscription which purports to show a father and son as the joint progenitors of another son;

68

he deduces from this a form of communism in happy Arabia. Joseph Muller disputes the authenticity of this, and reports in opposition, in his paper on the sexual life of primitive folk, Strabo's communications on the relationship of polyandry among the Minyers in happy Arabia: All brothers had one wife there jointly; whoever comes first, places his staff before the door, goes inside, and has intercourse. Men of another family who do this are considered adulterers and are punished with death. Strabo reports further, that the Minyers also copulate with their mothers and sisters, so that a kind of family communism exists. According to Joseph Muller this is not always complete promiscuity; for one must atone for a penetration with his life.

Strabo tells finally an amusing story how a king's daughter of remarkable beauty deceived her fifteen brothers all of whom desired her. She made staffs like those of her brothers, and placed one before her door, always, careful that there stood the staff of a brother other than the one who was coming. Since at one time all the brothers were together and yet a staff leaned before her door, the deceit was discovered. The story is silent about what then occurred.

## CHAPTER SIX

# ADULTERY

*Hebraic laws—The Koran on adultery—The penalty of stoning—Difference between free and unfree women—A Turkish concept—Moslem traditions—Persian penalties—The Turkish legalist Ibrahim Haleby on adultery—The crown witnesses—Penalties for adulterers—The single instance of a stoning in Islam—Freedom from punishment in certain cases—Corrective punishments—The pretended adultery of the prophet's wife Aischa—Warning of the Koran on defamation—Political consequences of the defamation of Aischa—South Slavic view of adultery.*

71

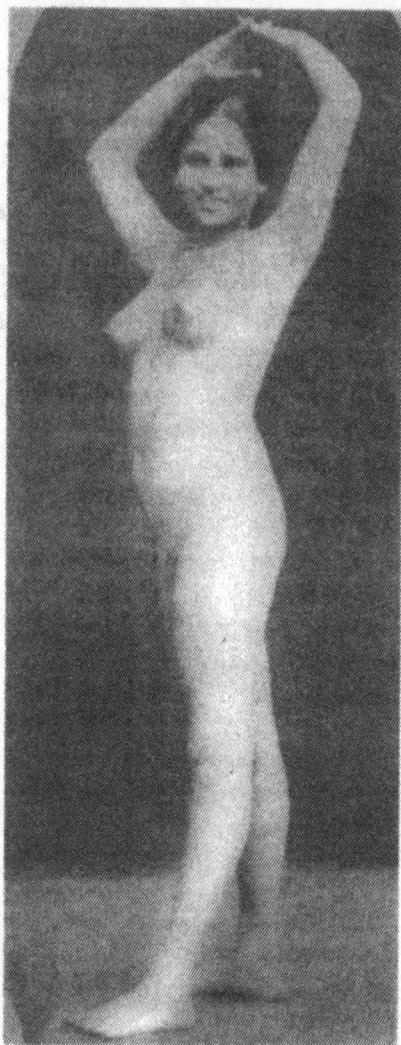

*Sixteen-year-old Malarabian*

In ancient times the death penalty was prescribed for adultery among the Hebrews. Moses orders it in 3 book XX 10 and in 5 book XXII 22. In the latter passage it is said: Both the bride who breaks faith with her groom and her seducer shall be stoned to death. This law was later mitigated. In the language of Jesus the son of Sirah, XXIII 19: Adulteresses and adulterers shall be punished; but no further mention is made here of the death penalty.

In the 4th book of Moses V 21 adulteresses are punished by God himself with bodily suffering and hopeless sickness: "The Lord make thee a curse and an oath among thy people, when the Lord doth make thy thigh to rot and thy belly to swell. And this water that causeth the curse shall go into thy bowels to make thy belly to swell and thy thigh to rot."

The Koran is inexhaustible in its condemnation of adultery. In Chapter IV it says: "If any of your women be guilty of whoredom, produce four witnesses from among you against them, and if they bear witness against them, imprison them in separate apartments until death release them, or God affordeth them a way to escape." If slaves after marriage are guilty of adultery, "they shall suffer half the punishment which is appointed for the free women." Slaves are thus punished more lightly because they did not receive such good upbringing, says

73

Ullman in his Koran Commentaries. According to Sunna, adulterers who are free born should be stoned; if they are slaves, they should receive only a hundred strokes of the whip.

The Turk Omer Haleby says the following to adulterous women—for the law mostly had the women in view: "You who commit adultery, know that the Bastonnade and the death penalty threaten you. Hear what happened to Ammewije, who committed adultery: she was sentenced to the punishment of stoning; but since she was pregnant, the sentence of the law was accordingly suspended. After her delivery, and after she had enjoyed the fruit of her crime for some months, she appeared before the prophet carrying the child in her arms, with a piece of bread in its hands. 'O Sir, she cried, you see the child already in a position where he can dispense with his mother's care; do not change the lawful penalty for my crime on his account any longer. I could be surprised and condemned by death to atone for my sin in Hell; it is better that I lose my life in this world than the sacred happiness of the hereafter. . . .' Know, O daughters of Islam, that the bitter tears and the obvious repentance of the religious Ammewije wiped out her sin in the eyes of God and Man. For God is right and generous!"

In Persia, if a man finds his wife in *flagranti*, he may immediately kill her. If it is, however, difficult to obtain the evidence, for according to requirement of Ali: *Necesse est videre stylum in pixide*, it is hardly possible, then he gets a divorce; of course the wife must then relinquish her claim to any of the marriage goods.

The Code of Ibrahim Haleby deals expressly with the kinds of adultery and the accompanying penalties which the Turkish law fixes.

It says there: Adultery is an act of uncleanliness, in which one makes himself guilty with a person with whom he has no legitimate right so to do. The evidence of the crime is: either the free confession of the guilty; or the testimony of witnesses before the court. In the first case, the guilty ones must repeat their confessions four times at four different terms of the court. Then the crime is acknowledged and the penalty fixed. They receive no corporal punishment if they excuse themselves on the ground they did not know the law or that they did not know the severity of the offense. For example, if a husband sleeps with his wife after a complete contractual divorce; if a master sleeps with his slave after her absolute freedom; if a master sleeps with a slave who has been given to him as a hostage, but who really belongs to one of his kinsmen; and if the guilty one declares that he did not know that he must not have done that—then his sentence is suspended. In all of these cases, the copulation, although it is illegitimate and contrary to law, does not call for any legal penalty whatsoever; for it does not prevent the father from recognizing and legitimizing the child which is born of such copulation. It is different, however, if one commits the crime with the slave of a blood relative; in this case, whether the guilty one pleads ignorance of the law or not—he is punished.

In case adultery is shown through witnesses, it is prescribed that four respectable and trustworthy men give testimony of the same tenor. They must appear together before the tribunal and testify in unanimity, but not under the name of the plain *Dschima*, a simple pretended union of the guilty ones, but under the name *Sena*, adultery. And they must say that they are themselves witnesses of the act, and they must have seen *kel mil fel mikhale, stylum in pixide*. In such case the witnesses shall have no scruples about having cast their glance upon that portion of the body of their neighbors which the Koran and shame forbid them to look upon under other circumstances. For in such a case man has the duty to consider the evil so that he may punish it. Besides these, however, neither ear witness nor substitute witnesses are acceptable by the justice; and even the eye witnesses are no longer acceptable if their testimony is in conflict at any point, for it is then not sufficient. For these depositions must coincide in every detail concerning the time, the place, and the consent of the woman. Rigorous circumspection and carefulness are the duty of the judge. The slightest contradiction in the testimony over the consent of the woman lifts the indictment from the accused. The testimony of the witnesses must be given in the presence of the putative adulterer; but the accused woman need not be present. The testimony of the witnesses must immediately follow the crime and the entire proceeding must be completed within a month. The witnesses are free to testify or not; both are praiseworthy. In the first case they serve the truth and receive the compensation of having uncovered a crime and having seen to its punishment, and they take part in upholding the law of the land. In the second case, his silence is a humane act towards his neighbor. For the prophet says: "He who shields his brother, will see his own wife shielded by the generosity of God on the day of judgment."

The penalty for adulterers who are *Mouchssin* is stoning. Those men and women are considered as *Mouchssin* who are of age, healthy in spirit and body, Moslem, free, and always married. If a man or woman is short any one of these six qualities, then the guilty one can be sentenced only to the punishment of whipping. Adultery committed during *Ramasan*, the month of fasting, is in every case penalized with death; there can be no mitigating circumstances. The same happens in case of incurableness and repetition, or it happens inevitably to the man if the woman dies during an act of rape.

The whipping consists of a hundred strokes for a free person, and fifty for a servant. The strokes must not be too violent, lest they bring about the death of the criminal; nor too weak, lest they do not fulfill the purpose of the law, which strives for correction. The strokes must be apportioned on all parts of the

76

body—with the exception of the head and the sex parts. The guilty man must stand up straight and lift up his shirt at the commencement of the bodily punishment. The sentenced woman must sit and be dressed, and she need not even lift a fur-lined dress. Besides this penalty, the court may also decree as a penalty for adultery, the punishment of exile. If adultery with a stolen slave is discovered, the robber must also indemnify the true owner of the slave in gold.

The penalty of stoning must take place in public. The sentenced man should stand free in the middle of the field, but the sentenced woman must be buried in a grave up to her bosom. The witnesses of the crime must throw the first stones upon the sentenced ones; then follow the attendants of the court, then the people all take part in the stone throwing until the criminals show no more sign of life. If the witnesses refuse to take part in the procedure, or if they do not appear on the day set for sentencing, or if they shall have died in the time between the sentence and its execution—then the death penalty is lifted from the guilty ones.

In case an adulterer is sentenced, not as the result of the testimony of witnesses, but because of his own confession, then the attendants of the court must throw the first stone.

Those so punished are not refused the honor of a burial.

If an adulteress finds herself in a condition of pregnancy, then all punishment is lifted for the moment. And if she herself answers for her crime, then she retains her freedom until after her delivery; and then again so long as the child needs her milk and her motherly care.

At the time of Mohammed IV, at Constantinople, the wife of a cobbler, caught in adultery with a Jew, a linen dealer, was stoned to death. Since the origin of Islam, this punishment decreed by the Koran for adultery had not been administered, because the prophet, as this penalty was about to befall one of his most valiant fieldmasters, had demanded a milder inter-

77

pretation in the name of heaven for a rigorously given law and the indispensible requirement that the testimony be by four trustworthy witnesses, so that neither at that time nor since then had the penalty decreed by the Koran been meted out to anyone. This occurred in the reign of Mohammed IV under the highest judge of the land, Bajasisade Achmed Efendi. This author of "Significance of the Will in Acts of Devotion of the greatest Imam" as strict in orthodoxy as he was learned, did not rest until he had in his power several witnesses whom he suspected of concealing what they had seen, whereupon, before the Mosaic of the Sultan Achmed, he had a grave excavated, and had placed therein the wife of the cobbler and the Jew, who several days before, in the hope of saving his life, had become a Moslem, and who was therefore crowned with special favor, but the woman was buried before the entire people under a heap of stones. The Sultan betook himself to the Palace of Falsipascha on the racecourse so that he might himself see this drama of rigorous enforcement of the law.

The Moslem who bestows his favor upon a free woman must not be considered as an adulterer. Likewise, neither a man nor woman will receive the death penalty if they have committed adultery in a foreign land or in a section which is revolting against the legitimate ruler. In both of these cases only a corrective penalty must be decreed.

Furthermore, foreigners are punished only if they commit adultery with a woman of the land, and native if they commit adultery with a foreign woman.

Corrective penalties are merited particularly: for adultery with a near relative; for an unclean dealing with a minor; for a deed which a man commits in the darkness through mistake: toward a strange woman, a slave of his wife's, his father's or his mother's; for Liawta or pederasty with a person of the male or female sex; for the contemptible business of pimping; for unchastity with animals; for marriage with a widow or a di-

78

vorced woman, so long as she is not yet out of the *Iddet*, the period which she must wait before marrying again; for the free intercourse of both sexes, if a man and a woman who do not see fit to obey the law, meet in a familiar manner, chat together, drink and have a meal secretly; for every deficiency of respect in the attitude of a man towards a woman who is strange and not related to him; for the neglect of the equality which a man owes all his legitimate wives, but this holds true only if the man repeats his offense after having been once warned; finally, a corrective punishment is merited for the disobedience of a wife to the will of her husband.

Just as in all of these laws the judge is required to mete out punishment only after great consideration and sufficient proof of the offense, so the believers are admonished to adhere to the strict letter of the truth in their complaints, accusations and testimony.

In the Koran XXXIII, 58, it says: "And they who shall injure the true believers of either sex, without their deserving it, shall surely bear the guilt of calumny and a manifest injustice."

Koran XXIV, 4-15, 18-20, 23-25, deals with false complaints of adultery. The occasion for it was the following: Aischa, the third and most beloved wife of Mohammed, who accompanied him on his expedition against the Mozalek race in the fifteenth year of the hegira, one night wandered from the road. Safan Ebn Al'Moattel, one of the most distinguished generals, also happened to remain behind, and found Aischa sleeping in the morning. As Aischa awoke and saw Safan, she threw her veil over her face. Safan, without saying a word to her, had her mount his camel and brought her back. Through this coincidence, a certain enemy of Mohammed, Abdallah Ebn Obba, attempted to cast aspersions on Aischa's virtue, which caused Mohammed great grief. For his own peace of mind, and for the consolation of Aischa, her father Abu Bekr, and Safan, the following verses were written into the XXIV chapter, wherein this calumny was considered as a test, and for solacing the soul of the one concerned: ". . . But as to those who accuse women of reputation of whoredom, and produce not four witnesses of the fact, scourge them with four score stripes; for such are infamous prevaricators, excepting those who shall afterwards repent and amend; for unto such will God be gracious and merciful. . . . As to the party among you who have published the falsehood, think it not to be an evil unto you; on the contrary, it is better for you. Every man of them shall be punished according to the injustice of which he hath been guilty; and he among you who hath undertaken to aggravate the same shall suffer a grievous punishment. (Abdallah Ebn Obba, for his punishment, was condemned to die as an unbeliever, rather than as a Moslem.) Did not the faithful men and the faithful women, when ye heard this, judge in your own minds for the best; and say, This is a manifest falsehood? Have they produced four witnesses thereof? Wherefore since they have not produced the witnesses, they are surely liars in the sight of God. . . . Had it not been for the indulgence of God towards you, verily a grievous punishment had been inflicted upon you, for the calumny which ye have spread; when ye published that with your tongues and spoke that with your mouths of which ye had no knowledge. . . . When ye heard it, did ye say, It belongeth not unto us, that we should talk of this matter: God forbid! this is a grievous calumny. God warneth you, that ye return not to the like crime forever, if ye be true believers."

The calumny of Aischa did not remain without serious consequences in the history of Islam. The first general of the schismatic Motesele, the digressor, who disputed the right of the son-in-law of the prophet to the throne, was quoted as a declared opponent of Aischa, to whom Ali, the consort of her stepdaughter Fatima, never denied that he did not believe blindly in her innocence after investigation of her adventure with

Safan, but like other sceptics he must keep his silence because of this heaven-sent chapter. Since she herself witnesses the battle from a camel, it was called the battle of the camel. The adventure of the favorite wife of the prophet remained forever a cause for war between Persians and Osmen, between Shahites and Sunnites, and if a religious peace was effected between these two folk, these were constantly the main provisions: Forbearance from all abuse of the companion of the prophet, the highly revered, who watched the holy battle on the *Imam,* and the mother of true believers, Aischa the chaste.

The desire to protect the honor of his own house, of his own most beloved wife, was sufficient reason for Mohammed to provide protection also for the honor of other women: four witnesses must verify the adultery, otherwise the accusation is deemed calumny. It is also said in the XXIV chapter: "They who shall accuse their wives of adultery and shall have no witnesses thereof, besides themselves, shall swear four times to God that they speaketh the truth, the fifth time that they imprecate the curse of God on them if they be liars." The following however, prevents punishment of the wife: "If she swears four times by God that he is a liar. And the fifth time she imprecate the wrath of God on her if he speaketh the truth." Ullman sees a similarity here to the IV book of Moses, chapter V 11-31, and writes: Mohammed seems to have known the law therein contained, and to have changed it intentionally to suit his purpose.

Among the Christian Balkan folk the morals are much more lax. For instance, the southern Slavs do not consider it wrong for a single man to lie with the wife of another if she gives herself willingly to him. *Eh, dala mu je*—"for she has endured him" is said in his defense, while the adulteress, to excuse herself can sing the generally useful song: "Every woman is a loveable gad-about, who does not endure it but twice or thrice; for between today and tomorrow one becomes

81

black earth." But if a married man uses another woman, they say angrily: "he paganized himself with her"; and "in the other world the woman will be hanged with limbs outspread on the posts of hell; and while drops fall from her sex parts, her lover must stand under her with open mouth to catch the drops."

CHAPTER SEVEN

# MARRIAGES AND WEDDINGS OF THE SULTANS

*Original marriages of interest—Marriage of one with a right to the throne with a slave—Marriage feasts—Expensive offices of honor—The wedding year 1612—The wedding palms, symbols of manly power—Dowries—Bridal presents—A ninefold marriage—The festival—Decrease of the rich dowry—Dealings with daughters of a Sultan—Age of the bride—Difference between virgins and widows—The bridal night of a princess—Disadvantages of marriages with a princess.*

*A Fellah from Cairo*

The mariages of Osman rulers were originally, just as among the European princes, very often tied up with important political questions. I have already mentioned as an example an Osman Byzantian marriage. The Sultan Murad also married his first born son, *Bajesid Jildirim*, the ray of weather, for political reasons, to the daughter of the master of Crimea who brought the greatest part of the fortune of her father to her bridegroom as dowry. As soldiers of the bride there went to Crimea the Judge of Brussa, Chodscha Efendi, and the standard bearer, Aksankor, with the *Tchauschbaschi Timurchan*, and as companions to the bride, the wives of the judge and standard bearer and the nurse of Bajesid with a following of three thousand men and women. The prince received the messengers with honor, gave his daughter over to the three women and determined who was to accompany the bride and lead her horse. The wedding was brilliantly celebrated at Brussa. There appeared not only the messengers of the neighboring princes of Eidin, Mentesche, Kastamuni, and Karaman, but even ambassadors of the Sultans of Syria and Egypt, bearing rich presents. They brought Arabian horses and Alexandrian goods, and Greek slaves, male and female. Ewrenosbeg, alone, a Greek renegade, brought a hundred of the most beautiful boys and girls, the sons and daughters of his people, as slaves. Each of the first ten slaves carried aloft a plate of goldpieces, each of the following ten a silver bowl of silverpieces, the other eighteen: gold and silver pots and basins with enameled cups and saucers, goblets and glasses set with jewels, "so that," as Idris says, "the Koran description of paradise was fulfilled: And there went about them—the holy—everlastingly young children with basins and pots and goblets." These presents were called in Turkish *Satschu*, strawwork, because the customary wedding presents, gold and silver coins, were strewn over the head of the bride.

A later marriage also of interest of a daughter of Bajesid with the Mohammedan prince, Enkel Timur, was celebrated with the permission of the latter on the Plain of Jenischepir, east of Brussa; but that did not deter Timurs from disturbing the Osman kingdom and relieving Bajesid of the throne. Timurs' marriages were but imitations which Dschengischan's writings and life give as grand examples of the might of ruling houses. Constantly to further and secure this through marriages was Thimurs' aim from the beginning to the end of his government, which accounts for the fact that his weddings constitute a permanent chapter in history.

As Timurs was first rising to power. he wooed the hand of the princess Turkan-Chan, the sister of the Shah Husein; and he supported the throne of Husein as long as his sister lived; but on her death four years after the marriage, he broke the bonds of the blood relationship and vassalage and arose in open warfare against Husein, the master of Chorasan and Transoxanien. A truce was consummated, but war again broke out, until after the pillage of Balch and the death of Husein, Timurs succeesed to the throne without opposition. Of eight princesses who were in Husein's harem, Timurs took half for himself, but he took only two as consorts, and divided the other four among his friends, relatives and brothers in arms.

The campaigns of Timurs proceeded thenceforth not only

with friendly dealings and treaties, but also with marriages. After the first campaign against the aforementioned Husein of Churesm, Timurs through an embassy obtained his daughter Chansade as a consort for his oldest son Schihangir, and Husein Ssofi made a feast which compared in brilliance with the famous wedding feasts of the Arabian Caliphs. The trousseau of the bride consisted of costly crowns, a golden throne, arm-bands and earrings, necklaces and belts, chests of jewels and pearls, beds, tents, sofas, and canopies. As a welcome the nobles of the kingdom strewed gold pieces and pearls over the head of the bride, the air was permeated with the odor of musk and ambergris, the roof was covered with tapestries and golden cloth; in all of the cities through which the bride passed she was met by *Scheichi* and *Kadi*, *by Imame* and *Molla*, and all of these celebrations were doubled at her entrance into Samarkand. The pavilion wherein the marriage took place represented heaven with precious stones as stars, the top of the pavilion was of ambergris and the curtain of the innermost chamber of gold stuffs. Several tents filled with chests, dishes, clothes, and other merchandise were placed about the streets and near the palace. The astronomers arranged the horoscope for the happiest moment of the wedding, and this was an exhibition of such splendor that nothing like it had been seen in the east since the most beautiful time of the caliphate. The following year, with slightly less splendor, Timurs celebrated his own wedding with the Princess Dilschadaga, the daughter of the Sultan of Dschete, after he had captured her on his second campaign against her father. Besides those wives already mentioned, Timurs married the Princess Tumanaga, the daughter of Emir Musa, because of whom he united the twelve royal gardens of Samarkand, which was named *Bagni bihischt,* the garden of paradise. This tie of relationship, however, saved the Sultan of Dschete from his downfall just as little as it did the Shah of Chuaresm or the Sultan of Osman.

87

In the year 1636 Timurs celebrated a double wedding, that of the Princess Begisi, his grandchild, with the Prince Iskender Mirsa, and his own with Tuwelchanun, the daughter of Keser Chodschah, the mongolian prince, whom he married in his seventy-second year as his ninth wife, and whom he favored with the newly laid most glorious garden of Samarkand, called *Dilguscha*, heart opening.

The young bride—as Hammer writes—could not seduce the old conqueror with any faithlessness towards the bride of victory and conquest; at the preparation of the wedding feast the campaigns were terminated and Timurs rose from his bridal bed to a conquest of India.

The beloved favorite of the Tartar emperor was called *Tscholpan*, morning star. He depended on her to such an extent that he took her with him on all his trips. This bloodthirsty despot could also be extreme in his love; strikingly enough not only in his sex love, but also in his family love. His only daughter, Sultana Becht, could demand everything of his love.

In spite of the bad result caused by the relationship of the Osman court with the Tartars, he still stressed the importance of a convenient relationship. So Sultan Murad II proceeded with great pomp to Adrianapolis to the fiery wedding with the daughter of the prince of Siope. Elwanbeg, the overseer, in whose family reposed the high office of being messengers for wooing the bride was sent to Sinope with the widow of Chalil-Paschas, who was brought up in the harem of the Sultan Mohammed, to bring the bride in full state. The prince of Sinope received the embassy with proper nobility and courtesy; he turned his daughter over to the consort of Chalil-Pascha. Wherever the procession passed through, the princess received a most hearty welcome, and then the wedding of the Sultan was celebrated in Adrianapolis.

Also in the winter of 1438 was the festivity of the marriage of Murad II with another, a Serbian princess devoted to Adrianapolis.

In the same year Murad also celebrated the marriage of his son Mohammed with the princess of Sulkdr. Suleimanbeg, the Turkish prince of this country, had five daughters; in order to choose one of them as a bride for the heir to the Osman throne, the woman Chisr Agas was sent to look on the possible brides, and she chose one in the name of the Sultan for his son, and she placed an engagement ring on her finger. The second time this matron went with the bride-wooer, Siridschi-Pascha, to fetch the bride, who was accompanied to Brussa with her dowry by the most noble of her country. Judges, *Ulema* and *Shahs*, went to meet the princess on her joyous journey; the wedding itself was celebrated at Adrianapolis midst many other festivities and also with poetry for a period of three months.

Since then, however, Osman history records but few marriages of sultans or the sons of sultans with princesses: there was a strict law for those with rights to the throne that they marry only slaves, and no further word is mentioned of a desirable relationship. Nevertheless more space is taken in Osman history with marriage festivities which took place at the marriages of the daughters of the sultans, but with whose hands and hearts were made happy, not foreign princes, but favorites of the court. So at Constantinople Sultan Suleimus the Great celebrated with "until then unheard of festivities," the marriage of his sister with the Grandvizier Ibrahimpascha. A pavilion and a throne were erected on the hippodrome for the Sultan. He named two viziers as leaders of the bride, Ajapascha, who, emulating Romulus, laid the foundation for Germany—and Janitscharenaga, who went to Sserai to praise the Sultan who had treated them royally and who expressed high praise of Ibrahim. For, seven days the *silihdare, sipahi, ulufedschi, chureba, dchebedschi, and topdschi*, and on the eighth the *janitscharen* and the viziers were brilliantly entertained. On the ninth day, determined as the evening for taking the bride from Sserai, the Sultan, "as if between two walls of gold cloth and silk covers, with which the windows of the streets through which he passed was bedecked," proceeded to the palace of Ibrahimpascha.

The "wedding palms" began the festive journey as a true symbol of manly strength; one of them consisted of sixty thousand, the other of sixty-four thousand little pieces; on them were to be seen "the strangest pictures of trees, flowers, and fabulous animals, an entire creation and world of wonder." Six days thereafter it pleased Suleimus to go to the Sserai placed on the Hippodrome of Ibrahimpascha, and midst various displays of wrestlers, dancers, and archers, races and other contests, to take from the poets their wedding writings.

The wedding of another Ibrahim with the Sultana Aische, the daughter of Murad, took place with just as great a show. Through an entirely new extraordinary favor, this occurred threefold at Kanun with the hundred thousand ducats, the determined dowry of the princess; the leader of the bride was the Kapudanpascha Kilidsch Ali, whose present merely consisted of some fifty thousand ducats, and who in addition to this paid all of the expenses of the sugar works and the wedding palms. In old Sserai, in order to complete the engagement, he and the Beglerbeg of Rumili, Mohammedpascha, were dressed in golden wedding clothes, and in all, after the registration, apportioned three thousands kaftans. The Sultan's teacher, the learned Seadeddin, the historian, added the sum of three thousand ducats as a present, from which it can be seen that wedding officials find it pretty costly at such marriage ceremonies.

On the ninth day of feasting the bridegroom entertained his guests in his Sserai on the Hippodrome—the same at which the Grandvizier waited upon the former Ibrahim, and now again belonged to an Ibrahim. Forty wrestlers and singers

90

entertained the gathering with their offerings in wrestling and song. In the afternoon the wedding procession started, led by men upholding two twelve ell-high wedding palms, and a smaller one beset with jewels.

One year distinguished in Christendom as in Turkey with joyous wedding feasts of unusual splendor was 1612. In France and Spain, Portugal and Germany, reports Hammer, the double wedding of Ludwig XIII with the Spanish Infanta Anna of Austria, and the Spanish prince with the Princess Elizabeth Bourbon, the oldest sister of the king of France, was celebrated. At Constantinople there took place the double wedding of Machmud, the son of Cicala, with a sister of Mohammed III, and Mohammed the Bull, the Kapudanpascha, with the oldest daughter of the reigning Sultan Achmed; at the same time the youngest princess became engaged to the Grandvizier among the *Mufti* and the *Viziers*.

The princess-bride of Machmud was the widow of a former vizier, Mustafa Pascha. The celebrated were none the less brilliant. The bridegroom gave races with mace and bars, and the banquet cost twenty thousand dollars. Twenty days thereafter the wedding of the Kpudanpascha, Mohammed the Bull, was celebrated with greater pomp, because it was the marriage of a virgin. The outfit of the bride consisted, according to Hammer, of twenty-seven gifts: the first jewel gleaming headdress and golden slippers inlaid with turquois and rubies, the oldest and newest symbol of the highest rule of women; then the Koran in golden bands with brilliant clasps; a jewel casket of crystal in which were to be seen immense diamonds and pearls, worth one hundred and sixty thousand ducats; armbands, necklaces, belts, headdresses, ear—and finger—knuckle-rings, as the seven spheres in which the beauty of the harem moves; together with twenty-seven bridal presents borne by twenty-seven carriers. Eleven crowded wagons followed full of maids-in-waiting and slaves as servants for the bride, each one attended by two black eunuchs; twenty-eight slaves in golden clothes on horse, accompanied by twenty-eight black eunuchs. Two hundred and forty mules with tents, tapestries, gold and silver cloth, carpets and cushions. Thus were the gifts and the following of the bride ushered into the house of the bridegroom. A few days later she came herself. Her procession disclosed five hundred *Janitschares*, then eighty Emire, some in their felt caps, others in their green turbans; then came the *Imame* and *Shahs*, the *Viziers*, *Muderries*, or professors, and *Danischmende* or students, the *Kiadeskere*, the *Mufti* on the left and the *Kaimakan* on the right, each filling the highest place of honor; for according to the arrangements of the ceremony the right side is the place of honor for the officers of the court and the generals, the left the place of honor for the deserving of the law, so that there could never be a dispute about the rank between the *Aga* and the *Ulema*, since each takes his place. The Turkish military music followed the Egyptian with half drum beats and castanets, accompanied by wedding music from the zither and harp players, the laborers from the arsenal with axes and hammers, with poles and crowbars to tear down the stalls and houses which hindered the procession in the streets or the free movement of the immense wedding palms. After the wedding palms, "which through their heaven reaching height represented the symbol of manly power and through the richness of their multifarious fruits the fertility of women," there went twenty officers of the chamber as representatives of the *Defterdar*—bride—leaders, behind whom three wedding torches were carried by many slaves: the third was of enormous size, streaked with gold, and illuminated more through the brilliance of its precious stones than through its flame. The scion Efendi, as house chancellor and arranger of the wedding festivities, followed with fifty officials of the court of the princess.

Then the wedding carriage of carmine velvet, and behind it

a larger one bedecked with gold, whose golden curtain hung down to the ground on all sides; in it rode the Sultana-bride, surrounded by black eunuchs.

Her wagon of state followed drawn by four gray horses, then eight wagons of maids and eunuchs intermingled, finally her most beautiful slaves, twenty-five in number, with flying veils and hair. Such reports of wedding pomp are not to be found only in the year books of Osman history, but also at the place itself, so thinks Hammer, because the customs of the east have constantly been related to those of the Romans and the Greeks since ancient times. In the palms are represented the phallus, in the carmine veil of the carriage, the flame, in the wedding torches, amours and hymens, in the Egyptian accompaniment to songs of half drums and castanets, the mutual desire, of fascinating music and an extravagant accompaniment to the pleasure.

Double sorrows, as history relates, followed at the foot of the festivities of the double marriage: "The youngest daughter of the Sultan who was engaged to the Grandvizier Nassu, died, and on the day after the last pictured wedding, the Sultan grossly mishandled the Sultana, the mother of the princess married to the Kapudanpascha. She had strangled from jealousy a black slave which the Sultan had given to his sister, and in addition pleased him, as she had already done to several others as soon as they apeared to be in the good graces of the Sultan. Sultan Achmed, finally made furious by such murders from jealousy, beat his consort miserably, stabbed her in the cheek with his dagger, and trampled her under foot." A dervish, who, fool or assassin, threw a huge stone at the Sultan, luckily striking him only in the shoulder, was beheaded.

At the time of Mohammed IV, the marriage of his daughter Chadidsche with the second favorite vizier, Mustafa Pascha, was celebrated for fourteen days with marches, processions, street feasts, and plays. The engagement present of the bride-

93

groom, called *Nischan,* was extraordinarily rich: Thirty bearers brought sweet-meats, twenty *Janitshares* each carried a sherbet filled barrel out of whose opening grew a tree with branches heavily laden with fruit. Forty others carried two gardens, six feet square, adorned with golden plants and silver springs, ten others with flower-covered caskets of sweet-meats on their heads. Twenty soldiers came with as many wedding caskets full of silk cloth, muslin, shawls, and gold embroidered bath towels; thirty-four with as many caskets in every one of which were three pieces of rich cloth for dressing the bride. The ornaments were carried by twenty soldiers in silver plates on embroidered cloths; among these were: a cap of ˌfine velvet with several decorations of diamonds, four diamond belts, the great and the small *Chasseki,* the favorites of the Sultan, and the princess-bride; three remaining diamonds for the bride, the crown-prince, and the Sultan; three diamond turbans for the bride, the great *Chasseki* of the Sultan, and the daughter of the small *Chasseki,* determined as the bride for the *Kaimakam* Mustafa-pascha; two Korans in gold embroidered, jewel-set binding for the bride and the crown-prince; a pair of emerald earrings of a hundred carats, three pair of diamond armbands for the mother of the Sultana, the favorite of the Sultana, and the bride; diamond buttons for his majesty the *Padischah.* Furthermore for the bride alone: sables, ermine, and lynx, three lead-horses whose covers were beset with pearls, sapphires, rubies, and tur-quois; two gardens of sugar, forty palms, eighty-six mules with all kinds of womanly finery, half covered, half open, so that the pearl embroidered pillows, the golden veils, the brilliant display shone out. The procession closed with twelve wagons of slaves and thirty-six black eunuchs.

The spectacle of the jugglers and the rope dancers lasted three days. On the fourth day the bride was accompanied by the viziers and the notables from her royal retreat to that of the bridegroom's. Two lofty, immense palms, then two small silver ones glorified the procession, in which the bride rode in a carriage decorated with silver and stripes of gold plate, drawn by six white horses. The Sultana Chasseki, the mother of the bride, arrived in a silver-decorated carriage, followed by ten other carriages filled with slaves and eunuchs. The bride was "conducted to the bridal chamber only for the purposes of the ceremony, for, not yet ripe for the consummation of the marriage, she had been engaged merely for a relationship of the highest favor, or as a design for profit on her widow's estate, which the bridegroom owes to royal protection with a restitution of the dowry if she dies before the marriage is consummated."

In the year 1708, at the time of Sultan Achmed, both daughters of prior Sultan Mustafa II, Emine and Aischa, were married, one to the Grandvizier, the other to Nuuman Koprilisade, the second son of the worthy Koprili. The marriage festivities took place with the same pomp as ever; but the sum expended became ever less; one notices the decrease and the impoverishment of the cities and the courts. The dowry amounted to but twenty thousand ducats, a fifth, yea, a tenth of the dowries of former princesses. The engagement present which the Grandvizier brought to the princess and which was open for display, consisted of a headband, a necklace, armbands, rings, a belt, diamond ear- and knuckle-rings; the seven rings of the seven spheres of eastern women; further, a jeweled mirror, a veil set with diamonds, slippers and socks embroidered with pearls, bath slippers of gold set with jewels, two thousand ducats and forty dishes of sweet-meats. After these two Sultanas, who were nieces of the reigning Sultan Achmed, were married, the latter also considered the marriage of his own daughter, the four year old Fatima. In vain did the Grandvizier seek to thwart the winning of her hand by Silidarpascha, the known favorite of the Sultan; he nevertheless was chosen with a dowry of forty thousand ducats; and in addition, his royal domain was enlarged by the Island of Cypress. The feast was brilliant, for there was no greater lover of feast than Sultan Achmed. This partiality he showed somewhat later, as he celebrated a nine-fold wedding, wedding means also circumcision in the language customs of the orientals, the marriages of three of his daughters and two of his nieces, and the circumcision of four of his sons, with a brilliance which reminded one of the splendid feasts of former times. The description of this nine-fold celebration of five married princesses and four circumcised princes filled sixteen folios in the book of the historian of the kingdom. Raschid, drawn from the detailed wedding book of Wehbis is, says Hammer, well worth relating in detail, even at the neglect of all of the arts recorded by the historians of the kingdom, the art of rope- and sword-dancing, of juggling and swinging, of cup-and-ball and card play, of bull-dogs and buffoonery, because it has reconstructed in minute detail the order of rank and the clothes and the sequence of events of the ceremonial feast, and so records new and remarkable things. Hammer has devoted much time to it. I mention here only the names: The five bridal pair were Nischandschipascha Mustafapascha, the son of Kara Mustafapascha, the Governor of Rakka; and Alipascha with the three daughters of the reigning Sultan; Sirke Osmanpascha with the princess Ummetullah, and the Governor of Negroponte, Silihdar Ibrahim, with the princess Aischa, who, engaged but never married to the deceased Koprilisade Nuumanpascha, was now married to his successor. For the requirements of the feast there were furnished: ten thousand wooden bowls, seven thousand nine hundred hens of European extraction from Rodosto, Amedschick, Schehrkoji, Asiatic hens from Sandschak Chudawenghiar, a thousand four hundred and fifty Calcutta hens, three thousands young hens, two thousand doves, a thousand ducks, a hundred cups, fifteen thousand lamps, a thousand lamp rings in the form of half moons, and ten thousand tankards in order to sample the wine; a hundred and twenty pipe carriers in leather coats and hose, with oiled pipes were stationed as a police watch over the feast, so that it was ruled, not by clubs, or canes, but only by oiled waterpipes which propriety prescribed.

We have already seen how the amounts which princesses received from the court as dowry always became smaller. Sultan Selim had three daughters; two of them received as much as a hundred thousand ducats. Fatima was married after her father's death by her brother Sultan Murad III to Siawuschpascha with a dowry of two hundred thousand ducats. That was a thriving business for Viziers and favorites. Known renegades were rewarded in this manner. So the Vizier Achmedpascha, The Fisher, received the hand of a grandchild of the great Suleimus, and through her became immensely wealthy. He married his daughter in great style to the Janitscharenga Dscighalesade; the present of the best man Siawusch consisted of sixty thousand ducats, the wedding palms alone cost a thousand ducats, the dress of the bride a hundred thousand, the distributed sweet-meats twice that much. These expenses were borne by the mother-in-law, the old Sultana Mihrmah, Sunmoon, the daughter of Suleimus, and the widow of the Grandvizier Rustem, who were protected by a daily income of two thousand ducats. The Kapudanpascha was in a like manner rewarded for the conversion of his father by the hand of the Sultan's daughter, just as the Genoan and the continental renegades Cicala and Paggi had prior thereto become viziers and sons-in-law of the Sultan. A display of apparent splendor was granted to the wedding of the continental renegade Paggi, whose Turkish name was Chalil. An entire week the business of the couch and the gate were set aside, for three hundred palms exalted the marriage procession; on the birthday of the prophet the contract of marriage was signed in ancient *Sserai* by the head Eunuch in the name of the bride, by the best man, the Vizier Mohammed, in the name of the bridegroom, and by the Sultan's advisor, the historian Sae-

97

deddin, with a dowry of three hundred thousand ducats. For three days the trousseau was brought into the palace of the bridegroom by forty eunuchs on three hundred rows of mules. According to ancient custom it was necessary for the bridegroom to provide servants for the harem to the extent of one hundred and eighty thousand, before he could touch the trousseau of the bride. For three days the law makers and officers of state were entertained royally, then they came with elephants lions, horses, camels, giraffes, gazelles, falcons, parrots, and fruits of all kinds, made of sugar. The bride was conducted under a red satin canopy on a horse bedecked with jewels, accompanied by her eunuchs on foot, and the bridegroom with exceptional wedding palms.

But the times gradually changed; to marry the daughter of a Sultan remained no longer the share of a specially favored or beloved Grandvizier, but it became a service, an offering for the favor of the Padischah. The Princess-brides received smaller dowries, so that it became necessary for the vizier sons-in-law to provide more of the marriage favors. In addition the brides were either so young that they soon survived their old husbands and could quickly find a new attachment, or too old: so Mustafa III married his thirty-four year old sister, the Sultana Aischa, to the Vizier Silihdar Mohammedpascha, the inhabitant of Sandschak Tirhala, with a dowry of but five thousand ducats, a twentieth part of the dowries under Sultan Suleimus, the law maker, a forty-eighth part of those under Murad IV who married off the Sultana Kia, the consort of Melek Achmedpascha, with a marriage portion equal to a year's Egyptian tribute. The thirty-four year old sister of Mustafa III, Ssaliha, a widow, was married at the same time to the Grandvizier Raghib "as a sign of highest favor." Days before, in order to get into the good graces of his engaged bride, the Grandvizier sent her ten silver bowls with silver covers on a silver table, a silver dish of sweet-meats, thirty dishes of flowers and fifty of fruit. Fourteen days later the Sultana entrained for the palace of the Grandvizier without a festive procession, for she was a widow; for the same reason her eunuchs followed in their everyday turbans and without music. Nevertheless this wedding is of particular interest, because at its mention the historian relates an intimate ritual: After sundown, according to previous custom, the Kislaraga came to lead the bashful bride to the arms of the bridegroom.

It is the custom of the court for the princess to take the bridegroom ungraciously with pride and repulsion and barely to be able to tolerate him. After the silent scene lasts for some time, she suddenly arises unwillingly and withdraws into her chamber; the eunuchs seize that moment to remove the slippers of the bridegroom, and to place them at the entrance to her door.

This ritual is of the greatest importance, for through it the bridegroom takes command of the possessions of the harem, whose entrance is only available to the husband. The eunuchs draw back, the bridegroom goes into the "innermost chamber, where the princess sits on the place of honor on the sofa." He throws himself at her feet and remains kneeling with his arms forming a circle, awaiting a word of favor from the silent ungracious mistress. She says: "Bring me water!" He fetches it on his knees, at the same time beseeching her to permit him the favor of letting her veil be lifted. This is embroidered with flowers and jewels, and her hair, braided with gold and pearls, hangs to the earth in seven braids. She has barely disposed of the water when the slaves bring her two bowls, in one of which are two roasted doves, in the other candied sugar, and place them down on low tables in the middle of the room; the bridegroom urgently implores the bride to taste some of it; she answers proudly and arrogantly: "I do not like it"; the bridegroom, in despair, takes to other means of supplication to soften the inexorable one. He calls the eunuchs who pour out rich presents at her feet. Made tractable thereby, the bride permits the bridegroom to take her arm and to lead her to the table according to the customs of the court. He gives her a piece of roasted dove and she sticks a piece of candied sugar into his mouth. The ban is lifted; the bride again takes her place on the sofa, the eunuchs retreat, the pair remain alone for an hour during which the customs of the court permit only the most formal conversation. The Sultan meanwhile occupies himself in the public hall of the harem, where he receives the good wishes of the viziers and the nobles after he has met the sultanas of the harem; music, dance, and shadow play, which the young married woman, naturally without her husband, attends, shorten the night. Finally the young wife, exhausted, desires to go to bed; the gathering breaks up. The first slave, escorted by a eunuch, advises the bridegroom that the bride is in bed. He steals into the bedroom, undresses himself quietly, approaches the feet of the bride on his knees, touches and kisses them gently, and if she suffers this willingly, he moves higher up and arrives finally in a position to receive the greatest favor of a princess of the Sultan. On the following day the bridegroom goes to the bath accompanied by the officers of state and the worthies of the court; the day is called Day of Sheep Feet, for the newlywed, on his return from the bath, has placed before him a bowl of sheep feet. On the third day the Sultan sends his son-in-law an iron club with which to beat the bride to death if on the third day she has not yet given him the right of a consort. History relates no such martyr death.

Even older than the above mentioned bride was the Sultana Fatima, who, already past half *Sakulum*, at the time of Mohammed IV was married to the Governor of Silistra, Jussufpascha, with extraordinary pomp; but here the bridegroom had to be well comforted with the marriage portion of an Egyptian ransom, six hundred thousand ducats. In remarkable contrast, at the same time another Jussufpascha was married to another

Fatima, the sister of Mohammed IV; this second Fatima numbered but two and one-half years.

The two and a half year old Fatima, just as the more than
fifty year old Fatima, these two Sultana-brides, seem to an
observer of Osman court life as characteristically unnatural
sacrifices to blind servile ambition and as an offer to money-
mad royal politics.

The Sultans regarded their daughters and sisters finally
only as possibly good to sell or possibly wares frequently to be
bartered. In order to fill the state treasury the only daughter
of Mustafa III, beloved by him more than life, the princess
Schahsultan, became engaged to the Grandvizier Hamsahamed,
and simultaneously the widow of Raghibpascha, the former
Sultana Ssaliha, who had meanwhile become much older, was
again married to the Kapudampascha. The Grandvizier had
to send his bride forty thousand ducats, a hundred and twenty
thousand piasters for merchandise, eighty thousand for out-
fitting the house, and besides this he had to contribute an
enormous amount of gold to the treasury of the Sultan.

Alibeg, son of the Grandvizier Kara Mustafa, elevated
himself by means of the hand of the little princess Rakije,
later through the sisters, the five and six year old Aischa and
Emine, who were engaged to Hasan and Nuumanpascha, in a
short time to the governorship of Damascus and Erserum; but
as Hasanpascha soon thereafter fell into disrepute, his bride
was simply taken away from him and the subsequent favorite
and Grandvizier, Ali Pascha von Tschorli, was favored with
her hand.

The strangest engagement indubitably, likewise occurred
at that time: in all seriousness they celebrated the engagement
of the barely three month old princess Hebetallah with the
Silihdar Hamsapascha.

Naturally such brides were often dealt with by men to
whom they never belonged. Many princesses did not come

101

really into the marriage bed until they were married seven or eight times. A princess Aischa was engaged at the age of three to Ipschirpascha, at ten she was married to Mohammedpascha, the Governor of Haleb, and when he lost his head for counterfeiting money, she was married to Ibrahimpascha, the *defterdar*, Governor of Cairo; and after his death to Dschanbulnsade, the married Governor of Ofen. Her sister Fatima passed even more often as consort of viziers from hand to hand. She was married the first time to the Vizier Kenaanpascha, the second time to the Vizier Jussufpascha, the third time to the Kapuda Sinanpascha, the fourth time to Ismailpascha, and the fifth time to Kasimpascha; the latter was originally a surgeon, and at the circumcision of the prince Mohammed, the follower of the fourth Sultan of that name, he knew of an astringent powder which stopped a great flow of blood which had left the prince powerless; later, therefore, when Mohammed became Sultan, he conferred upon him the governorship of Temesvar.

As Kasim, conquered by Souche, was about to be beheaded, the Sultan recalled with gratitude that the general had once as a surgeon stopped his bleeding, who now had the power to command the flow of his blood, and in order to save his head, he granted him the hand of his sister, who, after nineteen years of marriage with four husbands, nevertheless came to the hands of her fifth husband as an untouched virgin. She had preserved this virginity "as a result of an exceptional obstruction"; the historian does not describe the latter very adequately, but he does relate that the fifth husband, the former surgeon, artfully put the bride to sleep, removed the obstruction through a well-meant incision, and thereby acquired the highest favor of the princess and the special graciousness of the Sultan. So that he made his fortune, first through stopping, another time through creating a flow of blood.

It should be noted that marriage for many Moslems with daughters of the Sultan must be painful, because one can have

102

no other wife besides a princess-wife; and, in case one shall already have been married to others, he must be divorced from them.

This custom is also prevalent in Persia. Polak says: "If a *Chan* marries a princess, or if such a one is promised him as a wife, then the unwritten law demands, for the law makes no distinction, that he shall hàve no other wife near her, in fact he is compelled either to divorce all other wives which he had previously had or at least to send them from the house and to refrain from having any further cohabitation with any of them."

On the other hand one must treat a princess-consort with extreme care. In general, the husband in the Orient is the unquestioned master over all of his wives, but in this particular case he is the miserable knave and slave.

When in the year 1541 the Grandvizier Lufti sinned through insufficient care and mistreatment of his wife, the sister of the Sultan, he was deposed from his position, divorced from his wife, the Sultana, and exiled to Demitoka.

## CHAPTER EIGHT

# THE POWER OF WOMEN IN THE SULTAN'S HAREM

*The gateway to blissfulness—The slaves as mistresses—Sultana Churrem—Roxelane, the Russian—Her command over Suleimus the Great—Sultan's harem and the sublime porte—Under Murad II—The Venetian—Power of the servants—Drowning of charmers—Under Osman II—Mohammed III and his wives—Baffa—Sultana Mondgestalt-Kosem, the Greek—The Pole Tarchan — Tragedies of jealousy — Sultan Ibrahim, the wife-slave — The Murder of a Sultana-mother—Wealth of the Sultan's wives and favorites—Schechuswar—Mustafa III—Good influence of women—Power of servants —Luxury of the wives—Catastrophes—The Crete—Spring rose drinks.*

*Eighteen-year-old Greek*

Power of women in the Osman domain sounds almost para-doxical.

The harem bears in the Osman custom of speech the beauti-ful name: *Dari* or *Deri seadet.*—The house or the gateway to blissfulness.

Through the gateway to blissfulness the way leads into the sacredness of blissfulness, into the innermost part of the court, into the chambers of the women. But blissfulness does not always rule there; tyranny and caprice and misfortune pre-vail there more than elsewhere, and there the rulers and tyrants most frequently become slaves themselves. Suleimus the Great, whom one could designate as the most solid of all Osman mon-archs, Suleimus, the most powerful and most important of all independent Osman rulers, was given to servility to the most beloved of his wives, let her dictate to him the ruin of his friend and favorite, Ibrahim., He then felt for the first time her future power, and at her wish finally turned over the sceptre of highest power to her son-in-law Rustem, who, however, also could not rule according to his own reason, but according to that of his harem and his mistress. This beloved bedfellow, and at times. truly faithful consort of Suleimus, the Sultana Chuerem the happy, was, according to Hammer, Russian born, whom French historians of her people called Roxelane. She exerted influence on war and peace in the kingdom, governed not only the domestic, but also the foreign policies. She sought a desired opportunity to disclose in a wide field the generalship of her son-in-law, the Grandvizier Rustempascha, and also to have her oldest son, the prince Selim, the Governor of Magnesia, designated ambassador of the Sultan to the rulers of Europe; and in furtherance of this it was determined to declare war against Persia. Her son-in-law also succumbed to her power. Under Rustem's governorship the ruinous influence of the harem over important affairs first became apparent, and just as this influence of the harem appeared at first to serve and strengthen the purposes of the command of the Grandvizier, in fact the command of the Grandvizier since then began to be undermined, because the harem, once it had discovered an opening, in time its power, instead of assisting the Grandvizier, exercised itself more against him, and later, not only the women, but even their watchers, the eunuchs, ruled.

Under Murad II the castrated caretaker of the palace and several women, all "Pillars of the harem" became mightier and more influential than all the associates, favorites, and advisors of the Sultan.

Two Hungarian boys, brothers, were first circumcised as slaves under Sultan Selim, and then, because the Sultan was very much pleased with their service as pages, were castrated for service in the harem; the younger was called Dschaafer and the older Chasnefer; the latter, through awakened spirit, developed through his studies, insinuated himself into the favor of the Sultan Selim, then the Sultan Murad, at first to the position of *Odabaschi*, guard of the page room, and then to the position of *Kapu Aga*, overseer of the palace, and was clothed with good-nature and power under three Sultans—Selim, Murad, and Mohammed. He held his first position for thirty years in the service of the court. He restrained the abuse of his power, but near him, however, with less good-nature and a greater

abuse of their power ruled the women. First, the Sultan's
mother, Nur Banu, the "Lightwoman"; following the mother
in supervision was the first of the Sultan's wives, Ssaffije, "the
clean", a Venetian born of the house of Baffa, whose kin the
poet Baffa claimed to be in his poems, and whose father was
the Governor of Corsica, and who was captured from Corsicans
on the road from Venice to Corsica, to be taken into the harem
of Murad. She ruled her husband as crownprince and as emperor for such a long time that he, although of very lustful
temperament, remained hers alone. The mother and the sister
of Murad, Sultana Esmachan, who was married to the Grandvizier Sokolli, were unhappy because of this; whether it was
through fear that through such power the Venetian would de-
tract from theirs, or whether to make certain of a successor to
the throne through the birth of a great number of children—
they did not rest until they had aroused Murad's lust with two
slaves, a skilled dancer and a Hungarian, more subtle and vivacious than beautiful, antagonizing the Venetian for some time,
so that he shared the pleasures of his bed with them; but although Murad found such great pleasure in his multifarious
affairs that he possessed these two three times in one night,
Ssaffje nevertheless remained wielding power as the mother of
his first born, Mohammed. Especially was this so after the
death of the Walide, the mother of the Sultan, Nur Banu. On
her deathbed she implored Sultan Murad to be very careful of
the grasping hand of his wife Dschanfeda, "Soul offering", who
so far as Kiajai-harem, head mistress of the harem shared the
favor, although not the bed of the Sultam with her former
slaves, supervised the business of the household, and exerted a
great effect on the outside government.

Through this, which is Hammer's report of Murad's dependence on the acquiescence to women, is laid a great portion
of the weakening and softening of the character of the Sultan.
Under his rule the ministers and ambassadors were named and

placed by the women of the harem.

Siawusch became Grandvizier through the influence of his consort, the sister of the Sultan, and her mother the Sultana Walide. While she still lived, his sworn enemy the Sultana Chasseki, the mother of the crownprince Mohammed, who held the ear of the Sultan, could do nothing against Siawusch: Siawusch thought to bring her and her son into disrepute with the Sultan, so that he might preserve the throne for his own children. When Walide died on the Ruhr, not without suspicion on the part of the Sultan that she had been poisoned by the crownprince Mohammed and his mother, Siawusch fell into disfavor, and it was only at the prayer of his consort, the sister of the Sultan, that he was permitted to retain the pension of a retired Grandvizier, three hundred thousand Aspers.

After the death of Walide the influence of Chasseki, the Venetian favorite, and several women who tended them in the harem, and through whom the Sultan ruled, increased. The head mistress was the already mentioned Dschanfeda; two other influential women were: Dame Rasije, whom the Sultan wooed with true love while yet a crown prince, and who later demanded that her protege Schudschaa be elevated from gardener to shah; and the Jewess Kira, who provided the harem with wares and decorations. The princesses of blood, whose influence and credit demanded high posts in the kingdom for their husbands and favorites, either attained their wishes, or if they were refused, saved their heads and fortunes.

At that time lived the three daughters of the Sultan Selim, the sisters of the Sultan Murad; namely, the widow of Solollis, the widow of Piale, and the consort of the Grandvizier Siawusch; then the old, very wealthy woman Mihrmah, "Sun-moon", the daughter of Suleimus the Great, the widow of the Grandvizier Rustempascha, whose daughter married the Vizier Achmedpascha, who had given him two daughters. These two great-grandchildren of Suleimus the Great both came, first the elder, and after her death the younger, into the harem as consorts of Kapudanpascha, the Genoan renegade, Cicala, who through this double tie attained the greatest power and worth. The jealous and power seeking widows of the Bosnian Sokolli and the Crete Piale also did not rest until they were again married. The widow of Piale, who while gazing into the mirror one day, saw her husband touch the neck of a slave in passing, and had immediately killed him with a dagger, was maried to the third Vizier Mohammedpascha; Esma, the widow of Sokolli, was small and ugly, but lively and full of spirit, and still capable of bearing children; she had three hundred slaves of whom not one survived the night when she had touched the Pascha; this gentle princess, after she had secretly hoped to be made happy by the conqueror Daghistan, Osmanpascha, gave her hand to Kalailikos Alypascha, the successor of Oweispascha, the Governor of Ofen, an acknowledged valiant fighter in all tests of weapon and riding arts, who soon however, was overtaken by deserved misfortune, because on account of his ambition for the hand of a Sultana, he chased out his first loving wife with her children. The separation of the wife and children was followed by the tears and curses of Ali's former consort; "by tears," says the historian, "which the mountain fields would have liked to quiet; curses which shortened the life of the bridegroom, tor the following year he was buried on a hill near Ofen. There to this day Turks visit his grave as a *Gulbabas* of the father of roses, a champion of faith and blood-letting in the holy war, while Ali was but a martyr of his ambition for three horse-tail standards and the hand of a Sultana."

The Vizier Achmedpascha, the successor of Sokolli, attained the highest office in the kingdom, not only through his service as a second Vizier, but also through the influence of his consort, the daughter of Mihrmah; besides the two daughters who became wives of Cicala, he had a third, who married the rich Hasanpascha, and a yet unmarried sister-in-law, a daughter of Rustempascha, the Sultana Aischa, through whose hand the former Governor of Semendria and later of Gustendil, who fell into disfavor and became the state secretary Feridunberg, was taken back into favor and reinstated in his former position.

The credit of the widows of Sokolli and Piale required a high station for the sons of Sokolli and Piale, whose life would seem to have been taken against the law, if they were really sons of Sultanas, or what is truly the fact, the sons of other women; the son of Sokolli at first became Governor of Haleb, then Vizier of the Port, and the son of Piale received the Sandschak of Klis. Dschaaferpascha, the son-in-law of Sokolli, was already sixty years old when, through the favor of women, he received the governorship of Anatoli and then of Rumili. While these changes in Viziers and governors was occurring through the women, the Sultan occupied himself in the harem with his slaves, " especially with two with whom his mother and sister had seduced him, trying all kinds of methods of guaranteeing to himself an heir." When he finally became impotent, he ordered to be thrown into the sea six Turks and Jewesses "as witches, who, through magic words, were said to have robbed him of his power to beget children, and to have charmed him into failing desire."

Of the eight women who ruled the kingdom through the Sultan at that time, there were four outside of the *Sseiai*, the three sisters and the old aunt, the daughter of Suleimus; and four within the *Sseraiit*, the Sultana-favorite, Chasseki, the mother, Walide, Kjaja, the head mistress of the court, and Wekili Chardsch, the caretaker of the harem. These were the persons nearest to the Sultan, the women who surrounded him and who shared in his government.

Through their influence the governorships and the positions of Grandvizier were sold; Hasan, the eunuch, and then Ibrahim became Grandviziers only through Walide; through his wife, the sister of the Sultan, Chalil rose first to the position

112

of *Kapudanpascha*, then to that of Vizier-Kaimakam, representative of the Grandvizier.

Osman II had as his most beloved Sultana "a Russian
peasant of extraordinary beauty," who, freed from the
bonds of slavery, as her countrywoman Roxelane had once
been, became none other than the free and powerful consort of
the Sultan, exercising her will against any concession for right.
When she presented the Sultan with a son, she became all-
powerful. After six weeks she went with the new born babe to
meet the Sultan at Adrianopolis, where she was received with
great festivity by all the Viziers at the command of the emperor.
The pleasures of the harem daily took more command over
Osman; the Sultana-Chesseki, the Russian consort, mother of
the crown prince, enjoyed in full the concomitants and honor of
her rank; but, as a result of all her power, a tragic fate befell
her; a friend of actors, she asked the Sultan to dedicate a
brilliant feast in her honor, and at her request the Sultan
ordered a great play, which represented the Polynesian war
with a storming of batteries and the explosion of mines. An
unlucky discharge of flint caused the death of the crown prince.

In order to drown his sorrow, Osman took to himself three
consorts at the same time, but not from purchased slaves as
had thus far been the rule and custom of Osmans, but from
among the free daughters of his dependents, which, according
to Hammer, was against all the canons, an innovation dangerous to the state, because they feared a weakening of the power
of the ruler as a result of a union of the Sultan with daughters
of mighty families; the law therefore eliminated, not Christians, but foreign princesses and free daughters of the country
if the relationship gave rise to a fear of a usurpation of the
throne from the normal successor. The ruler's wife must be
a slave in innocent youth, torn from the circle of her kin, without protection, without ties, without family care; she should
receive the highest protection only as Sultana-Chesseki, as moth-

113

er of the prince, as Sultana Walide, as mother of the reigning Sultan. The Sultan himself is "not the son of a free woman, but the son of a slave, so that he can rule unimpeded, and for the consolation of the slaves, his servants, who were not bought with gold, but were forced into the yoke of slavery, birth from a free woman shall give way to the son of a slave on the throne." Osman wished to violate this basic maxim of the rights of honor of Osman Sultans, and now lie simultaneously with four lawful consorts, which each of his dependents wished to prevent according to the laws of Islam; he married the daughter of Pertewpascha and wished to become legally married with the daughter of the Mufti. He was, however, so quickly put to death that his marriage plans could not be carried out.

After the death of Murad II it became possible for the widow of Baffa, as Sultana-Walide, as mother of the reigning Sultan Mohammed III, soon to acquire greater power than theretofore. Her son thanked her for being able to ascend the throne without difficulty. She had kept the death of her husband secret from the Viziers, so that the Bostandschibascha would not write about it, but she merely hurried with the news to the mother of the new ruler. Mohammed III was a weakling and never outgrew the domination of his mother.

Until the Moslem year 1005 the treasury of the petticoat government of the Sultanas amounted to no more than nine thousand nine hundred and ninety-nine Aspers, and until then no loan had ever been made by the petticoat government. Until the year 1005 dwarfs, deaf-mutes, and other servants of the court and harem were favored with loans. Now things changed. The conquered Cypernia was given up to the jeweled Sultan-mother, Walide, so that the island of Aphrodite, already presented as tribute by the Roman emperor and the Egyptian Queens Arsinoe and Cleopatra, was returned to the women as such.

The soul of the government of Mohammed III remained

ever, in spite of the machinations of the viziers, the Venetian Baffa, who under Murad II as Sultana-Chesseki, Sultana-favorite, and consort, now under Mohammed as Sultana-Walide, Sultana-mother, ruled her son, although as mother, as Hammer says, she trembled for the duration of her power, for she could not accompany her son on his expedition into the field. She desired power to such an extent that, in her fear lest she lose some of her command through her son's departure from the state, forbade everything to prevent this, even neglected all of the ties of true believers to the Father, and in desperate tyranny decreed the massacre of all Christians.

Immediately upon his ascent to the throne Mohammed had made a present to the Sultana-Walide of three thousand Aspers daily, almost three hundred thousand Aspers for the winter, and as much for the summer, to be paid in new coin. Soon a million Aspers were added for the petticoat government. Her son-in-law Ibrahim, whom she had twice attempted to elevate to the position of Grandvizier, from time to time entertained her slaves in his garden at Jenihissar on the Bosporus, and the cost of such a feast was estimated at six thousand ducats. The Sultana-Walide Baffa ruled not only the harem but also in the entire kingdom, to its certain ruin. Yet she did much for the good of the state; so she erected a mosque named after herself at Skutari, at which an academy and intermediate school were founded. From time to time she also decided to pay the troops or to finance another war from her immense fortune; but still more were the slaves which she presented to her son suited to keep her in continual favor.

The most noted of all women who succeeded in obtaining power and command of the Osman court was the Sultana Kosem or *Mapheiker*—Moonfigure, the wife of Achmed I, the Sultana mother of Murad IV, for whom she conducted the government as he ascended the throne at the age of twelve. When Murad IV was but seventeen years old, he began to feel his own strength, and to be tired of the guardianship of his mother, who until then, in her business as Kislarage of Mustafa, had ruled in the name of the Sultan and had named the Grand-viziers. He was irritated over the too great protection which she afforded to her dealings as Kislarage and to the new Ka-pudanpascha, her son-in-law Hasan. In order to make his unwillingness known, and to cause his brother-in-law and his mother to tremble, he had the office of Kapudanpascha taken away from the husband of his sister. In order to pacify the Sultan, Walide spent ten thousand ducats on a feast which she gave her son besides a present of horses with jeweled fittings. And so it became possible for her to rule the harem as Walide for several years more. But the consort of Murad, Chasseki, Greek by birth just as Walide Kosem, disputed the rank of the latter; to be sure, not with lasting effects; for she was more wasteful than generous and because of that had less power over Murad than his mother, who showed herself to be a highly understanding, politically minded, happy, generous woman, and so she acquired the great influence which she had already had under the government of her husband Achmed I through her beauty and understanding, and as mother of ten children, five sons and five daughters. This power she likewise exercised through the first five years of Murad's reign as guardian.

The affairs can best be made clear by the fact that it was she who had Koprili appointed Grandvizier. Koprili was secret-ly introduced to Walide by Kislaraga, and answered her ques-tion whether he was not afraid of making mistakes in his determined service as Grandvizier, with his desires in respect to the following four points: first, that every one of his sug-gestions be sanctioned; secondly: that he be given a free hand in the choice of officers without being obliged to accede to the intercession of anyone, for weakness results from such inter-cession; thirdly: that no vizier and no grandvizier, no trustee, whether he received his trust through purchase or gift, encroach

116

upon his authority; fourthly: that no blackening of his character will be accepted; if these four points were promised, he would with the help of God and the grace of Walide undertake the office of Grandvizier. Walide was satisfied and swore her promises thrice with: "By God the Almighty!" A short time thereafter Kosem had played out her part in every respect under Murad IV; but at the time of the rule of her other son Ibrahim I and then her grandson Mohammed IV, she again attained her old influence.

Under Mohammed IV, at the beginning, she forced the Sultan's mother Tarchan, the true Walide, into the background. Tarchan had very little control over her son: Mohammed IV, since the birth of his son, went around continually with the thought of murdering both of his brothers so as to ensure the throne for his son and himself. His mother, a Russian, truly a Pole, the Sultana Tarchan, who was not inclined to offer the life of her younger sons to the older, but in the conduct of life exercised the same motherly duties towards all, had the foresight to lock the boys in a room of the harem to which there was no entrance except through hers. Unaware of this, the Sultan came one night with drawn dagger into the bedroom of his mother; two of her watching slaves awoke her with nudges, for they did not dare cry out. She fell into the arms of the Sultan and begged him to stab her rather than his brothers. The fratricide was thus checked; the two watchful slaves were hanged for their deceit. The fear of the mother that one of her sons would kill another remained alive; and when she was compelled to undertake a trip at the command of the Sultan, she asked for the escort of the representative of the Grandvizier, the Mufti and the general, for she recognized the escorts her son gave her as the implements of fratricide. So frivolous joy and the glamor of commanding did not always accompany the position of Sultana-mother.

In the name of the young Mohammed IV, his grandmother

Kosem reigned, so that all the strings of the empire found themselves in her hands, while the young, the true Walide, Tarchan, lived in the new *Sserai* with the old one, but was for a long time only a shadow of the Sultan-mother. Under her grandson Ibrahim, the influence of Kosen was to be sure diminished in great part by the whims of the commanding favorite, but by that time she had already engineered many innovations with an eye towards the trousseaus and dowries of the Sultanas, her granddaughters. Before then it had been customary for Sultanas pledged to paschas, immediately to leave the *Sserai*, their court, and to become a burden upon their consorts. Through Kosem this was now changed, so that princess-brides, often two and three year old children, were engaged to the paschas, but were not given to them, on the contrary they were raised to maturity in the *Sserai*, at a great burden to the treasury of the kingdom because of the great cost of their slippers, veils, and belts. The Sultana-Walide Kosem had increased her own widow's portion to about three hundred thousand piasters.

Finally, however, came the catastrophe; the naming of a new Grandvizier without the consent of the Sultana-mother Kosem bared the secret of a disunited harem, and that in the new rise to power of the old Walide, who until now had held the reins of the government, she had exceeded her power. The new light was that of the young Walide Tarchan, the mother of the Sultan, or to a greater extent, that of the black eunuch Suleimus, the Sultan's overseer, who with his entire band of eunuchs revolted against the disciplinary measures of the old Walide. So the young Tarchan opposed the old Walide Mahpeiker, *moonfigure*, and while she organized the eunuchs of Suleimus's court party, the *Aga* of the army interceded for the old Walide; at that moment, however, as Kosem was preparing to carry on a civil war, and—as many historians believe—to murder her grandson the Sultan and thereby make his mother innocuous, Kosem herself was murdered. So ended the most powerful and most noted of all Sultanas, the only one in the history of Osman who witnessed the government of seven Sultans, under four of whom, Achmed, Murad, Ibrahim, and Mohammed, she was for thirty years, as consort, mother, and grandmother, not only the ruling power of the harem, but also the commander of the kingdom. Even on the very night when she was murdered, her corpse proceeded from the *Sserai*, escorted by her entire household, into the old *Sserai*, where she was washed, and, according to the usual laws of dead bodies, placed in the tomb of her husband Achmed in the mosque built by him.

Hammer says concerning her: "A magnanimous, high minded queenly woman, of high spirit and noble heart, but with a mania for power. She spent her yearly income from her subjects in Asia and Europe—each brought her yearly fifty thousand dollars—in a most worthy manner, for the erection of the great Walide-Chan, named after her, for her mosque in Skutari, for the mosque at Constantinople, begun by her and later completed by the mother of Mohammed IV, for the irrigation from the Nile into the cloister of Chalweti at Cairo, for the maintenance of the Seide or the descendants of the prophet, and for the poor at Mecca, for the freeing of delinquent debtors, for pensions for widows and orphans. She did not depend upon advisers and counsel in apportioning these good deeds, but visited herself the hospitals and churches. She granted her slaves their freedom after several well rendered services and married them with rich dowries to deserving men of the court; she provided marriage portions for poor girls; men and women in her service thought well of her. These good deeds are mentioned not only by the time honored historian Mohammed Chalife, at that time head chef in the "great chamber", but also the historian Scharihul-Minarsade; yet the latter does not neglect to add that Kosem filled her private chest at the cost of public funds, and that after her death there were

119

found in her house twenty caskets of ducats, and among her clothes, two thousand seven hundred shawls valued at fifty thousand piasters. But she also donated for good purposes fortunes which would otherwise have been dissipated. She treated her people with the greatest kindness. The pages, whose fate it was to endure many whippings from the eunuchs, had in her court but five watches a week and two days off. So much generosity, kindness, charitableness, and graciousness, in a word, such a good heart did she possess that many historians said no evil word of her and in fact barely mentioned her intention to kill her grandchild; moreover, if she is to have known of this murder and to have taken part in the formation of its plans, parallels will be found in history among other spiritual and generous occupiers of the throne. She who was endowed with her great qualities had become a criminal only because of her mania for power. She, the mother of the greatest tyrant Murad IV, and the greatest wastrel, Ibrahim I, the Greek Kosem who was named Moonfigure because of beauty, through the commanding glance of four emperors— her husband, two sons, and her grandon—was revered more in history than Agrippina, Nero's mother, through her kindness, her desire for power and the tragic finish in Osman history of a female Caesar."

After Kosem's murder, however, conditions became no better. The rule of women continued to prevail. The weakness of Mohammed was so great that he dragged the harem along with him to war, and the soldiers grumbled, "the army of women is not much smaller than that of men; Sultan Murad IV was taken to the field with one wife and two pages, while now there are over a hundred wagons for the harem; that of the Sultana-Chasseki was streaked with silver, the wheels had silver spokes, the saddles and reins of the horses were trimmed with velvet." During the reign of Mohammed IV the eighty-year old revered Walide Schechsuwar, a Russian born, died; as a

Mohammedan she was such a religious woman that she never stepped from the sofa to the ground before she had taken water for her hands and had washed herself carefully, and that she prayed to the chapter on the knowledge of unity fifteen hundred times a night; the kingdom historian Wassif therefore bestowed upon her extraordinary praise, namely; "that she was clean as Mary, prudent as the Queen of Saba, discreet as Miriam, the sister of Moses", also, "that she was as religious as Raabia Aduje, one of the most holy women of Islam".

Of Mustafa II, Hammer relates, that he had an especially sensitive passion for his own niece, Nuri Chanumsultan, the consort of the governor of Rumili, the successor of the Kapudapascha; she was a beautiful, young, spirited princess whom Mustafa visited daily, and who, through her conquest of the Sultan, also obtained influence over his affairs. Through her intervention Bekir, whose wife had been a married slave of the Sultan Machmud, became *Reis Efendi*, Minister of the Interior; yet easy come, easy go; through his wife through whom he had risen, he was again demoted, because his wife, called into the *Sserai* and asked where at the time of Machmud I many costly things had been placed, neither could nor would give any explanation.

One can see by the role which Nuri Chanum played with her uncle Mustafa III, that not only the favorites but at times even the merely related women had occasion to obtain authority.

At a much earlier time this incident transpired: As Sultan Murad II once turned back from Asia to Europe, the prayers of his second sister, the wife of the western captured Machmud-Tschelebi, Governor of Boli, awaited him. Moved by the supplications of his sister, Murad determined to reestablish peace with the *Walachei*, the Serbians, and the Hungarians. This was effected in July, 1444 at Szegedin, for a period of ten years on the following conditions: first, that Serbia and Herzegovina be returned to George Brankovich; secondly, the Walachei remain under Hungarian rule; thirdly, that a ransom of 70,000 ducats be paid for the release of Machmud-Tschelebi. This shows the human feeling of the rough ruler; a feeling that was not killed by twenty years of unbroken continuous warfare. This acquiescence to the requests of his sister, which facilitated peace in Asia and Europe, is one of the nicest pages of the laurel-wreath which Osman history wound around this tremendous campaign of Islam.

The wives, sisters, aunts, and daughters did not always utilize this royal favor for peaceful purposes. So the daughter of Suleimus the Great, the widow of the Grandvizier Rustem, drove him to a conquest of Malta and at her own cost equipped four hundred galleys.

It was worse if women attained influence in the harem who found themselves in humble and the lowest positions and yet from there conceived and executed the most important affairs. The Jewess Kira or Chiera has already been mentioned. She was a power as caretaker of the harem under Sultan Murad, and therefore a target for the flaring up of mutiny of Sipahi. because she had involved herself in the granting of a loan of horsemen and had attained an unworthy position through bribery. In full revolt the Sipahi demanded her head. Since the Grandvizier-Representative Chalil and the Walide were in conspiracy with her, and Chalil feared that the loss of the head of the Jewess might cost him and the Walide theirs, he sent a message to the Tschauchbaschi of Sipahi saying that Kira and her sons had been placed in jail; and the sly Chalil sent this message with the victims themselves; the Sipahi fell upon Kira and her three sons, tore them to pieces and hung their torn limbs on the doors of those officials with whose help Kira had sold offices. The fourth son of Kira alone saved his life by conversion to Islam; as a Moslem he was called Ajsak Mustafa Tschausch; the revenue from the estate of which his mother had been deprived approximated no less than five million asper. If this treachery split up the Grandvizier and the harem of the Sultan, the incident resulted in his removal as *Kaimakam*. Kira had also had influence in foreign affairs. The business dealings of the ambassador Soranzo and also of his successor, Bailo Giovanni Correro, were carried on mainly through Kira, and in foreign business through the assistance of the Jewish physician, Solomon Nathan Eschinasi. The influential head mistress of the court Bschanfeda has also been mentioned heretofore. She made her brother Governor of Diarbekr; when he was accused of extortion, only immense presents and the influence of his sister saved him. When, however, the brother of Dschanfeda, after having overcome this difficulty with dire necessity, leaning on the power of his sister permitted Erserum, a Janitshare, to be burnt to death, the Janitshares arose so strongly against him, that the Sultan, in spite of the fact that his sister ruled the harem, was compelled to have him thrown into the seven dungeons.

The greater the influence of the women became, the weaker became the Osman Sultans who had once filled the west with fear and terror. So Sultan Achmed III was nothing but a lover of women and birds, of tulips and carnations, of mirrors and lamps, and the greatest accomplishment of his reign was that he had brought up thirty-six children. He occupied himself only with his wives, their sewing and caressing, and entertained them with ever new entertainments of tulip bulbs and candy feasts.

The worst period of the lascivious rule of the harem was that of the wastrel Ibrahim I. Ibrahim, says Hammer, was nothing but a wastrel and debauchee. Under his reign, at the whim of one of his wives, began the twenty-five year Venetian war, which resulted in the ruin of Kandia, like Troy. Ibrahim sank more and more into the puddle of his harem lust. At the beginning of his reign, since he was the only descendant of the Osman royal tree, it seemed praiseworthy to the viziers to

123

favor the inclination of the Sultan for women through many presents of slaves, and they emulated him. He himself, whenever he rode around the state or entered upon a journey for passion, presented the watchers of the gates with four or five bags of gold to pray for his children and descendants; soon, through the birth of half a dozen sons, the fear for the dying of the Osman line disappeared, but the Sultan's lust grew so insatiable, and so unlimited, that while the authority and influence of the women rose, his own diminished. Concurrently with the commencement of the rule of the harem, the nervous system of the twenty-four year old man was so in accord with his limitless desires, that he once enjoyed what he wanted twenty-four times within twenty-four hours. We already know from the first chapter of this book that the court physician, Hammalsade Mohammed Efendi knew of no remedy for exhaustion, tediousness, and other symptoms of sexual diseases, other than continence and rest, and he therefore fell into immediate disfavor and was exiled to the island of the Princesses.

The inability to satisfy his overpowering desires harnessed the Sultan Ibrahim even more to the yoke of wives and favorites, of concubines and watchers of the harem. His mother Kosem thought to satisfy the insatiable lust of her son by furnishing him ever with new slaves.

So Ibrahim remained a plaything of his women. Of the latter seven bore the title Chasseki, "most favorite," until at last the eighth, the famous Telli, "the wiry," was solemnly united to him as consort. Another was called Ssadschbagli, "she with the tied up hair." Each of these most favorites had her own court, her Kiaja, the income of a Sandschak as pin money, each had a gilded wagon set with precious stones, a boat, and a costly riding outfit. Besides the Sultana-favorites, Ibrahim had slave-favorites, two of the most famous of whom were *Schekerpara*, "piece of sugar," and *Schekerbuli*, "bag of sugar." Sultan Ibrahim was not satisfied with all this. He desired also the wives of his viziers. And this was cause for rebellion. The Sultan demanded of the Governor of Siwas, Warder Alipascha, that he deliver up to him the wife of his friend, Ipschirpascha, the beautiful Perichan, the daughter of Marukchan. Warder Ali defied this command and was to have been persecuted and annihilated by Vizier Achmed Pascha. He, however, arose and with a fully outfitted army proceeded to Skutari to save the eight heads which the Sultan had prepared for slaughter, the heads of the Grandvizier, Mufti, Dschindschi, Chodscha, the Chief Justice of Mullakab, Begtaschaga, Tschelebi Kiaja, Mussliheddinaga, and Karatschausch, and to take revenge on Achmedpascha. He was captured by the very Ipschirpascha, the honor of whose house he had protected from the lust of the Sultan. When he stood before Ipschir, he asked him, "Is this the reward for my not permitting your wife to come to shame, and for my warning you yourself at Tokat?" For an answer Ipschir severed Warder's head from his neck, and Ipschir, that extraordinary paragon of faithfulness and gratitude, sent the head of the man, who became a rebel because of him, to the Sultan Ibrahim at Constantinople. His wrath was not satisfied by even this. He commanded, "as a shameful manifestation of his lust" that the lowest revenge be permitted a free rein, and that the wife of Warder Ali be tied at night on four horses and shamed publicly, because her husband stood in the way of the Sultan's lust.

The despotism of the wives of Ibrahim, of the Sultan's inordinate debauchery, the slavery into which the harem threw him, and the tyranny of the Grandvizier Achmedpascha increased from day to day. Achmed Pascha, says Hammer, a descendant of Mutafa Tschausch, the son of a Greek priest, had elevated himself from a low station, through the favor of a woman of the harem whose adviser he had been, to the position of Grandvizier, an unusually able, well versed in the affairs of state, but a highly despotic Grandvizier. In order to attain his ambition to be also the son-in-law of the Sultan, he divorced his wife, the daughter of Chanedansadeaga, the former ambassador to Vienna, who had at one time assisted him, exiled his wife and her mother from the capital, but called her back again, at which the Sultan took the former wife of the Grandvizier for his harem, and therefore permitted him to marry his youngest daughter Bibisultan. On this occasion the wedding palms were driven at their highest, through the extravagance of the Sultan; two of these, as high as Minare, swelled with gold and silver, exceeding in size and splendor Atheneus' description of the splendor of the Egyptian phallic celebration; in splendor and prodigality Ibrahim placed the greatest function and the brilliance of his government.

For the eighth, Chasseki Telli, "the wiry," formally married to tne Sultan himself, the palace of Ibrahimpascha on the hippodrome, presented to her by the Sultan, is said to have been trimmed entirely with fur; in place of carpets, in place of tapestry, only fur, "the softening of the softest easy chair and couch of hair." The Grandvizier and the Defterdar Tschalid-schisade exhausted themselves in a tremendous fiscal measure to produce so much fur, and when it became impossible in spite of all tyranny which was brought to bear on the market, they had to be satisfied with trimming one Kjoschk of the palace with sable and lynx. When the Sultan saw this, he found that in one spot the colors of the joined materials did not flow into one another very accurately, so that the fugue remained unpretentious, and the entire thing therefore displeased the wastrel so much that he removed the finance minister and caused him to be incarcerated.

Sultan Ibrahim was a particular friend of grandiose illumination. Of one of his Grandviziers it is written, according to Hammer, that the illumination of the great mosques during the nights of Ramasan consisted of ringed lamps, which were called moons, because at night they were supposed to represent

126

ever so many half moons, just as those which cast rays of gold in the daytime in the reflection of the sun from the spires of the towers and domes. Under Sultan Ibrahim and Ibrahim the Grandvizier originated the lamp-and-tulip feasts which took place every year in the spring in the garden of the *Sserai* or in one of the palaces on the banks of the Bosphorus. The bed of tulips was illuminated with lamps—"the splendor of the ancient flower festivals at Sais was transferred from the banks of the Nile to the banks of the Bosphorus." This was the most brilliant of such flower festivals; through the wonder of the illumination, and it certainly was the most brilliant festival ever given by a Grandvizier to a Sultan, through the number of visiting Sultans and Sultanas, princesses, mothers and favorites, with which the Grandvizier Ibrahim entertained in his palace of lust at the behest of the Sultan Ibrahim and his entire harem. There were present at this festival besides the Sultan: four of his sons, seven Sultanas, his daughters, the Sultana-favorite, mother of the four princes, four mothers of dead princes, and the five Sultana-consorts, the first, second, third, fourth, and fifth wives, altogether twenty Sultanas, then sixteen slaves, trusted favorites of the Sultanas, ten trustees of the Sultan, and the Kislaraga of the officers of the innermost court.

In order to satisfy a momentary whim of the rulers of the Sultan's harem and their slaves, it was necessary at this time to keep the rooms open all night by candlelight, and as a reason for the lack of payment of the merchants, he even decreed the exposition of their robbery. Another time a power in old *Sserai* rode through the entire market with the order that all places of business be immediately closed. In one and the same instant not only all the rooms but all the doors of Constantinople were locked; then on the same day criers announced that everything again be opened. The reasons for both the closing and the reopening remained unknown, sprang from the mere caprice of the Sultan and his harem.

The extravagance in furs, says Hammer, was so great, that gray fox, lynx and ermine was no more to be seen, but only sable remained in the market, and that increased in price tenfold and more. Floral displays, the splendor of clothes, and play went hand in hand with Ibrahim's taste for women, amber, and sables. Ibrahim loved flowers as a symbol of the grace, color and perfume of women. Instead of a propensity for diamonds which usually graced the turban of the Sultan, he used to stick flowers on his head or behind his ear, which was considered a shameful thing in Turkey, for this was the custom only among courtesans. Ibrahim devised a kind of loose dress, trimmed inside and out entirely with sable, and then for himself a certain dress of state, with knots of precious stones, each of which cost eight thousand piasters.

The splendor of the dress of the women of the harem exceeded all, present, past, and future; the finest English cloth, the most delicate French silks, the richest Venetian velvet and gold cloth were joined in a most striking combination. If a merchant came to the Dardanelles with silks or rich wares, and his ship, kept back by the north wind, came to Constantinople, the women of the harem immediately sent express messengers in speed boats to the Dardanelles, where the wares were often, without negotiations, taken by force.

The Sandschak of Boli and Nikopolis were given to the third and sixth Chasseki as pin money, the fifth received the Sandschak of Hamid, and the seventh, the most beloved of all, the governorship of Damascus, just as the consorts of the Persian and Egyptian kings had once received the income of cities for their veil, belt, and slipper money; besides this the women of the harem created the most desirable positions for their advisers and the heads of their houses, transferring and removing deserving office-holders. One of the most important opportunities of the kingdom at that time was the utilization of the necessary snow from Olympus for cooling the Sorbete in the

Sserai. The Judge of Brussa, Idris, gave rise to this opportunty himself when he ventured forth himself into the snow region and there suddenly got lost, so that it was rumored that he had been buried in an avalanche; his office was immediately filled with a protege of the laundress of the harem, and when Idris reappeared, it nevertheless remained with the new officeholder; the laundress later became engaged to this same protege of hers, and when a Sultana, the former occupier of the palace of the former Grandvizier, died, the laundress of the harem received her palace.

The Sultan's passion for the softest furs was finally the cause for the hardest pressure.

Open discord rose all the more when the Grandvizier, as part of the fur passion of the Sultan, served his own lust for robbery.

The monies were accounted for as expenditures for sables and amber, but the Sultan's great desire for amber and sables was only the apparent reason for them. Sultan Ibrahim's partiality for furs increased all the more since a seer and story teller from Ejub, who told fairy tales all night in the harem, brought a carpet of a once famous Padischah of former times, who loved sable to such an extent that all clothes, cushions, tapestries, and carpets in his palace had to be of sable. From now on Ibrahim dreamed of nothing but sable, and a royal command issued to all the nobles of the kingdom, that they deliver up their sable furs. No one, neither the Ulema nor the Aga was spared from this demand for sables. Only a few had sufficient free will and courage to express the general bitterness over such unworthy pressure.

Fortunes were actually gathered as a result of the confiscation of sables and amber, and therefore, just as before, a wagon beset with jewels was created for the *Chasseki*, and now a jewel bedecked skiff for the Sultan. Furthermore, two *Chasseki* received formal crowns. Not satisfied with such tragic management of finances within the domain, the Sultan and the Grandvizier so far forgot the good of the kingdom, that a messenger was sent to Persia merely to bring on two elephants five hundred pieces of gold cloth and furs. The Walide Kosem, who offered her son friendly advice, and promised him that she would no longer stir up any open discord, was banished from the *Sserai* in the garden of Iskendertschelebi. Several days later the Grandvizier celebrated the marriage of his son with the eight year old daughter of the former Grandvizier Kara Mustafapascha, in an unheard of lavish manner. Street artists, card tricksters, Chinese shadow play, and dances intermingled with one another. Among those invited were the influential heads of the Janitschares, who were the frankest opponents of sable and amber expenditures; the Grandvizier hoped to rid himself of them at this feast; they were already sitting in the hall when they got wind of the contemplated onslaught from one of the trusted ones, and quickly ran home.

That brought about a catastrophe. The Janitschares arose and gathered in the *Sserai*. There promptly appeared the Sultana Walide Kosem, with a black turban, in a black veil, accompanied by black slaves fanning her.

"Isn't it cheap to create such disturbances? Aren't you all the most graciously treated slaves of this house?" she asked. Thereupon the old Wusslihedding, crying, took the floor: "All-gracious woman, gratitude no longer permits us to gaze quietly upon the ruin of this illustrious house and kingdom. Be gracious, do not oppose yourself, you will interfere not with us but with the noble laws." The Walide, no matter how much compassion she felt for her son Ibrahim, nevertheless had enough reasons to examine and to fear him. Because she offered him well-meaning advice, she was, at the behest of the favorites, banished from the *Sserai* in the garden of Iskender-schelebi, and was to have been exiled to Rhodus. Sultan Ibrahim had repeatedly mistreated her daughters, his sisters Aischa,

Fatima, and Chansade, and his niece Kiasade, in that he compelled them to serve as maids to the favorites, to bring them coffee, and to hold the basin of water for them to wash themselves. These insults to the princesses, the woman, especially the mother, could not forget; nevertheless Kosem pleaded once again for the continuation of the government of Ibrahim under the guardianship of the Ulema and the Viziers. Finally a certain Hanefisade spoke: "All gracious woman! You are the mother not only of the Sultan but also of all true believers; give up this position, the sooner, the better. The call of the Minares of Aja Sofia will rise above the noise of the fifes and drums, the cymbols and timpanies, which ring out from the *Sserai*. The markets are being plundered, favorite slaves rule the world."

The Walide attempted once more to quiet the rebels and said, "How is it possible to place a seven year old child (Mohammed IV) on the throne?" "According to the interpretation of our learned ones," answered Hanefi, "it is not permitted that an adult who is off his mind rule, much better that it be an intelligent boy; upon this is based the content of our code: with an intelligent boy a wise Vizier can promote order in the world, a demented adult disposes of him through murder and plunder, through corruption and bribery."

"Well," finally said the Walide, "then I will fetch my grandson Mohammed and tie a band around his head."

When the conspirators gathered before Ibrahim, he remonstrated with them: "Traitors, am I not Padischah, what does that mean?" But the answer rang out: "No, you are not Padischah; in that you care nothing for truth and faith, you have ruined the world; you have spent your time in play and lust and dissipated the treasury of the kingdom for things of no consequence!"

The prison into which Ibrahim was brought consisted of but two rooms, a chamber and a foyer; from above, the light

131

came through a small opening. On the following day all of the windows were walled up except one through which he was given food, and it looked out only upon the lifted wall of the canal opening. Here Ibrahim was confined with two slaves, an iron lock was affixed to the door, and this was sealed into the stone with melted tin. So was "condemned to languish the sable and amber loving wastrel, in strict confinement, near the stinking gutter of the *Sserai;* but yesterday the idol of the *Sserai,* today its outcast." He broke out into imprecations and curses, cursing the people of Turkey because of their faithlessness to his rule. He was strangled with these very curses.

The slaves and Sultana-favorites of the Sultan Ibrahim, according to prior customs, retired immediately after a change of government into the old *Sserai,* only *Mahpeiker,* Moonfigure, or *Kosem,* after she had placed her grandson upon the throne, remained and ruled now in his name. The favorite wife, *piece of sugar,* had fallen so into disfavor with Kosem, that she treated her very highhandedly, robbed her and her trusted friend Hamida, the daughter of the sultanly Hebamme, of all of their possessions, and banished them to exile to Ibrim in Nubien. A slave of Hamida, who was with the wife, *piece of sugar,* at the moment of her seizure, represented herself to be Hamida, and as such she was put on board the boat, which was going to Constantinople, so that the slave served her mistress with cunning and faithfulness. Two trustees of the wife, *piece of sugar,* were questioned minutely concerning her treasures; there were found two hundred and fifty bags of pure gold, an enormous mass of costly clothes and merchandise, a mere two hundred covers, one embroidered with pearls, two with gold; she who swam in such richness, was placed on the boat without clothes, without money, from the highest luxury into the deepest poverty, so that she considered herself fortunate to receive from the Governor of Egypt five hundred piasters for her necessities. Her trustees were tried, strangled, beheaded.

The fate of a favorite often ended so sorrowfully, only to become better, when the favorite later, often after many years, as mother of the reigning Sultan, again appeared in the sultanly harem.

## CHAPTER NINE

# WEDDING CUSTOMS OF THE PEOPLE IN TURKEY

*Armenian wedding prayers—Greek wedding songs—Albanian—Mazedo-Wal-achen and Roumanian—Bulgarian—Serbian—Montenegrin—Spanish—Arabic Jewish—Jesiden—Turkish—Bedouin—Persian—Kurden—The sign of virginity—The significance of the wedding bed sheet—Among the Fellahs in Palestine and Egypt—Bulgarian and Roumanian customs.*

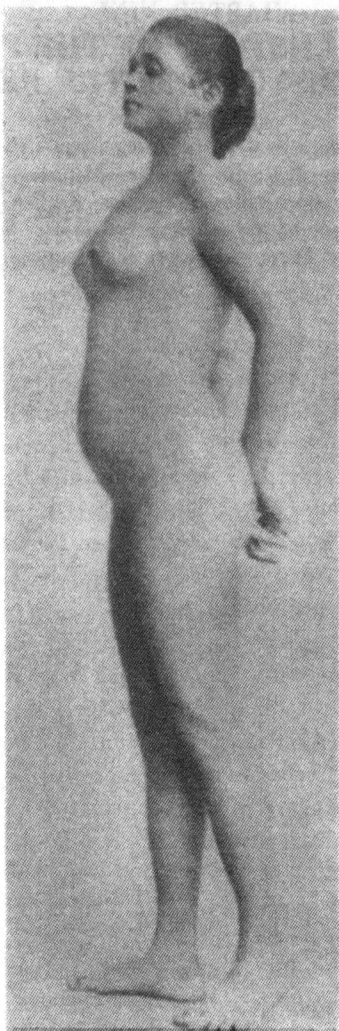

*Seventeen-year-old Hindoo*

Concerning the wedding customs of several oriental folk I have already written in detail in my book, "From Kaspi to Pontus." Other authors have also devoted sufficient care to these subjects; Bodenstedt, Schweiger-Lerchenfeld, Ami Boue, Adolf Strauss, Fredrich S. Krauss, Kanitz, and Hahn. Finally, my friend D. Theophil Lobel-Efendi, Ottoman censure inspector, published a book several years ago in Amsterdam, in which everything concerning wedding customs in Turkey was printed, together with many collected anecdotes which he himself assembled. With an eye on this rich and easily attainable material, I believe I shall need make but short work of this chapter and touch gently upon only that which is least known.

Of the Armenian customs, which Bodenstedt has rendered in great detail, I wish to recall merely the prayer which the priest says at the close of the wedding: "Everlasting God and Creator of the entire world! We ask and implore You, who worries full of pity for your creatures, consider, O friend of man, our prayers graciously! Just as You closed the weddings of our fathers according to the laws of Moses, so you have, according to the understanding and divine direction of your own child, taught us new làws, and erected the holy cross for the sacredness of marriage for those who believe in You and Your Son. Give now, O Master, through the everlasting cross, strength and power to those who lean on You. Withdraw from them the spirit of hypocrisy and insubordination and all wicked passions; preserve them from ignominy, from dark roads, and from uncleanliness in their conduct of living. See to it that this cross be an inspiration and the foundation stone of a firm foundation upon which the house of sacred marriage will be erected. Decorate her head with the crown of beauty, send over her the soul of the Holy Trinity, which does what is necessary for them, and brings them fame and honor, now and forever, to all eternity. Amen! Bless them with all! Holy and invaluable Father, who has blessed and made sacred this cross in the name of Your own child, through the hand of Your sinning servants, through the benediction of Your holy spirit! I now pray to You also, O Master, send Your holy spirit down as an inspiration for the structure which we are now creating here. Take these two unspoiled to each other, accompany and lead them to the hour when I shall place the crown of honor upon her head; for the honor is Yours alone, and to you alone is born the fame and the power, now and forever, to all eternity. Amen!"

At the weddings of the Greeks, many songs are sung: While the bridegroom washes himself at the wedding toilet, they sing:

Wash the young rich man in a silver bucket,
The duck brings the water and the magpie the soap.

While he is being shaved they sing:

Silver razor, go slowly, slowly,
Leave nothing protruding,
Lest you break the heart of our young rich man,
Our beautiful star.

When the bride is being combed she cries hot tears; from the

138

throats of her friends standing near her, is heard a song reminiscent of Heinrich Heine:

You have beautiful golden hair which hangs down on your
    shoulders,
The angels comb it with golden combs.

While she is being clothed, the song continues:

    While your mother was giving birth to you,
    All the trees were bedecked with flowers,
    And the small birds sang in their nests.

After the finish of her toilet, finally:

    Today the heaven beams,
    Today the day shines,
    Today the eagle and the dove become one.

The bride, however, recites with feeling this song: "I had in my home a cotton bush with outspread branches, I cared for it and sprayed it and hoped sometime to possess it; but a stranger, a foreigner came and took it from me. How often have I said to you, dear mother, do not let this stranger into the house. How often have I said to you that he is laughing at you, that he is deceiving you, that he will take away the cotton bush. How often have I begged you that you hide me, mother, that you hide me, so that the stranger would not take me!"

When the priest proceeds with the ceremony of marriage, he says, "There are being married the man of God (follow the name) and the maid of God (follow the name) in the name of God, the Son and the Holy Ghost, now and forever, and to all eternity, Amen!" Then with the "wedding crown" he makes the sign of the cross three times over the head of the bride and says: "There are being married the maid of God and the man of God in the name of God, the Son, and the Holy Ghost, now and forever, and to all eternity, Amen!" Then he places the crowns upon the heads of the bridal pair.

Before the door of the bridal chamber the men bring a serenade: "Awake and kiss a body like a Cypress, a white neck, breasts like citrons, like cold water.' In many places the custom prevails that on the third day after the wedding the female relatives and friends of the young woman come and lead her to the fountain. The newlywed here with a previously determined bucket of her own draws water from the fountain and then throws into it food and bread. After a dance around the fountain they return.

In Cappadocien, relates Naumann, there prevails a custom of strewing a mixture of corn and coins over the heads of the newlyweds. A crowd of street-arabs then squabble over the money.

Among the Albanians, reports Hahn, children are engaged while still in the cradle; it even happens occasionally that a prospective mother, before the event, before she knows whether the child she is about to bring into the world is a boy or a girl, before her delivery, has already arranged an engagement for this child. These engagements are not made known to the growing children until they attain a marriageable age, namely, when the girls become twelve and the boys eighteen years old. Love is not the originator of marriage. The Albanians know no love for the thoroughly despised womanly sex. The wife is the worker and supporter of the house; she is nevertheless fully satisfied with her fate, so that kind treatment of her on the part of her husband would not be right and would appear to indicate his degradation. In case of war the Albanian women are true comrades of their men, they are the sanitary troops, and not infrequently in cases of need, the deciding factors.

140

meal, one of the branches is placed at the fireplace of the groom's house and the other in the bride's house. In the evening they sing the following song:

> My mother does not wish me to marry
> Says, I shouldn't worry her at all,
> Says, I am much too small,
> Small, small like a partridge,
> O, mother, I beg of you,
> Marry me off.
> I am no longer nine years old. . . .

Sunday the wedding, *Numta*, is held.

Before the bridegroom goes to the wedding, the barber comes, whose first operation is washing his head. While this is going on, in the house of his parents assembled girls and women sing the following song: "At the proper time comes the barber, wash my head, my beloved barber. Wash my eyes and face, things suddenly appear so light. And I see a black-eyed boy, pretty and bold in combat, and he holds a ring in his hands, a silver ring, a pure one. O bolder, bolder boy, I have been told of your courage, as the best silversmith in the village, you have long been known to me. I give you a silver coin for your wife to wear on her neck."

After the head washing the bridegroom is shaved; at that the gathering sings: "The barber comes at the proper time to shave the bridegroom. Barber, as true as you live, make him beautiful for me, beautiful for the present and the future, and more beautiful for his wife. Gaze but upon his eyebrows, like the heaven with its stars; gaze but upon his forehead, happy, he who is his father; gaze but upon his nose, happy he to whom it belongs; gaze but upon his teeth, happy, they who are his parents; gaze but upon his neck, it seems a tart; gaze but upon his breast, it looks like a beautiful nightingale; gaze but upon

143

him with his belt on, he looks like a bridled horse."

After the shaving the singers turn to the bridegroom and sing the following song to him: "You mother is beautiful, like the morning star, her face beams so with the decorative cloth. We go to you, we meet you on the way, the way is crowded for both, you stepped from the road so that we should not be crowded; take this bag and make a present, a necklace for the bride to wear around her neck with a locket, not that I wish it, not that I prepared it, I give you a seal for it and seal it." On the bride's leaving the house of her parents, on the way to the church two women hold a tart, *Kaniskulu*, over the head of the bride, and a third woman, who stands behind the bride, has a flask of wine in her hand.

At the separation of the bride from her parents and brothers and sisters the following song is sung: "Do not cry, wife and bride! Do not cry! You are spoiling your beauty!" "It should spoil it, wherefore then do I need it? I will cry! . . . As my father is crying over me, so will I cry!" . . . These same words are repeated again and again, but the father is merely replaced with the mother, the brothers, the sisters. The song then closes: "I know not what awaits me, I will cry!" . . .

When the wedding procession passes before the house of the newlyweds, the mother of the bridegroom carries a child towards the bride. It is the symbol of the sacred purpose of marriage. The bride takes the child in her arms and kisses it; at that a second and finally a third child is brought to her, and she does the same to each. On crossing the threshold she is given a plate of butter; she takes a little butter with her fingers and rubs it on the threshold and the gateposts. After she has wiped the butter from her hands with a handkerchief, she takes an apple in which are placed gold or silver coins, according to the circumstances of her fortune. With the coming of night the bridegroom retires to the bridal chamber. After much persuasion the bride is brought to him. She hesitates at the door

144

and does not wish to enter; she is pushed in by force and the door is shut from the outside. Early Wednesday morning the young wife betakes herself to the fountain in the company of several women and musicians where she fills a bucket with water; after this has happened, she spreads butter which she has brought with her on the fountain.

Among the Bulgarians the wedding day always falls on a Sunday or holiday. After the services, the godfather approaches the bridegroom and places a boy in his hands, while the godmother places a girl in the arms of the bride. At evening the young pair disappear into the wedding chamber, but the guests rejoice undisturbed until the morning. After sunrise the married couple again come among their guests and the young man proclaims loud and joyously that he succeeded in forcing the innocence of his bride. . . . After this declaration all stroll over to the fountain of the house, to which each of two maidens carries a bucket perched on her shoulder. The best man fills the buckets with water at the fountain and puts them under a tree, he then throws a handful of small coins into each bucket. He then breaks two green twigs from the tree and with them tears the headdress from the young wife. When this has been done, the ushers then dance three times around the buckets with the young wife, after which she upsets the buckets with her foot.

Among the Serbians, that folk of happy songs, of numerous songs, the wedding feast is naturally commanded by song. Surprisingly enough Serbian songs deal less with happy than with unhappy love and marriage. So one song says:

A deep snow falls on Saint George's Day,
No bird dares fly over the snow,
Yet the maiden flies over the snow,
She fears not snow, she fears not woe.
She complains: My feet are not frozen

145

If they are not bare.  But my heart if being broken
And will almost leave me frozen,
Yet my mother lets me not move it,
My own mother is the cause of it,
She wants me to marry an old man.

Other songs deal moreover in this sacred moment with
faithlessness and unchastity; a folksong complains:

Woe to the land where the armies tarry,
Where maidens themselves to the men hurry.
And the men say to them, who themselves dishonor:
You would not have run so, if you had any honor.

On the morning of the official engagement in Serbia, the
bridegroom comes to his chosen one and gives her an apple
decorated with gold coins, Jabuka, which the maiden takes, and
rushes with it to her mother.  The bridal gift and especially
every present is named after the apple: *Jabuka.*

It is noteworthy, remarks Lobel-Efendi according to Ernst
von Dombrowski, that it is just among the Serbians that the
custom of the apple prevails at the engagement, and not among
the other more conservative races of the occident where an
engagement ring is in vogue, for the following comes from a folk
song of about the eighteenth century:

One gives an apple on the discovery of love,
The basil for its fragrant odor;
Yet one gives only a ring at the engagement.

Another Serbian song follows:

On the meadow, under the maple, runs the brook,
There comes here a young maiden to draw water;

146

Under Belgrade's white embankments she carries water.
Carrying a golden apple, Mirko approaches her:
"Take, O maiden, this apple, and become mine!"
The maiden takes the apple and throws it back him:
"I do not want you, nor your apple, go from here!"

On the meadow, under the maple, runs the brook,
There comes here a young maiden to draw water;
Under Belgrade's white embankments she carries water.
Carrying a golden necklace, Mirko approaches her:
"Take, O maiden, this necklace, and become mine!"
The maiden takes the necklace and throws it back at him:
"I do not want you, nor your necklace!  Go from here!"

On the meadow, under the maple, runs the brook,
There comes here a young maiden to draw water;
Under Belgrade's white embankments she carries water.
A golden ring in his hands, Mirko approaches her:
"Take, O maiden, take this ring, and become mine!"
And the maiden takes the ring and puts it on her hand:
"I want you now together with your ring!  I am yours!"

At the wedding feast the banquet lasts the entire night.
When the guests begin to leave, the young wife, the *Mlada*,
stands on the threshold and kisses each one on the cheek, at
which each presses a small present, mostly gold, into her hand.
In some neighborhoods the young Serbian wife, early in the
morning after her wedding night, pours water on the hands of
her guests and brings them a towel for drying them.  As a
reward for this she receives the "spilt money," *Poljevacika*,
which is thrown into the wash basin.  The freshening is quite
necessary; for the wedding feasts of the Serbians are very
active; one uses the saying: "Like a Serbian wedding," to express active jubilation.

The wedding customs of the Montenegrins are different

from those of the other south Slavics. The position of the Montenegrin woman is reflected in several sayings. "You are not worth as much as a maiden!" Another proverb says: "Men are beaten with a ball of reed, women, however, with a stem of reed!" to which it should be noted that it is considered the greatest insult if a man is beaten with a stem of reed, and it can only be effaced with blood. A worthy Montenegrin, cultured in customs of the land and in the beliefs of the land, says, on introducing his wife: "Pardon me, this is my wife!" . . . I record this although it is possible that a misunderstanding exists. It may also be merely an idiom, somewhat as they say in German: "Permit me to introduce my wife." After the services the young wife is given a child by her father-in-law; she caresses and fondles it as a sign that she now understands her future role as mother; with the child in her arms she steps into the hall among her guests. A basket of fruit is brought to her here, which she distributes among those present. This also has a significance: it is supposed to serve as a symbol that her house will always be well stocked.

Lobel-Efendi says that the Arabic Jews have adopted the manners, customs, speech, and thought of the Arabs. The female sex lives among them in the strictest confinement, in the harem, from which only few emerge, and then only with thickly veiled faces. In contrast to those religious western Jews who cut their hair short after the wedding, and who carry the rest of it covered by a head cloth, the Spanish Jews in Turkey do not touch their hair and wear it free. The Arabian Jews cover their necks; the Spanish do not do this either. Arabian Jews are married at a very early age. Especially the female sex quickly assumes the yoke of marriage; we often find here mothers who have not passed their twelfth and grandmothers who have not passed the twenty-fifth year.

Polygamy, which the Bible does not forbid, is prevalent among the Arabic Jews, though not to the same extent as among the Mohammedans; they do not recognize the restriction which Rabbi Gerson has thrown on polygamy. During his more than four year stay in Arabia, Lobel had become acquainted with a number of Jews who had two wives at the same time. Lobel knew a Jew in Bagdad who took as his second wife the niece of his first childless wife. How joyous and happy the first wife felt when her niece made the uncle and their joint husband a father!

The wedding customs of the Arabian Jews in Turkey are the same as those of their Mohammed neighbors, except that instead of the Imam, the Rabbi, the *Chacham*, performs the marriage according to the laws of Moses. Marriages among the Spanish Jews are, except for love marriages, more often than not engineered through marriage brokers. The marriage brokers, usually rabbis, take all pains to obtain a wife for every man and a husband for every woman. They negotiate with both sides and make provision for the marriage potion and the dowries. For their commission they receive three per cent of the dowry, of which the parents of the bride pay one per cent and the parents of the groom two per cent. If two friendly families determine to marry their children to each other, a third person is nevertheless called in as a broker to arrange the terms and take care of everything. For the most part the marriage brokers do not wait to be called. No sooner do they see in their notebooks of marriage candidates, a young man' who they think earns enough to support a wife, and not very much is needed for this, than they shower him with propositions and spread before him an entire inventory of girls from which he need only choose. One is pictured to him as more beautiful, more lovable, and richer than the other; in short, all of the best things are said, all his wishes anticipated. The main thing is to win over the youngster; a broker makes short work of his parents and the parents of the bride. The least obstacles are presented by the parents of the bride if they are not wealthy. The parents of the bridegroom place the greatest emphasis, however, on the dowry. Among the Spanish Jews, as everywhere generally in Turkey, there are so many girls that the parents count themselves fortunate if they can get rid of a girl. The marriage brokers do not let a marriage candidate go, once they have caught him, until he has promised to look upon a bride. The first meeting of the young people usually takes place at a prearranged promenade, or at a respectable gathering in the house of the girl's parents.

The engagement, Spanish: *Esposoris,* occurs in a circle of relatives and most intimate friends in the house of the bride's parents. In the presence of witnesses a contract is drawn up in which are contained the conditions upon which the marriage will take place. The Rabbi then reads these conditions to the witnesses and the bridal pair, and lets them take an oath that they will marry each other, and that in the event of a default the withdrawing party will pay to the other a certain sum of money. This ceremony is called "*Kinian* and is very formal, for the Rabbi gives first the bridegroom and the bride one end of a tablecloth to hold while he holds the other end. Meanwhile he says the following: "You promise to marry this beautiful maiden, then follow her name, daughter of N. N. according to the laws of Moses and these stipulated conditions." He says the same to the bride. After the bridal pair have said "yes," they let the cloth drop and sign the engagement contract, which the witnesses countersign. They then fix the wedding day and the father of the bride gives his future son-in-law a part of the dowry. If any obstacle arises after this engagement ceremony which prevents the celebration of the second ceremony, the closing of the marriage, the bridal pair are nevertheless bound, so that only a legal divorce, according to the laws of Moses, can release the tie.

In the time between the engagement and the wedding the bridegroom is free to visit the bride as often as he wishes. He can even take her for a walk or a ride, but always in the company of her mother, an older sister, or her brother. If a wedding day is fixed for a Sunday, the wedding declarations, called *Pregon, begin* on Friday. The *Pregonero,* the crier, goes on Friday in the houses of the bridal pair, and on Saturday during the hours for prayer in the synagogue, and announces the wedding that is to take place on Sunday.

In Constantinople, just as in other sections inhabited by Spanish Jews, there is a custom that the newlyweds, right after the services, jump three times over a plate filled with fresh fish. This is a symbol of rich fertility; and the married people usually live up to their expectations. On the Saturday following the wedding, called *Schura,* the young married man, who for the entire week has borne the name *Hattan,* goes with his young wife, his parents, and hers, to the synagogue.

The marriage customs of the Jesiden or devil worshipers are of particular interest. It is said that the Jesiden worship a hen or a peacock, called *Melek Ta-Uss,* King peacock. Their wives are not lacking in a certain beauty; they are the true companions of their husbands, whose life, full of work and danger they share; they are very well treated and can devote themselves to their traditional open baths without fear of insult. The law strictly permits but one wife, but the leaders nevertheless have several wives; concubines are entirely forbidden. Marriage between relatives is encouraged. For bad conduct the wife may be sent home, and the husband is authorized, with the permission of the *shah,* to marry again, while the wife is denied this. By "bad conduct" of the wife can be meant only adultery. At an earlier age, when the Jesiden were independent, the death penalty was fixed for an adulterous woman, while an adulterous man went free. According to the prevailing custom, the woman was simply sold to the man. From this comes the resulting right of ownership, which operates very strictly against the woman if she, so to say, breaks her contract.

At one time the parents demanded a great sum for their daughters; and since the Jesiden were not wealthy, many girls remained unmarried. This strange situation in the provinces of the orient was the source of numerous complaints of the poor in the community. Marriage is among the Jesiden also an opportunity for festivities. They are made sacred for all by no religious ceremony, the publicity which one gives them is their only consecration. Bridegroom and bride appear before the *shah*, who takes cognizance of their mutual understanding. The bridegroom presents his bride with a ring or a piece of gold. They then fix the day for the entertainment, and on this day they drink sorbet, which is plentiful or meager, according to the fortune of the entertainer, and dance. Lobel-Efendi recalls from Layard the following Jesiden wedding: The musicians play on their instruments; the bride, covered with a veil from head to foot, and stuck behind a curtain in a corner of the room, must remain there for three days; then she is taken by her husband from her retreat. The court of the house is filled with dancers during the festivities, and day and night one hears nothing but the happy cry of the women, the sound of tambourines, and the noise of flutes. Early on the third day they seek out the young husband, lead him in triumph from house to house, and give him at each place a small present. He is then placed in the midst of the dancers. Finally they lock him in a dark room and set him free only for ransom.

Among the Turks, the engagement—Turkish: *Nischan, Nischanlanma*, called the sign— consists in the closing of a contract, in which are contained the mutual promises of marriage, and besides that there is noted the sum which would have to be paid for a breach of the promise. The wedding day is also fixed on the closing of this contract. The bride, *Gelin* or *Nischanlykyz*, sends the bridegroom, *Guweji* or *Nischalyn*, a beautiful silk packet, *Boghtscha*, containing: dayshirts, handkerchiefs, a nightshirt, a shawl, and a silver tobacco box; the bridegroom sends the bride only a silver vanity, like a mirror in silver cream —this must never be missing—and jewel boxes.

During the entire time of their engagement the bridal pair must not see each other. The broker, and this for only the last thirty years and only in the large cities, arranges a rendezvous. The bridegroom sees the bride only through her veil and—at a certain distance. He must not come close to her, much less speak to her. Engagements by parents of children five or six years old, which was often the case in earlier times, happen very seldom today. The wedding, *Dujun*, is celebrated in the houses of both the bridegroom and the bride; and true to their code, the women remain in the harem and the men in the Selamlik.

The wedding festivities usually last for five days: from Monday to Friday. On Wednesday the bride is led midst great pomp to the bath, to which all the friends and also all the poor women of that quarter of the city in which the bride lives, are invited. Early Thursday the bride leaves the house of her parents in the company of her mother, sisters, relatives, servants, slaves, neighbors, guests, and those sent by the bridegroom, to go to the house of her future master and ruler. Not the bridal pair themselves, but two of their named representatives, *Wekil*, conclude the marriage in their name. At the marriage services the Imam says among others the following prayer. He recites the sentence of the Koran: "Marriage is my law, and I recognize him who recognizes my law." He then continues: "Allah, let this union be accompanied only by happiness and blessings. Let peace and domesticity govern these married people, may lasting love and rest rule in their family. But never discord and estrangement, obstinacy and hate! O Allah, join them as you once joined Adam and Eve; as you joined Mohammed, peace be with him, with the great Chadische, God be satisfied with her; as you joined Ali with Fatima, God grant him peace and be satisfied with her! O

153

Allah, give these newly married people good children, a long life, and great wealth! O Master, give us joy from our wives and our children and lead us on paths of righteousness! O our Master, grant us earthly and heavenly happiness and save us from the curse of hell. Blessed be Allah, the Master of the world! Peace be with the prophet and praise be with God!" Then: "Blessed be Allah, who said in His book: 'Marry your virgins!' Peace and blessings be over our prophet Mohammed, who loved the poor and the orphans! Peace and blessings on the family of the prophet, and his descendants who are great and all-knowing. May it please Allah who is the source of blessedness and happiness, to bless and make happy this marriage which have now brought to a close." Those present say: Amen! "May the Master grant the young married couple long life, health and wealth, and bliss in both worlds!" Amen! "May the Master crown all their deeds in this world with his sanction, and may he give them their share of everything which leads to happiness on the other world." Amen! "May God permit consideration and love to prevail between the newly-weds!" Amen! "May God keep them worthy, take them into the circle of the religious, the faithful, the wise and the holy." Amen! "May God make them happy, them and their children, and may they survive their successors." Amen! "May God let those faithful present here share in the happiness of both worlds, and may they enjoy a long life." Amen! "May God insure the position of our Padischah, the ruler of all true believers, in his kingdom, and may our Padischah and Caliphs, through the intervention of our Master and Prophet, be granted a long life!" Amen! "Praised be God, the Creator of the world, Amen!"

The final act: After the evening prayers and after he had kissed the hands of his parents, the bridegroom slinks quite slyly into the bridal chamber where his wife is hiding, and in the presence of an old matron, waits in expectation for what is his. Hardly does the bridegroom enter the bedroom than the young married woman rises; he runs to her, takes her hand, and asks her for her name. She does not answer immediately; he repeats his question and now she says her name very lightly. He asks her permission to take off her veil; she looks shamefully at the ground and gives no answer. He repeats his request, and since no answer follows, he takes off her veil and gives her a wedding present, the *Juz Gorumlug*, namely, to see the face, usually a costly ring; she grasps his hand suddenly and kisses it.

She gradually takes courage and begins to enjoy herself with her husband. Meanwhile the matron gives the young couple their wedding meal; she serves them black coffee, and after she has received a tip, she withdraws.

Lobel-Efendi next reports several Arabian customs which are derived from the Turkish or Mohammedan, according to observations of Burckhardt, who has made interesting observations on the love life and the wedding customs of the Arabs, especially the desert Arabs, the Bedouins. According to Burckhardt the Bedouins are perhaps the only people in the east among whom we find a true love pair according to their own will. It is customary when a Bedouin entertains danger or warfare, to leave his wife or his beloved with the pretty saying: "I go to battle and to death for your eyes." And in a Bedouin song, which sings of warfare:

> I shall color my lance a bloody hue,
> For the eyes of my maiden will I die.

The warrior ties the reins of the first horse which he has taken as booty around the hand of his beloved wife.

While in the cities the Mohammedan customs keep both sexes separate, among the Bedouins free intercourse is permitted between them. They learn to know each other, and the love which sprouts in two hearts, blossoms forth through the

155

years, until the two branches are joined into one tree. But everything happens in an honorable manner, seldom, or more accurately never, does it happen that there is the slightest deviation from righteousness. The bridegroom brings a lamb before the tent of the bride, and here before witnesses he cuts the neck off the offering. Just as the lamb's blood trickles to the ground the marriage is deemed consummated. There follow dances and eating contests. With the coming of night the bridegroom retires to a wedding tent which he has himself erected, and there waits for his bride. The maiden, innocent in her shyness, seeks to reach a strange, friendly tent, until several women catch her and drag her to the bridegroom, who draws her to him by force. When she is held there, the young wife must give vent to a cry of terror; only a maiden must do this, however—for a widow who already knows the mysteries of marriage, it is not only not proper, but dishonorable.

Among the Bedouins of Mount Sinai the maiden, returning from the meadow, where all the girl herd, is captured by her beloved and his assistants, and led by force to the tent of her father, where the robber throws a mantle called an *Aba* over her and says: "No one shall cover you but me." Thereupon they lead the ever careful bride after the bridegroom has dressed her anew and decorated her richly, on a camel into the tent of the bridegroom. If the virgin is not really compatible with the young man, she can be rid of him again the very next morning; she need merely flee to her parents. But if she is satisfied with her unlooked for lot, for there is not always a prearranged understanding, then she must remain fourteen days in the new house, without taking a single step out of it. Particularly are prescribed her nightly ventures.

Among several tribes of the Sinai it happens that the maiden, after being covered with the Aba, flies into the mountain and lets herself be sought for. The evening passes before the bridegroom finds the bride—night falls, and the pair cele-

156

brate their wedding night in the open. With the breaking of dawn the bride flees again to the house of her parents. She remains there for days; she merely makes a rendezvous with her husband at night. Not until she feels that she is about to become a mother does she go to live in the tent of her husband.

Among the Sinai Bedouins the bridegroom must pay a price to the father of the bride, each according to the family and the beauty of the chosen one, somewhere from five to twenty dòllars. Widows and divorcees require half the price paid by their first husbands.

In many sections, on the contrary, maidens are cheaper than widows and divorcees. And it happens, as among the Bedouins in Dschebel Schammar, that the maidens are often married for a short time to strangers, so that they can then be considered widows or divorcees.

In Persia, as Dr. Polak relates, the girls go veiled from their ninth year. In the poorer families they consider them fit for marriage in their tenth or eleventh year; cases have been recorded even in recent times, where according to the purchased dispensation of the priest, marriages take place even in the seventh year; but in good houses the daughters are provided with dowry after their twelfth or thirteenth year. He who desires a maiden for his wife must pay her parents a purchase price, *Schir-e-buha*, a milk price, and besides this, promise to the bride, each according to her physical beauty and development, an appreciable wedding portion, *Maerieh*. The assignment of the price attains at times the sum of 500 ducats. The parents therefore spend money for the cultivation, nourishment, and clothing of the girl and all possible necessaries, and they must also provide the remaining house necessities. If a maiden has a beautifully built body, her antecedents are rarely inquired into, she can become the wife of the leader of a tribe, the most respectable office holder, and even of the king, as daily examples prove. Children in their cradles are often pledged to each

157

other, especially cousins; intrafamily marriages are usually the rule. Before the wedding the bride goes to the bath with her playmates; on this occasion the bridegroom sends her a quantity of henna to color her hair and nails. The bridegroom also goes to the bath accompanied by his friends. After the wedding services the young wife is taken to the house of her husband by her relatives, and she finally sees him now for the first time. Respectability demands that he unveil her by force and that she offer opposition. At the moment when the veil is lifted the husband cries out: "Bismillah errahman, errahim! In the name of God, the most gracious!"

The Turkish Kurden, successors of the Kurduchen, Kyrtier, or Gordyaer of ancient times, live in the eastern provinces of Asiatic Turkey. The women enjoy just as much freedom as the men and are just as brave. As an example of this courage, the Kurden, Kara Fatma of Rowandiz, a district in Taurus, at the outbreak of the Crimean war, assembled a squadron of irregular troops and hurried to Constantinople to take her place beside her monarch against the Russians.

The Kurden women and girls usually go around uncovered, and if they are of the rich and comfortable class, the *Assireten* aristocrats as opposed to *Goranen*, the back-bending working class, they tie a red cloth around their heads.

The usual age at which they are accustomed to marry is fourteen to sixteen for girls and sixteen to twenty for men. Mutual inclination plays an important role in their marriages, so that opposition of the parents is not very rare.

Dr. Wutz wrote to Lobel-Efendi concerning the Kurden wedding ceremony: An hour and a half after sundown the bridegroom is led to the door of the bedroom by his most intimate friends and there turned over to waiting women. These lead him to the bridal chamber where almost everything is placed within his reach. The women thereupon withdraw and wait in an antechamber for that which must now occur. After

158

the young married man has fulfilled his marital duty, the nightdress of the bride is turned over to the women, from them to the mother of the bridegroom and then to the men. The latter tie the trophy into a stick and carry it singing and accompanied by music throughout the village. It is then brought to the mother of the bride, who alone is excluded from all the festivities. The predetermined dowry, or rather the purchase price is now paid over, and the wedding festivities are over.

The display of the wedding-bed sheet also occurs in several other folk of the east and the Balkans. For in the entire orient it is one of the worst deceptions if a bride who has been taken as a virgin appears to have been devirginated.

Among the Hebrews, if a man complains that his wife did not come to him a virgin, then her parents must take the sheet on which he lay with her on the first night and spread it before the elders of the city. If it really does not show the signs of virginity, then, as is related in the 5th Book of Moses XXII, 13 to 21, the woman is taken to the gates of the town and there stoned by the people. If the signs are, however, discovered, the husband is fined as a defamer, he must pay her father a hundred shekels of silver, and he must keep his wife without being able to divorce her.

The custom of utilizing the sheet of the wedding bed as a means for determining the virginity of the bride is very old. In much the same manner as among the Hebrews, it is accepted by the Subbas, an Asiatic folk. There the husband shows the bloody sheet of the bed to several trusted men on the morning after the wedding. In earlier times, especially in the larger cities like Bagdad, Bassorah, and Mossul, it was carried in procession through the streets; this happens now only in villages.

Among the Fellahs in Palestine, the women relatives appear on the morning after the wedding at the house of the young couple. The important purpose of this visit is the determination of virginity according to the display of *Alamet el*

159

*bokara*, the signs of virginity, which are to be found on the sheet of the wedding bed. This sheet is then preserved in the *Sanduka*, hope chest, of the newlyweds. For if the women Fellahs do not enjoy a good name, they must be in a position to show the *Alamet el bokara*.

A similar custom exists, according to Schweinfurth, among the lower classes of city Arabs and among the Fellahs in Egypt. The *Lelet el dachle*, the night of the entrance, the bridal night, is full of festivities. The invited and uninvited eager participators assemble, and the Talba and Rababe chant, and belly dances take command of the situation. The bride naturally cannot be seen by the male public. She sits on a couch in a separate room, surrounded by female relatives, deeply veiled. Between twelve o'clock midnight and two o'clock in the morning, the bridegroom wraps a white, gold embroidered handkerchief around the index finger on his right hand, steps before the bride, who is at that moment unveiled by her friends. While her mother, supported by the other women, holds her tight, the bridegroom kneels down, places his right hand under the clothes of his bride, and breaks the hymen with his covered index finger, which he does without delicacy, but bores in violently and breaks it on all sides. After which he leaves the room, goes to the father of the bride, kisses his hand, and shows the guests the bloody cloth; this ceremony is accompanied by soft music; joyously, singing and dancing the men go out into the street and carry the bloody trophy throughout the entire town showing it to all people. Immediately after the departure of the bridegroom the bride is placed into a sitting bath. Her mother goes to her and rubs a powder into the opening. The powder consists in equal parts of white sugar, crystalized sugar, black pepper, and pine qarad or the husk of *acacia nilotica*. This powder burns the wounded area and the bride cries out terribly. The guests hear this over the entire house and in the street, and they answer with cries of joy and loud

160

music. For respectability demands that the bride lose her virginity painfully. She does not remove the powder from that area until it serves its purpose. The above mentioned burning takes at least two and sometimes nine days to heal, and the young man must not approach his wife during this time. Very often the bridegroom has not the courage to undertake the reported operation, or he does not do it completely enough. Then the devirgination is performed by the *ballane*, a woman who must not be missing at any wedding. The *ballane* alone must undertake the rupture in a case where the hymen is *kelib*, tough; more is said of this in the chapter on kinds of vulvae.

The Bulgarian writer, Tscholakow, says that in Bulgaria, there is a custom in the country after the first full act of coitus on the wedding night to remove the sheet from under the bride and to inspect it for signs of blood. If these are found, they proclaim the chastity of the bride from a hilltop. If not, they chase her back to her parents

Krauss notes this tale as mere air; but I do not know in what part of Bulgaria it was supposed to have been discovered. I recall that as a boy, I saw the same custom practiced at the weddings of several lower class Jews in Riga; and although I did not understand it at that time, it took a firm hold on my childish memory.

Among the Roumanians in the country, the mother-in-law entertains the guests in her house on the day after the wedding with a "bridal-supper"; this occurs if the maiden is found to be pure. If this is not the case, then the "day of the bridal supper" is not observed.

On the discovery later, if the bride is still innocent, there is a stereotyped saying in Dalmatien and Montenegro: "It will be sufficient *piza* for the bridegroom to be here, and also for all the wedding guests." We shall not go into the question here of whether this saying was originated as the remains of the quickly disappearing courtesan of the bridal night, or as Krauss thinks,

161

merely a low attempt at dishonoring the bride. It may be gathered, however, as Krauss himself adds, that "among the southern Slavs there once took place a courtesanship on the bridal night, and in Montenegro it happens perhaps even to this day."

## CHAPTER TEN

# PHYSICAL ASPECTS OF THE BRIDE AND GROOM

*Wishes of the Fellahs in Palestine—South Slavic wishes—The bride as virgin—Mohammed's expression—Persian severity against unchastity—The virgin in the Koran—The breasts—The hair—Indian hair remedy—Mohammed and the hair of man and wife—Incidents of beards among women—Cutting the hair of boys—Arabian police laws for hair dressers—The beard—Baldheadedness—Pubic hair—Shaving the sexual area among the Moslem women.*

*Singhalese Girl—Fifteen Years Old*

The Fellah youngster in Palestine wishes his bride to be thus: She should be light in weight, and she should have pretty red cheeks, and eyes as large and brilliant as a gazelle's or as large as coffee saucers; and she should have beautiful white teeth—and other similar things, for which no man has poor taste. The southern Slavs, on the other hand, prefer wide hipped women with heavy buttocks. They consider fleshiness a requirement for fertility. Above all, they must not be too extraordinary; or else they may be subject to ridicule.

The person chosen for a wife should be a virgin. The prophet Mohammed said: "Go, take a virgin for a wife." The Arabs designate virginity with the word *sabah*, morning. If a girl gets married in Persia, she must be a virgin and provided with a hymen, *dachter-e-bakere;* there is no excuse for deceit in this respect, in addition the wife in such case can be deserted after the first night on the mere word of the husband. Omer Haleby recalls the oft repeated admonition of 'the prophet and says: "This admonition having been given, it is advantageous for true believers to take a virgin as a wife rather than a woman whose body has already been pierced by the thorn of evil. But life with the sun, the fragrance of the rose with its scent rising to its head—that surrounds a virgin whose thighs are yet free from any contact." An Indian poet pictures the virgin as a shy rosebud, whose calyx has not yet been determined, and the poets of all times and in all countries have repeated this simile.

Pure and unspotted virgins are the ideal of all Moslem love yearning. Mohammed has promised this to all true believers as the most beautiful reward of heaven for all who are worthy of it. So in the Koran II, 23: "Bear good tiding unto those who believe, and do good works, that they shall have gardens. . . . There shall they enjoy wives subject to no impurity." . . . And in the same chapter it is said: "The people are impregnated with an urge and desire for wives, children, gold and silver, gentle horses, herds and acres. But all this is nourishment for this life; but the most beautiful return is to God. Say yourselves: Can I give you a better report than this? The religious will receive from God a garden through which brooks flow, and there they will spend their time. There shall they enjoy wives subject to no impurity. . . ."

These are the houris. The word houri in Arabic means: Girls with large eyes in which the black and white are sharply differentiated." These heavenly virgins are of an exceptional nature, believers will always find them in a state of virginity; they remain ever beautiful, they never give birth and they never age. The Koran returns to this heavenly promise in many places. So LXXVI 12-13 and 21; LV 70, 72, and 74: "In the garden of paradise are good and beautiful damsels; houris, locked in tents, who have been deflowered by neither men nor genii"; XXXVI 55-57; XLIV 51-54: ". . . and we marry them to black eyed houris"; LII 17, 20: ". . . with large eyed houris"; 27-39: "Under thornless lotus and bananas with blossoms and far shadows, and by rippling water and fruit in quantity, inconceivable and unpromised, there shall you live; and on raised polsters. . . . See, how we herd the houris in separate compartments and keep them virgins for the loving enjoyment in old age for the companions of righteousness, for the holy."

In Chapter 78, verses 31-33, it says: "But for the pious is

prepared a place of bliss: gardens planted with trees and vine-yards, and damsels with swelling breasts." The "swelling breasts" are also desired, however, on earth. A Bosnian song follows: "O foolish boy, place your hand under my armpits and take out the two apples." The maiden is satisfied with everything, that they are "not yet ripe"; but therefore also "not green, but her own to caress." Among the Hebrews the normal development of the breasts was a condition precedent to the marriage of their maidens. In the Song of Solomon, IV, 5: "Thy two breasts are like two young roes that are twins, which feed among the lilies." In Ezekiel, XVI, 7, it is said symbolic-ally: "Thou hast increased and waxen great, and thou art come to excellent ornaments: thy breasts are fashioned and thine hair is grown."

In other places also in the Old Testament the rich growth of hair of a woman is mentioned. In the II book of Samuel it is related that the Hebrew women anointed their hair. They braided it and ruffled it: Judges, XVI, 13; Isaiah, III, 24.

In the Kamasutra the Indian women employ the following remedy for care of, their hair: Myrobalanen fruit, provided with the milks of *Euphrobia antiquorum*, Soma and *Calotropis gigantea* and the fruit of *Vernonia anthelminthica* bleach the hair white. A bath with the roots of Arabian jasmine, *Wrightia antidysenterica*, Kavanjanik, *Clitoria Ternatea* and *Slaksna-parni*, makes the hair grow again. If one strokes it with an ointment which one obtains through the proper cooking of these same things, the hair becomes black and never stops growing.

A Moslem song begins thus: "Honor to him who has be-stowed the beard of men and the hair of women as decorations."

Mohammed fixed the greatest price, death, as a penalty for him, "who disfigures the face of a man through spoiling his eyelashes or eyebrows, or the face of a woman through spoiling her hair." It was likewise deemed a crime "to perform an oper-ation which makes another lose his mind or one of his five senses, or which makes a woman sterile." Mohammed has also forbidden through Allah the use of false hair and has damned "those who deal in it as well as those who make use of it."

As welcome as the decoration of hair is to women, so unwelcome is it to them when it appears as a beard. And yet the latter is prevalent in the orient. Dr. S. Weinberg of Elizabethgrad reports on his treatise on Ethnology, chapter XXIV 280, from his own calculations after a walk on the Pera street in Constantinople; he counted 151 women between the ages of 18 and 50 of whom 11 had beards; on a second walk 273 of whom 33 had beards; on a third walk 243, resp. 26; on a fourth walk 667, resp. 70; on a fifth walk, finally 105, resp. 9. All in all he met 1,439 women between the ages of 18 and 50; of these 149 had beards, about 10 per cent. He saw all varieties from a flowing beard to a short cut beard. Only one old woman of the entire 149 had sidewhiskers.

The boys of the Bedouins in Palestine have their heads shaved on the seventh day after their birth.

Among the Jews in Palestine, Asia Minor, and Persia a custom exists of giving a boy his first haircut at the grave of a pious man. The grave in Jerusalem most visited for this purpose is that of Rabbi Simeon ben Jochai, the so-called composer of the Sohar or foundation of the Cabala. On the anniversary of the death of the pious one, on the 18th of the month of Ijar or on the 31st of the Sephirah, about the middle of May, Jews from far and near, even pilgrims from inner Asia assemble here. According to the nightly prayers and the lecture of the holy writings, a flame of fire from the finest oil rises from this grave to the heavens. On the next morning, after the morning prayers, they lead the boys with music, song, and dance to the grave of Rabbi Simeon, and at the door of the house of prayer the first haircut is given.

The hair of Moslem boys, especially in Bosnia, is entirely cut off for the first time after they have passed their fourth year. This always takes place either on a Thursday or a Sunday. The hair is then weighed and the father of the boy distributes among the poor as many coins as the number of Turkish drams that it weighs. The size of the coin depends upon the wealth of the spender. The Barber who goes through this procedure also gets a present.

In the Sultan's house such occurrences are occasions for great feasts. Under Sultan Achmed II the Grandvizier Daltaban clothed the barber in sables, which made known the joyous fact that the Prince Machmud was having his head shorn for the first time.

The old Arabian police laws provided special regulations for hair dressers: "They shall have narrow waists, and shall be reserved in their manner. The razor must always be new and sharp. The barber must eat nothing that can give his breath an objectionable odor, like onions, for this odor does not please people when a barber approaches them. The barber shall arrange the forehead and both temples of the subject in a comfortable manner; he shall not cut the hair of a child without the consent of its father; he shall not shave the cheeks of a young man whose hair is just beginning to grow, nor the beard of a man who is impotent."

Of Persia relates Polak: The barber takes away the superfluous hair at the extremities and on the head with a knife. Priests, especially people who still wear turbans, have their heads shaven bald. According to the newer mode the parts around the temples and the crown remain undisturbed; in the first part it is placed in two locks before and behind the ear, in the latter it is joined in a braid or a kind of Chinese queue. The women hide their hair entirely. The hair must be shaved from the genitals and from the arm pits according to the law of the ritual.

Among old Hebrews the shaving of a beard is considered an outrage—at least in certain cases. In the 2nd Book of

Samuel X:4, it reads with respect to this: "Hanun took them and shaved off their beards."

It is reported in Osman history that a cut beard was once the cause of rebellion and murder: An old Turk named Sukundkodscga, who complained that his land was overtaxed by two hundred aspers, instead of having his burden lifted, had his beard cut off. Hurt more by the removal of his beard than by the reduction in his income, the complaining Turk and his son Suklun Schah Weli and a third one, Sulnunoghli placed themselves at the head of several Turkish tribes, attacked the land assessor, the judge and the Sandschakbeg and beat them to death.

A decorated beard is abhorred by the orientals no less than a cut beard. Osman historians tell of many superstitious indications; the despotism of the women over their slave Sultan Ibrahim developed to such an extent, that one of the favorites even induced the Sultan to decorate his beard with precious stones, and show himself to the public, which was taken for the poorest taste, for in all the orient, Pharaoh alone decorated his beard in this manner.

In Samson's hair lay his strength. In the Book of Judges XVI:17 Samson says: "There hath not come a razor upon my head; for I have been a Nazarite unto God from my mother's womb: if I be shaven, then my strength will go from me." And so it came to pass.

The laws of the Hebrews forbade the baldheaded from entering into priesthood. Baldheadedness is widespread in the orient and particularly characteristic.

While in civilized Europe the idea is prevalent that baldheadedness is the prerogative of the learned, two types of it are met in Turkey, and both happen through nothing less than an overstraining of the nervous system, namely: Turks and Spaniards.

An Austrian doctor, Schweiger, followed up the causes of

oriental baldness, and in a letter from Widdin, March, 1885, for the information of a colleague, Dr. Gelber, presented the following results in the Austrian monthly for the Orient, XI:4: The oriental women, to whom indolence is generally known, distinguish themselves more through passive than through active sin. Usually the helpless children suffer as a result of this. The primary duty of nursing is neglected by midwives, mothers and wet-nurses alike. The newborn child, in the first eight days of his life, is placed on the flat hand of his nurse once daily, is sprayed with a little warm water, and then dressed in rags, and to be sure, colored rags, to spare frequent changes. A well-padded hood is placed on the head of the infant and tied fast under its chin. This manipulation is repeated in the following weeks only once in two days, for they fear that the child will catch a cold if he grows too quickly. This is also the ground for the superstition that the infant must not have his head washed with any pressure, for the scabs which form on the skin of his head are healthy for his eyes. These scabs are nothing but filth, and mixed with the secretion of the hair oil, they form a good mourishment for various plant and animal parasites, which use up the secretion, hinder the development of the hair, and have already taken effect on the roots. Therefore, the well-placed broods of trichophytes and microspores are not in the least disturbed by the fresh air, the enemy of all low organisms; among the Turks as well as among the orthodox Spanish Jews the head dress must never be removed, neither by day nor by night. At night the fez is merely replaced with a cloth of similar shape. Under this head dress there develop various eczema which ruin the growth of the hair.

Young men as well as girls are considered ripe in the Orient if hair sprouts in the region of the genitals. In a Bosnian song a youngster asks a maiden: "O you Magdelan, have little hairs begun to sprout on your skin?" And she answers: "Yes, by God, O Martin! They have risen until they have climbed onto my belly." . . . In a Montenegrin song the maiden answers the question: "O you maiden, young and fair, have you sprouted the little hair?" with a quite simple answer: "O little boy, full of cheek, come yourself and take a peek."

Every Friday the Moslem women religiously clean the genital region and remove the hair, usually through an Aurum salve, or they permit themselves to be shaved in the bath by expert female barbers.

Concerning Persia Polak reports: "The maidenhair is removed according to the law of the ritual with a preparation of Auri pigment, *Zernich,* and chalk; they call this *hadschebi keschiden,* to undertake that which is lawful; elegant women, however, tweeze their hair out until it finally stops growing of its own accord. Men must also follow the same prescription; a derivation of this, just as they let the hair remain on their forehead is considered a separate sign of emancipation in law. This ritual finds its source in this, that at prayer and at every religious dealing, just as after every excretion the washing of the genitals is commanded, and the hair cannot be sufficiently cleansed." Krauss believes that this custom is also in vogue among the southern Slavs, "because the men draw back in fright from mated evil—smelling maidenhair."

On the day before her marriage, the Fellah bride in Syria takes the greatest care of her body. Accompanied by friends and relatives she goes to the bath. There she is washed, scrubbed, rouged, and decorated. It is an important duty of the friends with the aid of a plaster made of honey and other ingredients to rip all the hair from the body of the bride—she becomes smooth and shiny, like a small immature girl. They then return to the house. Here the hair of the bride is braided and beauty marks of gold paper are stuck on her face, the eyebrows are painted with charcoal and the fingers and feet with henna.

It is similar, says Schweinfurth, among the lower classes of

172

the Egyptian city-Arabs and the Fellahs. Several days before the wedding the bride takes a bath. On a fixed evening she comes together with her friends and they remove the hair from every part of her body except her head; for this they need a sticky Colophonium heart in a turgid state, which they pour on the hair which is to be removed, and after it cools, they tear it off violently with the hair. A less painful method, but one requiring more care, is to obtain an ointment which contains certain ingredients dissolved with Auri pigment and silver leaf. Twenty-four hours after this procedure there follows the *lelet el henne*, the night of henna. The bride and several friendly girls and women who have come to the house fill their hands with henna-paste, tie henna-paste on the soles of their feet, and keep their fists clenched in their sleep, so that the henna brei should not fall off. On the next morning this is removed and there begins the process of beautifying the eyebrows and lids, which are colored with antimony or a bluish tint. The women folk spend the rest of the day chewing gum in order to make their teeth shine sharply.

## CHAPTER ELEVEN

# SEXUAL LEXICON

*Respectable and unrespectable designations—The hymen—Menstruation—Coitus — Onanism — Lesbian love — Procurers — Adulterers—Prostitution—Pederasty—Designations for the vulva;—for the penis—Poetic and flowery expressions—Gonorrhea—Chancre—The seat—Simple oaths.*

*A Slav from Bruenn*

Havelock Ellis says, according to Roth, that there exists in Queensland a respectable and an unrespectable vocabulary, so that there is a word for vulva that can be used in the best society, while another which is banned. So also among the peoples in the Orient there exist for all things related to sex life simple and embellished, frank and symbolic designations.

It is not unpoetic if the Turks use the word *Sabah,* which means the morning, to designate the hymen.

Holy writings always have flowery language for menstruation. In the 3rd Book of Moses, XV, 19-24, it says: "If a woman have an issue . . ." In the 3rd Book of Moses, XX, 18, however, it speaks more precisely of "fountain of her blood" or "from the bloodflow of her body." In the last mentioned chapter it also speaks of "monthly sickness." In the 3rd Book of Moses, XII, 2, and in Ezekiel, XVIII, 5, it talks merely of "the usual sickness of the women." In the first Book of Moses it is related that "it ceased to be with Sarah after the manner of women"; and in the first Book of Moses, XXXI, 35, Rachel excuses herself before her father: "Let it not displease my lord that I cannot rise up before thee; for the custom of women is upon me." The expression "monthly-flow" is also used in many places. The Koran calls menstruation simply "The monthly"; so it is in the 65th chapter. The Turkish expression for menstruation is: *al baschi* or *haiz;* Arabic: *el Hizat, el tems;* Persian: *eladet, ras eschar;* Hindoo: *kamerie.* For failure of menstruation they say in Arabic: *kulet* (or haps) *el heis;* in Persian: *kalilet* (or habs) *el ade;* in Hindoo: *lou e kammer bend;* in Turkish: *silyk* (or eksiklik) *kusur.* The Serbians designate the period as "womanly blood."

The Koran says: "You happen to women and they are a cloak for you." Among the southern Slavs the woman is called "the bed" of the man; Sekula the wonder boy says in a Bulgarian minstrel song to his mother as he counts his booty for

177

her: "I brought home a pretty little wife to share your housework and my bed."

For coitus the Bible as well as the Koran says: "to lie with", "to live with". Moses more often uses the expression "uncover". In the 2nd Book of Samuel, XIII, 1-14, there occurs the term "weakening". The Turkish term is: *sikisch*, they also use: *bili jatmaklik*; the Arabian: *dschamea*; the Persian: *mudschema*; the Hindoo: *mudschema, nal some*. There are innumerable south Slavic term sfor the practice of coitus; they say: *jebati, jebucati, jebiti se, peysti*, in the most common use. It is described as: *Jahiti*, riding; *Navschriti*, consummating; *Mrdati, Trti*, rubbing; *Poklopiti*, covering; *Prcati, Prtschiti, Kundatschiti*, creating; *Sigrati se sigre*, playing. A more delicate expression: *Saprtschkati*. Finally they say: *poljubat*, to kiss the vulva, for coitus; and for the practice of *coitus a retro* they have the special term: *podjebavati*.

The Koran and the Bible use the Hebrew or Arabic term for the sperm. The southern Slavs say: the oil; see Krauss, I, 289. Holding back of the sperm is called in Turkish: *As or Srok*; onanism: *Eummaira*. The expression for onanism among the Arabs and the Turks is: *itlam*; the Persians say: *muscht zenni*; the Hindoos: *scheiten kari*. The southern Slavs employ the following terms for onanism: *Odrati Kurac*, for men; *Pisdu guliti* or *oguliti*, for women. Besides this they say: *Kurtschati se, si alter alterum fricat*. To designate lesbian love they say in south Slavic: *Pisdecati se*, approximately: the female sex part in onanism. For pollution it is said in the 3rd Book of Moses XVI: "If anyone is deprived of his semen . . ." The Turks call the flow of semen: *motelim*; in Arabic: *suret enzal*; Persian: *dscherian emenni*; Hindoo: *dat, tant*. *Besevenk* is the Turkish term for procurer; it is regarded as in German as a derogatory term. Yet, under Sultan Mustafa III, a procurer once became Grandvizier; that was Ali Moldowandschi, of whom Hammer said in his history of the Osman kingdom: "Moldo-

178

wani or Moldowandschi means only seller of slaves, a name which the Bostandschi Ali acquired in an honorable sense under Sultan Osman's reign, when he was sent out against the street thieves, and he sold the servants which were brought in together with their children. From the simple Bostandschi he elevated himself in the train of Chasseki to the position of a favorite of the Sultan."

For adulterers the southern Slavs have the word: *Preljub*, for men; and *Preljubniza*, for women; in private they say: *Pogan, Heide; Pogana, Heidin.*

Prostitution is called in the Testament as well as in the Koran simply: harlotry. In Turkish they also have the expression: *Kahba.* The southern Slavs say of men: *Jebac; Jebalac, Jebatsch, Kurvitsch;* also: *Pisdólow, Pisdolovac;* of women they say: *Jebica,* also *Jebitschina.* In all the Balkan states the harlot is popularly called: *Frajle, miss.* The derogatory term in south Slavic for harlot is: *Kurva.*

For pederasty Ibrahim Halevy, on page 253 in chapter 6, uses the Turkish expression *Liavata.*

Among the southern Slavs *coitus in anum* is called: *U dupe jebati.* Among the Bulgarians they say indefinitely: *da ti go vkaram.*

For the female sex part the Bible has the expressions: "Genital slit", "womanly separation". The womb is called: lap, body, motherbody. In Ruth I, 11, it is said: "Are there yet any more sons in my womb"; and in the first Book of Moses, XXV, 24: "there were twins in her womb". For the vagina the Turks and Arabs say: *ferzedscg, kus, danat;* the Persians and Hindoos: *kus;* for womb the Turks use the word: *raam;* the Arabs say: *rehm* or *beit el olet;* the Persians: *betschedan;* the Hindoos: *zedane.*

The Bible employs known terms for male as well as female sex parts: "Genitals", "Nakedness". In the first Book of Moses, IX, 23, it is said: "Shem and Japheth covered the nakedness

179

of their father Noah". In II Book of Moses, XX, 26: "that their nakedness may not be discovered". For the male sex part there is found finally in Ezekiel, XXIII, 20, the expression: "Gland"; and in the 5th Book of Moses, XXIII, 2, the designation: "Urethra".

The vulgar, coarse expression of the Turks for Penis is: *El sobb;* the more delicate: *Dkor* or *Palawer;* the Turks also say: *sik, erkegen aleti;* the Arabs: *er, kazib, beker;* the Persians: *kir;* the Hindoos: *dendi.* The Koran usually employs for the male sex part the term: *Nakedness,* for the female: *Ornament.*

The Serbian and Bulgarian expressions for penis are: *Kurak, Kurek, Kuro, Kur, Kurtschina, Kurcekanjo.* If one wishes to avoid the outspoken word in good company, he says, especially in Bosnia: *Kudrac.*

Among the southern Slavs the female sex part is called: *Pitschka, Pitschiza, Pika, Pica, Pisda, Pishdra, Pisdra, Pisdura, Pisdurina, Pisdetina, Pisdekanja, Pisdenjac;* also, particularly in Bulgaria: *Putkata, Pitschica, Ozngarica, Dupka;* particularly in Serbia are found the following descriptions: *Manda* or *Mandra,* the enclosed room; *Koka,* happiness; *Curka,* the plump hen; *Vratscha,* the gimlet-hole; *Vagasch,* the rut; *Rupa,* the hole; *Schupak,* the excavation.

South Slavic terms for the glans penis are: *Glawitsch; Njuschka; Propfkeil;* the head. For the testicles: *Muda, Heljbice, Mudica, Kita, Klupkofi Jaja, Jajeta, bucekanja;* they are also described as: the bagpipe (Krauss, II, 253). In Turkish they say *Kesa,* namely: the bag. The Bosnians often express themselves quite poetically: "O my maiden of Silaj"—says a song from Krauss, I, 244—"you may well weave with me: I have a spool with two coils." And she answers: "Beneath the navel sprang up the sugar melon, it is neither ripe nor green, but it first aspires to a reddish hue."

Another song renders a lusty comparison: "Why have you risen up in a circle, like the oxen in the fold? Why do you

180

wave your beard, like the maidens their pitschkas?" The word fold is also often used to describe the pitschka, the female sex part. Thus sings a maiden in a song from Krauss, I, 255: "I liked to sit under the nut tree and stroke my fold."

Just as the southern Slavs call the penis: "rat", so compare the male gland to animals. So the expression snake for penis is widespread. In the Berlin Museum of folk lore can be found a wood carved figure from New Guinea which represents a woman in whose vulva a crocodile is pushing his snout; at another figure which comes from the same source, a snakelike crocodile is creeping out of the vulva, and at a third figure one sees a small round snake similar to the penis at the entrance to the female sex organ. These figures are reproduced by Ploss and Bartels.

In Turkey urine is called: *sidik, boul*; in Arabic: *boul schakh*; in Persian: *pischab*; in Hindoo: *karura, muter*. Urine drops are called in Turkish: *damalajan, sidik*; Arabic: *boul mutekathir*; Persian: *sinselet eboul*; Hindoo: *pischab ke topka*. Gonorrhea is called in Turkish: *belsoklughy*; Arabic: *harak el boul*; Persian and Hindoo: *suzzak* or *korra*. The Turks and Arabs call chancre a Frankish pestilence; the Turks say: *freng sameti*, the Arabs, *gru el freng*; the Persians: *zachm atescheg*; the Hindoos: *bad ke zachm*.

For the seat of man the Bible has the expression: "the buttocks." In the II Book of Samuel, X, 4, one reads: "Hanun cut off their clothes in the middle even to their buttocks." Turkish expressions are: *got deligi* or *beuzuk*; Arabic: *ayn ettiz* or *makat*; Persian: *gun*; Hindoo: *tschotter* or *pitschari*. The rectum is called in Turkish: *doghru baghersak*; Arabic, *miai mustakim*; Persian: *makat*; Hindoo; *tundri*. The southern Slavs say: *Dupe; Zadnjica*, namely: the rear end; they describe it as: *Prkno; Zrcalo*, the mirror; *Tupi Kraj*, the stump. They also say, especially the Serbians: *Gus, Gusiza*; the Bulgarians: *Guso*.

The southern Slavs just as the Russians take their oaths

181

from the sexual lexicon. "You should dishonor his mother's soul" (the original expression employed the common word), or: "Dishonor your own mother"—one hears that as casually as "Good morning" or "Good evening". They go even further and even say: "Matri tuae eum in anum introducam." Or: "I sodomize your father!" Even the greatest Being is drawn into the curse, and the God who is known to the cursed one—he is often also the God of the curser—is considered in the same manner as the father and mother of the one cursed. His parents and he himself are made relatives of dogs and he says: "A dog has slept with your mother"; or: "You are a dog and the bastard of a whore"; or: "You were brought up like a dog." A milder reproach is: "You were brought up in the gutter." One says of a stupid one: "Your father did not finish you."

If a southern Slav wishes to express her deepest dislike for anyone, she bands forward, lifts her dress high with her left hand, strikes her buttock with her right hand and cries: "Na ti ovo! Here have this!" They call this pretty art, *Pokasati prkno*, showing the rear. They say from hate as well as from love—the tone alone makes the difference: "Osch pitschke? May you not have a pitschka?" Krauss relates in his book on this showing among the southern Slavs, I, 201, an anecdote about one "who married his wife as a punishment." For the expression of the idol of Berlicheingenthe southern Slavs use the following variation: "Ajd u Kurak!" Or they pull their hose up or down and show the scorned one their organs! Another rendition: "Penis meus tibi in anum introiat!" is not very unusual.

The expressions are indispensable to the southern Slavs. If the people, however, wish to be more genteel and avoid the out-spoken original words, they change them a little and instead of saying *jebem ti*, they say *jerem ti*, and instead of *Kurac* for the male organ, *Kudrac*.

Instead of a direct command like that of the idol of Berlichingen, they say: "Write me in anum!" . . . Instead of "God bless you," they say to one who sneezes, in a friendly manner: "Drive your nose in anum!" Instead of indicating anger with the the words "Leave me in peace!" they say: "Ride in anum!" Instead of: "It is all the same to me," they say: "My anus is dark." To a stupid person they say: "Even my penis has a head."

## CHAPTER TWELVE

# MENSTRUATION

*Beginning and end of the period—From Persia—Early maturity—Expediting methods—Restraining methods—Syrian—Serbian—A Moslem tradition—The harmfulness of those who menstruate to their neighbors—Ethnographic parallels—Biblical reminiscences—Cleansing baths—Uncleanness of those who menstruate—The concet of Tabu—Good and bad characteristics of those who menstruate, according to Plinius—Superstitious observations of the Syrians—Among the Jews of Palestine—European abnormalities—Menstrual blood as a medicine and love potion—Comparison of animals with humans—Menstruation and coitus—Ordinance of the Zendavesta—Biblical rules—Precepts of the Koran.*

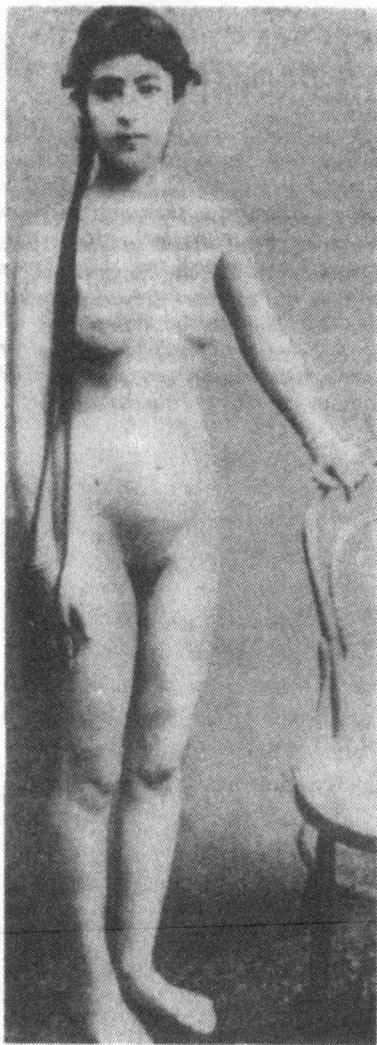

*Twenty-two-year-old Persian*

In the Orient menstruation usually begins about the thirteenth year and stops with the thirtieth. The Oriental woman ages quickly. At the age of 35 she is already old.

Polak says concerning Persia: The "Scherifen", female descendants of the prophet, from Arabian sources, menstruate and give birth longer than full blooded Persians, but this is not deemed to be caused by their race, but it is explained as a miracle. The women in the Orient control their menses much more easily than the women of Europe, for they count according to the monthly calendar in use there, so that they can determine exactly the first day of their menstruation. This holds true for the day of birth as well, which falls precisely on the day after the tenth menstrual period.

Legally the maiden in the Orient should not get married until she has attained full puberty, "with the beginning of menstruation and when pubic and arm-pit hair begins to show itself," just as under the laws of Moses; the poorer classes do not, however, abide strictly by this law, as Polak reports of Persia, and this holds true also for the rest of the Orient; they seek to increase their capital as soon as possible, and the consent of the *Mulla* is easily purchased. Girls of unfulfilled menstruation and quite flat breasts marry, but both develop quickly in marriage. Dr. Polak tells of cases in Persia where pregnancy occurs before menstruation has set in. This begins in northern Persia at about the thirteenth year, but in southern Persia at about the ninth or tenth year; the latter age is also true for Jewish maidens who, in spite of their apparent anaemia caused by the straitened circumstances of their life, menstruate earlier.

In Schiraz Polak saw women twelve years old who were already mothers, while in Teheran a woman rarely gives birth before the thirteenth year. Women of 30 are often grandmothers; daughters and mothers become pregnant at the same time. Menstruation therefore ceases approximately between the thirty-second and thirty-fifth year and with it also the *facultas generandi*, after which time change of life begins.

The root of Alizari, *Rubia tinctorum*, is considered among several nomadic tribes of Asiatic Turkey as a method of fostering menstruation, and this is also used by the same tribes in childbed to bring about the cessation of the childbed flow. In Constantinople, reports Rigler, the domestic doctors and the women believe that they must let the blood from the arm and foot at the same time; thus the blood is drawn to the upper part of the body and the period is skipped. If a Moslem woman in Syria has to ride on a horse while she is in a condition of menstruation she must, so says Eijub Abela, first place some earth under the saddle on the bare back of the horse; then the riding will not harm her.

If a Serbian woman wishes to disturb the regularity of her menstruation, she must merely wash herself at the beginning of the period, and pour the water over a red rose. A Moslem tradition, which is traced back to the prophet Mohammed, provides that the woman may take drugs to suppress her regularity, but only on the condition that these drugs be harmless and that her husband consent.

Belief in the harmfulness of menstruation is spread over the entire world. I have heretofore mentioned cases of the description of Caucasian women in my book, "Between Kaspi and Pontus." I wish here to recall several more: Among the negroes in Surinam the woman must live in solitude during her period; it is considered frightful for a man to approach her; and if she sees anyone coming from a distance, for her own protection she cries: Mi kay, mi kay, I am unclean, I am unclean! . . . Among the Negroes in Issing, says Trusen, in every place there is a separate building, some hundred steps away, called the *Burnamon*, which is set aside for the women during their monthly cleaning. Women of the kingdom of Angora wear a band around their heads as long as their period

lasts. A similar separation can be observed among the Hottentots of Ceylon and among the Kalmucken.

In England a line from Ellis says: "You are repulsive,
menstruating woman—everyone carefully avoids your body!"

The talmudic laws oblige the Israelites after every menstrual
period, likewise after childbirth, to bathe in well-water which
has not yet passed through the earth, that is, while it is running,
such as the approach to a well, or in wells which are located in
cellars, usually in cellars of synagogues. Well—and running—
water in a bathtub which has left the earth useless. The bath
is also prescribed for Moslem women after the conclusion of
their menstrual period or childbirth.

A menstruating woman is considered "unclean". She must
visit no sacred place, among the Moslems not the mosques,
among the Christians not the churches, among the Jews not the
synagogues.

On the question of "Uncleanness", Havelock Ellis remarks
in his book on the Sex-urge and the feeling of puberty: In the
earlier periods of culture menstruation was considered a process
of cleansing, as a dangerous release of rotten fluid, therefore
named catharsis from the Greek; therefore also the medieval
opinion of Boethius on women: *Mulier speciosa templum addi-
ficatum super cloacam.* . . Among the later Jews the holy books
"soiled" the hands of the reader just as the touching of an unclean subject. Among the Syrians, says, Lucian, the dove is held
so sacred that whoever touches it is deemed unclean for a day.
So it seems that unclean should mean righteous, sacred. This is
carried to such an extreme among the heathen semites that
unclean animals become sacred animals. An unclean one in a
religious sense brings misfortune to him who first greets him in
the morning, according to Arabian belief, and the condition of
a sick person becomes worse if he even approaches him.

Wallhausen, in his book on Remaining Arabian Heathenisms, says: among the ancient Arabs clean signifies: unsacred

189

and permitted; unclean: sacred and forbidden. Jastrow says the same of Babylonian semites. Wellhausen thinks also that in pre-Islam times the designations applied to women depended only on whether they were in or out of the menstrual period. Frazr adds that the interpretations of sacredness and uncleanness are not yet differentiated, so that women in childbirth and during menstruation are on the same plane as divine kings, rulers, and priests, and have assumed the same measure of ceremonial cleanness. To exclude such persons of the outer world, so that the feared spiritual danger which they have attained shall not leave him, is the purpose of the "Tabu". After all, thinks Ellis, the woman must not be thought of as in a condition of degradation and uncleanness because of menstruation, but—according to age old creation—as a being who will be raised to supernatural power in the highest region.

Plinius relates in his nature studies, VII, 13, and XXVIII, 23, long rows of different good and bad characteristics of those who are menstruating: Hail storms, thunder and lightning pursue a woman who uncovers her body while in menstruation. This also results in all other kinds of weather and storms. On the sea a storm can be quieted if a woman uncovers her body, also if she does not menstruate in time . . . If a woman goes about naked in a cornfield during her menstrual period, the worms, beetles, and other insects fall off from the corn stalks.

But also at other times, when they are not in a menstrual condition, the women can, as Plinius claims, rid the garden of worms if they go about naked therein. Plinius reports also that the Kappadociers and Kantharides believe they can make their land fertile by having menstruating women walk through it; but this method must be tried before sunrise, or else the seeds become rotten.

Superstition is bound hand in hand with sanitary, aesthetic, and religious observations. The Syrian Eijub Abela relates that in his home it is believed that: If a menstruating woman sits at the bed of a pregnant one, it is to be feared that the new born child will have a "Milk-crust".

The Jews in Palestine say: No live animal or menstruating woman shall be permitted to go into the room of a sick person. A Syrian superstition forbids menstruating women to salt or prepare food. Hammer-Purgstall has already remarked in one place in his history of Persian literature that the belief in the harmful influence of menstruating women on baking and cooking is widespread generally in the Orient. Plinius, VII, 13, likewise speaks of the evil influence of a woman when she is menstruating, on plants, fruit and bee-hives. She chokes the power of life, makes flowers wilt, causes fruit to fall from the trees, deprives the corn of its power to grow, kills shoots. But this belief is also current in Europe. In the great refineries of north France, so reports Ellis according to Laurent, a woman who is wearing the cloth is strictly forbidden while the sugar boils or cools, for otherwise the sugar would become black. For the same reason no woman is permited at the opium gathering in Saigon: that opium would become changed and bitter.

Ellis relates: In 1878 an associate of the British Medical Association turned to the Medical Journal with the question of whether it was true that the ham which is salted by a woman in her menstrual period becomes rotten; he knew that this had happened a number of times. Another answered: There is no harm done if meat rots after it had been salted by a woman while in her period; that he could affirm with certainty. . . .

That the effect of a menstruating woman may also be a good one has already been told us by Plinius. According to an expression of Aelian, a woman in her menstrual period is in a true measure joined to the world of stars. The menstrual blood is used in many ways as medicines and love charms.

The source of the secret strength which is ascribed to the

female organs, lies, as Ellis says, in the primative conception of the blood; not merely menstrual blood. Every kind of blood is the subject of a similar feeling among wild and barbaric folk. All possible precautions must be taken with reference to the blood. In it resides a godly principle, or, as the Romans, Jews, and Arabs believe: life itself. The passage of blood is "tabu": it sanctifies everything with which it comes in contact. Now the woman is the chronic display of bloody manifestations.

A sect of the Valentines ascribed to the menstrual blood the worthiness of the sacrament, and profited therefrom as from the blood of Christ. Menstrual blood is useful as a love potion; I spoke of this before in the chapter on love charms. Similarly in Kamasutru, the Hindoo primer of love, it is prescribed "as a drink, furthering potency and long life": "The first menstrual blood with *asparagus racemosus, Asteracantha longfolia, Melassesaft,* paste from *Piper longum,* honey, cow's milk, and melted butter from goats." Also: "The first menstrual blood with *asparagus racemosus, Asteracantha longfolia, Gmelina arborea,* with four parts water boiled to the proper consistency." Plinius reports of the Kappadocians, that they believe that the blood of a menstruating maiden would make the weapons effective and the coats-of-mail impenetrable. This notion has remained to this day in Germany. For they say in Bayern: A piece of clothing touched with the menstrual blood of a virgin is a preventative for cuts, bruises and relieves burns.

In the middle ages, remarks Strack, menstrual blood was a remedy often turned to for leprosy. Strack also relates the use of menstrual blood as a method of love charm: In Germany, he says in his discussion of examples, girls to this day smuggle drops of their menstrual blood into the coffee of their beloved, to assure themselves of their love.

Ellis says: It is worthy of note, that among animals this period is the only time they have sexual intercourse, while among humans this is just the time when sexual intercourse is forbidden, often under severe penalties, sometimes even the death penalty. Ploss and Bartels have already joined in remarking on this point. They relate that in medieval times the preachers warned their listeners against the sin of sexual intercourse during menstruation. Ellis declares: The injunction against sexual intercourse during menstruation is a fundamental element of the rites of wild peoples, an element which is universal only because, as is now generally recognized, the grounds of human psychological development are the same all over. On the psychological side, continues Ellis, the primary normal and fundamental characteristic of the menstrual condition is the disclosure of the compelling sex-urge. . . . Ellis recalls the old Hindoo doctor, Susruta, who claimed: The urge to chase men is one of the signs of menstruation (Schmidt, Comments on Hindoo Eroticism, p. 390). In this connection it is said in an Arabian book, "The Perfumed Garden": that women during menstruation have a repulsion for sexual intercourse. Hippocrates offered unfruitful women the advice to give their husbands access to their wombs at the beginning of the period. In ancient times as well as in medieval there was current a belief that sexual intercourse during menstruation would bring about a miscarriage.

In connection with the last-mentioned notion a south Slavic opinion seems proper. Krauss relates that among the southern Slavs they say of an unworthy official: "his mother must have conceived him during her period, and he must have fallen from her vagina onto a dung heap." Among Iranians, so say Ploss and Bartels, menstruation is considered as a creation of the evil spirit. According to the Avesta the women are shown to a separate place and there enclosed. If they go around with a man during this time they receive 30 strokes of a strap the first time and then 50. For the man, says Zoroaster, there is no expiation. He must atone in hell until the resurrection of the

193

dead. If the man has engaged in coitus with his own menstruating wife, he becomes unclean and either receives 200 strokes of a strap or must pay 200 dollars.

According to Mosaic law both individuals are exiled if a man has lain with a menstruating woman. The 3rd Book of Moses, XV, 19-24, contains the following rigid admonitions to menstruating women: "And if a woman have no issue, and her issue in her flesh be blood, she shall be put apart for seven days: and whosoever shall touch her shall be unclean until the even. And everything that she lieth upon in her separation shall be unclean: everything also that she sitteth upon shall be unclean. And whosoever toucheth her bed shall wash his clothes, and bathe himself in water, and be unclean until the even. And if it be on her bed, or on anything whereon she sitteth, when he toucheth it, he shall be unclean until the even. And if any man lie with her at all, and her flowers be upon him, he shall be unclean seven days; and all the bed whereon he lieth shall be unclean." . . . In another place it is said: "And if a man shall lie with a woman having her sickness, and shall uncover her nakedness; he hath discovered her fountain, and she hath uncovered the fountain of her blood: and both of them shall be cut off from among their people."

The Koran is not as strict as the Old Testament, although it prohibits sexual intercourse during the time of menstruation. In chapter II it says: "They will ask thee also concerning the courses of women: Answer, They are a pollution: therefore separate yourselves from women in their courses, and go not near them, until they be cleansed. But when they are cleansed, go in unto them as God hath commanded you, for God loveth those who repent and those who are clean." Moslem authorities have commented prolifically on this section of the Koran.

In Sidi Khebit, an ancient law book for Mohammedans, it is said: "He who visits a menstruating woman with the intention of satisfying his lust, loses his power and spiritual comfort."

The modern Osman author of a book on the secrets of love, Omer Haleby, says in this connection: "Mohammed commanded us ever to do the opposite of that which the Jews do, with the exception of things relating to sexual connection."

CHAPTER THIRTEEN

# CHASTITY AND THE FEELING OF SHAME

*The first doctor in a Moslem harem—Modern customs—Dr. Spitzer in the harem of the Sultan Abdul Medschid—Doctors' visits in the harems of private people—Strange questions of a doctor—Consultations per procuram —Persian customs—Content of the sense of shame—Clothing and the sense of shame—Bible and Koran—Veiling the face—The history of veiling—The face and regio sacropublica—Uncovering of the sex organ—Admonitions of the Koran—Nakedness and chastity—Religious and superstitious sources of the sense of shame.*

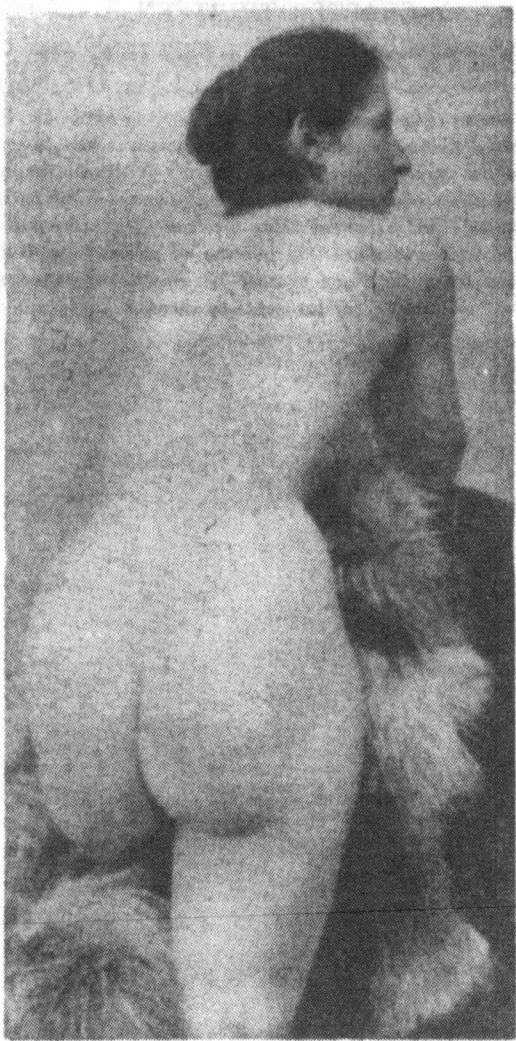

*A Greek Woman—Age Twenty-four*

The family life in Turkey is often to this day a mystery to strangers. Even the Christians and Jews do not lightly let their domestic affairs be investigated.

The most difficult, of course, is to obtain a glance at the intimate life of the Moslem wife. The first non-Moslem doctor to step into the harem was the Christian Dschordschis Ben Bachtjeschuu, doctor to the hospital of Dschondschabur in Persia. According to one of the manuscripts discovered in the Viennese library of Arabic doctors and the biographies of the doctor Ibn Ossaibije, Hammer-Purgstall reports the following in his history of Arabian literature, p. 1189: Dschordschis Ben Bachtjeschuu, with the given name Ebu Bachtjeschuu, doctor of Dschondschabur, author of the Kenasch or the book of Pandects, died about the year 154 according to the Moslem calendar or 771 according to the Christian. As the Caliph Manssur was building the city of Bagdad in the year 148 (765), he became subject to stomach trouble and impotence. He was advised to summon Dschordschis, the most renowned doctor of his time, the director of the hospital and medical school of Dschondschabur. Dschordschis came and brought with him his pupils Ibrahim and Isa Ben Schehla. The Caliph spoke with Dschordschis Persian and Arabic and marveled at the spirit and calmness of the doctor, had him dressed in beautiful clothing and commanded the chamberlain to conduct the doctor to a dwelling in the best part of the city. Dschordschis cured the Caliph to his great joy. Manssur showed his gratitude by sending the doctor 3000 ducats and three beautiful slaves; when these presents came Dschordschis was not at home and they were received by his pupil, Isa Ben Schehla. Dschordschis, who had left his old wife at Dschondschabur because she had not been in a position to undertake the strain of the journey, cursed the youngster for having accepted the slaves; he immediately returned them to the Caliph with the message: "As a Christian I must touch no woman other than my own wife." From this moment

Deschordschis was granted free access to the harem of the Caliph Manssur.

In more recent times, Dr. Sigmund Soitzer, love doctor of Sultan Abdul Medschid, induced by the latter's own wishes, entered the royal harem. He made reports of this in detail in his day book, and these disclosures deserve mention here as a noteworthy document: "Friday, August 11, 1845, I met the Sultan apparently disturbed. When I questioned him about this he said in a moving voice: "I have already spoken to you about the sickness of my third wife. She and her child feel very bad. The latter, Reschad-Efendi (heir apparent after Abdul Hamid II), is irretrievably lost. But very little hope is held out even for the recovery of the mother. Merjem Hatan (the Armenian Maria Dudu) and a doctor obtained by her, called S., have treated her in vain for many months. But I wish to leave nothing undone and would especially desire that you see her. For know that this woman is the only female being with whom I have found true love. I depended from youth with my whole heart on her upbringing. If you think it possible to save her, then you will take over her treatment, if nothing can help, do not hesitate to advise me. In that tragic case, you will approve of the methods theretofore employed by the doctors, so as not to frighten the sick one, and you will have nothing more to do with her. Above all I demand of you truth." Tears sprang to his eyes as he said the last words.

"He now had the eunuchs instructed to open the gates of the harem and meanwhile he led me into the ante-room in which he paced to and fro in impatient haste until the appearance of the negroes. These had finally opened the doors, which were closed again after we had passed through. We found ourselves in a corridor which no stranger had been permitted to step into before me. For even those women and doctors who had until now come into the harem, were certainly not in the position of being led in by Selamlik. We needed about ten minutes to wander through this corridor, which was often broken in corners. The two eunuchs went ahead, then came the Sultan, and I followed at a distance with sunken glances. Whenever we came to a corner, the Sultan called to me smiling: 'Restez!' At that I remained stationary, while unveiled women who somehow found themselves in our way and whose stifled voices mingled with the rustle of their clothes and the slamming of hurriedly closed doors fell upon my ear, were scared away. I did not move until the Sultan, who seemed delighted with the happenings in spite of his inner emotion, permitted it with the order: "Avancez!" So we came to a second portal at the end of the corridor, at which the *Kislar-Aga*, the watcher of the harem, saluted the Sultan, at the same time staring at me with wide-open eyes.

"We stepped into a chamber where we waited for a while, until sufficient preparation were made for our appearance into the inner sanctum of the harem. We then proceeded: first the Sultan, and I behind him, and the *Kislar-Aga* beside me watching my glances carefully. Through a splendid cabinet with richly gilded walls, we reached a wonderful, truly royal hall, which received its light from above, and whose ceiling was borne by two rows of grandiose marble pillars. Along both sides of the hall to the end I saw a number of doors covered with heavy red portiers, which gave a conception of artistic spaciousness. Each of these doors led to an apartment. The first one on the left is that of the Sultana mother; after this came the chambers of the legitimate consorts and those of the remaining odalisques. The Sultan approached the fourth of these doors and lifted the curtain, behind which the chamber was not yet to be seen, but a small foyer was found there under a second separated curtain.

"At the first step I attempted to take into this foyer, following the Sultan, the *Kislar-Aga* gripped my arm so that the other, looking back, indicated that he wished me to be let free. Just

201

at that moment a young maiden unveiled, unconsciously crossed the hall; my companion threw a grim glance at her. The Sultan then stepped into the chamber and motioned to me to do likewise. In the middle of a wall of the richly decorated room, I naturally lacked the leisure to examine it more closely, I saw a bed overhung with the finest Lahore-shawls, and on this under covers of similar material lay the sick Sultana, her face hidden with a silk shawl. The Sultan drew near her and asked in a tender tone: 'How are you feeling, Efendim?' 'I feel quite well, Efendimus,' replied a wonderfully soft lovely voice. 'This is my doctor,' added the Sultan, 'with whom I am altogether satisfied; it is my wish that he also treat you.' 'You need but command,' answered the sick one. The Sultan then asked her to let me feel her pulse, at which she offered me a delicate beautifully formed but quite fleshless hand, which seemed to give all indications of a consumptive suffering. The Sultan then asked me if I did not also wish to see her tongue. At my affirmative reply he himself drew back the shawl which covered her head, and I saw before me the most beautiful female head that I had ever seen in my life, and through the suffering expression, the pale complexion and the clear eyes resulting from the sickness, appeared even more striking. After I had done that which had been requested of me, the Sultan replaced the shawl.

"In the meantime Merjem Hatan had entered the room, and there transpired between her and me a sprightly, lengthy conversation in which she gave me to understand her conclusions with reference to the condition of the Sultana. While this was taking place I noticed that the curtain over the door was lightly lifted until through a small opening thus formed, a voice interrupting the American doctor added: 'You are not explaining the things properly. Let the doctor come to me.' It was, as I soon discovered, the Sultana-Walide. For after we left the sick-chamber, the Sultan led me to that of his mother, without entering himself. Through the separation in the curtain we consulted in detail concerning the condition of the sick one, at which Merjem Hatum with the greatest forcefulness defended the treatment of S. against the opinion of the Walide. The Sultan led me from the hall into the previously mentioned little chamber where he anxiously asked me for my opinion. I told the Sultan that whatever my notion of it was, I could not undertake the responsibility of the treatment by myself, and that my professional examination, thanks to his presence, was promising, furthermore, that etiquette would not permit me to render judgment and that it seemed necessary for me to have a consultation with the former attending physicians."

Dr. Spitzer later relates: "Yesterday, the 16th of September, 1845, in Beglerbei, as I was about to come before the Sultan with Hamid Bey, the first chamberlain, he informed me that I would again be taken to the harem, and he advised me not to make known my opposition to any kind of visit at this time. So forewarned I stepped before the great master, who immediately came to the point. 'I know,' he said, 'that you do not care for this course of conduct. You fear to trespass against etiquette in this undertaking; you also believe that you cannot accomplish much with the women, and you are worried lest I be angry if your treatment does not have the hoped-for result. You can rest easy on all of these things. I have once placed my trust in you and I know your medication can at least do no harm. If heaven gives its blessing she will be cured. Whatever your doubts if the opposite happens, they are quite unfounded. For I shall not lead you to one of the younger women, but to my mother, who is a very calm, understanding matron, and from whom you will receive no opposition or hinderances in the practice of your art. For some time her health has been undermined and lately she feels so indisposed that she cries bitterly, and I with her.'—Tears came to his eyes as he said the last words. He now left through the entrance to the harem, but soon came back with the report that the Sultana-mother had taken a walk to Tschiragan. He asked me to go there and indicated two eunuchs whom he ordered to accompany me and to introduce me to the Sultana as his doctor, and to ask her in his name to let herself be treated by me and if necessary to help overcome my timidity.

"Arriving at the court of Tschiragan, I saw in the distance a couch upon which there sat a woman covered with a veil and a mantel. It was the Sultana-mother, whom I approached respectfully, following my black companions. After these had advised her of the Sultan's wishes, she received me in a very friendly manner and invited me to be seated. Through the half-transparent veil I saw an influx of a happy red in her cheeks, as I spoke to her of the delicate trouble, of which her son had informed me with relation to her health on that day. Calmly and impartially she answered my professional questions, and the full beauty of her fine white hand impressed me no less than the regularity and energy of features of this 35-year-old, yet very well preserved Georgierin. On my leaving, she parted with me graciously, implored me to advise her of the necessary medicine, and took from the pocket of her *Federsche* mantel, a gold-filled purse which she presented to me through the above-mentioned eunuchs.

'I then hurried back to Beglerbei to the Sultan to give him the report of my visit. While repeating that his heart was set on the most careful treatment of his mother, he said with a moving tone: 'We are not dealing with a tree which must blossom and bear fruit again, but to see at least that it does not rot!' With naive kindliness he also asked me whether I could not give his mother the same medicine which not long before, at a quite different indisposition, had such good results with him. 'Well, was it necessary to do it with anxiety?' he added. 'The Europeans always criticise our family life from a false point of view. Are we not all humans like you? Have you discovered anything unpleasant about me or mine? Be

204

dispassionate, we have had an opportunity for mutual understanding. *Dost olduk,* we have become friends!'"

In general, the appearance of doctors in the harem is today very mechanical in the following manner: If a doctor comes into the harem, the inhabitants disappear or veil themselves promptly. A eunuch precedes the doctor and chases the women out of the way. He finds the sick one in a bed which is made on the floor or on an ottoman, deeply veiled and surrounded by her female household and relations. Of the face the doctor sees only the tongue; only when he is well known for years in the harem does the patient unveil her entire face, and then only if it is absolutely necessary. Testing, seeing and examining other parts of the body rarely occur. It often happens that the sick one hides herself behind a curtain and merely stretches out her hand for the doctor to feel her pulse. The most frequent question which a Turkish woman asks of a doctor is this: whether or not she is pregnant; if in the affirmative: whether she will give birth to a boy or a girl.

In the provinces where no emancipation at all is yet to be found, and the doctor is precluded from the harem just as before, instead of the female patients, their husbands, brothers or sons go to the healer. A man sits before the doctor and complains of symptoms of a sickness which is affecting his wife as though it were his own. The doctor is clever enough to recognize the modesty of the women and the jealousy of the men and advises the allegedly sick guest to do that which the truly sick woman can do at home. To be sure, such treatment at a distance is rarely accompanied by good results.

In earlier times in Persia, when a doctor was summoned to a sick woman, he was merely permitted to feel her pulse, yet, according to Polak's assurance, civilization has now progressed there to such an extent that at a serious disease the doctor must undertake a general physical examination. Only once did a prince demand of Dr. Polak that he should determine the condition of a sick woman while standing behind a curtain through a small opening of which she stretched out her hand. The wives of peasants and even wealthy ones visit the doctor themselves.

Nevertheless, the very last thing that the Oriental woman shows the doctor is her face. The face is the focus of female modesty in the Orient—a thing worthy of note on which I shall elaborate later.

The primitive state was nakedness. I Book of Moses, II, 25: "And they were both naked, the man and his wife, and were not ashamed." But with sin was also born a sense of shame; only a few pages after the original state of nakedness the Bible reports; I Book of Moses, III, 7: "And the eyes of both of them were opened, and they knew that they were naked; and they sewed fig leaves together, and made themselves aprons." The first thought was the same for man and woman, and she has still remained as God, in the last-mentioned chapter, verse 21, "unto Adam also and to his wife did make coats of skins, and clothed them." It did not become necessary for men and women to have separate clothing until later. In Book V of Moses, XXII, 5, it says: "The woman shall not wear that which pertaineth unto a man, neither shall a man put on a woman's garment: for all that do so are abomination unto the Lord thy God."

Nakedness was soon considered a shame and penalized. Isaiah 47, 2-3, says: ". . . uncover thy locks, make bare the leg. . . Thy nakedness shall be uncovered, yea, thy shame shall be seen." . . . And in Hosea, II, 10, is repeated: "And now will I discover her lewdness in the sight of her lovers."

In his work on remaining Arabian heathenisms, Wellhausen relates as examples of the sense of shame that among the heathen Arabs insufficient clothing was forbidden. If persons appeared naked among them it was always under special circumstances and for a particular purpose. Women in mourning bared their face and bosom and tore their clothing. Messengers do likewise when they bring bad news; mothers who want to make an impression on their sons take off their dresses; men who are forbidden to take revenge give expression to their despair by tearing their clothing from their bodies or by drawing their garments from behind over their heads.

When Mohammed made known the Koran, the Arabs adopted the custom of going naked about the Kaaba in Mecca. The Koran declared itself against this and commanded in chapter VII: "O children of Adam, we have sent down unto you apparel, to conceal your nakedness, Say: who hath forbidden the decent apparel of God which he hath produced for his servants?"

The women particularly were commanded to dress in outer clothing when going out: "O prophet," says verse 59, chapter XXXIII, "speak unto thy wives, and thy daughters, and the wives of the true believers, that they cast their outer garments over them when they walk abroad, thus will be more proper, that they may be known to be matrons of reputation, and may not be affronted by unseemly words or actions." The Arab women of that time were already wearing as outer garments those which are in use even to this day in Arabia and Egypt, made of white cloth and covering the women from head to foot, leaving only a small opening for the eyes. In another place in Chapter XXXIII Mohammed provides that his own women should remain the most unattainable of all. It says there: "And when ye ask of the prophet's wives what ye may have for, ask it of them from behind a curtain." According to Ullman: a curtain here means one between you and the wives; or a curtain means a veil which veils his wives. The reason given for this is cleanliness: "This will be more pure for your hearts and their hearts. . . . It shall be no crime in them, as to their fathers, or their sons, or their brothers, or their brothers' sons

207

or their sisters' sons, or their women or the slaves which their right hand possess, if they speak to them unveiled."

It is not impossible, thinks Ellis, that the Mohammedan requirement of veiling the face is derived from the fear of an evil glance. One must not forget that this requirement is not of Mohammedan origin but had long been in vogue among the heathen Arabs and was related by Tertullius in "De Virginibus Velandis", XVII. In ancient Arabia men also veiled their faces if they were particularly beautiful, to protect themselves against an evil glance. According to Wellhausen there is much in the thought that the veiling of the female face is a ritual of a protective measure.

Durkheim also says: The veil often has the purpose of warding off the influence of magic. Originated in this manner, the requirement was preserved, and changed more and more in its meaning. Among the Moslem women veiling became a religious law, which made the face the focus of the sense of shame. Emín Bey remarked, says Ellis, that women of many African tribes which go about naked, cover their faces with their hands under the influence of the sense of shame. Martial has already written: if an innocent maiden sees a penis, she does so through her fingers. When Casanova was in Constantinople, he was assured by the Count de Bonneval, a Frenchman converted to Islam, that he would be foolish to bother to try to see the face of a woman when he could so much more easily gaze upon more piquant things; the shyest Turkish woman knows modesty only in relation to her face, and nothing makes her blush so long as her face is veiled. There where, as among the Mohammedan folk, the face has become the focus of the sense of shame, the baring of the rest of the body, such as the *regio sacropubica*, but in any event the limbs and the upper part of the thigh are shown quite unconcernedly. I can verify this sentence expressed by Ellis. In the most active street in Constantinople I saw deeply veiled women remain standing, lift up their cloak unembarrassed and scratch themselves in the sex region. In Beyrut I once witnessed a scene where Turkish women prostituted themselves, throwing themselves upon a bed for coitus without letting their veil drop. And yet the Koran has forbidden the baring of the sex region no less than the baring of the face. In chapter XXIV it is said: For women who can bear no more children and who can no longer marry, it is no shame if they lay aside their outer clothing, but they must be careful not to disclose their "ornaments". Here quite clearly unveiling is permitted, but the uncovering of the ornaments remains no less prohibited than before.

Chapter XXIV proceeds in greater detail as follows: "Speak unto the true believers, that they restrain their eyes, and keep themselves from immodest actions: this will be more pure for them. And speak unto the believing women, that they restrain their eyes and preserve their modesty, and discover not their ornaments (namely: their naked body) except what necessarily appeareth thereof; and let them throw their veils over their bosoms, and not show their ornaments, unless to their husbands, or their fathers, or their husbands' fathers, or their sons, or their husbands' sons, or their brothers, or their brothers' sons, or their sisters' sons, or their women, or the captives which their right hands shall possess, or unto such men as attend them, and have no need of women, or unto children who distinguish not the nakedness of women. And let them not make a noise with their feet, that their ornaments which they hide may thereby be discovered."—that means: neither their naked bodies, nor any kind of ornament which the Oriental women used to wear on their knees. In Isaiah III, 16, the Hebrew women are reproached with "their stretched-forth necks and wanton eyes, walking and mincing as they go", whereby they sought to bring notice to their hidden parts. The Talmud is of the opinion that the above-related golden, silver and other costly ornaments about the lower part of the foot, are purposely brought together and tied with a golden knot over the knuckles; they serve "among respectable maidens as a protection of chastity." Among Turks and Arabs there is also a method of preventing the premature defloration of immature girls or the marriage of aged slaves, which consists of the infibulation of the pudenda with silver-wire.

Occasionally one finds the notion that the sex organs are hidden at an early age so as to prevent disagreeable evaporations in the neighborhood. This idea does not seem to me to hold much weight. For no folk in the orient is so sensitive as to permit themselves to be bound by a mere unpleasant odor. The Koran, which permits the ornament to be displayed before "slaves and old people" and "before children who do not notice the nakedness of women" notes, however, in the same chapter a qualification of this with respect to slaves and children: "O true believers, let your slaves and those among you who shall not have attained the age of puberty, ask leave of you, before they come into your presence three times a day; namely, before the morning prayer, and when ye lay aside your garments at noon, and after the evening prayer."

The concept of modesty is remarkably undefinable. I might say each folk interprets it differently. Herodot, I Book X, relates that among the Lydians and especially the barbarians, it is deemed a great shame for a man to be seen naked. In another place he tells of the women of Gindamer, that they wore as many belts of leather on their clothing as the number of times they had intercourse; and those women who had more belts than any other were considered most enviable. Rudeck reports in his history of the public morality in Germany, that there, in the middle ages, one undressed fully on going to bed, and it was not necessary to have any covering in the bath. Of the Empress Theodora, relates Prokop, an historian of the sixth century, that she "often appeared quite naked before the public, and would have liked to have gone

210

about naked all the time if that had not been prohibited to women, who were required at least to wear short trousers."

Among the southern Slavs, says Krauss, man and wife strip themselves of all clothing for coitus. Johnston relates concerning the Massai, that they wear *penem suum insueta longitudine praiditum* publicly. On the well populated bridge Karako, which leads from Galata to Stambul, one day about noon, I saw a dervish going about his business with the *ingens membrum suum* hanging exposed. Only the Europeans took notice of him. But the Turks did not find this at all offensive. He was a penitent, I was told; he chastised himself by baring that part of his body through which in his opinion he had sinned most. No one dared or wished to stop him. Undisturbed he went to Pera, where the police, on the demand of a European, asked him to transfer the exposure of his chastisement in his own home, or at least in a Turkish quarter.

If the uncivilized folk cover their sex organs, it is not always from a sense of modesty. Ellis says that, according to Somerville, the men of the New Hebrides carefully cover their penis, but they do it from fear of Narak, the evil charm; they believe that the glance at the exposed gland is highly dangerous both for him who has uncovered it and for the one who looks. They therefore wrap many ells of calico or other material around the organ, until it is about two feet long and unspeakably enlarged in thickness; they then tie the end with blooming grass, and carry it drawn up in the middle of a belt. But the testicles remain uncovered. A passage from Sunna also interprets the hiding of the sex parts as being derived from superstitious fear. It is there written that no man, unless he is alone, must uncover himself or wash himself while nude, from fear of God and evil spirits; one imagines that Hiob must have fared so poorly because he took issue with this precept. The Turkish writer Omer Haleby closes with this and says: "The laws of modesty forbid every Moslem to consider certain

211

portions of his own body. How much more must you, O women! watch yourselves to consider that which shame hides with a thick veil! Did not Aischa declare that she often bathed in the same water with the prophet, and that both drank from the same glass, and that nevertheless they did not see each other? And did not the prophet say: 'Whenever you approach your women, cover yourselves as much as possible, for the glance then unnerves the soul and weakens your power.' Therefore, O women, be decent in your glances and in all your dealings and gestures."

## CHAPTER FOURTEEN

# WICKEDNESS

*Virginity among the Iranian and Hebrew folk—Zoroaster's precepts—
Mosaic laws—Violation of virginity—The Koran on debauchery—The writings of Hamsa the Druse—Persian customs—Albanian punishments for the
unchaste—A Christian-oriental custom—South Slavic notions—Nobler com-
positions in song—Rape is an outrage—Lascivious songs and feats—The
south Slavic Kolo dance—The sex urge and the seasons—Ethnographic and
historic parallels.*

*Dancers from Port Said*

Among the peoples of ancient times it was only the Iranians and the Hebrews who had any understanding of the Moslem word chastity. To be sure, in China, Hellas, and Rome they honored the virgin, but they did not deem it sinful in certain cases to deflower her without her knowledge, and they held every sex act permissible so long as it did not infringe on the rights of another; for example, intercourse with a widow or with any other woman who was mistress of her own person.

Among the other folk a virginal maiden was preferred as a wife above all things; but it was not very unfortunate if the bride turned out to have been previously plucked.

Among the Hebrews and Iranians, however, the virginity of the bride was an absolute necessity. The sex laws of the Iranians and the Hebrews are identical, word for word: "Thou shalt not commit adultery; thou shalt not covet thy neighbor's wife; thou shalt not practice sexual intercourse except in marriage; thou shalt not be lavish, neither with your body nor with your presents"—these are the Iranian precepts.

After lies, debauchery is the greatest crime in the eyes of Zoroaster; whether it be debauchery in the form of onanism, unfruitful and unrespectable, or in illegitimate love. The loss of germs is considered a serious one in the presence of God. An Iranian without a wife is deemed the lowest of being. If a man makes a maiden pregnant and then sneaks away, she has the right, if she becomes a mother, to kill her seducer.

On a similar level of morality stand the Mosaic laws in the 5th Book of Moses XXII 28-29: "If a man find a damsel that is a virgin, which is not betrothed, and lay hold on her, and lie with her, and they be found; then the man that lay with her shall give unto the damsel's father fifty shekels of silver, and she shall be his wife." If the seduction was of a maiden who was engaged to another, and if it happened inside the city where she could have called for help, then both are stoned; the maid because she did not call for help; the man because he has seduced the wife of a neighbor; for the engaged are considered as good as married.

If the violation of virginity was committed with force on a yet unbetrothed virgin, then the man had to pay the father of the girl fifty shekels of silver and marry the girl with this additional penalty; that he could never be divorced from her. Finally if it happened outside the city, and the damsel was betrothed, then the man was deemed guilty of adultery and sentenced to death; but the maiden was not penalized, because her cries for help would have been in vain.

In the II Book of Samuel XIII 1-14 history relates the case of the rape by Amnon of his sister Tamar. He received no public punishment, but his brother Absalom, after having reproached him, had him killed by his servants. The violation of the virginity of a maiden who is pledged to another was, according to III Book of Moses XIX 20-22, punished with the flagellation of the evildoer; besides this they had to offer up a ram as a sacrifice for the crime.

The Koran follows the Bible in relation to its writings on chastity. Chapter VI prohibits "marriage with wicked and lewd women" and demands that slaves which are taken as wives be chaste and not wicked, nor must they have had any lovers. Chapter XXIV: "The wicked women should be joined to the wicked men, and the wicked men to the wicked women; but the good women should be married to the good men, and the good men to the good women." Marry those who are single among you, and such as are honest of your men servants and your maid servants; if they be poor, God will enrich them of his abundance. And let those who find not a match, keep themselves from fornication." Chapter XVII: "Draw not near unto fornication; for it is wickedness and an evil way." Chapter VII 29: ". . . but be not guilty of excess; for He (God) loveth not those who are guilty of excess." But one must not complain of women without sufficient cause, lest she blame this for her free undertakings and voluntary acts. In Chapter XXIV it says: "Moreover they who falsely accuse modest women, who behave in a negligent manner, and are true believers, shall be cursed in this world and in the world to come; and they shall suffer a severe punishment."

As an example of ideal chastity, the Koran tells the story of Joseph in the house of Potiphar, and in chapter XII the verses relating thereto, 22-35 and 50-50, are the most beautiful passages in this holy book: "And when he had attained his age of strength, we bestowed on him wisdom, and knowledge. . . . And she in whose house he was, desired him to lie with her; and she shut the doors and said, Come hither.' He answered, 'God forbid! Verily my lord hath made my dwelling with him easy; and the ungrateful shall not prosper.' But she resolved within herself to enjoy him, and he would have resolved to enjoy her, had he not seen the evident demonstration of his Lord. So he turned away evil and filthiness from him, because he was one of our sincere servants. And they ran to get one before the other to the door; and she rent his inner garment behind. And they met her lord at the door. She said, 'What shall be the reward of him who seeketh to commit evil in thy family, but imprisonment, and a painful punishment?' And Joseph said, 'She asked me to lie with her.' And a witness of her family bore witness, saying, 'If his garment be rent before, she speaketh true, and he is a liar; but if his garment be rent behind, she lieth, and he is the speaker of truth.' And when her husband saw that his garment was torn behind, he said, 'This is a cunning contrivance of your sex; for surely your cunning is great. O Joseph, take no further notice of this affair: and thou O woman, ask pardon for thy crime for thou art the guilty person.' And certain women said publicly in the city, 'The nobleman's wife asked her servant to lie with her; he hath inflamed her breast with his love; and we perceive her to be in manifest terror.' And when she heard of their subtle be-

217

havior, she sent unto them, and prepared a banquet for them, and she gave to each of them a knife; and she said unto Joseph, 'Come forth unto them.' And when they saw him, they praised him greatly: and they cut their own hands, and said, 'O God! this is not a mortal; he is no other than an angel, deserving the highest respect.' And his mistress said, 'This is he, for whose sake ye blamed me: I asked him to lie with me, but he constantly refused. But if he do not perform that which I command him, he shall be surely cast into prison, and he shall be made one of the contemptible.' Joseph said, 'O Lord, a prison is more eligible unto me than the crime to which they invite me; but unless thou turn aside their snares from me, I shall youthfully incline unto them, and I shall become one of the foolish.' Wherefore his Lord heard him and turned aside their snare from him, for he both heareth and knoweth. And it seemed good unto them, even after they had seen the signs of innocence, to imprison him for a time. . . . And the king said, 'Bring him unto me.' And when the messenger came unto Joseph, he said, 'Return unto the lord, and ask of him, 'What was the intent of the women who cut their hands; for my lord well knowth the snare which they laid for me.' And when the women were assembled before the king, he said unto them, 'What was your design, when ye solicited Joseph to unlawful love?' They answered, 'God be praised, we know not any ill of him.' The nobleman's wife said, 'Now is the truth become manifest: I solicited him to lie with me; and he is one of those who speak truth.' And when Joseph was acquainted therewith he said, 'This discovery hath been made, that my lord might know that I was not unfaithful to him in his absence, and that God directeth not the plot of the deceivers. Neither do I absolutely justify myself: since every soul is prone unto evil, except those unto whom my Lord shall show mercy; for my Lord is gracious and merciful. And the king said, 'Bring him unto me: I will take him into my own peculiar service.' And when

Joseph was brought unto the king, and he had discoursed with him, he said, 'Thou art this day firmly established with us and shall be entrusted with our affairs.' "

Hamsa ordered chastity for the Druses in the following words: The animal passion of the sex urge is derived from the four elements. Whoever violates his religion stands between asses and oxen, according to that saying in the twenty-fifth chapter of the Koran: They are like unreasoning animals, yea, they stray from the path of righteousness even more than these! Whoever keeps himself free from bestial passions stands higher than the most ennobled angel. If he is drawn by an unchaste remorse, he must humble himself for seven years, and crying, visit the initiated; if, however, he is drawn by no remorse, then he dies a faithless one and an unbeliever.

In Persia, if the misfortune of defloration of a maiden is discovered, an arrangement is made to keep the shame from her and her parents. She is married to a poor Mirza with the understanding that after a short time he would divorce her, so that she can then marry a respectable man; or they give her as a wife to a young immature boy; or on the day of the crisis she is helped by an operative concept which several Persian chirurgs well understand.

In the orient the maiden is not asked about the wishes of her heart, but is forced to accede to the will of another in the choice of a mate. There are not many instances of a girl escaping marriage with an unloved man, sanctified by tradition. Among the Miredites in upper Albania, there exists, as Hahn reports in his Albanian Studies, the following method: If a virgin wishes to save herself from marriage with a hated man, without inviting the accompanying revenge of the rejected wooer and his family on her and her family, she goes to the priest and says: "From now on I wish to be considered and to live as a man!" And the priest brings this knowledge to the entire company and gives the girl a male name. The virgin dresses in man's clothing and the whole world deals with her henceforth as a man. But woe is her, if she, as a man, becomes pregnant; then her penalty is death.

Among the Christians in Turkey, there exists the general custom that a bride must cry loudly so that the groom may hear her from a distance when he comes to take her to the church. For if she does not complain loudly of her innocence, it is a sign that she has nothing more to complain of.

Among the southern Slavs if a single man goes astray with a maiden, it seems to be no greater sin than "if a person plucks a little flower." If one considers merely the erotic songs gathered by Kraus, the southern Slavs are extraordinarily sensuous. At the glance of a woman, says Krauss, the southern Slav immediately thinks of marriage. This discovery is given support by the unembarrassed expression in their roundelay songs. So one says: "I would rather stand near you than be vizier in Bosnia; I would rather undress you than eat dinner with the emperor; I would rather sleep with you than take my soul to paradise."

Another Bosnian duet runs: "O thou maiden of Koraj, thou would choose to tarry in paradise." . . . "And she would choose to be in paradise, for she will be quartered by Zeumpten." According to Milena Mrazovic unchastity is severely punished among the Bosnians; they avoid the wicked maidens and exclude them from better society. That may be. But that unchastity is therefore seldom seen is really unthinkable according to the numerous lascivious songs which circulate there. So in Bjelinaer Bezirke in Bosnia they sing this duet: "O you maiden of Dubica, your shirt reaches to your buttocks, the gayly decorated corset to your ribs; how would you like to sleep with me? . . . "Quiet, do not fear, how can I resist? *prehende penem prehensumque introducas.*" Or in another Bosnian village:

220

"O brunette maiden, would that I could seduce thee,
  Would that you could succumb to me. . . ."
"No, by God, I would not think of it,
  I much sooner would laugh at it."

In another Bosnian roundelay song the boy asks:

"Tell me, O maiden, painted vessel,
  Where do you rest your bottom tonight?"

And the answer comes promptly back:

"There where I sleep with the rest of me,
  In no case have I a place for thee."

The Bosnian song often pictures the monk as obscene: "My mother sent me to gather vegetables with the monk. But the monk gives me no rest, he is ever gazing in the piza." Among the Moslems in Bosnia the songs are also not very chaste. A Bosnian-Moslem poem runs: "O thou little maiden, wouldst thou the piza give me?" "O thou little laddie, who could ever resist thee?—Lead me into the little forest, lift up my skirt, gaze at my nakedness, cut two little prongs of wood and rub stiff your little prop."

In the act of promiscuous intercourse, the south Slavic city woman strikes her flat hand on her sex part and declaims: "My merchandise, my desire, whoever desires me, to him I submit; I have hidden myself from no one." And like the city woman, thinks and sings the peasant woman. *"Dala sam i datschu, a pre sam i satschu,* I have promised and will give, even sooner will I give, and so will I live."

In numerous variations do they sing the song of the mother driving the daughter into wantonness.

A Bosnian song: "The wastrel stands with the mother at

221

the door.  Penum suum fricat, and offers twenty pieces of silver. "What shall I do mother, shall I submit to him?"  "Submit, O daughter, your mother has also submitted."

In another song the daughter does not let herself be persuaded by her mother, but says:  "If she has promised it to you, let her give it to you."

In a Bulgarian song, which is sung in the neighborhood of Sofia, the daughter asks:  "Shall I submit to him, mother?" The mother says:  "You are young, you will penem fragere him."  The daughter, however, comforts her worried mother with the words:  "I am young, I will penem calefacere him."

The greatest outrage among the southern Slavs, according to Krauss, is rape.  A maiden who falls prey to a wastrel as a result of her own carelessness is considered deflowered, in direct opposition to the old Hebraic moral, where, as I have shown, in such case the maiden is not punished, but the man is chastised. Among the southern Slavs a promiscuous maid easily finds a husband, but not so with a raped maiden.  This is especially so with reference to such women who, unmarried, have become mothers, but who have given themselves out of love; and, as Krauss says, even one who is purchased with money is preferred to a ravished one.  The debaucher is marveled at or avoided, depending on the circumstance under which he receives his punishment.  But the nearest relatives of the maiden think to take his life.  In earlier times, if it was the wish of the family of the ravished maiden, the debaucher was castrated.

It is therefore not surprising that in one of the songs of Bosnia which otherwise flow with obscenity and jubilation of lust, in such case the ravished maiden in a melancholy tone complains to her mother:

"O mother, to speak of the shame!
And yet I must to thee complain.
Do not think that I would lie;

222

Believe that your child the truth will speak.
I betrayed myself and fell asleep,
Under the cherry tree in the thicket.
And while upon the bank I nodded,
Someone came to me and prodded,
Drove it in from the side in silence—
O mother, do not think I'm lying.
As he himself to his feet did take
And I did from my sleep awake—
O mother, so great is the shame,
I have lost my head and name."

Such songs are sung among the southern Slavs at the
roundelays of Kolos, which are not in the least lewd. The
greatest importance, says Krauss, is given to the contents of the
songs. In the roundelay songs sex and passion cease and the
full freedom of song rules. The roundelay songs are set aside
for the maiden, in the beginning they dance them alone. A
roundelay for boys alone is seldom seen; finally the boys and
girls dance together. Every roundelay has an introducer, and
at the same time one who sings a prelude. They start the dance
at first slowly, then gradually more quickly and lively, after
which with the upper part of the body bent forward and the
eyes cast to the ground they sway their hips. The hind parts
play an important role at the Kolo; "for they who can shake
them best are considered the most excellent dancers."

That is the beloved "rear-end dance" of the Balkans, while
in Constantinople and Asia Minor the belly dance of the Armenians and gypsies is preferred. The boys lounge around and
look on, they catch fire and place it where it best pleases them.
They are livelier, do not merely hold hands, but embrace each
other, and dance body to body, and thigh to thigh. In order to
show their welling passion, the boys step on the toes of the girls,
bite their necks, tear their necklaces with their teeth, and snap

at their ears. The music is furnished by *Dudasch*, the bagpipe-player, who dances alone in the midst of the Kolo. In Bulgaria near the Dudsch they also have a fiddler with a three-sided *gusla*. The song is lascivious throughout. Pregnant girls are not permitted to dance in the roundelay.

In Serbia they play at masquerade, at which the main person is called *Turiza*. Masked beyond recognition, *Turiza* makes unceasing noise, in the meantime swaying the body with an obscene motion.

The real sexual transgressions among the young people occur mostly in the first harvest time after they are finished with bringing home the fruit from the fields. It seems as though the young men behave themselves as though mad with love for two or three weeks; they dance the roundelay to exhaustion for nights at a time and sing obscene songs until they are hoarse. The wildest cancan can not be compared with the south Slavic harvest *Kolo* when it is danced in the light of the full moon by highly decorated maidens with welling breasts, ornamented with strong smelling flowers and leaves, and by drunken boys. The sensuously arousing power of this dance is astounding, the surge of the sexual passion encompasses them in every respect and they do that which their forebears did before them—"they dash to the thickets with the women."

Krauss thinks that these harvest dances are fundamentally caused by a religious motive. This opinion meets its counterpart in Dr. Havelock Ellis' book Modesty and the Sex Urge. Johnston tells of an unrespectable African dance which represents the beginning of the act of mating, but so modified with the passage of time that its true purpose cannot be recognized.

Among the gypsies and Slavic folk there was in earlier times commingling with full sexual freedom. Until the beginning of the sixteenth century, relates Kowalewsky, there took place on the banks of the river near Norgorod, such erotic feasts on the eve of the feast of John the Baptist, who in heathen times was called the Godly Jarilo. Half a century later the church endeavored to destroy all traces of these old feasts. A general characteristic of those feasts was the domination of voluntary sexual intercourse.

Among the Esthonians it was customary even until the close of the eighteenth century to gather together around the ruins of an old church and to light a fire, and sterile women danced about naked, but young maidens hurried to the woods with boys to indulge in their lusts. Even to this day I saw remains of this old Baltic feast in my Lapland home; but they spring barefoot over the fire merely to attain health or to become fertile.

Ellis has assembled data to show that there are seasonal changes in the human organism, which regulate themselves with the seasons and have a particular relationship with the sex functions. Laycock has already given even earlier interesting examples of the principle that the bodily system undergoes a change especially of a sexual nature at the time of the spring and autumn equinox. Westermark gives instances which tend to prove that the late spring or early summer brings with it an increase in the sex instinct, and considers this a remnant of the ancient copulation time. Cook found that among the Eskimos passion was at a low ebb during the long winter night; no sooner does the sun appear than the people tremble with sexual passion. Both periods, spring and autumn, the time of the awakening of nature and the time of the gormandizing to overflowing, appear according to Ellis to be the most general period in the entire world for erotic feasts.

In classic Greece and in Rome, in India as well as among the North and South American Indians, spring is the season of love, while in Africa the harvest time is selected.

If one considers closer the feasts which are celebrated all over the earth, he will of course find that they occur in all four seasons. But usually only two seasons are celebrated by one people.

In Australia marriage and conception takes place during the hot season, and among many races the conception is celebrated by a feast when the roots are ripe; a particular characteristic of this feast is the moonlight dance which represents a symbol of the sex act. With their spears which are supposed to represent the male sex organ, the men take a trip on the thickets which impersonate the female organs. According to Miklucho-Macleay the best time for conception among the women of New Guinea is usually towards the end of the harvest season. Guise writes about the year-round feast that takes place at the time of the root and banana harvest, where the maidens are ceremoniously introduced to the secrets of the sexual life and marriages are arranged. Johnston relates in his work on Central Africa, that at certain times there sexual orgies are indulged in, serious and ceremoniously. In New Britain, report Ploss and Bartels, according to Weisser, young maidens are carefully protected from the young men. But at a definite time a trumpet signal is given towards evening, and all young maidens are given permission to go into the thickets to have intercourse with the young men. In old Peru, in December, when the fruit of Paltay is ripe, at a feast which follows a fast of fifteen days, and which lasts for six days and six nights, men and women meet in a certain place in the garden fully naked; they all undertake a race to a hill and every man who catches a woman is obliged to have sexual intercourse with her.

Dalson writes similarly of the Bengal folk: Die Ho, an Hindustan tribe which engages only in agriculture, have their main feast, *Magh Parak,* in January, "when the gardens are full of corn and the people full of the Devil"; this feast of the harvest at the completion of the work of the whole year takes place at the time of the full moon. All rules of duty and respectability are set aside, girls and women receive unlimited freedom and become bacchantes. They believe that at this time men and women "are so overladen with the power of life

226

that it is absolutely necessary to open a safety valve." Die-Ho folk are at other times quiet and formal, decent and respectable toward women; the maidens have an innate sense of respectability, modest demeanors. But at the time of the Magh Parak they shed everything, their clothing inclusive. Everything is steeped in vulgar speech; they become animal-like in their sexual excesses and acomplish things with which only the fantasy of bacchanalian feasts and the famous orgies of Pan can compare.

The all-fools'-day of the middle ages was just such an orgy. There occurred a parody of a fair, then they danced vulgar dances in the church, shame and shyness vanished, passion reigned undisturbed. This feast, says Ellis, can easily be traced to the Roman saturnalia. Mannhardt, in "Forest and field cults," was the first to show how closely the spring and early summer feasts in Europe were connected with the wooing of love and the choice of a life companion. The principal season which is associated with erotic ceremonies in all Europe is the time of the summer solstice, the eve of midsummer or St. John's Day. Erotic ceremonies command the feasts of the German Easter holidays, the Celtic Mayday, the Walpurg night, of which Grimm writes that it has the same derivation as the Roman Floralian and the Greek Dionysian.

CHAPTER FIFTEEN

# PUBLIC PROSTITUTION

*Harlots among the Hebrews—Old Arabic punishments for harlots—The Koran on harlotry—Prostitution in the Moslem domain—The law of the Sultan Ghasan—Prostitution in Cairo—Harlots as the cause of pestilence—Arabian police laws against harlots—Sultan Suleimus' laws of conduct—Reminiscences from Osman history—Florid clothing and walks of women forbidden—Freer customs among the Bedouins—Prostitution almost un-known among the Bedouins—Omer Haleby on prostitution—In present day Turkey—In the inland—The Greek women of Sille near Konia—The daughters of the Algerian tribe of Ulad Nail—In the seaport towns—On the caravan bridge in Smyrna—In Galata—In the Christian Balkans.*

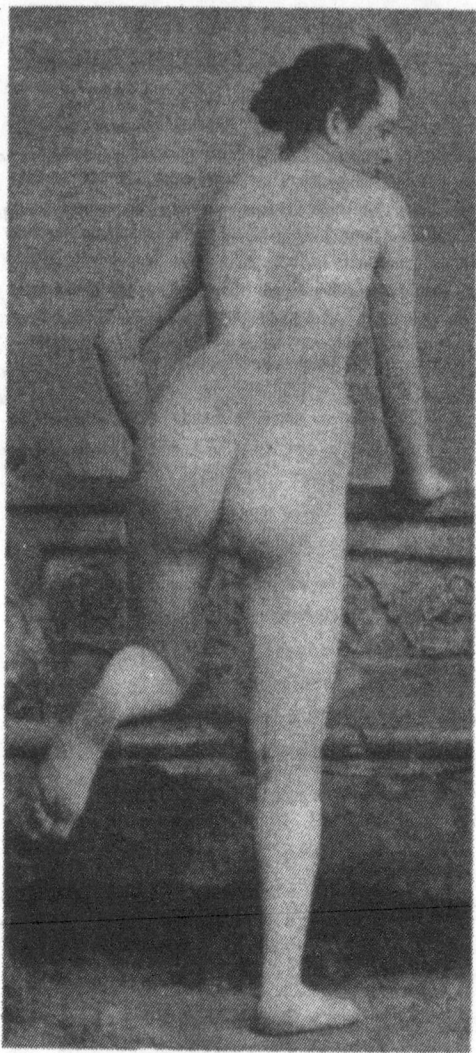

*South Hungarian—Eighteen Years Old*

On prostitution the Old Testament says in the 5th Book of Moses, XXIII. 18: "Thou shalt not go, being the hire of a whore, into the house of the Lord thy God for any vow." In the 2nd Book of Moses, XXII, 15 and 16, every dishonorable association is forbidden under severe penalties. In the 3rd Book of Moses, XXI, 9, it is said: "And the daughter of any priest, if she profane herself by playing the whore, she profaneth her father: she shall be burnt with fire." The burning occurs after stoning as a public degradation after which comes death; and the shame marks of the stones become apparent on the burnt one. Moses, 1, Book XXXVIII, 24 and 3; Book XX, 14. In spite of this "harlots" were no novelty among the Hebrews. Under Antiochus all kinds of lewdness were indulged in with women on a sacred plane.

The heathen Arabs buried their daughters alive if they had become harlots. So says note 4 in Ullman's translation of the 81st chapter, page 523, according to a commentator. Abdallah Ebn Obba, who defamed Aischa, and claimed that she was unfaithful to the prophet, led no faultless life himself. He is said to have forced his slaves to let themselves be used as public slaves and to give him a certain sum of money therefor. The Koran prohibits this killing of two birds with one stone in chapter XXIV: "And compel not your maid-servants to prostitute themselves if they be willing to live chastely: that ye may seek the casual advantage of this present life. But whoever shall compel them thereto, verily God will be gracious and merciful unto such women after their compulsion."

According to Sunna a whore and a whoremonger, if they

231

are slaves, are punished with a hundred strokes; free born persons who take to such life are stoned. The Koran says in "The Light", the XXIV chapter: "The whore and the whoremonger shall ye scourge with a hundred stripes. And let not compassion towards them prevent you from executing the judgment of God; if ye believe in God and the last day." Some true believers are to be witnesses of the punishment; IV, 19: "If any of your women be guilty of whoredom, produce four witnesses from among you against them, and if they bear witness against them, imprison them in separate apartments until death release them, or God affordeth them a way to escape." A little further in the same chapter the Koran commands: "The whoremonger shall not marry any other than a harlot or an idolatress. And a harlot shall no man take in marriage, except a whoremonger or an idolator. And this kind of marriage is forbidden the true believers." XVII, 34: "Draw not near unto fornication; for it is wickedness, and an evil way." VII, 31: "Say, verily my Lord hath forbidden filthy actions, both that which is discovered thereof, and that which is concealed. . . ."

Prostitution was not in the least suppressed in Moslem lands by all these Moslem laws, just as "whoredom" among the Hebrews by the biblical warnings.

The Moslem Sultan Ghasan of Persia saw fit to declare a new law which attempted to do away with whoredom. We can gather from this law that prostitution at that time was a well organized establishment. There were *Charabat*-houses, brothels; and besides these, "loose women" walked the streets in large cities usually preferring the "neighborhood of mosques, public buildings, and churches", and of course near the barracks, just as today and at all times and all over. Sultan Ghasan commanded the *Charabat*-houses should "pay a greater price for maidens than the others, because they use them more." As the higher price for the purchase of maidens, who were intended for the business of prostitution, did not in the least decrease it, the Sultan ordered the *Charabat*-houses closed. This measure led to many complications. The owners of the houses had bought the maidens and they declared themselves discriminated against if they were prevented from being repaid gradually through the practice of their trade. This seems to have impressed the Sultan; he ordered a slower procedure: "for interesting reasons the brothels have long been tolerated, and since prostitution is strongly entrenched, the evil cannot be eradicated with one blow." Therefore the next thing they tried was merely "to free those women from the *Charabats* who wished to be free"; the others, however, who for lack of another means of existence had to remain at a horizontal trade, and who declared themselves understanding of their situation, were permitted to go back. Nevertheless, it was strictly forbidden to sell new women and girls to the Charabats. And finally the Sultan determined a price for each freed prostitute, which returned her to her former social status, and permitted her to be married, legally. This was the best method of preventing those freed from slipping back. After some time they had finally attained their purpose, and the historian Wassaf says of the newly developed time of chastity and purity: "Each man saw his passion only in the eyes of his beloved; one heard only the guitars about Nahid, the Venus of the heaven"—and no longer about prostitutes as formerly.

This condition did not last long, and soon again and to this day all oriental historians complain of the ineradicable prostitution in Moslem countries.

When in the year 146 the pestilence afflicted Cairo, the Sultan Almalik Alaschraf Barsebai questioned the wise men of the land about the cause of the epidemic. And the wise men declared: "It is the wrath of God because of the scandal of the wicked women day and night in the streets and at the market." As a result of this the Sultan commanded the appointment of a *Muchtassib,* a police chief, "of great stature" who would command the respect of the women. They chose as "overseer of the women" in accordance with the wishes of the Sultan, "a man of great stature, Daulat Hadscha Assahiri, who was famous because of his strictness, his ungraciousness, and his tremendous patience." At the installation the Sultan declared his innermost request, that the new *Muchtassib* "would judge the conduct of the women with his keenest eye, and especially, under no circumstance to permit any one of them to show herself on the street." Behrnauer reports this according to Arabic sources in his comments on Arabic police laws. Dozy also relates in his "Dictionaire des vetements des Arabes" that according to Ibn Ayas' history of Egypt, the named Sultan in the year 940-1436 forbade the women to leave their houses, so, "that only the woman who had to wash the dead women, in the performance of her office and in order to be able to leave her house, was able to obtain a badge of permission from the *Muchtassib;* she wore this badge openly upon her headdress so that all could recognize her calling from afar."

The laws of conduct in the Kanuname of the great Osman Sultan Suleimus also hold a significant place in the necessary restrictions of that time. The laws of Suleimus the Great decreed that the practice of whoredom be punished according to the fortune of the guilty one with a penalty of 1000 Aspers for the richest, and 30 for the poorest. Seducers of boys and girls pay therefor with the sacrifice of their manhood. Whoever watched the wife or daughter of another in order to scare her, and kissed her, received a sharp admonition and paid one Asper for each word and each kiss; whoever acted likewise towards servants received but half the penalty, he paid one Asper for two kisses and for two words. The complaint of seduction was not given credence without witnesses; if the one complained of swore to the contrary, then the woman or girl received an even stricter admonition and had to pay one

Asper. The father who lay with a slave of his son paid no fine. Whoever had traffic with animals paid one Asper for each transgression.

If honorable women, who belonged to the veiled class, abased themselves, the judge freed them with warnings and a fine of twenty Aspers; but unveiled and unhonorable women with an admonition and a fine of two Aspers for each offence. The laws of conduct of Suleimus were not enforced very rigidly against the indulgence in wantonness, in fact, they were for its encouragement rather than keeping it in check. Except for the capital punishment of stoning which the Koran prescribes for adultery, one could pay for his evil with monetary fines according to the law book of Suleimus.

One, therefore, can not believe that in polygamy wantonness, prostitution, and the mania for women would decrease. No people is so rich in erotic literature as the peoples of the Orient.

Sultan Achmed II universally decreed a pointed police ordinance which declared the status of the gypsies to be, as the historian Mohammedgirai remarks, "to that day and from that day on the women of these hordes are all harlots, the men all procurers."

Not even the sacredness of the harem is inviolable before the wild passions of an aroused people: When in the year 1688 an uprising threatened the Grandvizier Siawuschpascha, his first fear was for the defilement of his harem, which the gang of robbers was approaching; "since he could not endure this, he placed himself with his Aga before the gate, in order to ward off the storming cavalcade with arrows and muskets. More than a hundred and fifty lustful robbers fell dead, just as many were wounded. Finally, however, Siawusch, who so bravely defended the honor of his harem until his last breath, succumbed, a martyr to his chivalrous disposition. Now the stream of robbers poured unrestrained into the harem, divid-

235

ing the occupants as booty and mistreating them shamefully. The female slaves were carried away on their backs like caskets of stolen riches. The sister of Siowuschpascha and his consort, the daughter of Mohammed Koprili, had their hands and noses cut off, and the stunned women were chased naked through the streets."

No such shameful mistreatment had ever occurred at any of the previous uprisings and plunderings of the palaces of the ministers; but they later became so prolific that the historian deemed it sufficiently important to remark about a rebellion in Constantinople at the time of Sultan Achmed III: "The police were strictly managed, over ten thousand rebels were assembled, without anything being pilfered or robbed, nor a single woman ravished; no warehouse was plundered, no boy attacked, no drunkard seen."

The era of the last mentioned Sultan Achmed III was exceedingly unfavorable for the freedom requirements of the women. The luxurious clothing of women, which became fashionable especially during the time of the sojourn at the court of Adrionapolis in the year of the war, was restrained by an ordinance, that no woman must wear a cape longer than one span, a kerchief larger than three spans, nor a band wider than one inch, the use of ermine was entirely denied to the general classes. The enforcement of this clothing ordinance required the co-operation of the judges of Constantinople, Galata, Skutari, Brussa and Adrianopolis, as well as the Janitshcaren-aga and the Bostandschibaschi.

This law, of course, was soon forgotten. For there are also many prohibitions in Constantinople which, according to the saying of the people, last only from noon to afternoon.

Sultan Machmud I was therefore compelled to reinstate the former "law of luxury against the great cloaks of women, the embroidered petticoats and hoods, the two ell-long capes of silk coats, and against the too fine and transparent veils, the too scanty outer clothing which disclosed too much of the face and figure." Several women who were accused of wishing to evade the perverted thought of the Moslems, were drowned, one of them, known by the name of the Devil's overseer, was, as the historian of the kingdom says, "wrapped in the dress of the blue watered silk of the waves of the sea." And again it was of no avail.

The first governmental measure of Sultan Osman III which emanated from him personally was the threefold injunction against taverns, the walks of the women, and the clothes of the Rajah. This ruler commanded further: Women must not show themselves upon the streets on Tuesday, Thursday, or Friday, because on those days the Sultan himself wished to go out. It seems, says Hammer, that Osman III wished to let the women atone for the prison-like existence of half a century, and to inflict upon the city that which was merely the despotic custom of the harem. When the Sultan entered the harem he wore boots which were set with large silver nails, so that their noise on the stone plates of the entrance would advise the harem and the slaves at a distance of the presence of the master, and permit them sufficient time to withdraw to their tents and chambers; for the unwanted presence of the women could inconvenience the exclusive possessor of them, to the extent of half a thousand; none must dare to intrude on her master through the fascination of her glance, and the noise of the silver boots banished the rule of the petticoats.

With regard to the clothing ordinance, Mustafa III walked in the footsteps of his brother Osman, in that he, no less strict in his feeling against the luxury in clothes and the appearance of women upon public walks, renewed the restrictions of his brother. In order to supervise its full enforcement himself, he strode, like Osman III, untiringly through the streets of Constantinpole and its suburbs. The first measure of his Grand-vizier, the barbaric Serb Daltaban, was a clothing restriction directed against the Moslem women. The women, "who from time immemorial had worn their clothing tightly so as to reveal their figure, and who veiled themselves with thin muslin through which the face could be seen", were decreed wide outer garment and black forehead bands in order to veil the face. The women and maidens of the Bedouins fared better. The Bedouin is none the less an avid defender of his honor and especially the honor of his harem; for his own honor or that of his wives he fights to his last drop of blood; but that does not prevent him from granting them human freedom. Their conduct sounds like fairy tales and nightly song in the pale moonlight. Youngsters and maidens gather in groups, repeat in harmony the verse first sung by a soloist, accompanying the singing with hand clapping and all kinds of movements of the body. Two or three veiled maidens dance opposite the youngsters, whom Bedouin custom forbids to call the maidens by name, and they are permitted to be addressed only as "young camels." The very same melody of the night song is also that of the fight song; on a happy occasion the women sing lightly for hours at a time in the meadows, and in case of death their tone assumes the death wail of complaining women.

While among the Bedouins in spite of all free communion of the sexes prostitution is practically unknown, it becomes more and more entrenched in every Moslem country where women are still kept under strict supervision, and it must constantly be preached against. The Turk Omer Haleby therefore warns the true believers: "There are people who will tell you that there is no verse in the Koran directed specifically against prostitution. Answer to this: in that the holy book damns adultery, sodomy, and the loss of semen, it also prohibits prostitution. True, it does not appear in so many words, because prostitution is not even to be conceived among the Moslems because of their laws and customs. Prostitution is the result of monogamy, it vanishes in the polygamous organization

238

which grants the individual every possible satisfaction, even to excess. Flee, O true believers, from everything which prostitution curses! Flee from prostitution for it is the work of idolators, Jews and Christians! Flee from it, for it deprives you of your health, opens your body to the influence of demons and the disorganizing winds of evil! Flee from it for your own sakes, for the sake of your wives, and for the sake of your friends! Flee from it as one of the things prohibited by the teachings of the prophet!"

At another place, Omer Haleby vouchsafes that prostitution in the Moslem countries and namely in Stambul is only "entrenched through the numerous contacts of the true believers with the Jews, the idolators, and the Christians." This seems to imply that prostitution was unknown here during the first century of Islam. Finally Omer Haleby, in a sort of resume, again answers the question whether it permitted to have intercourse with a prostitute: "There are various opinions of this. Some say: Yes, if one pays the maiden generously, and it is done for purposes of health in order to free oneself from an excess of semen in the absence of a legal bed fellow, and not for perverse reasons. Others deem coitus with a prostitute absolutely unpermissible and proscribed by the Koran. My opinion is this: In principle it is never allowed for one to sleep with an unbelieving woman, because this alone is already prostitution and filth and can later result in a bad example for our women and daughters. But since it is necessary for us to live in the midst of a crowd of unbelievers, and the prostitutes who surround us, praised be God, belong to these unbelievers, I believe that one may have traffic with them if that traffic will save us from adultery and blood shame."

The brave Omer Haleby must none the less have known what every informed person knows, that even among the Turkish and Arabian women and even in the innermost province of Turkey prostitution is tolerated. Angora has been notorious for its immorality since ancient times and has not improved its name with the Turkish rule. The Turkish Wilajet Kastamuni is entirely infected by syphillis. Throughout the entire Turkish Konia, where I myself observed, on certain days of the week from the neighborhood of the Greek village Sille, the women came over when their husbands were working in the fields, and earned substantial sums through prostitution with the Turks. Similar to the Greek women—as Regla relates in his remarks on El Ktab 71, note —the Moslem daughters of the tribe Ulad Nail at Biskara conducted themselves in the Algerian province of Constantine. They permit themselves to be deflowered by a youngster of the tribe and then they wander from place to place, to Algiers, Constantine, and Oran, in order to offer themselves in prostitution in such houses in which are permitted to enter only circumcised ones, Moslems and Jews; these prostitutes accept Christians only with apparent shame. When they have then saved some money, they return home and marry themselves usually to the man who deflowered them and they remain true to him. If conditions in the innermost Turkey are as pictured, then one can conceivably find that morals in the seaport towns have remained even less pure. Namely, on the shores of Arabia and Egypt Islam is no hinderance for prostitution.

In Smyrna there is a special harlot quarter at the caravan bridge, a rendezvous place of oriental colorful life—inhabited for the most part by Greeks and Armenians. Prostitutes of all nationalities are to be found in the Constantinople port district, Galata.

The immorality in several Christian Balkan states is well known. Even in the better hotels in Bucharest and Belgrade there are, among the servants, those whose special duty it is to bring in transient women; these women can usually be had for twenty francs, they often belong to the so-called better classes, but come only to strangers from whom they need not

240

fear discovery. The earnings do not serve to lighten the necessities of life, but are spent for perfumes and useless baubles. In smaller cities and smaller hotels the chamber maids themselves offer themselves to strangers; this kind depends on this income equally with her serving; she must often even share her harlot money with her employer. Strict regulation was invoked only in Bulgaria through Stambulow, and in Sofia and Philippopel the prostitutes are confined to a separate quarter whose houses bear the inscription: *"Publitschny dom*, public house."

The Serb thinks, as is expressed in a song, that it is easy to distinguish a harlot from other women: "I place seven, eight maidens together and recognize which of them is a harlot: Every harlot has a narrow waistline, a respectable maiden, however, has a broad waistline."

Wantonness is not considered evil among the Christian Balkan folk, so long as it results from love; if one wishes to excuse and explain it by the hot temperament of the southerners, then a woman who is bribed by money is, in every case, socially disreputable and avoided.

## CHAPTER SIXTEEN

# THE SEX ACT

*Defloration—Lubricating the penis—Among the Hindoos—Among the Serbians—Uncleanness of Coitus—Among ancient peoples—Moslem laws and observations—Abstemiousness among the Moslems and the Druses—The Turk Omer Haleby on the act of coitus—Superstitious fear of the demon at coitus—Washing and perfuming after coitus—The Hindoo method—A Turkish kiss-poem—South Slavic kisses—Parallels from Ovid—Delicacy and passion—Erotic and pig-like—Beating and biting at coitus—Sensuality and strife, love and anger—The best time for Coitus—Turkish notions— South Slavic conceptions.*

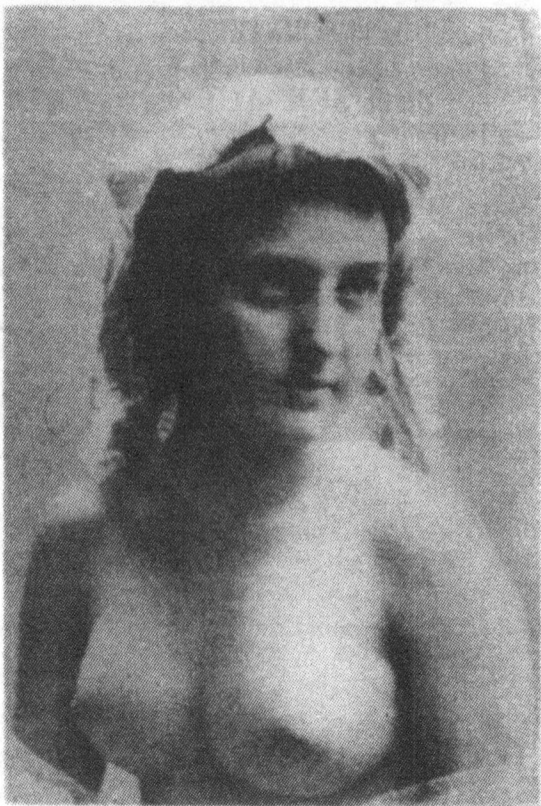

*Seventeen-year-old Czech*

Defloration is not always a simple thing of pleasure. A well known Bosnian song reports a difficult case: "The vagina wound a ruffle around the member. As it rode in with good humor, the buds burst about it. It felt bad, for the vagina had dressed itself; it was well timed, for it kept itself watchful." In order to facilitate the first immission of the penis in *vulvam,* one must lubricate it.

Among the Hindoos, in order to make the penis "prevailing" the following was done: They stroked it "with honey mixed with the powder of *Datura alba,* pepper shrubs, and *Piper longum.*" It is also said in the Kamasutra: "*Euphrobia neriifolia* and *Euphrobia antiquorum,* cut into pieces, provided with a powder of red arsenic and sulphur, pressed seven times and rubbed into a powder, rubbed on the penis with honey, makes it prevailing."

The Serb does not like to have any difficulty with defloration. He besmears the opening of the vulva and his own organ and the testicles with grease. A Serbian song runs: "The mother sent Marie to the roundelay, she had greased her vagina with tallow, so that it should not rip through." A Polynesian song also describes the greasing of the vulva with tallow, Kryptadia III, 332, number 50. The Serb prefers for the purpose the fat of fish. He sings: "Give me, O God, long limbs with which to wade in the deep sea, with which to catch the pike, with which to take the oil from the pike, with which to grease the mouth of the vagina." A Bosnian singer goes even further in that he demands of his partner in the roundelay that she furnish him with the butter with which to anoint his organ so that he can have his way with her more easily. Another Bosnian song prescribes honey for this purpose; it goes: "My mother sent me to the milk chamber for a small scale with which to weigh a litre of honey with which to stroke the penis so that it may tear through the heart of the vulva."

The sex act was considered unclean even in ancient times.

245

Herodot relates that among the Babylonians after intercourse both husband and wife had to bring a sacrifice of incense, and then, at daybreak, had to take a bath.

The Assyrians considered themselves as unclean after coitus as if they had touched a corpse. Among the Jews, as is said in the 3rd Book of Moses, XV, 18, every act of intercourse renders both parts unclean until evening. Mantegazza recalls in "La Donna," that a newly married Lapland woman has to hide her face from her husband for two months and must not give herself to him until after this period. Schellong relates in the Timebook of Enthology, 1889 ,I, 18, that the Papuas in Kaiser-Wilhelmsland practice coitus only in secret; whoever permits himself to be seen doing it is considered idiotic or weak-minded. In Tahiti, however, remarks Ellis, according to Tautain, on the wedding day the marriage is consummated before witnesses. Among the Subba in Arabia, the newlyweds must remain together for the first eight days and must come in contact with no one, for they are considered unclean.

Elsewhere the newlyweds may come in contact with other people, but only separately, they must not be seen together for a long time. The Catholic Maljsoren in upper Albania consider it shameful, so reports Hahn, if the young married man is noticed going to his young wife or leaving her. If the young pair, in a somewhat numerous family, have no separate room, then man and wife meet secretly until the birth of their first child.

The Koran admonishes the Moslems in Chapter IV, 46: ". . . come not to prayers . . . when ye are polluted by the emission of seed, unless ye be travelling on the road, until ye wash yourselves. But if ye be sick or on a journey, or any of you come from easing nature, or have touched women, and find no water; take fine clean sand and rub your faces and your hands therewith. . ." Several other passages return to the same situation; in so many words: Koran, V, 9.

246

Omer Haleby comments on this question in "El Ktab" in the following manner: "Coitus was introduced by the Creator and is therefore the key to the warehouse of nature; it is practiced as a song of praise to the almighty God, to him who makes women fertile. But it is also the concentration of all the assaults of the devil whose function it is to insinuate himself into the drunkenness and joy of humans in order to deprive this pleasure of its purity and to pervert its heavenly purpose. This gives itself expression in "the irregular coitus" and a disturbance in the sex organs. Omer Haleby goes on to say, "that at the moment of the union of the man with his wife the genii and evil spirits attempt to reach into the womb in order to make the children sick, to effect a miscarriage, or to ruin the being morally." One must therefore approach the act of coitus with a proverb and at the moment of the emission of seed call God's name repeatedly. So also says the Shah Dschallaleddin Abu Soleiman Daud: "At the moment of the beginning of coitus it is good and praiseworthy to say: "Bismillah!" repeating the word of the prophet: If one of you who approaches his wife says: "In the name of God! O my God!" then you put the devil to flight, for it is as if you said: "O God, remove the devil from the good deeds which you point out to us."

Zoroaster had already commanded likewise: The marital act is sanctified through prayer. One calls out: "I entrust to you these seed, O Sapondamad, daughter of Ormuzd!" Every morning the husband prays to Him who creates the germs.

The laws which forbid Moslems from visiting women on the days of the month of fasting, Ramadan, may also have been written for such reasons; on the nights of this month, it is, however, permitted. In the Koran, II, it is said: "It is lawful for you, on the night of the fast, to go unto your wives; they are a garment unto you, and ye are a garment unto them. God knoweth that ye defraud yourself therein, wherefore he turneth unto you, and forgiveth you. Now, therefore, go in unto them; and earnestly desire that which God ordaineth you, and eat and drink, until ye can plainly distinguish a white thread from a black thread by the daybreak; then keep the fast until night, and go not in unto them." In the same chapter and in the one entitled "The Pilgrimage" it is said: "The pilgrimage must be performed in the known months: whosoever therefore purposeth to go on pilgrimage therein, let him not know a woman, nor transgress."

I wish to mention here that the laws of the Druses command continence after conception and during nursing time, and besides this permit mating only once a month.

Omer Haleby ordered a delicate procedure at coitus: "When you wish to begin the act, draw your wife gently to you and say sweet things to her, which will flatter her, and she will be a worthy partaker in your pleasure. Caress her lovingly, and she will do likewise to you. Kiss her cheeks, her lips, her breasts, her neck, and play with her hair. If she is naturally cold, and if you see that her state of passion does not coincide with yours, place your hand upon her clitoris, and if it is absolutely necessary, stroke her there gently or energetically, but without going as far as onanism; for the law bans such practices in general. This delicacy your wife must also show to you; she must co-operate with you in this enchanting play, just as the holy prophet had on many occasions commanded."

The Hindoo textbook of love also advises rubbing the vulva with the hand before beginning coitus, and the practice of intercourse only when the woman has already become filled with desire. One cannot satisfy an elephantine woman, a woman *Hastini*, as she is called there, that is, one who possesses an exceptionally large vulva, unless he has aroused her passionately through rubbing her vulva. Ovid likewise says: Lovers shall not hold their hands motionless in bed; their fingers shall practice in that mystic sanctuary where love loves to penetrate.

When you have found that region which a woman prefers to have touched, no foolish modesty shall hinder you from permitting your hand to tarry there. You will see a moving brightness in the eyes of your beloved, a brightness like that of the rays of the sun when they refresh themselves in the waves of the sea. She will say pleasant things, give vent to love signs, moans and a delicate cooing.

When "all is ready for the penetration," when the woman becomes aroused in this manner, and "through short gasps and light cries" shows that she is in a condition to receive the *Semenliqueur* with benefit, then, says Omer Haleby, the man should lay himself upon her, face to face, belly to belly; not violently, but nevertheless with an energetic gentleness, and begin to penetrate with several effective strokes. At this moment, in order to drive away the devil, both should cry out: "In the name of God!" And at the instant of the dying flutters, at the instant of the emission, when the woman remains lying motionless as if in ecstacy, then the man must add the rest of the sacred formula: "The generous and the gracious!"

If one acts this way, then, according to the opinion of Omer Haleby, the enterprise will be successful, and the child which is conceived in this moment will never feel the hand of the demon. After the finished act of coitus, they wash themselves, perfume themselves, and again thank God.

The Hindoo method of approaching the woman is just like that of the Turks: Vatsyayana, the author of the Hindoo textbook of love, advises a delicate procedure at wooing: "to him who can approach his adventure without too much haste. The women are like flowers and must be wooed very gently. If they are wooed involuntarily by people who do not yet possess their trust, then they learn to hate sexual union."

Another Hindoo writer, Bhartrihari, said: "Happy are they who kiss the honey from the lips of the young women who rest in their arms; who kiss the loosened hair, the half closed eyes; who kiss the cheeks damp with perspiration; for they have developed the capacity of enjoying love."

In connection with the use of kisses in sexual intercourse, the Kamasutra ordered the following rules for the Hindoos: During the first coitus one must not proceed too violently, in order first to awaken trust. Later, however, very quickly and with particular violence, in order to arouse passion. One must press kisses on the forehead, the hair, the cheeks, the eyes, the breasts, the lips, and inside the mouth; among the inhabitants of Lata, also on the joint of the thighs, the arm-pits, and the region below the navel.

A beautiful Turkish poem translated by Grunfeld follows:

I do not want the moon to see your face,
When it draws over you at night,
Nor that the daytime sun shall warm you,
Nor that the crying Kerem shall harm you.

I do not want the rain to drench you,
When it waters all the other flowers,
I do not want your mother to love you,
Nor should she shower her child with kisses.

I want to be your moon and your sun;
And if you are thirsty, I am a present for your mouth.
I want to love you now and forever,
And I alone want to kiss your mouth and hair.

The southern Slavs know quite another kind of kiss called: "jezicati se," which means: "The man sticks the tip of his tongue deep into the mouth of the woman." The southern Slavs believe, "that the women become immensely sexually aroused through this, and submit to the man without any opposition."

But there is nothing new under the sun, and particularly so in the methods in which men make love. For Ovid says in his "Ars amatoria", XIV Elegie, book III: "There is a place for revelling. There nothing will save you from being freed of the light tunic which hides your enchantment, and there you will hold the thigh of your beloved on yours; there his tongue will glide between your rosy lips, deep into your mouth."

Man desires above all that the woman shall not be lacking in passion at coitus. An epigram by Martial, X, 60, runs: "You ask whether Chloe or Phlogis is better at love? Chloe is the more beautiful, but Phlogis, a Vulcan, kept young by Nestor; Chloe feels nothing of this. One can believe that she is absent or made of marble. If God would but give Phlogis the figure of Chloe and Chloe the fire of Phlogis!" The Balkan Slavs love to have their women to shake and toss during coitus.

And so sang Ovid: ". . . do not be niggardly with sweet words, with provoking delicacies, let your bed tremble with unchaste motions. . . ." In numerous songs the southern Slav incites himself to penetrate as deeply as possible. A Moslem song in Doboj in Bosnia runs: It "should break through the teeth of the vulva and press so deeply into its yawning abyss that it can no longer utter a chirp." In West Serbia they sing: "O maiden, you shall choose me as a pole perch for your limbs, with which to be yoked to yours; I shall drive it into the utmost depths, even unto the anus!"

From the erotic they often stray into the realm of swinishness. Thus, when they call in a song to the maiden: "O maid, maid, accept it as a jest if one of my buds is drowned in your urine!" It is even worse when they claim that "a good vagina must stink"; or if a man provides himself with all kinds of filth which accumulates around the organ and the prepuce, because he believes that a penis so covered heightens passion. Or if they demand that the woman sing a certain evil song at coitus, which is expressed colloquially with the filthiest

251

words. Another song which I cannot translate fully because of the demands of respectability follows, and I leave it to the reader to complete it: "There is no rain without thunder and lightning, and no fish without water; there is no vagina without buttocks, no breasts without nipples, and no coitus without ———."

A Russian saying goes: he who loves a woman, burns her up. The Hindoo textbook of love has already devoted an entire chapter to the mishandling of the beloved, the man as well as the woman, in order to arouse passion.

As the author of the Hindoo text says: "The enjoyment of love is a kind of combat." So Hesiod conceived it in his Theogonie of sensual pleasure, and the strife as essential.

Propertius said: there is no furious wrath in a woman without violent love. If one is to believe in her faithfulness, she must show it through insults. "God of the Cythere, my enemy's a feelingless beloved. My rivals may count the teeth of my beloved on my breast. The bluish lines can show all whom I have near me." . . .

In Lucian, Ampelis says to Chrysis who is bewailing her beating by Gorgia: "O my beloved Chrysis! The oaths, the tears, the kisses—all are merely the incidents of the beginning of love. Only when one beats the one he loves—that is the proof of a great love. . . . You can wish for no more than that that your beloved shall treat you in this manner."

The mishandling of the woman in order to arouse sexual passion is customary among all Balkan peoples. For the same purpose, the men let themselves be insulted and beaten by the women. The greatest gluttony shows itself at coitus if they bite each other; the Balkan Slavs have a special expression for this: *griskati se*. In a song the mother asks her little daughter who is returning from the field: "Why have your eyes become so overcast, why is your white face bitten by teeth?" In another song the maiden rejoices: "With his teeth he had bitten

252

wounds on my breasts." The newly married southern Slavs parade with such signs of their husbands' love just as the Hindoos.

The Turk Omer Haleby also acknowledges this through the sentence. "A woman marvels at him who scorns her and beats her."

According to the Turkish conception, as is elucidated in El Ktab of Hodscha, Omer Haleby Abu Osman, it is best for coitus to occur in the evening, after the digestion of the evening meal, when the body is in a regular, normal condition between warmth and freshness, between satiety and oversatiety, in a word, when it is in the most ordinary condition. In any event it is good if one does not take to coitus on an empty stomach; "the son of Omer never lay with a woman unless he had previously eaten." According to the opinion of the wise Dschellaleddin Abu Soleiman Daud, one should not have intercourse if he is tired, worried, annoyed, or if he has taken a physic. The best rule is to have intercourse only then "when the need therefore is predominant and the desire for the completion of coitus is compelled through forceful methods, or through lascivious glances, or through erotic thoughts; only when the accumulation of the semen animate one and draw him to sexual intercourse."

The southern Slavs believe, as is sung in one of their songs, that a woman is found "sweetest" eight days after a happy delivery of a healthy child. The southern Slavs consider dawn the best time for the practice of coitus. If one wishes to visit his beloved, so it says in a widespread roundelay, he must come to her at the break of dawn; "then every body is most amenable."

The Serbians say in a song: "Take"—the orignial expression calls the thing by its vulgar name—"take the old one in the evening, for she will roast you a little hen; the young woman at the break of dawn, for you will receive a shirt from her; but the maiden everytime, as often as you become erect."

253

CHAPTER SEVENTEEN

# THE KIND OF SEX ACTS

255

*Girl from Morocco—Twelve Years Old*

The oriental love-physiologists measure the degree of pleasure at coitus almost entirely by the dimensions of the sex organs of the persons involved. A small vulva is almost always desirable among women, and a powerful penis particularly embellishes a man.

One knows Ovid's little saying, by the use of which one can recognize without fail at a glance the superiority of a woman or a man: "Among women—small feet, small vulva; among men—large nose, large penis."

Among the Egyptian fellahs, according to the report of Schweinfurth, women are divided into three groups with respect to the shape of their vulva: the *Schelenkijeh*, the *Ennabijeh*, and the *Kelbijeh*. Among the *Schelenkijeh*-women the hymen breaks with a long split; the loss of blood at the devirgination is only slight, several drops. Among the *Ennabijeh* the hymen is entirely closed; but it breaks at the least poke, like a grape; the loss of blood is very slight. The women of the third category are called the *Kelbijeh*, like a dog, among whom the hymen is thick, fleshy, and resistant, and the loss of blood at its opening is considerable. The defloration of the female fellah is usually effected, as has already been related in another chapter, not by the bridegroom, but by another person designated therefore, the *Ballane*, who breaks the hymen with her finger. Particularly the *Kelbijeh*-women must be deflowered only through the *Ballane*.

South Slavic roundelay songs which deal with this subject treat zealously of the narrowness and width of the vulva and the dimensions of the penis. In Zabrgje in Bosnia, Krauss heard a roundelay song from the mouth of a newly married peasant who was describing her own defloration: "When I was yet a goatsherd, my vulva was like the smallest coin. A short time thereafter I was married, they bent me around like a violin bow, drove a thing in me like a crowbar and drew it out like a coulter."

The southern Slav expects a narrow vulva from the woman whom he is going to make happy; the great wide one is an abomination to him. A Bosnian song runs: "A maiden sits on the bank of the brook; she measures her vagina to see if it is deep. An ell long, three ells wide, it holds eighty Oka."

Martial complained in his Epigrams, XI, 71: "Lydia is as wide as the rear end of a bronze horse; like an old shoe which has fallen into the gutter; like a mattress robbed of its bedsheet. They say I have brought Lydia to a receptacle of the sea; but I believe that I have worked myself into the receptacle."

A Bosnian Pope, whom his wife accused in a song of being a sodomist, countered with the following words about the size of her sex organ: "A goose can go in there, two Turkish penes can go in there, and a board of pine wood and a German cat."

Since the men among the Balkan folk wish their women to have a narrow vulva, it is generally customary for the women to spread alum in the opening, in order to draw together the sex organ cleverly if it is wide.

The good Poppea, Nero's last consort, seems to have labored under a wide vulva, which is not surprising, for Nero was her fifth or sixth husband. As the "Secret of Poppea" the following method is offered in the discreet sexual literature: "In order to appear always as a virgin, wash your sex organ with a water which has attained a milky color through alcoholic benzoate; then dry the neighboring region with fine linen and rub it energetically."

As a method of narrowing the vulva, the Kamasutra advises the Hindoos: "Use a salve of the fruit of *Asteracantha longifolia*"; such salve draws together even the largest vulva, the so-called "elephant cow", for a whole night. In case, however, they wish to widen a vulva which is too narrow, the "gazelle" vulva, they use: "A pleasant smelling powder of the roots of

*Nelumbium speciosum* and blue lotus, also from *Terminalia tomentosa*, rubbed into an ointment with honey."

The possessor herself falls in love with a small fine vulva. In a Bosnian song a maiden becomes enchanted by thinking about her vulva. The maiden runs to a nut tree, lifts up her right foot, and shows her vulva and cries out: "O my happiness, how beautiful is your cut!"

Just as a small one makes a woman happy, so on the other hand, the large one is preferred among the men. The Arab distinguishes himself through the display of powerful glands. I have been told, and this belongs here in part, that from childhood on they rub the penis long and energetically on a stone or in sand after urinating in order to rid it of after-dripping water.

At Turkish weddings of great courts the so-called wedding-palm is carried in the train of the bride as an emblem of upright standing manly power, as I have already related above.

At any event, even though a large penis is desirable, it is not the sine qua non. In Bosnia they sing a song: "One asked a maiden which penis was best, and she answered: Whether a long one has its end stuck up, or a thick one filled out, it matters not as long as it satisfies in abundance." Among the Moslem Slavs the following song is current: "He has nothing, a fold or an inclosure, may God kill him! But if he has a hearty penis, God helps him of necessity!" The small penis is a condition of ridicule and avoidance.

Proudly in contrast to this, a Bosnian peasant calls to his neighbor in the roundelay: "O thou maiden, see how huge I am; man's gift to you." In another song a maiden describes a penis by the smith Athanasius according to her taste: "Like a worm, neither too long nor too thick, at its end is a wedge with which it feels efficiently when it presses into the vagina."

In a Bosnian song a maiden is asked if she has already eaten at night. She replies: "I have eaten nothing at night

259

but a little head of garlic, I felt very bad—until he penetrated me, as thick as my arm"; she then became well and no longer felt hungry. The initiation by such a large member frightened her: "O mother," says a young blood, "how big and ruddy is our neighbor!" Often initiated maidens also seem to feel anxious before an enormous pointing instrument. In a popular little song widespread among the Balkan folk, a maiden says: "I will not submit, you have an enormous penis." But after the wooer has declared: "Submit, or I will cut it off." She absolutely refuses to consent to this and cries: "Don't cut the darling, the sweet bit."

On several occasions in the Old Testament the desire of woman for a large penis is also evinced. Prophet Ezekiel, XXIII, 20, says: "For she (Aholibah) doted upon their paramours, whose flesh is as the flesh of asses, and whose issue is like the issue of horses." Stallions are brought into relation with sexual love in another passage also; so in Jeremiah, V, 8: "They were as fed horses in the morning: every one neighed after his neighbor's wife."

Of all the peoples of the Orient the Hindoos have undoubtedly done most to bring sexual love to a position of the most thorough study, have inaugurated the finest, exact division of men and women according to the dimensions of their sex parts, and have written up most of the kinds of the practice of coitus.

According to the Kamasutra, men are divided into three groups according to the dimensions of their penis: Hares, steers, and stallions. I wish to repeat here that the southern Slavs, as can be read in the wordy Intermezzo, designate men with small glands as hares, and that the Bible, as I have recently brought out, brings men with large glands into a relationship with asses and stallions. The Kamasutra also divides women into three classes: Gazelles, mares, and elephants. This gives rise to three proper forms of intercourse between men and women: the hares with the gazelles, the steers with the mares, and the stallions with the elephants; and six improper forms, those which do not take place between the corresponding groups. Of these forms they consider those which take place between steer and gazelle or stallion and mare of greater pleasure; that between a stallion and a gazelle the greatest pleasure, for it is a union of the largest penis with the smallest vulva. On the other hand the union of a hare with a mare or a steer with an elephant-woman gives a lesser pleasure, and the union of a hare with an elephant, the least.

Similarly the Kamasutra classifies man and woman according to the degree of their passion as weak, middling, and strong. Finally there are three classes, each according to the time when the seed comes to the men and the women. At the first coitus, thinks the Kamasutra, the passion of the man is the greater and the duration of his accomplishment short; with the repetition of coitus his passion becomes ever cooler and his seed requires more and more time to be ejected. Among women, however, all this is quite reversed.

The Koran has prescribed all kinds of coitus for the Moslems. It is said in the II chapter: "Your wives are your tillage; go in therefore unto your tillage in what manner soever you will: and do first some act that may be profitable unto your souls." Omer Haleby says in his El Ktab, the book of the secrets of love: "The strong and healthy virgin is that tillage which returns joy and drunkenness a hundred fold, if one entrusts his seed to her." But the virgin is also a source of remorse for him who does not know how to fertilize her with cleverness and gentleness, and disturbs the flower coarsely and vulgarly.

Therefore, the Turkish love-physiologist, just as the Hindoo, advises a delicate procedure, particularly at defloration and towards all women who have as yet enjoyed little of love.

"Do not attempt," he warns those who are too headstrong,

261

"to tear down the resistance of the closed calyx with a powerful stroke. Learn to control your desire. And if nature has made you too strong, do not hesitate to put off the finishing of your work of deflowering until the next day or even until the day after that. Do not forget, O people, that serious consequences can result from a rough handling of a delicate flower, and that such disturbances through the bursting of the womb either to the right or to the left can result in nervous diseases of the woman and even in her sterility. Use the virgin which God has entrusted to you with moderation; cultivate your tillage as humans, who err in the direction of duration rather than ephemeral swiftness."

Among the southern Slavs "in the case of ordinary pleasure, the woman usually lies at the left side of the man, so that he can lean comfortably on his left arm when he lies upon the belly of the woman." In a Bulgarian song a woman asks the man "to lie on the right side for a change, because her left side hurts her."

A Bosnian song extols coitus in *gremio* in the following manner: "The sister-in-law sits with the brother-in-law *supra ova*. He cries: *"Abi, stultas testiculos mihi frangis."* The woman thereupon seats herself backwards on the sitting man. This kind is called in Bosnia: *mlivo sije,* she filters flour. This is just as bad for the woman. A Bosnian peasant in another roundelay song commands the maiden "to take a lower position" in order to raise the centre of her love.

A special kind is the *srpski jeb,* the Serbian coitus; in a song it is described with the words: to choke the women. Krauss described this method in his book on "Manifestations", I, 220: The man grabs the woman from the front below the joint of her foot, makes her fall backwards so that she must hold fast to the ground with her hands in order not to break her neck. Then he places the girl's legs upon his shoulders like a yoke, he holds her tight in his arms with all his power, and kneeling, drives his organ into her, at which he throws himself upon her with all his weight, untroubled by her sighs and groans.

One must gather that Krauss thinks that marriage was primarily derived from the stealing of women, and that the robber did not truly become the husband of the kidnaped one until he had lain with her. He must have taken her against her will, overpowered her with his own strength, without beating her half dead or otherwise stunning her. It was, however, easiest to approach the woman in the "Serbian manner", if she refused to submit to the will of the man. Besides this, it can also be that the man in this manner shows the woman his superiority in every sense of the word from the very first moment, while she prefers to consider this worthy of her master, and she later retains this conception. This is now firmly entrenched through custom.

The heroes of these songs proceed in this manner, if they lie with their stolen brides; and a constant turn in these songs runs: "He raises her feet towards the ceiling and thrusts his large one between her thighs." Other verses relate the case in a flowered manner: "They play all kind of games together, but mostly the game of break-the-neck."

The following is a variation of the *srpski jeb:* The man raises the girl's legs in front of him and then moves back and forth. In another song it is called: "to make a Greek wagon or a hand-barrow."

The Bulgarian kind is the same as the Serbian. But there is also a special Bulgarian kind: Man and wife both squat down; "this kind can also be accomplished while riding on a horse."

I have heard of a similar "Arabian kind". In the entire Orient, the Arabs, just as the Armenians, are famous for the enormity of their sex glands, which are said to make it possible for them, while sitting on the ground, to have intercourse with a woman who is sitting backwards before them. The "Dalmatine kind", also called the "Italian", is very much like the method of dogs.

## CHAPTER EIGHTEEN

# PEDERASTY AND SODOMY

*The loving of boys among the Greeks and Romans—In 1001 nights—In the Old Testament—In the Koran—Abdul Wahib against lewdness—Loving of boys in the Osman history—At the court of the Sultan Bajesid—At the court of the Usurper Mohammed II—Christian boys a sacrifice to lewd-ness—Pages of the Sultans—From the beloved of the Sultan to the Grand-vizier—A chief justice as seducer of boys—Murad IV and his beloved page Musa—Seduction of boys in the baths—Moslem opinions on pederasty—Bosnian songs—Depravity in Constantinople—Licentious fellows in the coffee houses—Loving of boys in Chorasan and Albania—Unchastity with animals — Biblical restrictions — Old-Egyptian — Modern-Egyptian — Ethno-graphic parallel from Russia and Sicily—In Bosnia—Bosnian sodomy songs—Osman doctors permit unchastity with animals—Parallels from Algeria and from the Balkan states—A reminiscence from a journey in Alexandria.*

*Nineteen-year-old Czech*

The depravity of loving boys was nowhere so widespread as among the ancient Greeks and Romans. Catullus and Tibullus sang the praises of their beloved boys with an intimacy which only a poet could express in order to arouse his beloved maiden. According to Catullus, pederasty was quite general in his time in Rome, and particularly in the army. Xenophon relates that to be sure, they forbade the soldiers the companionship of slaves and booty, as it made the march more difficult; but they could not help permit each, soldier a boy. The source of the depravity can easily be sought in the Orient. The original stories of 1001 Nights is a conglomeration of pederastic and sodomistic practices.

In the Old Testament in Book 3 of Moses, XX, 1, severe punishments are promised: "If a man also lie with mankind. as he lieth with a woman, both of them have committed an abomination: they shall surely be put to death." This kind of depravity was not limited to individual cases, but appeared like epidemics in entire neighborhoods. In the first Book of Moses, XIX, 4, it is reported that two angels accepted the hospitality of Lot in Sodom: "But before they lay down. the men of the city, even the men of Sodom, compassed the house round, both old and young, all the people from every quarter: And they called unto Lot and said unto him: "Where are the men which came into you this night? Bring them out unto us that we may know them." In vain did Lot plead with them to retract their demands; in vain did he compel himself to offer the horde his two virgin daughters. The penalty which was inflicted upon Sodom for this crime did not prevent this depravity from being retained by all nations more or less throughout the years. It is also related in the New Testament: "that men desert the natural use of women, and arouse each other, driven in their lust to shame, man with man." And concurring with the Bible the Koran, in many verses, points ever-warningly to the fate of Sodom. So reports the VII Chap-

267

ter, 79-81: "And remember Lot, when he said to his people, Do ye commit a wickedness wherein no creature hath set you an example? Do ye approach lustfully unto men, leaving the women? Certainly ye are people who transgress all modesty. But the answer of his people was no other than that they said the one to the other, Expel them from your city; for they are men who preserve themselves pure from the crimes which ye commit. . . . And we rained a shower of stones upon them. Behold therefore what was the end of the wicked." XI 71-84: "And when our messengers came unto Lot, he was troubled for them, and his arm was straightened concerning them; and he said, This is a grievous day. And his people came unto him, rushing upon him, and they had formerly been guilty of wickedness. Lot said unto them, O my people, these my daughters are more lawful for you: therefore fear God and put me not to shame by wronging my guests. Is there not a man of prudence among you? They answered, Thou knowest that we have no need of thy daughters; and thou well knowest what we would have." XV 57-81: "And the inhabitants of the city came unto Lot, rejoicing at the news of the arrival of some strangers. And he said unto them, Verily, these are my guests: wherefore do not disgrace me by abusing them; but fear God and put me not to shame. They answered, Have we not forbidden thee from entertaining or protecting any man? Lot replied, These are my daughters: therefore rather make use of them, if ye be resolved do do what ye purpose. As thou livest they wander in their folly. Wherefore a terrible storm from heaven assailed them at sunrise, and we turned the city upside down: and we rained on them stones of baked clay. Verily herein are signs unto men of sagacity. . . ." XXVI 55-59: "And remember Lot; when he said unto his people, Do ye commit a wickedness, though ye see the heinousness thereof? Do ye approach lustfully unto men, leaving the women? Ye are surely an ignorant people."

Following the example of the Bible, the Koran also prescribes punishments for this wickedness in chapter IV 20: "And if two of you commit the like wickedness, punish them both." But how severe this punishment shall be is not said. Yes, it is expressly provided that in certain cases there shall be no punishment. And these cases are: merely repentance! . . . "but if they repent and amend, let them both alone; for God is easy to be reconciled and merciful."

The teachings of Abdul Wahib preached fearfully against this unnatural lust, which was all too popular among the Turks. Almost all of the Sultans were guilty of this depravity which had blossomed in the Osman kingdom since the time of Bejesid. Bajesid, says Hammer, elevated through the wings of war and plundering, began to neglect the kingdom and himself also, in that he, the first of the Osman princes, drank wine against the laws of Islam, and assisted his Vizier Ali-pascha in luxurious and unnatural activities.

Sultan Mohammed, the usurper of Constantinople, was a notorious lover of boys. On the day after the capture of Byzantia, he arranged a festive meal in the royal palace and partook inordinately of wine. Half drunk, he commanded the chief eunuch to bring to him the fourteen year old son of Notaras, the last of the great rulers of the Byzantine Empire, whose beauty had kindled a fire in him. The father, amazed at the tyrannical command, replied that he would never of his own free will have his son submitted to such shameful lust, that he would rather have the Sultan send his hangman. The eunuch returned with this answer, and Mohammed sent his hangman for Notaras and his entire family. Notaras followed him with his sons and with Cantacuzen. The hangman left them standing on the threshold, and he dragged the youth forth as a sacrifice to the sultanly lust, the others he put to death.

Notaras, who had not conducted himself honorably at the capture of Constantinople, at this moment again discovered the lost dignity of soul and spirit, and he reminded his sons to die like Christians, and he finished his speech with the words: "Thou art right, O Lord!"  The sons were decapitated before the eyes of their father; Notaras asked the hangman for several moments of prayer, which he said near the guillotine, after which he also was beheaded and he fell on the still trembling corpses of his sons.  The bodies were thrown away naked and unburied.  The heads were brought to the tyrant who thirsted not only for wine but also for blood, just as Marius had the head of the Consul Antonius brought to him at mealtime.  Mohammed's natural cruelty was again inflamed through a stranger whose daughter the tyrant loved passionately, and to please whose father he commanded the execution of all Greeks whose lives he had granted several days before.

For the satisfaction of their shameful lust the Osmans enticed the crowd of Christian boys, who were no longer merely recruits for the *Janitshares*, as up until this time, for "Adschemoghlan," but were brought into the innermost service of the court as *Pages*, as *Itschoghlan*," because of their beautiful bodies and exceptional spirit; and from now on they were demanded for this career for the possessors of income bringing fiefs, and the first officers of the army and the state.  So the unnatural demoralization of the East, whose origin even in ancient times was blamed by the Greeks on the Persians and by the Persians on the Greeks, insinuated itself into the Osman domain; it throve not only through the example of Sultans and viziers, but also through those learned in the law, particularly through the position of the judges, so excessively that it became the most excellent favorite depravity of the court, the army, and the people, the most remarkable means of honor and wealth, and not rarely the secret reason for war with the Christians, the booty of which was said to fill the thinned ranks of recruits and *pages* with a new growth of power and lust.  Notwithstanding, the law of Islam could never be twisted so as to

270

tolerate such shamefulness, for it is damned as unnatural, in open defiance of everyone in the Turkish realm engaged in this demoralizing practice.

If, as indications from Herodot and other historians do not permit of contradiction, the shameful custom of boy-loving is originally Persian, or even Medician, and intimately bound up with the luxury of eunuchs, it enervated them in their long Medician wanderings as well as the Persians: so the Turks invoked a new manly class, in that they lifted the ancient Medician tie of this groups with the eunuchs, and divided the original Persian luxury into two, one group merely for service in the harem, and the other for service in the city. The Medicians and the Persians castrated the most beautiful boys not only as unnatural watchers of the harem but also for the practice of their unnatural lust, and thus sinned doubly against nature, against the freedom of woman and the dignity of man.

The ancient Greeks praised the unnatural in the Theban *host of the loving* and in the Macedonian *host of the immortal* as a more lofty and more pure union with youth for freedom and country; the Turks profited by this arrangement, debasing their Janitshare boys and pages; but with few exceptions these remained uncastrated, and the numbers of white eunuchs were mostly replenished with Georgian and Circassian slaves, and not with European.

Greek, Serbian, and Hungarian boys were not castrated as eunuchs, but circumcised as Moslems and instructed in the use of weapons; and after they had satisfied the lust of their lords and masters, the road was open for them to the first place in the state and the army through favor and capability. The greatest men of the Osman domain came from this school. The son-in-law of the Sultan Suleimus, Rustem, elevated to that position and to the position of Grandvizier, was a former pupil of the page's chamber of the Sserai and won the favor of Suleimus as a subject for his lust. Rustem was born a Croatian.

The demoralization of the Ulema and judges was ever worse than that of the sultans, the paschas and the viziers. As the "greatest violation of the law" Osman history considers the act of the chief judge Tschiwisade, "infamous for his ignorance and shameful conduct with boys." The Grandvizier once dared to address the Silihdar Jusuf Pascha, the "war-wealthy plutocrat of the kingdom" and pilferer of Egypt, in a high-strung unrespectful tone with the following words: "It is time you stopped being a young man," an unrespectful reference to the fieldmaster's relation to the Sultan, but just as inappropriate as unrespectful in the mouth of a Grandvizier who had attained his position and power in the same manner. The Grandvizier received an apropriate punishment for his unthinking expression. As he went as usual after this transgression to seat himself at the table in the divan, the head chamberlain came to demand the seal of the kingdom from him.

Under Sultan Murad IV, the troops, during an uprising, desired the head of the betrayed Musa, the Sultan's most beloved personal youth. The Sultan turned over the threatened youth to two high officials in Obhut; these, however, Redscheb and Dschanbulasade Mustafa Pascha, delivered Musa to the rebels. When the Sultan discovered Redscheb's shameful part in the death of his beloved youth Musa, he took terrific revenge on Redscheb, his brother-in-law and Grandvizier, for this "crime against insulted majesty." The Dschanbuladsade was not punished for the outrage until later. The Sultan seized upon the slightest occasion to order his execution. In spite of his many accomplishments in the field, in spite of the hand of the Sultana Aische, whom Dschanbuladsade had married, Murad's unreasonably implacable revenge could not pass him by, for he, with the Grandvizier Redscheb had at first vouchsafed the life of the favorite Musa and had then sacrificed him as a prize to the madness of the rebels.

The Grandvizier Silihdar Mohammedpascha in his youth had been a page in the Sserai and a favorite of the Sultan, and as such rose to *bearer* of the *table cloth*, the *horn*, the *cloak*, and the *sword*, and soon after the ascension of Sultan Mustafa to the throne he was honored with the hand of the Sultana Aische, and, after he had passed through the pathway of Viziers, he was elevated to the greatest dignity of the kingdom. But forgetting his own past, in 1771 he formulated, during the Danube expedition, in order to establish better breeding, strict laws to deprive all the rascals of this situation. There then took place in the public divan the following circumstance which the historian of the kingdom discussed under the heading, "Extraordinary tale," and must truly appear in the mouth of a historian of the kingdom as a strange example of ruling demoralization and total lack of breeding. The Grandvizier reproved the general of the edge-tool makers, Gurd Aga, with harsh words because of his overstepping the compulsory laws; the master of the petitioners, Munib Efendi then said: "What does this mean? When the Padischah strongly forbids the wearing of jewels, the ministers and nobles nevertheless permit themselves small knives set with stones which catch the eye; and this is overlooked without even taking notice of it. Who will prevent me from keeping in my service a small boy of eight years, who grants me additional days of life and serves as a health amulet, as a child of the soul to wind a band about my head, instead of expelling him as a sacrifice to the lust of another?" All were silent, the historian adds, no one contradicted the under-state secretary, and those who agreed with him secretly rejoiced.

Almost all over the orient youths were the masseurs in the baths, who offered themselves for pederasty, and never in vain. To be sure, the Moslem law says: "If a man engages in pederasty, his wife may demand a divorce if she so desires," but there is no example of such divorce.

The Turk Omer Haleby likewise condemns pederasty and declares: If onanism is banned, how much more must be *coitus in anum*, whether it be with a man, with a woman, with a eunuch, or with an animal. If you are told: Everything which can satisfy the senses is permitted—then answer: this is profanity and untruth; this is an unclean coitus. And have intercourse in this manner neither with humans nor with animals." Omer Haleby, however, recognizes so many exceptions, that the rule becomes entirely abrogated. He says: "But whatever occurs to your own wives in case they themselves agree, you can practice *coitus in anum* only in case sickness prevents you from entering the vulva, and if you have only one wife. Then you engage in sodomy with her only for the reason that you wish to remain true to her, but not as a perversion; and if you sin, then God is merciful towards the repentant and he forgives." At another place Omer Haleby contends that it is also permissible for a man to engage in sodomy with negro women if he is afflicted with a venereal disease; whether these be believers or unbelievers, fetish or devil worshipers. One must nevertheless never forget at the moment of the emission to cry out: "In the name of the merciful and gracious God!" for this formula eases the healing and protects the negress employed from catching it.

Bosnian songs sing the praises of pederasty with men and women:

"O little boy in cloak of cloth,
Let me enter in your anus!"

A Sarajevoen song describes the pain of a boy plagued with pederasty. Another Bosnian song runs:

274

> "Three reins, three strings,
> Three penes are at her anus,
> I pulled on the string,
> The penis rode into the anus."

In all the cities of the orient boys of various nationalities peopled the public houses in no smaller number than girls. In Turkish baths boys are offered to one. On holidays one sees such boys in their striking rich womanly costume, with false hair, singing and dancing, parading about in the streets and enticing wastrels. In Constantinople one meets them with pale haggard faces, in wide gold embroidered pantaloons, usually in the coffee houses of Galatea.

In Stambul there exist separate houses of prostitution, called the houses of Imam, in which boys only practice the functions of prostitutes. The Russian physician, Dr. Rafael-witsch, in the year 1846 recalled ten such institutions of un-natural debauchery. Since that time, according to a report made to me by a Turkish police official, the number has increased threefold. The "loving of boys of *Chorasan*" is an old pass-word in the orient. According to Saalebi, the Arabs use this expression for the reason that the inhabitants of Chorasan, because they were warlike and restless and remained apart from their wives for a long time while on their journeys, became involved in this perversion. An Albanian proverb says: "Who-ever drinks 40 oka of Skutari water becomes a rascal; but whoever drinks 40 oka of Tirahean water becomes a lover of boys." As Hahn assures us, the frightful depravity is not equally intrenched in all regions; while among the Tuscans sexual love is the rule and unnatural love of boys the exception, it is quite the reverse in the neighboring region. Here the lov-ing of boys among the unmarried men is a national passion. Just as elsewhere men vie for the affection of a lovely maiden, here they woo the favor of the boys, and it happens occasionally

275

that there occurs murder and a death struggle between men on account of the rivalry over a boy. The depravity is widespread in violation of law among the Christians as well as among the Moslems. It is remarkable, however, that it is encountered only among unmarried men, and that this unnaturalness usually sees its finish at the moment of marriage.

Another ineradicable evil of the orient is lewdness with animals. In this connection it is said in the 2nd Book of Moses XXII 19: "Whoever lieth with a beast shall surely be put to death." In the 3rd Book of Moses XVIII 23: "Neither shalt thou lie with any beast to defile thyself therewith: neither shall any woman stand before a beast to lie down thereto: it is confusion." In the 3rd Book of Moses XX 15-16: "And if a man lie with a beast, he shall surely be put to death; and ye shall slay the beast. And if a woman approach unto any beast, and lie down thereto, thou shalt kill the woman and the beast: they shall surely be put to death; their blood shall be upon them." This wickedness was taken over from heathen peoples. Moses warns the Israelites in the 3rd Book of Moses XVIII 3: "After the doings of the land of Egypt, wherein ye dwelt, shall ye not do: and after the doings of the land of Caanan, whither I bring you, shall ye not do." Michaelis reports that among the Egyptians several of their worshipings to God involved unchastity with animals. In his "Journey writings of upper and lower Egypt," Sonnini relates that in about the year 1800, "the Egyptians chased male crocodiles from the female who were lying on their backs, in order to engage in sodomy with the latter." In my book "The Romanoffs" I gave a description in passing of the customs under the Romanoffs from Peter the Great and his dispensing with the uniformity of war; in the fourth chapter I said: "Indecent assault is inevitably followed by the penalty of death," and the fifth chapter says: "Unnatural chastity between men and men, the ravishment of boys, and lewdness with animals is punished with burning at the stake." It is reported that the women on the coast of Guinea let themselves be mated by animals; they are said to give themselves particularly to apes. Darwinians can find support for their theory on this. The priests there are said to confine themselves to intercourse with asses, as Blumenreich writes. In Sicily the goatherds are reputed to make use of their goats frequently. In Serbia, as Krauss recalls, Kara Gjorje is once said to have engaged in sodomy with goats. In Bosnia every stratum is ascribed to a particular preference for a particular animal. So they say that Frenchmen prefer house goats for their needs, while other Catholic cults choose hens and cats. The Greek orthodox popes and the Moslem Hodschas prefer young mares. In Bosnia, as Krauss has seen with his own eyes, women give themselves not only to dogs, but also to cats.

In rare cases, say famous Osman doctors whom Omer Haleby quotes, it is permitted to make use of "animals of large structure": the goat, the mule, the mare. Such cases, however, are "purely medical matters" and must only "be utilized as a means of cure, only in the interests of health." So one may use a female animal if he suffers from gonorrhea or another infection of the penis; chancre and wounds and sores of every kind are excepted. Experience teaches that under the influence of such coitus, the man can be rid of his evil without making the animal sick, since the pus is annihilated through the great heat in the vulva of the animal and through the strength of the animal mucous secretion. "If you are sick and without medical help," thinks Omer Haleby, "or if you cannot afford a doctor, use an animal; but, in order to avoid the penalty which the law of Islam provides, this must be stopped at the moment that you have regained your health." When the French had conquered Algiers, says Regla, the courts of justice were overburdened with cases involving unchastity with animals. They surprised the Arabs daily in the stalls of the cavalry in the practice of coitus with young mares. The good Moslems were

277

astounded when they were punished because of this and they excused themselves by offering the reasons which I have mentioned above from Omer Haleby. In Christian Balkan states as well, coitus with animals is considered a means of ridding one of gonorrhea. But they utilize for the most part a hen. First it is plucked alive, then the diseased one presses his penis into it, while a helping friend gradually kills the animal, so that in its death tremor the vagina is convulsively drawn together. In order that the cure may be permanent, one must roast the dead hen, and it must be fed to a stranger who is passing through; he takes the disease along with him. All of these things belong also in part to the chapter on venereal diseases; I mention them here, however, because I believe that the health giving foundation of unchastity is only a cloak for the excuse of engaging in coitus with animals. Krafft-Ebing in his "Psychopathia Sexualis," reports similar cases in other countries, in the section written by Mantegazza: among the Chinese there is a respectable "sport," which consists of sodomizing a goose, and at the moment of emission, having its head cut off. I myself was in a house on an expedition to Alexandria when the same thing happened to a hen. In the same house several Arabs gave a personal exhibition to the European guests: how one practices coitus with an ass. This latter procedure is considered all over the orient as the lowest that can be thought of, and they designate a very hateful person as an ass.

278

## CHAPTER NINETEEN

# EUNUCHS AND SEXUAL PERVERSIONS

*Female eunuchs—Excision of the ovaries and mutilation of the Clitoris—
In Egypt—Among the Copts—Male eunuchs—Their role in the orient—The
Bible on eunuchs—The Koran on mutilation—Origin of the creation of
eunuchs—Semiramide—Potiphar—Eunuchs in Osman history—The character of eunuchs—Their position in Persia—The eunuchs in Rome—Division
of eunuchs into three categories—The crushing of the testicles—An historic
incident—Eunuchs as husbands—The feeling of revenge of eunuchs—Eunuchs in India—Eunuchs beloved by women—Men among women, women
among men—Coitus through the mouth—Monumental representation of
coitus through the mouth—Mouth-coitus among the Romans—Brothels for
oral-coitus in Algiers—Mouth-coitus harmful to women—A praise of
gypsies—Lesbian love.*

**279**

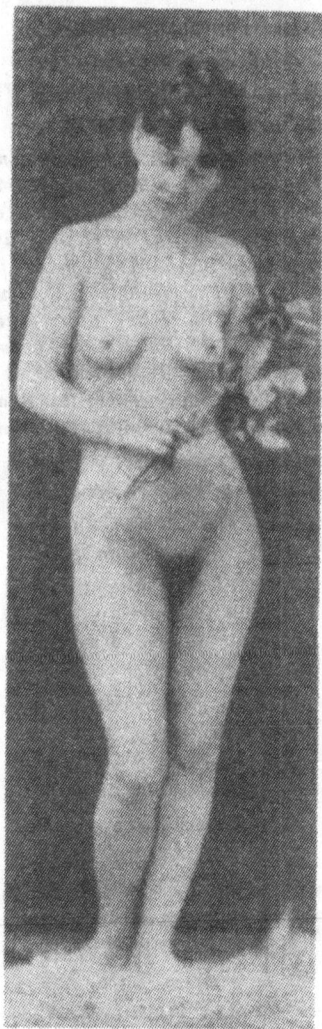

*Twenty-year-old Slav*

Female eunuchs are a remarkable thing in the orient. They cut open the belly of young maidens in order to extirpate the ovaries. They cut the clitoris to the root, they then close the vulva and sew together the labia pudendi. In this manner they create beings without sex and without desire.

In Egypt the operation takes place among maidens between five and nine years of age. According to some statements the clitoris is mutilated; according to others the labia pudendi are merely partly cut away, because they frequently assume immense proportions among the women of that region and result in a lascivious temperament among the southern women during the erection at coitus; in this way they do away with the hindrances to sensual pleasure, for too large lips of the vulva prevent the desired deep penetration of the penis, or at least make it more difficult. According to the accounts of the native doctors, this operation, which is called *Chasath* and which is the practice of specialists, is performed only to prevent nervous diseases and hysteria. This representation can, however, rightly be questioned. All unprejudiced reports maintain that the barbaric operation arises from sensual motives. Strabo has already written of this, and Xanthus, a Greek historian, discusses the castration of women which was practiced in ancient Greece; this was accomplished there at the command of King Gyges; in the first place, so that he could use the women without expecting any results, and in the second place, in order that the women might retain their youth and beauty for a longer time.

The castration of maidens is still at the present time prevalent, particularly among the Copts. The operation encompasses both the shortening of the small labia pudendi and the sewing up of the maiden, so that intercourse can no longer be consummated through the female organ, but must follow an unnatural course, as with a boy. An incomplete seam, that is, a clever tightening, will often be found, in order to bring about a simulation of lost virginity; this operation is usually performed several times on maidens whom one uses for marketable love.

The role of male eunuchs in the orient is many-sided. The eunuchs are not merely the watchers of the harem, they also serve as willing subjects for all possible kinds of perversions; and the Latins coined the word for them: "Men among women —women among men."

In my book on the court and the harem of Abdul Hamid, I have devoted a separate chapter to the eunuchs. I give here a supplement with the aim of dealing with the part of eunuchs in the sexual life of the orient, for I have only touched lightly on this question in my above mentioned book.

In the 5th Book of Moses XXIII 2, it is said: "He that is wounded in the stones, or hath, his privy member cut off, shall not enter into the congregation of the Lord." Visiting at sacred places was denied to eunuchs. As is related in the 3rd Book of Moses XXII 24, animals with crushed testicles must not be brought as a sacrifice to Jehovah.

The Turk Omer Haleby says concerning eunuchs: it is absolutely contrary to the principles of morality of Islam, and he asks: "Have we not, as watchers of the honor of our wives, the severe penalties laid down by the Koran, the laws against adultery? Did our Prophet need eunuchs? Does the Arab of the desert and the tent employ these incomplete people? The Osmans have established the institution of eunuchs, have adopted it from the demoralizing customs of the Greeks and the decadent peoples. According to its source, it is more Christian than Moslem; for it is the basis of the famous sect of Valesians of the third century. One can only condemn the custom which the Turks invoked with the Padischah on the point of white and black eunuchs; it is everlastingly united with the practice of castration."

The Moslem law prescribes severe penalties for wounding or mutilating an organ of a man or boy. The destruction of a member of which man possesses but one, demands the entire price of blood. To this group of organs of which there exists but one belongs the genital organ. The price of blood is: blood for blood, retaliation of like with like; whoever mutilates the organ of his neighbor, has the same thing done to him. This has nevertheless failed to hinder the creation of eunuchs in Moslem countries even to this day.

According to Marcellus, Semiramide was the first to have commanded that young boys be castrated. Cicero relates: In Greece there has long prevailed the ancient belief that Colus, the Heaven, was castrated by his son Saturnus. In Egypt eunuchs have been known to exist from the earliest of times, and Potiphar is said to have been a eunuch. At the time of Cyrus Ethiopians were already known all the world over as eunuchs; their tribute to the Persians consisted of boys. The Colchians also paid their tribute in castrated boys.

From the very beginning the Osmans were lovers of eunuchs. When in the year 1547 the ambassador of the Indian Sultan Aladdin appeared at Constantinople to implore the Sultan for help against the Portuguese, besides rare animals and parrots of wonderful hue, besides costly spices and foods, hearts and balsam, he brought as a rarity: a slave who ate only human meat, and as the most desirable present: negroes and eunuchs.

Under Sultan Achmed III at the beginning of the sixteenth century, the Grandvizier Ali Pascha published the most note-worthy and humanitarian law in Turkey, that from then on negroes would no longer be castrated in Egypt. This surprising command of the Grandvizier impressed the officials and judges of Egypt so that they were rewarded and credited through the restraint of such compulsion and evil; from a side remark of the historian of the kingdom, it seems reasonable to believe that humanity was not the reason for this, but that the primary purpose of the Grandvizier was merely to rid the Sserai of negroes. This law of the Grandvizier was moreover poorly enforced, with the result that the institutions of eunuchs has held its own to this very day.

The description of the character of eunuchs which I have given in my book on the Court of Abdul Hamid will be supplemented here with the sketch which Dr. Polak draws of the eunuchs at the Persian royal court:

The eunuchs, so he says, are avaricious, covetous, vain, and superstitious, but absolutely not malicious, cruel, and treacherous, as they are usually described to us. They love ostentation and are particulaly partial to beautiful horses and birds. They also have a passion for plants and flowers, which they cultivate with special care. One can hardly find a single beautiful flower in the royal manors, for the eunuchs always secretly appropriate them for themselves. They take .preference over all servants of the house; they bear the title *chadsche*, patron. One entrusts them with the keys to all sacred possessions; they receive splendid clothing and personal servants for their needs. Contrary to their lawful destiny, they are permitted to take a wife, so the first eunuch of the king, Baschir-Chan, after the death of Mehmed Schah, married one of his most beautiful wives, in which choice the woman agreed for reasons of her own. At the time of Feth-Ali and Mehmed Schah, a number of eunuchs attained the highest positions and dignity of the realm. It was one of these, Georgier, whom Agha Muhammed Chan, the first prince of Kadschar, had captured upon his expedition of plunder. Two of them, Muhammed Eddauleh and Cosruw-Chan Vali, are even today held in great esteem among the Persians; the first as Governor of Ispahan, provided safety in roads and streets, broke up the castles of robbers, and strengthened the lax control of the Shah in the rebellious province of Aribistan; the other, successively Governor of Yezd, Kurdistan, and Kaswin, distinguished himself through his exceptional bodily strength, of which the most adventurous anecdotes were related all over the land. Under the Shah Nassreddin the influence and power of the eunuchs were very much decreased; the white ones were entirely banned from the harem as a result of overpowering jealousy.

In Rome the eunuchs were watchers of the women as well as subjects for lewd practices. In Ovid II Bagoas, the eunuch, is requested not to be a very strict watcher: "O thou Bagoas, who art neither man nor woman, thou watcher of my mistress, permit her a little freedom!"

The Romans, both the earlier and the later people, divided eunuchs into three classes: the *Castrati*, the *Spadones*, and the *Thlibiae*. The *Castrati* were those whom one had robbed of all outer genital organs; they were the most sought after and the dearest. The *Spadones* were merely robbed of their testicles. Among the *Thlibiae* one could distinguish no outer sign of emasculation, for their organs are permitted to remain, and their testicles are merely crushed. The islands of Chios and Delos furnished most of the eunuchs for the Roman kingdom for a long time.

According to Suetonius, Domitian forbade any further castration and raised the price of eunuchs which were still on the market. The successor of Domitian, Emperor Nerva, indorsed the first edict. But the decrees of both rulers were soon observed less and less, and the number of eunuchs grew anew. Heliogabalous afforded them gratuities and high positions. In order to stop the enormous growth in the number of eunuchs in Rome, Aurelius determined a norm, according to which each Roman citizen was permitted to have just so many eunuchs, as his income warranted as declared before the senate. As a result of this, relates Flavius Vopicus, the price of eunuchs rose enormously.

At that time castration was also frequently ordered as a penalty for adultery. Horace recalls an instance of this kind. Valerius Maximus reports of an operation which was performed on Attienus when he was discovered *in flagranti* by Bibienus, and of a like fate which overtook Marcus Pontius when he was surprised by Cervius.

Epistle 60 in Book II of Martial tells us the same thing in a humorous vein: "Thou are trifling with the wife of a military Tribune, O youthful Hylus; Be careful or you will be castrated. You think that is not allowed? What you are doing, is that then allowed?"

According to Omer Haleby there are among the Turks, as among the Romans, three classes of eunuchs: "The complete, the incomplete, and those of the third category." A complete eunuch is one who as a child has been robbed of his genital organs, the penis, the testicle sacks, and the testicles. An incomplete eunuch is one who has had his testicles cut out after he has reached manhood. To the third category belong those eunuchs who had their testicles crushed during infancy. The crushing of the testicles takes place while the boy is placed in a vessel of warm water; when he is asleep, they are pressed with the fingers until they can no longer be felt. For castration one holds the testicles with the left hand, stretches them, makes a cut with a knife over the left one, so that it springs out, cuts it off, and leaves only a piece of surrounding flesh.

Hammer reports an historic instance of the crushing of testicles in the second volume of his Osman history in which he tells of the murder of Sultan Osman: "Daudpascha, the Grandvizier, came with his Kiaja Omer, the Dschebedschibaschi and the police lieutenant Kalender, who bore the surname Oghri, "the childrobber," in order to complete the work of the hangman. Sultan Osman, full of the lusty power of youth, defended himself for some time against the four ravishers, but the Dschebedschi finally threw the noose over his neck; the "Oghri" crushed his sex parts with his hands, and the gruesome deed of the first murder of a ruler which leaves a spot on Osman history was consummated. An ear of the murdered one was brought, as a sign of the consummation of the deed, to the inciter thereof, the Walide-Sultana, the mother of the Sultan Mustafa."

In Egypt the removal of the entire penis was always thought proper. This operation, according to Trusen, was performed particularly in Siut by Coptic priests, and also by Christian doctors. For this purpose, the child is buried lengthwise in fresh sand, so that only the head and the parts to be operated upon remain free. The genitals are completely severed from the body with a single stroke of the knife; the bleeding is quickly checked by pouring boiling lead over the wound. After forty days everything should be healed and only 16 or 17 per cent are said to be killed by this operation. Even if only part of the penis is hacked away, not much remains. Fritsch produced before the Society of Ethnology in Berlin in the year 1894 an exhibition which showed the remnant of a eunuch's penis as small as the size of a nut; this is discussed in greater detail in the annals of that Society XXVI 445-458. Often, as Rigler relates, the bleeding is attempted to be stopped merely through the use of astringents or through burning. I have depicted other methods of operation and stilling of bleeding in my book on the Court of Abdul Hamid, according to statements of a Hollandish doctor. Among several peoples in Africa and among the Skopzes castration is a religious ceremony.

Only eunuchs of the first class offer a complete guaranty that they cannot practice coitus; those of the other two groups, however, can indulge up to a certain age and they are all the more harmful to morality and good customs because they are capable of satisfying women without making them pregnant; yet in relation to this last matter, remarkable cases have occurred wherein eunuchs have succeeded in fertilizing women.

The eunuchs of the first group approach the female sex in the matter of their physical constitution, their intellectual and moral conceptions. They are beardless, their trachea re-

287

tains the dimensions which it possessed during childhood, their voice remains childish and piercing. They live longest, particularly if they belong to the black race. The eunuchs of the other two categories are not beardless, but their beard is light and thin. Their voice is deep and heavy. Their sexual demeanor is frequently vivacious. Their intellectual capacities approximate those of healthy persons, but they soon become weak and their body deteriorates and ages early.

Eunuchs are generally considered passionately wild. If they wish to take revenge for an insult, and they are insulted because one merely does not pay enough attention to them, they wait even for years with stone-like patience for a favorable moment. It is said of the black eunuchs: "If a black eunuch has made up his mind to kill someone, he kills him; and if he does not succeed in this, then he kills himself." The white eunuchs are considered less vengeful, but therefore more treacherous.

As has already been mentioned, the eunuchs of the third group often succeed in making women pregnant. In my book on the Sultan's Court, I relate several instances of eunuch love affairs. At the time of my sojourn at Constantinople, the eunuchs Muzaffer Aga and Faik Aga, of the harem of Abdul Hamid, two favorites of the Sultan, were exiled to Yemen, because they had engaged in intimate affairs with the women of the Sultan in the harem. Regla relates that a slave in the harem of Osman Pascha was made a mother by a white eunuch of the third category; the child came into the world dead.

At times the eunuchs served the women, not with their mutilated penis, but with their mouth. An Egyptian princess in Constantinople, Skutari, had such an affair with a black eunuch, who as a result of this died of consumption in 1887.

The Hindoos considered the eunuchs in part as a special kind of courtesan, who satisfied their lust through mouth-coitus.

Juvenal and Martial have already related that there are

288

women who are capable of loving eunuchs. Juvenal ridicules it in his VI satire: There are women who love the bashful eunuchs, their womanly kisses without passion, their beardless faces. With them they may enjoy according to the full extent of their desires, and they need never have recourse to abortions." And Martial says in VI 67: "You ask, Pannicus, why Gellia, your wife, loves eunuchs so much? It is because she wishes to enjoy love without acquiring any children."

When Domitian attempted to suppress the institution of eunuchs, Martial wrote in the 3rd epigram of his VI Book: "One makes a sport of violating the sacred right of marriage, a sport of mutilating innocent humans. You forbid this, Caesar! and you render a service to future generations. Under your rule no one will be a eunuch or an adulterer. But before you, *o mores!* the eunuchs themselves were adulterers."

Although the eunuchs, in spite of their mutilation, often played the part of men among women, they submitted much more to perverted men in the orient than women. They are above all, subjects of pederasty, and Omer Haleby says in this connection: "If these eunuchs permit themselves to be used *a retro,* they are the worst enemies of women, their most tormenting, wildest, most jealous watchers; and they are jealous not only of the women, but also of each other."

In India, the eunuchs who engage in such practices clothe themselves in women's dress. Since India has become Moslem, however, they wear men's clothing. For it is not the woman whom they seek, but the man as woman, and they do not wish to let themselves be deceived by anything unnatural in their perverted pleasure. The male is so much more welcome to these libertines than the most beautiful female quality that the Bayaders, who sing and dance for the Moslem princes, are often compelled to adopt male mannerisms in order to evoke more sensual provocation.

Just as they serve the women, the eunuchs also serve the

289

men with their mouth. Among the Hindoos eunuchs are used for oral-coitus, which is practiced by both sexes; they are courtesans alike for the lust of men and women. Coitus with the mouth, says the textbook on love in the chapter on the restoration of dead passion, serves this purpose among men of weak temperament whose youth is past; who are powerful, but exhausted.

Coitus with the mouth is called in India *Auparischtaka*. The Kamasutra says: The *Auparischtaka* is the means of existence of eunuchs who live as courtesans and practice the trade of a masseur. *Inter fricationem quasi complectens membris suis amatoris femora premat; familiaritate aucta femorum radices una cum inguinibus contingat; et illius membrum, cum erectum esse intelligit, manu fricans excitet ridensque illum ob lasciviam quasi obiurget. Si a vira, quamquam indicia praebet illiusque naturam monstruosam intelligit, non invitatur, sua sponte incipiat; si autem invitatur repugnet aigreque accedat.*

Not only eunuchs engage in the *Auparischtaka*, but also, it is said in the Kamasutra, "The subjects of their masters and friends practice it with each other." Furthermore, the men do this with their women and the women likewise with their men. "Out of passion for this kind of pleasure," says the Kamasutra, "courtesans desert their generous and wealthy lovers in order to throw themselves away on slaves and elephant leaders." They call this kind of oral-coitus: the *Krahe*. Such scenes of enormous size were often immortalized in architectural and structural masterpieces in ancient India. In the Elephanta-Temple there can be found a reproduction of the *Krahe*; it is again reproduced in the *Gravures* of Richard Payne, which deal with the cult of Priapus. On the sacred chariot of Mazupatam one sees a group of six persons of supernatural size: a man who is doing the *Krahe* with his tongue with five women. Other pictoral reproductions of this mouth-coitus are to be found in the Temple of Liva originating in the eighth century, in Bhuwaneschwara near Cuttak in Orissa and on the sacred chariot of Schander-nagor, where Krischna and a Gopi portray the act. Among the Romans oral coitus was the last resort of the old and the impotent. Martial IV 50 asks: "Wherefore, Thais, do you contend that I am too old? One is never too old to lick." In Algiers there are brothers where only oral coitus is practiced, mostly by Arabs. I shall not speak of this perversion in European cities, except to remark that many maintain that one should prefer oral coitus to every other form of sexual act for sanitary reasons, for it satisfies just as much and is least harmful considering the ever contagious venereal diseases.

The Christian Balkan peoples in Turkey believe that they can be rid of gonorrhea if they use a delicate maiden or permit a woman to perform oral-coitus on them. But in the latter case, add the southern Slavs according to Krauss I 237, there is a condition: that the woman devour the semen. In addition it is considered among the southern Slavs "as a sign of special love" if the woman places the man's penis in her mouth and sucks it until the sperm is ejaculated. Lascivious women do this to their husbands purposely, until they become impotent, and they have the best excuse for their debauchery." In numerous songs, Krauss I 210, the boy says to the girl: "You are biting the head off my penis." The husband also does this "out of special love" for his wife and "many men cannot enjoy a woman legitimately before they have excited her vagina by licking it." The gypsies have the reputation in the entire East of having attained the greatest perfection in mouth-coitus and of practicing it by preference. A Bosnian song jokingly asks a gypsy: "You son of a dog, do you caress your wife between her thighs, where her beard grows?" Hindoo women also engage in *Auparischtaka* in the harem among one another. One can designate this as a kind of lesbian love.

The "Lesbians" lie down as man and wife, belly to belly, and rub each other's vagina until they attain a high degree of immoderate pleasure. The French author Pierre Louys has described the life and love of Lesbians in his novel "Aphrodite," and has somewhat idealized this strange cult. Many maintain that women who indulge in this practice are incapable of possessing any love for men. Krauss reports, however, that he was told that "according to south Slavic notions no woman is more capable of satisfying a man sensually than one who has been aroused in a lesbian manner." A Turkish Sappho, who, as poetess and woman, lived according to the example of her Greek sister, is recalled by Hammer in his history of the Osman Kingdom in the description of the wonders of Amasia: "East of Ssamssum stretches the plain of Phanaraa, through which flows the Iris, and a little further out of Themiskyra, which is cut through by the Thermodon, is the habitat of the Amazons. At the Iris lies Amasia, whose name, a true rarity, from ancient times, through so many hundreds of years and in the mouths of so many barbarians has remained unchanged to this very day. In Amasia is found the grave of the poetess Mihiri, who, as the Sappho of the Osmans, immortalized her works and her single, although not virginal life of love. The Turkish beauties of Amasia, the very Amasia of Asia Minor, find rich material for romantic love stories and portrayals of the Chinese shadow play in the novels of Ferhad and Schirin, and the water falls which they believe to be a result of the canal which Ferhad built through the field for the milk of the creator of Schirin; and the walk of Kanli Binar, the "street of bloody fountains," they designate as the place where Ferhad, burdened by the message of the death of Schirin, stabbed himself in his bladder. The Amasiens of Amasia are satisfied with these new sagas instead of the old ones of their neighbor Amazons, of whom they no longer have any knowledge."

292

## CHAPTER TWENTY

# ONANISM AND ARTIFICIAL INSTRUMENTS

*Derivation of the word—Onanism in the Bible—Onanism in the Kamasu-
tra—Masturbation of women in modern India—Monumental portraits of
onanism—Ethnological parallels—The Koran on onanism—Omer Haleby's
warnings and teachings in relation to onanism—Onanism in the harem—
In Pera—Badana—In Persia—In Alexandria—Among the Christian Balkan
folk—The artificial penis—The artificial vulva—Prevalence of the artificial penis in the world and in all ages—Ethnographic parallels—In present
day Turkey—Bananas, cucumbers, and padlischan as penes.*

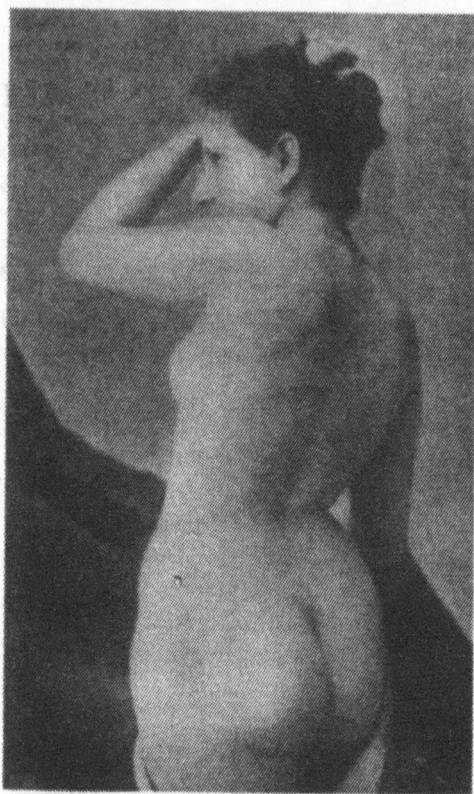

*Twenty-six-year-old Russian*

Onanism is derived from the name of that Onan of whom it is related in the first Book of Moses XXXVIII 8, that whenever he lay with the wife of his dead brother, he spilled the seed on the ground lest he should give seed to his brother.

In the Hindoo Kamasutra onanism is described in the following manner: "Just as the women occasionally quiet their desires without men, so it is also done by men who cannot procure a woman, to be sure, not in violation of the laws of nature, but with female beings such as sheep or mares, or through merely rubbing or touching the penis, as for example by the practice of the *walk of lions:* sitting with both hands placed on the ground, and with one foot stretched out, they rub the penis in the middle of the arm."

In present day India masturbation of women is an every day affair. A medical correspondent from India wrote to Dr. Ellis that he treated the widow of a rich Mohammedan and discovered from her that she "had begun to masturbate at a very early age, just as all other women." The same authority also testifies that there are to be found on the facade of a great temple in Orissa bas-reliefs which picture men and women masturbating alone, and also women whom the men are masturbating.

The Spaniards found when they first landed at Vizcaya and in the Philippines, that masturbation was prevalent there among the women. In Cochinchina, according to Lorion, it is practiced by both sexes, particularly, however, by married women. In Japan it is quite general and refined. Among the Nama-Hottentots Gustav Fritsch found masturbation so popular among young widows that it was considered a custom of the land; no secret is made of it, and it is dealt with as a usual occurrence of life in the legends and stories of this folk. It is likewise also among the Bastuos, the Kaffers, and the Balinesians. Eram asserts that masturbation is current all over the orient, particularly among young maidens.

The Koran II condemns "the habit of onanism"; from this Omer Haleby concludes that one must forbid in principle every restraint of seed, whether it be the method or the manner of the act. According to tradition the withholding of seed is permitted if both husband and wife agree upon it.

Dschaber says: "When the Koran was sent to the Prophet from heaven, Mohammed and his wife were engaged in the final moments of coitus, and the prophet held back the seed so that it should not spill on the genital organs of his wife. The prophet was asked about this. He did not expressly forbid this method, but he said: 'No breath of wind, no soul will be created by the creator until the day of general resurrection, except that this breath of wind will have its existence.' All souls which God will create, since then, have their existence on earth in human form. If therefore, coitus is not consummated, comments Omer Haleby, Allah will not prevent "your women from becoming mothers also in such cases." According to Omar, the Prophet expressly forbade "incomplete coitus or the withholding of the seed with a free woman, unless she consents."

Omer Haleby particularly warns the women concerning onanism: "Give no heed, O women of Islam, to evil advice; let yourselves not be seduced to onanism, pederasty, or Sapphistic practices, whether this advice is whispered into your ears by your servants, your eunuchs, and strange idol worshipers, or Jewish or Christian women. All of these practices will inject the deadly curse of sterility in your loins, will destroy your soul, will make tribute for the demon of your love, and will disturb the rays of chastity and modesty which you possess. Be the angel of the herd and not its hideous discord."

Omer Haleby then makes known in detail his personal opinions on onanism: Onanism is "every act which is accomplished with the hand, with the mouth of a woman, through a eunuch or a young boy, or whose purpose it is to bring forth the seed to the detriment of natural coitus and to the detriment of woman." Onanism with the mouth is widespread among the Christians, "as a remnant of ancient orgies, as they took place in certain heathen and idolatrous temples." It is unquestionable that this practice "is a legacy of those barbaric practices whose origin has been lost in the night of time." "O true believers!" says Omer Haleby, "leave such things to the Christians, the idolators, and the Jews; for it is certain that onanism, in whichever form it is practiced, is the cause of sorrow and a lack of courage, that, as has already been said by the wise Shah Dschellaleddin Abu Soleiman Daud, it weakens the sensual urge of nature, the desires and the organic growth. Many learned men misunderstand the words of the Prophet: 'Avoid adultery, for that is shameful and leads to evil; rather do anything that permits you to be diverted from adultery and the shame of blood.' These learned men contend in their misunderstanding: in certain cases, if no woman is present, as for example on a journey, it is permitted to come to the aid of nature if it demands it; and one may then have recourse to simple onanism, *Eummaira*, which is masturbation accomplished on oneself with the hand; but one must not do this in order to satisfy a perverted passion, but as has been said, only to assist nature."

In opposition to this contention and in "view of the fact that nature has a method of its own to help itself during sleep through exciting dreams," Omer Haleby condemns "such teachings thoroughly," and declares "with the Koran in his hand": "that onanism in every relation and of every kind must be considered a work of the devil, a deed harmful to the health of the body and the spirit, a deed which is capable of instigating the worst evil, and which is unworthy of a rational human being." And after this terrific condemnation the good Omer Haleby closes somewhat more leniently: "If, however, O true believer, you have fallen into this error, and this error is more of a mistake than a great sin, for it is even sanctioned by the Book of the Christians, then, O true believers, know that God is gracious, and loves to forgive, as soon as repentance enters our heart."

And this "error" prevails almost generally among the Moslems, and Allah has much to forgive. Particularly among the male and unmarried believers onanism is strongly intrenched. In Arabia, as among the Hottentots, it has become almost the custom of the land. It is seldom found among children and boys. The Moslem women also masturbate comparatively little. In large harems, where they are so often confined, they engage in Lesbian practices, but never with eunuchs, but with other women of the harem who strap an artificial penis about their hips and play the part of a man. Widows also do this among one another. The Turkish woman never engages in onanism with a man. In order to please her husband she sometimes acts as an object for pederasty, but she draws the line at rubbing his penis with her hand or engaging in "onanism with the mouth"; only the prostitutes in Algiers, Moslem women who must be numbered among the most accomplished prostitutes of the whole world, indulge in such practices. In Persia onanism is almost never found among virginal persons, except here and there among widows and women who are neglected by their husbands.

Among Perotian, Greek, and Armenian women in Constantinople there is known a particular kind of onanism called "the stick in the box." The maiden takes the penis in her hands and rubs its tip against her sexual organ, but is careful that the seed "falls to the ground," to use an old biblical expression. There are houses in the Perotian red light district where only *Badana* is practiced. In this way the maidens acquire a dowry and yet remain virgins, physically.

In Alexandria the *Badana* is engaged in with small negresses who have not yet attained the age of puberty, but who in spite of their delicate age go along to coffee-parties, in order to acquire knowledge.

Among the Christian Balkan folk onanism is understood only as the rubbing of the penis with the hand. It frequently happens that two rub the organs for each other. The southern Slavs say: "*Kurstschewanje slagje neg jebanje*, the mutual penis stroking is sweeter than coitus." Krauss noticed this particularly among the Serbian swineherds and remarked: Onanists there avoid the women.

The artificial penis is called in Latin, *penis succedanus*, *Phallus* or *fascinum*; in French, *Godemiche*; in Italian, *passetempo* or *Dilleto*; from the last word comes the expression employed in England, *Dildo*; the Hindoo name is, *apadravya*.

The corresponding apparatus for men, *cunnus succedanus*, is called in England, *Merkin*, which originally meant: imitated hair of the female secret parts.

The use of an artificial penis for sexual satisfaction was known as well in Biblical as in ancient Classical times. The first is substantiated in a passage from Ezekiel.

Lesbian women are said to have employed such instruments out of ivory or gold, which were covered with silk and linen. Aristophanes speaks of the use of an artificial penis, which was called the *Olisbos*, among the Milesierins.

Herondius, in his poem "The secret confession," lets two women glorify the *Olisbos* or *Bausson*," as the greatest ecstacy of life," and in another passage he mentions that these instruments were sold publicly.

Ellis says: "Throughout the middle ages, when the clerics always forbade the use of such instruments, until the age of Elizabeth, when, as Marston relates in his writings, Lucea went to bed with a glass penis, yes, even to the present day we can see such methods employed in all civilized countries. But throughout, they seem here to be utilized only by prostitutes and such women as conduct their lives on an aristocratic or half artificial plane. Ellis enumerates for pages such European instruments in which list there is nothing missing from the candle to the knitting needle. I naturally pass over these classes here and cast but a glance at the artifices of the orientals.

When the Spaniards landed in Vizcay and on the Philippines for the first time, they discovered that the women there employed an artificial penis in order to be able to satisfy themselves sexually. Among the Balinesians, say Ploss and Bartels, one finds a penis of wax in every harem, with which the women spend many hours of solitude.

According to the concurring reports of Ellis as well as of Ploss and Bartels, the Japanese women claim the highest degree of fulfillment through the use of artificial organs. They use principally two hollow projectiles made out of thin brass, of the size of pigeon eggs, one is empty, the other, so-called little-man, contains a small heavy metal sphere or some quicksilver, sometimes metal tongues which vibrate when set in motion. When both balls are held side by side in the hand, they are constantly in motion. The empty sphere is directed into the sex part first, until it touches the uterus; then the other one follows. The slightest movement of the pelvis or the hips and each individual movement of the abdomen makes the metal ball or quicksilver roll and the resulting vibration creates a tickling sensation, a gentle stroke like a minor electric current. These balls are called *Rin-no-tama* and are held fast in the vagina. The women who use these balls rock in hammocks and rocking chairs, so that the movement of the balls gradually creates the highest degree of sexual pleasure. Joest declares that this apparatus according to its name is also known to the Japanese maidens in the country, but it is chiefly used by the higher class geisha girls and prostitutes. Its use has spread throughout the orient.

In China one also knows of a supple, a rose-colored penis made of rosin, which is publicly sold and unceremoniously asked for by women.

In Canton, as Lamairesse reports, they create an artificial

300

penis from a gummy rosin mixture of certain malleability, color the product rosy, and send it out to all countries. In Tientsin they sell these instruments publicly, and give the purchaser an illustrated pamphlet in which are shown pictures of its use. It sometimes transpires in the theatre that a person affixes such an instrument to himself, in order to demonstrate to young women *ad oculos* how they can use it.

In Turkey and in Egypt they utilize such natural products which resemble the penis in appearance. The banana, in shape and size, seems to have been created for this purpose. Mythology tells of goddesses who were impregnated by bananas hidden under their clothes. The cucumber is considered the same as the banana. In Constantinople, the women employ the *Padlidschan*, seeds of fruit, which they roast, until they become hard.

Finally, there are widespread all over the East, Parisian fabrications which one can make larger or smaller according to her wish; it is filled with milk or another liquid and it bursts after a certain number of thrusts; and when the liquid then flows into the vagina, the illusion is complete in the greatest possible degree.

## CHAPTER TWENTY-ONE

# VENEREAL DISEASES

*The Bible on an unclean flow—Syphilis in Moslem countries—A word of the Grandvizier Reschad Pascha—Introduction of syphilis into Constanti-nople between 1827 and 1831—Present conditions—Sanitary reforms of Professor During Pascha—Syphilis in the Wilajet Kastamuni and Angora—Syphilis in Syria—In the army—Mildness of the disease in Constantinople and Smyrna—Women and priests as specialists for syphilis—Remedies—Opinions of the Turk Omer Haleby—Oriental folk remedies against syphilis—Moroccan remedies.*

*Barbary Negro Dancers*

In the 3rd Book of Moses XV, 2: it says: "When any man hath a running issue out of his flesh, because of his issue he is unclean." And it is prescribed that anything which comes in contact with such person is unclean; "And if he that hath the issue spit upon him that is clean; then he shall wash his clothes and bathe himself in water, and be unclean until the even. . . ." IVth Book of Moses V, 2: "Command the children of Israel, that they put out of the camp every leper, and every one that hath an issue, and whosoever be defiled by the dead." IIIrd Book of Moses XXII, 4: "What man soever of the seed of Aaron is a leper, or hath a running issue; he shall not eat of the holy things. . . ." A curse in IInd Book of Samuel III, 29: runs: ". . . and let there not fall from the house of Joab one that hath an issue or that is a leper. . . ."

Syphilis was practically unknown in the domain of Islam until the nineteenth century.

Even in the year 1832 Prince Demeter Maurokordato could write in a Berlin medical magazine: Syphilis is seldom found in Turkey. It then developed almost exclusively in the prevailing Christian provinces, in Moldau and Walachei. Things soon changed. The famous Hungarian scholar Vambery told me that the great Vizier Reschid Pascha had once complained to him: "We send our young people to Europe so that they may become civilized; but they come back—merely syphilized." Circumcision and the cleanliness of the Turks, the prescribed washings, the admonition that they cleanse themselves with a bath after intercourse, the lack of public houses—all this had long protected the Moslems from syphilis. The beginning of the disease in Constantinople can be determined almost to the day. When Maurokordato left the Osman capital in 1827 in order to complete his medical studies in Berlin, there were neither brothels nor syphilis in Constantinople. When he returned to the Bosphorus in 1831, everything had changed.

The police who had tolerated no lewdness among the Turks,

and who had watched the pleasure houses of the French very strictly, no longer bothered, and all kinds of wickedness flourished in Stambul as well as in Pera and Galatea: the time of reform had begun! Venereal diseases became general. The doctors of Constantinople possessed no skill in this matter, and they aggravated the condition. Since then entire states in Turkey have become diseased. The Wilajete Kastamuni and Angora are particulaly notorious. Professor von During Pascha has made numerous suggestions in recent times for combating the disease in these provinces. The government accepted his suggestions and the budget of the finance year 1315 provided the necessary money. Pascha demanded: the creation of hospitals in Kastamuni, Kenghiri, Erekli, Bartin, Dustche, and in Wilajet Angora; the enlargement of the existing hospitals in Bolu; a sum of 16,000 pounds for this purpose; a regular inspection of diseased areas by a commission consisting of two doctors and an apothecary, in order to send all afflicted persons to a hospital; the designation of 19 specialists for both provinces; the free rendition of all medicines to the patients. The measures were adopted in their entirety, but the evil was not easy to contend with.

There is no longer any province in Turkey today which is free from syphilis. In Smyrna, Konia, Brussa, and Beyruth there are very many brothels with Turkish women who also accommodate strangers; even the innermost Wilajets are diseased. In one of the twenty-three volumes of contemporary writings of the German oriental society, containing the letters of the Consul Wetzstein to Fleischer, it is mentioned that syphilis flourished disturbingly in Syria. In Damascus the disease is called *kotal*, which means the same as leprosy, also: "French disease" of the "genital region." One who is afflicted by syphilis is called *Mudschaen* or *Mudschasim.*

At the present time syphilis is widespread in the army.

The majority of those who are to be found in the Turkish military hospitals are afflicted with it.

In the everyday life of Constantinople public houses of pleasure are an unavoidable evil. In Galatea, for streets on end, one sees nothing but brothels. Syphilis is a very popular habit, for there has never been any supervision by police doctors. Fortunately, according to all medical reports made to me, the disease is not malignant in Constantinople. The same goes for Smyrna; here the favorable climate in particular alleviates these cases.

In Turkey the female quacks and the priest-doctors enjoy a good reputation for the successful dealing with syphilis. They attempt to effect a cure, as Professor Rigler reports, through a smoking with cinnabar or metallic quicksilver which is rubbed with mercuric chloride and the root powder of henna, made into a paste with a little of the white of an egg, and thrown on a coal fire; the sick one sits over the fire covered with a cloak. The ordinary man cauterizes the wound with tobacco juice.

Omer Haleby says: "*Teus'fia*, gonorrhea, is the result of too strenuous or too quickly repeated coitus; a result of weakness, or a result of the fact that the man has practiced coitus just before or just after the woman's periods. It can also result from an immeasurable use of spicy foods such as pistachios, bitter almonds, onions; or finally, it is a mere accompaniment to other sicknesses, a simple acidity of the blood. But all this is for simple gonorrhea, not for syphilis, nor for chancre and growths in the form of a cock's comb, a cabbage leaf, or a climber. These latter diseases are the result of prostitution and physical uncleanliness among strange peoples, where the dogmas of many sects even assist such uncleanliness. Flee therefore, O people! from whatever draws you to those unclean temples in this city of Stambul, temples which the so-called civilization of the Christians and the Jews has installed in such great number in the old quarters of Galatea, Hasskio, and Jenischehir."

As a preventative against venereal diseases of all kinds, Omer Haleby directed the Moslems to recourse to religious medicine, to the *nathrah*, the charming of water, which happens as follows: one places both hands on the water which serves for the general washing, and recites the last two chapters of the Koran, 113 and 114.

One then says: "Through these words I implore God for protection from choler, from acts of revenge, from all evil with which the wickedness of the devil can tempt your servant." As purely 'medical remedies against chronic gonorrhea, Omer Haleby finally offers: Injection with cubeben, *copaivabalsam*, red pepper.

In Persia, according to Polak, quicksilver is used exclusively for syphilis, and sometimes they mix tobacco with the coal dust of Nargileh and with cinnabar, and permit it to draw out the dampness. The effect is exceptionally quick and intensive, an application of eight or twelve times usually brings about a cure. More rarely an internal use is made of finely grated quicksilver.

In Morocco the cure of syphilis depends on the temperament of the invalid. The Moroccan doctor divides the four temperaments among the four elements and treats each according to the group of sickness to which he believes his patient to belong.

## CHAPTER TWENTY-TWO

# IMPOTENCE

*Impotence as grounds for divorce—Superstitious notions of the causes of impotence—Remedies for impotence caused by magic—A remedy of the prophet—Achmed's remedy—Omer Halebys' opinions—Age as a cause—A Bosnian song—Gereconomy—The incident of King David—Old and young—Camphor as an enervating medicant—Powder of cantharides as an aphrodisiac—Moroccan electuaries—Their interpretation—The recipe of Omer Haleby—Persian recipes—The guild of Osman electuary makers—Pastilles de Serail—Constantinople preparations—The excellent remedy of Omer Haleby—The advice of the Prophet Mohammed—Eggs, henna, and washings—Potency of uplifting spices—Herissah—Mohammed's potency—Tales of his favorite wife Aischa—Musk—The role of perfume at coitus—Further recipes of Omer Haleby.*

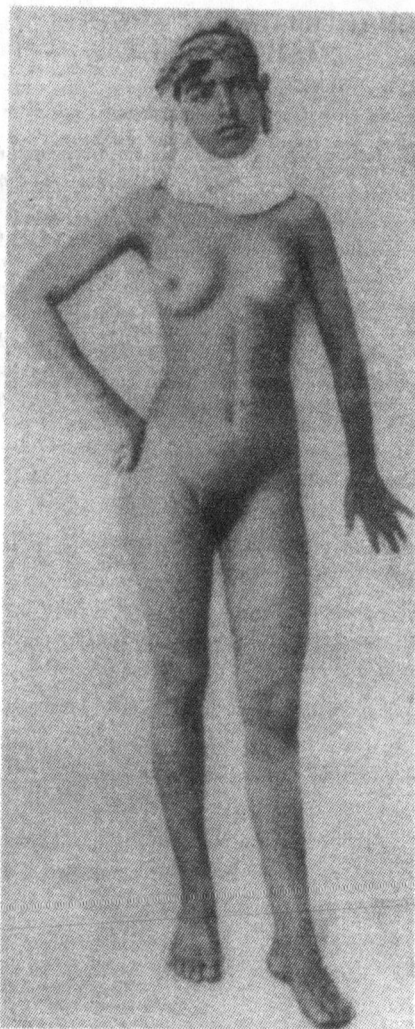

*Algier Girl—Eleven Years Old*

The question of potency and impotence plays a significant part in the character of orientals. At Turkish weddings, as has already been related, the so-called wedding palms are carried before the procession of the bride as an upstanding symbol of manly power.

If the husband is impotent, insane, or inordinately stupid, his wife may, under Moslem law, demand a divorce. The Levantines believe: if a bride sews anythings after the day of the engagement has already been fixed, then the groom loses his sexual power. In order to give this back to him, the bride must rip apart the sewed work. In Syria, if one is helping the bridegroom to put on his wedding clothes, he must be careful to see that his knots are tied and his buttons buttoned; otherwise his enemies have power over him, and if they wish him to be impotent or his wife to remain childless, they can have their wishes fulfilled. In order to protect the groom from such misfortune, the godmother of the groom, among the Syrian Christians, must move her hands as if in prayer while he is being dressed.

Similar beliefs exist among other peoples in Turkey: The groom is not in a position to accomplish his marital duties if he wears a bud in his buttonhole during the ceremony, or commits any other indiscretion, such as making a knot in his cloak immediately after the consecration of the marriage. The Turks call the buttons of knots, *sohor*, a magic word, which is supposed to exert an influence on the body and the heart of a person without direct contact.

According to Dschellaleddin Abu Soleiman Daud there are among the machination of magic operations, those which kill; those which invoke disease; those which separate a man from his wife in that they make her unfaithful to him; operations which arouse hate between man and wife or others which increase their love for each other.

In order to invalidate impotence which arises from curses

and magic, one must recite a verse of the Koran. Aischa said:
When anyone of the household of the Prophet was sick as a
result of magic, the Prophet himself spoke to the invalid and
recited the last two chapters of the Koran. Achmed commanded: The conjuror must place his hands over the water in
an arch through which the invalid must drink, and he must
recite the next to the last chapter of the Koran—then the water
is proof against magic. Thereupon the impotent one must
complete his washing and say his prayers. Finally he must
place the index finger of his right hand upon his penis, the
thumb on his umbilical cord, and gaze at the conjuror. The
latter sinks his glance into that of the sick one, recites to himself the last two chapters of the Koran, and says in a loud voice
and with powerful force: "Go, from this moment the charm
is broken, and you are no longer impotent!" If this is not sufficient, then the procedure is repeated three times, but a pause
of one week is permitted after each time.

In order to heal impotence which is not organic, Omer
Haleby says one can employ the "hygienic and pharmaceutical"
remedy. In the first stages cold local compresses are necessary;
one adjusts small rays of energy to the organ. One can also give
cold showers to the organ, and particulaly half an hour before
every coitus, morning and night.

Naturally age is also a cause of impotence. A Bosnian song
expresses itself drastically as follows:

>  An old man walks through a stubble-field,
>  His member drags after him like a hedge-pole.

A general opinion prevails that a senile man becomes
young again through marriage with a young maiden and the
reverse, but these age quickly. In the first Book of Kings I, 1-3: it
is related: Now King David was old and stricken in years; and
they covered him with clothes, but he got no heat. Wherefore

his servants said unto him, Let there be sought for my lord the king a young virgin; and let her stand before the king and let her cherish him, and let her lie in thy bosom, that my lord the king may get heat. So they sought for a fair damsel throughout all the coasts of Israel, and found Abishag, a Shunammite, and brought her to the king. And the damsel was very fair, and cherished the king, and ministered to him: but the king knew her not. Professor Ebstein calls this incident the beginning of the so-called Geroconomy, and he has written interestingly about attempts to bring back youth to senile people through contact with young persons, in a book on "the ability to lengthen human life."

In later times it was believed that this method could be profitably employed for strengthening weakened people of both sexes, although one could remark at the same time that, while the elders became more vigorous and acquired strength, the youthful persons apparently lost power and wilted through the intercourse with the older ones.

According to the opinion of the Arabian doctor Ibn Kilde, it is more sorrowful for a young man to approach an old woman than for an old man to find that he can no longer satisfy his desires.

The Serbians think entirely differently. If one is possessed by passion, if his penis *erigitur,* then he takes whatever there is to be had; if it necessary the devil eats flies:

> Every cow is black in the shade,
> And if I cannot have a maid,
> Any slut will do in a pinch.

Camphor, Turkish: *Kiafur;* Arabic: *Kafur;* Persian: *muschk Kafur;* Hindoo: *Kepur,* serves scorned women as a means of taking revenge on the inconstant man; the belief in the capability of this medicant to weaken sexual power is widespread. According to Rigler they employ as an antidote cantharides, called in Turkish: *kodos bodschigi;* Arabic: *zerarih;* Persian: *meges bra dagh;* Hindoo: *mekkien daghvala.* The powder of cantharides has become known in Morocco as an aphrodisiac, Turkish and Arabic: *mubehyat* or *muschteh;* Persian: *kuvetba;* Hindoo: *dova e kuvet.* The inhabitants of Moroccan cities use an elecuary, called the *madschun,* extensively. According to a report of Quedenfeldt in the 19th volume of the proceedings of the Berlin Association of Ethnology, the *madschun*-electuary has the following composition: honey, acorns, nuts, sweet almonds, a little butter, flour, sesame, hashish, and the powder of cantharides. One notices very little harmful influence of cantharides on the urogenital organs in Morocco.

The Mohammedans in Morocco know an electuary similar to *mudschun,* which consists only of sweet things and healing leaves, and is called *takanit.* Leo Africanus mentioned a root called *surnag* in Morocco, to which was ascribed the quality of increasing potency; another travelling writer reports a root of cabbage said to contain strengthening power, which was named after him, *Kersana.*

Omer Haleby gives the following recipe of a Turkish aphrodisiac: Take about 15 grams of aromatic *leaves of Stoechas* and leaves of saffron, about 20 grams of anis and wild carrots, 25 pieces of orange blossoms, 50 dried dates, 4 pieces of the yolk of an egg, 500 grams of clear well water, boil everything for 25 minutes in an earthen glass locked pot; lift it then from the fire, stir it gradually until it has become entirely regular, and then add: 50 grams of honey and the fresh blood of two doves. Let this stand for 24 hours during which stir it 3 or 4 times. Then pass it through a fine sieve, and you have the remedy. For a whole week take 1 to 2 teaspoonfuls half an hour before going to bed and before every coitus.

In Persia pills of pounded pearls, rubies, gold, amber, and

bernstein are bought as an aphrodisiac. Also quinine, taken evenings in doses of 1-2 grains, enjoys a good reputation in this connection. On the other hand, the Persians consider the use of camphor as a means of reducing potency, and because it is customary to place a piece of camphor in the mouth of a dead person.

The electuary makers, called *meadschindschian*, have long since organized a special guild in the Osman domain. They consider as their patron the attar dealer Obied, who with Hamsa, the Oheim of the prophet Mohammed, fell in the battle of Ohod, and lies buried at the foot of Mount Ohod. At the organization of the guild in earlier times, the *meadschindschian* appeared with mortar in their hands in which they pounded spices, or with silver plates over which their costly electuaries were spread, with which they gently stroked the mouths of the anxious ones in passing.

The Turkish wonder-remedies against weakened manly power have been famous for centuries. At first the Sserai of the Osman sultans occupied itself with the preparation of these oriental specialties. The third chamber in the palace of the sultan, the chamber of spices and sugar work, developed not only foodstuffs, but also electuaries of every kind. The pages of this chamber created a remarkable oil-skin which they gave to poor people afflicted with wounds and chancres. The most famous, however, in the sixteenth, seventeenth and eighteenth centuries were their amber—and *moschus*-patties, or *churse*, and their amber—and *moschus*-amulets, or *tensu*, which were provided with Turkish inscriptions, such as: "Easing of pain and healing of heart," and which were sold all over Europe under the name *Pastilles de Serail* as an infallible aphrodisiac.

Since the Sserai has instituted these concoctions, number-less Arabic doctors have occupied themselves with the development and sale of such power medicants at unbelievable prices, so that pearls and precious stones might be crushed to powder

315

in this medicine of Lulu and Elma. The oriental who can often call three or four wives his own, can conceive of no greater misfortune than that which places him on a level with his eunuchs. He therefore makes every sacrifice and pays three pounds for a little powder, if it can even give him slight hope of regaining his power.

A concoction against impotence used extensively in Constantinople harems is said to consist of powdered pastilles of hemp buds together with a mixture of honey, muscatnut, and saffron. According to an analysis of Professor Rigler, another aphrodisiac, much used in the harems of Constantinople for weakened men, consists of cannabis, carnations, moschus, cocoanut, honey, and pearls.

According to the opinion of the Turk Omer Haleby, one best combats impotence, "if he often strokes his penis and tickles his scrotum, just as the prophet has done."

Ovid in his 2nd Book advised the use of eggs and honey of Hymettus as an aphrodisiac. Omer Haleby also advises eating eggs. According to Ulema Dschellaleddin Abu Soleiman Daud, someone one day complained to the prophet that he begat too few children, and the prophet ordered him: "Eat eggs!"

The rubbing in of henna on the finger tips, on the skull, and on the feet, simultaneously arouses passion and combats physiological impotence; one must also shave the pubic hair frequently and rub henna around the genital region. "Stroke yourselves with henna," says Anas, "it youthifies, it beautifies, it creates an urge for sexual intercourse." Abu Rafi relates: "One day I found myself with our holy prophet; as I sat with him, he placed his hand upon my head and said: Good. Of all coloring cosmetics, make use mostly of henna. Henna strengthens the hand, animates for coitus." Omer Haleby adds an incident to this tradition: "According to my own experience there are few cases of inorganic impotence which cannot be alleviated if one rubs the penis morning and night with henna; 8 or at most

316

14 days are sufficient to bring about a complete cure in this manner."

Eggs, sea-fish, mutton in caraway-seed, anis and fennel, boiled, testes of steer, cocks and hedgehogs, carrots, asparagus, pistachio nuts, roasted nuts, Asiatic Khamis, which is known in Damascus, Bagdad, and Smyrna, as well as terfas or truffles from Algiers, are considered in Turkey as spices which strengthen potency. In particular "the terfas," a tubelike mushroom of exquisite odor and extraordinary taste, "makes coitus easier through its stimulating effect on the brain and through the elasticity which it lends to the entire nervous system." It is therefore good to eat *khamis* and *terfas* if one indulges excessively in coitus. Local cold baths of from 50 seconds to 2 minutes are also good early in the morning at rising. Self-chastisement also arouses.

One day, reports the traditionist Abu Horeirah, the prophet himself complained to the Angel Gabriel that he could not copulate sufficiently. "Why do you not eat *herissah?*" asked the Angel Gabriel, "in *herissah* lies the strength of 40 men." Herissah is, according to Régla, a kind of cake of flour and mutton; one cooks each separately, salts it and spices it with red pepper, chops the meat, and mixes it with the flour. Occasionally one adds to the mutton the meat of a young rooster without the testes and finely cut truffles.

Various scholars dispute the statement of Abu Horeirah, for the prophet enjoyed remarkable health and God showed him special favor in *puncto coitus*. Aischa said of her holy husband in this connection, and she must have known well as the favorite wife of Mohammed: "The nature of the holy prophet was as strong as the holy nature of the Koran." But the Turkish love-physiologist, Omer Haleby, in spite of this, takes sides with Abu Horeirah and says: "One must remember that the prophet was but a man; one must think of his strenuous daily accomplishments; one must remember the endless in-

317

trigues which he had conducted among his numerous wives and among all of his slaves, for they all wished to consummate marriage and to sleep with the messenger of God. If one remembers all of these things, the statement of the honorable Abu Horeirah is only natural; it merely shows us that Mohammed was granted more power from God, so that he might be able to satisfy all the needs of his high position favorably and fully."

According to Omer Haleby, the stimulants which are said to increase potency are either simple or complicated. One serves to facilitate coitus, the other to quiet coitus and to instill the required power. The employment of the first is derived directly from Mohammed, the others were advised by the traditionists and experimenting Hodschas.

Among the methods which played a part in the long life of Omer Haleby, one of the foremost was: Mesk or musk. The Koran says about this in Chapter 83 22-28: "Verily the righteous shall dwell among delights, seated on couches they shall behold objects of pleasure; thou shalt see in their faces the brightness of joy. They shall be given to drink of pure wine, sealed; the seal whereof shall be musk: and to this let those aspire, who aspire to happiness: and the water mixed therewith shall be of Tasnim, a fountain whereof those shall drink who approach near unto the divine presence." The Arab Dschaubair describes the preparation of musk: One takes small doves or delicate camels and nurses them for seven days with all of the best spices which have been sprayed with rosewater and with the extract of aromatic tips of leaves; one then takes a glass container streaked with oil, chokes the animals over it, and lets the blood flow into the glass which is then covered and protected against dust. When the blood is dried one adds a fifth of a gram of this to one gram of mesk and offers the mixture in a glass which has been streaked with *Gummi arabicum*. This is the best form of musk which I have ever seen.

Omer Haleby says: Musk is hot and dry and the most

delicate of all perfumes which are said to facilitate coitus. The prophet is said to have perfumed himself always with musk, and to have commanded his wives to wash themselves with it during the time of their period—from the beginning until the cleaning. It was Aischa's duty to perfume the prophet with musk when he dressed himself for the pilgrimage with Ihram. In conformity with the requirements of the prophet, his wives had to perfume their houses with musk on Friday in order to purify the atmosphere, invalidate the effect of evil charms, and heighten the pleasure of coitus.

It is a fact, according to the opinion of many authorities, that the sense of smell stands in a sympathetic relationship with sex powers. The fragrance of flowers often arouses lustful desires, as can be seen from the Song of Songs of Solomon, II, 7. The sensual eastern countries love a pleasant odor above all else. Omer Haleby says: "It is good to be perfumed with musk before as well as after coitus. If one adds the odor of incense of myrrh to the musk, by strewing these two over coals, one can be certain of great potentialities in having intercourse, and accelerate the emission of the seed and the final raptures. The fragrance of myrrh animates one for coitus, incense quiets one afterwards. One must use these things in small doses." The Arabs relate that Adam, on leaving paradise, held three things in his hand: A myrrh, a date, and an ear of corn, which are supposed to signify symbolically: the first aroma, the first fruit, and the first means of subsistence. According to the same tradition, the myrrh was the first seed which Noah planted on his exit from the ark. The myrrh is called in Turkish: *mur safi*; Arabic: *morr mekki*; Persian: *bol*; Hindoo: *hira*.

Omer Haleby gives the following recipe of still another perfume which has a good influence on potency: Put 2½ grams of olibanum or incense into 500 grams of rosewater, as many fragrant tips of leaves, also 50 grams of musk, myrrh, and camphor, all finely powdered. Pour this into a glass, seal it

319

hermetically, and place it in the sunlight for 24 or 48 hours. Then clarify it gradually, filter it, and preserve it in the same glass. If you wish to keep the perfume for a long time, add 75 grams of rectifying alcohol and three drops of Bagdad essence of roses. This perfume affects the brain, the heart, the genital organs and the consciousness. Pour a small teaspoon full of this into the washing water; sprayed on the clothing, it gives the entire body an excellent pleasant odor, protects it against insects and the evil influence of the demon. This same substance with less rosewater and less alcohol but with 1/6 of a whole Arabian gummi can also be prepared as pastilles the size of hazel nuts. One places these patties on three different heaps of charcoal "in the chamber of happiness" 25 minutes before the beginning of the coitus. If a man is entirely too weak in his love action, he doubles the doses.

CHAPTER TWENTY-THREE

# FERTILITY AND STERILITY

*Ancient Hebrew notions—The tomatoes in the Old Testament—A heavenly medicant for fertility—A modern Jewish method—Jewish superstitions—Sterility, a cause for divorce—Arabian and Albanian customs—The Koran on fertility and sterility—Instances of the famed fertility of oriental rulers—Menace of sterility as cause for an uprising—Advice of the Turk Omer Haleby—Superstitious methods for becoming fertile—Bosnian, Serbian, Albanian, and Syrian customs—The pomegranate—The tree of fertility on the Hermon—The apijun-leaf in Bosnia—Bosnian methods—Persian methods—Jordanvwater and Nile-water—Fertile making water of the Jews—Home remedies—Massages—Tampons.*

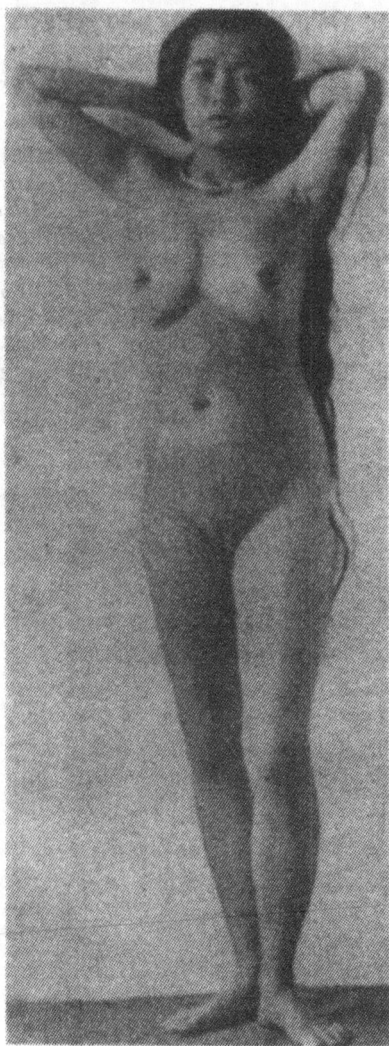

*Anamese—Fourteen Years Old*

Sterility seems worse for women in the orient than impotence for men. It was considered among the Hebrews and other peoples of ancient times as dishonorable; but the mother of many children was in an envious position. When Rachel finally conceived and gave birth to a son, she said: "God has taken away my shame." In the first Book of Moses XXX, 14-23, and in the Song of Songs, VII, 12; just as in other passages in the Old Testament, "tomatoes" are mentioned as remedies against sterility. Hamilton deems it "the fruit of *Mandragora officinalis*, a plant belonging to the solanaceous, also at home in South Europe, whose root was used as a means for charming and as an amulet." I have already discussed Mandragora in detail in an earlier chapter. The passage in the Bible which relates particularly to tomatoes runs: "And Reuben went in the days of wheat harvest, and found mandrakes in the field, and brought them unto his mother Leah. Then Rachel said to Leah, Give me, I pray thee, of thy son's mandrakes. And she said unto her, Is it a small matter that thou hast taken my husband? and wouldst thou take away my son's mandrakes also? And Rachel said, Therefore he shall lie with thee tonight for thy son's mandrakes. And God remembered Rachel, and God hearkened to her, and opened her womb. And she conceived and bare a son; and said, God hath taken away my reproach." For similar reasons Rachel stole the Theraphim images), as is recorded in the first Book of Moses XXXI, 34-45, when she left the house of her father, for at that time she had but one son, and she hoped to have more sons through the influence of the symbols of production. And for the very same reason we find the Theraphim in the house of Michal, the daughter of Saul, who was barren and had never given birth in her whole life; it is so related in the first Book of Samuel XIX, 13-16; and in Book 2, VI, 23.

In Judges XIII, the angel of Jehovah appears and says to the mother of Samson: "Behold now, thou art barren, and bearest not; but thou shalt conceive, and bear a son. Now, therefore, beware, I pray thee, and drink not wine nor strong drink, and eat not any unclean thing." And the woman bore a son and called him Samson. Now the Jewish bride knows an easier means of becoming fertile: at the wedding she must simply jump over a silver bowl three times, on which lie two living fish decorated with gold and silver leaf; meanwhile all guests cry out: *"Peru urwu! Be fruitful and multiply!"* and conception cannot fail.

If the newly married Jewess in Syria does not give birth precisely 9 months after the wedding, then an evil witch who lays traps for the women is at play. One must therefore lead the woman under the belly of a pregnant mare, for the latter also does not bring her foal into the world in 9 months, but in 11.

All other oriental peoples, just as the Hebrews of ancient times and nowadays, consider barrenness, Turkish: *haselsezlik;* Arabic: *aher, aker, akym;* Persian: *hamelbend;* Hindoo: *sen,* as the worst evil which can afflict a woman in this world. If a Mohammedan woman is sterile or insane, her husband is empowered by law to demand a divorce. The Mohammedan women of Bagdad is relegated to the position of a servant if she gives birth to no children. In the Albanian language child-lessness is called: *renje dallje,* namely: rootless.

In order to avoid the evil and shame of barrenness, they employ all possible preventative measures, they use all kinds of internal and external medicants, and they seek the shelter and help of female soothsayers and wise women. They begin early as maidens, as brides, and at the engagement and then during marriage to conform to numerous requirements to become fertile and also to bring only boys into the world.

It is said in the Koran, II: "Doth any of you desire to have a garden of palm trees and vines, through which rivers flow, wherein ye may have all kinds of fruit, and that he may attain to old age, and have a weak offspring?"

324

Mohammed sentenced anyone, who through any kind of machinations caused the sterility of a woman, to death; so also for anyone who causes a severe wound in the womb of a woman; finally, also, for one who injures a pregnant woman so that she dies before delivery or the newborn child dies soon after birth as a result of that injury.

When Mohammed's sons were all dead, Ebn Waijel called him jokingly, *al chautsar*, the childless. Therefore, the 108th chapter returns this joke with interest: "Verily he who hateth thee (the Prophet) shall be childless."

The history of oriental folk constantly relates astonishing cases of fertility: It is reported that Krischna is said to have had 161,000 sons. The Persian king Feth-Ali Schah had over a hundred wives, and since all gave him children, the number of his male descendants grew during a period of about 80 years to over 5000. He therefore acquired the nickname *Adam e ssani*, Adam the second.

When the Osman Sultan, Murad III, was 50 years old he had 102 children. Of these, twenty-seven daughters and twenty sons survived their father; nineteen sons remained alive only until the burial of their father and, according to the governmental law of fratricide, twenty-four hours later theirs followed.

Sultan Achmed III was distinguished for a fortunate fruitfulness. In the first ten years of his reign he became father of twenty-four sons and daughters.

Something noteworthy arose in the year 1595. The Grand vizier Ferhad issues a general order to the troops in which it was said: "Do you not know that those of you who do not obey your superiors are unbelievers and your wives become barren?" The troops at whom this word was aimed went to the Mufti to complain about this and to invoke an edict against the Grandvizier. "Brothers," said the Mufti, "if the Grandvizier has really said this it will do you no harm, you are

325

therefore neither unbelievers nor are your wives barren; go in peace."—"His Highness, the Mufti, gives no edict without money," sneered the aroused Sipahis, and they scattered this among the malcontents, spreading the spirit of rebellion. On the following day 48 million aspers in gold and silver were demanded from the treasury as payment for the soldiers and an increase in salary for the *sipahis*. The historian Selaniki, as overseer of the payments to the soldiers, prepared the shipment of booty, but the *sipahis* did not touch this, they desired the head of Ferhad who cursed them as unbelievers and their wives as barren; in vain did the Kadiaskere and the Mufti try to appease them; they met them with insults, the viziers with a rain of stones.

Sultan Murad III humored his enjoyment of the harem so excessively that the number of his favorites who had given birth to boys increased to forty, the number of children to over a hundred, and the number of slaves to half a thousand, and the price of the latter soon jumped in Constantinople a hundredfold. Finally, Murad III's power lagged behind his lust, which was ascribed to the magic knots of the Venetian Baffo, the jealous consort of Sultan Murad; and Jewesses and slaves who were said to have been employed for such enervating tricks of witchcraft were tortured by the eunuchs, some were thrown into the water and many were exiled to Rhodus and other islands. Suspicion of engaging in the use of magic knots led to frequent drownings of slaves who were denounced as witches.

Since barrenness is such a great misfortune for Moslem women, Omer Haleby advised them: "If the misfortune has befallen you, if the angel of sterility has established himself in your womb, if the time, the existence, and the power of this misfortune has become constant without any doubt, then, O women, choose one of your young and beautiful slaves to occupy your bed with your husband. When this slave has become a mother, adopt the child as your own, and worry over him as if he came from your own womb. In this manner, a true Moslem woman becomes worthy of the acts of desire of her husband, and preserves the highest conduct of the house, and the women, your friends and comrades, will not be able to point a finger at you and say: Look, she is unfruitful!" But this can not always be made clear to the women, particularly subdued, dutiful Moslem women cannot reconcile themselves to this idea, and they seek means rather to make themselves fruitful.

Superstition here finds a fertile field for play. There prevails among almost all Moslems and Christians in Turkey the notion that on the wedding night the ribbons of the underclothes of the young people must be braided with twigs of ivy, so that the marriage shall not remain childless. When the Christian bride in Bosnia dresses herself for the procession to the ceremony, she is careful to place her clothes on a sour cabbage barrel; otherwise, as many hoops as are on the barrel, so many years will she remain childless. The Serbian bride unties all the knots in her clothing before the procession to the church for the ceremony, so that she may conceive easily and give birth to good children. Among the other southern Slavs the bride must also see that her bridal train at the ceremony has no knots, lest she remain childless. The latter can also be wished upon her by enemies and rivals: If, for example, in the neighborhood of Elbassan in Albania, a Christian widower does not mourn once a year for his recently deceased wife, and marries another very soon, then the relatives of the first wife go to her grave and pour water thereon: this makes the second wife barren.

In Syria a barren woman is advised to pass under the belly of an elephant, or to stand under a hanged person who is still choking—two methods which can be considered effective because they cannot, as a rule, be done. In order to assure a young woman of many children, they advise these practices in Syria: When the bride reaches the door of the house of her bridegroom, she fastens a piece of sour dough over the entrance and steps on a pomegranate on the threshhold. The newly married maiden must be led to the chamber of her husband only by a married woman who has children, particularly boys, so that the young wife may become a mother just as she who leads her. The pomegranate also plays a part among the Latin Christians in Sidon. At the wedding, when the bride reaches the door of her new home, she must place over the entrance a handful of dough and a pomegranate, the first as a kind of life giving branch, the other as the holy symbol of fertility.

About an hour from the village of Radschar on the southern branch of Hermon, two great trees stand close together, which are called by the inhabitants of Schadscharat el Aschara, trees of Aschara, that is, trees of that Semitic goddess, the companion of Baal. The inhabitants of Radschar say: These trees belong to the great woman, Lis Sitt el Kebiri. One finds this Sitt el Kebiri again all over in Lebanon. It is not surprising that ancient religion is to be understood as synonymous with this great woman. One finds a group of similar trees in the neighborhood of the Venus temple at the village Afka, ruined at the command of the emperor Constantine. The trees are honored by Christians as well as Moslems. They hang their twigs on kerchiefs and lapels, signifying fertility. These are the remains of the ancient service of the female goddess, who was here worshiped beside Baal under different names; the Phoenicians called her: Astarte, Baalat, Baalkis; in southern Caanan she was called: Aschera; now the Syrian women honor her as Aschara.

The childless Bosnian woman seeks a leaf which is called *apijun* in the country, cuts the roots small, and lets it sour in a water which is called *voda omaja*, mill grist, for it is obtained from this. She drinks this medicine. She then winds her bridal belt about a freshly grafted fruit tree, and if the grafted shoot flourishes, she will also attain that happy position for which she strives. If a woman has as yet had no child in the twelfth year of her marriage, then according to Bosnian superstition, this charm will help her: A pregnant woman must look for a stone which has accidentally remained on a pear tree, *kruschka jagodnjatscha*, when someone was throwing down the fruit with stones. If she finds such a stone, she must shake the tree, but be careful to catch the stone with her hands so that it should not touch the ground. She carries the treasure in the left pocket of her frock, against her abdomen, pours a pail of water over the stone, and goes home. She then takes fresh grass, and makes this blessing over the pail: "This one and that one shall attain a desired position!" She thereupon offers the water to the barren woman to drink, and takes possession of her wedding clothes which she has not worn for such a long time, and she keeps it until the true owner begins to feel that she has become a mother, that she is nourishing a child in her body. The helping friend must take nothing from the other except the bridal clothes which she receives merely as a loan, not even a bite of bread; else her charm is ineffective.

In Persia a pilgrimage to Mecca is considered a tried means against barrenness of women. In order to assure fruitfulness in marriage, Persian maidens sit on the shaft of a horse-driven paper mill and let themselves be drawn twice around the hall. If a woman is smeared with pig's fat without her knowledge, it is believed in Persia that she must become sterile.

When I made a journey to Jerusalem, a Greek woman asked me to bring her some Jordan water; the Levantines drink this in order to relieve themselves of barrenness. In Egypt the women drink Nile water for this purpose. Among the Jews in Palestine, childless women drink water in which moss from the ruins of the temple wall has been cooked.

If talismans and superstitious means are of no help, if the

inspiration of the priest, the reading of certain passages from the Koran, or from the New or Old Testament are of no avail, if even pilgrimages to sacred places are fruitless, then they try all kinds of external and internal home remedies. Women have their barren nether abdomen region and their thighs gently massaged and rubbed with oil; they spray softening liquids in the genitals; or a woman is placed in baths which are impregnated with aromatic substances; or they place in the female parts shoots, tampons, of onions, viola, and mastix saturated with wine, or pessaries made out of carnations, cinnamon, bezoar, amber, and musk. Sad results follow unreasonable treatment, at times chronic inflammation of the womb and other severe women's troubles, particularly hysteria.

CHAPTER TWENTY-FOUR

# ABORTIONS

*Ancient Hebrew—Constantinople methods of preventing conception—The
simple method of the Serbians—Methods of checking past conception—
Bosnian abortives—The Hodscha-doctor and the bird-amulet—Abortions in
Persia—Self-help—Public institutions for criminal abortions in Constantinople—A statistic—Causes of forced abortions—The Moslem law and abor
tions—Complaints, imprecations, and warnings of Omer Haleby.*

*Syrian Girls—Fifteen Years Old*

It is remarkable that in spite of the passion for children, in spite of the desire for fertility, the prevention of conception and the disposition of its fruits is scarcely as prevalent anywhere as in the Orient.

Although childbirth was desirable among the Hebrews, they knew almost all possible means of preventing unwanted consequences. In the first Book of Moses, XXXVIII, 8, the following is related as the oldest contraceptive method: ". . . And Onan knew that the seed should not be his; and it came to pass, when he went in unto his brother's wife, that he spilled it on the ground, lest he should give seed to his brother."

In order to avoid fertilization, the following method is today employed in Constantinople, according to Rigler: the woman wears inside of herself a mushroom dipped in lemonade before the act; she then replaces it with a paste of aloe, *ruta graveolens* and *gummi,* or rubs herself with tobacco dust.

If a Serbian woman wishes to remain childless for the first year of her marriage, she can see to this as early as the engagement. Just before the ceremonial procession, she takes a curtain lock, unlocks it, places the key in one end of the room and the lock in the other, walks through between the key and the lock once and then back, and then locking the lock with the key she says: "*Kad ja ovaj katanaz otvorila onda i dete pon-illa,* I shall conceive a child when I open this lock again!" So she can now do as she pleases.

In Constantinople, in order to check conception which has already occurred, they turn, says Rigler, to several brutal methods: In the first months of pregnancy the woman drives a tobacco or olive stem into her uterus, in later months they are not afraid to puncture the ovaries and meanwhile she employs aloe, crocus and concentrated lemonade. The most certain effect is expected of the following internal medicine: One is helped by *tincture of hellebori nigri Dr. VI* with *tincture of opii crocata Dr. II* in doses of twenty drops daily; at the same time one must wash with thinned sulphuric acid, aloe, myrrh, and crocus together with prepared elexir and *porpretatis paracelsi;* finally, one must use sabina- and aloe-powder for massaging and spraying.

A Bosnian and Slavic method of performing an abortion, "*da dete u sebi otruje, da pobazi,* to poison the child in the body," is the following, related by Krauss: The peasant woman takes ¼ oka, that is somewhat more than ½ kilo *rubia tinctorum Linn,* and powders the stuff, boils it early in the morning and drinks the brew as hot as possible on an empty stomach. She repeats this several days in succession. Then at the earliest possible moment she brings a dead child into the world. Often, however, this cure also costs the life of the mother.

Another method employed by both the Bosnian and Slavic peasant women: They take hen-bane root, *hysciamus Linn.,* or in the popular tongue: *koren od bune,* also a corymb like a cluster of grapes, and finally, *datura strammonium Linn.,* or Slavic: *Sjemena ot tabule,* and then grind it all into a powder. They pour it into a drink and drink it; it is, as the women say, a terrible drink, as a result of which one may rupture the liver.

They often permit an abortion, Turkish: *tschodschuk, duschurmek;* Arabic: *mosket el olat;* Persian: *bescheh richten;* Hindoo: *noksan,* if they believe that the pregnant woman will have difficulty in giving birth. Among the Mohammedan women, there usually appears then, as Rigler relates, the *hodscha* doctor with an amulet upon which is pictured a bird with a large beak, and in a monotonous manner in various languages he recites his hocuspocus. The Moslems believe that the fruit of the body is in the same position as a bird which flies away at the birth of the child. The *hodscha* believes he is able to entice the bird with the unique amulet so that he can rupture the ovary prematurely.

In Persia, if an unmarried maiden, a widow, or a divorcee is said to have given birth, then she is certain of death. According to Dr. Polak, however, such an incident is unheard of; a child born out of wedlock, *haerum zade*, never finds itself in a position of ridicule. All pregnancies out of wedlock end in abortions, for the ovary is made to burst by means of a clamp. These operations are said to be performed with particular success by midwives, at least several of these are famous for this in Teheran and are visited by many. For the most part, the thing is engaged in quite publicly, and no hindrances are placed in its way. Only occasional unfortunate creatures wish to help themselves; they start terrific hemorrhages, make snakebites on their feet, and take purgatives of *sulfas cupri, drastica*, or the sprouts of date kernels; and if all of these methods are of no avail they let their lower regions be thrashed and stepped upon. Very frequently, says Polak, when I ask such unfortunates for permission to give them an abortive method, reproaching them with my gentlest oath, they refuse, answering: "Your oath may be good for Frenchmen, but we cannot give birth without being killed together with the child."

Pitzipios Bey relates in 1858 in his book, "The Reforms of the Byzantine Empire": "In all Moslem countries there are public institutions where women can be rid of the fruit of their bodies. In Constantinople in particular one can find many such institutions which are protected by the government, or at least tolerated, and one can always see Turkish women hurrying there in droves. One of these institutions, established in great style, is in Tschubali, in the neighborhood of Phanaos. At the time of the Christian emperor of Byzantium, there was to be found here the sanctuary of children born out of wedlock. In 1852 Kostakis, a Greek, a high police official, had the manager of this abortion establishment arrested: but a still higher functionary commanded Kostakis to leave the woman alone . . ." And in 1873 the Constantinople physician, Dr. Pardo, complained: "Oblivious to all indications of the danger which the crime of abortions involves for the life of the individual, the family and the state, and in spite of the publicity given it in the Constantinople Gazette of Medicine in the Orient, in spite of all contrary attempts of earnest thinking doctors of the land, the crimes did not cease, they increased in terrible proportions. Even the remonstrances of the Imperial Society of Medicine brought no result from the government. Apparently a new era had begun for the Turks, Midhat Pascha's reforms and progressive convictions ushered in a new age. But the country's practice of abortions remained; that is a deed, a deed which the civilization of the western reader cannot grasp in all its atrocity. This criminal abortion is one of the main reasons for the incredible decrease in population, in spite of the fact that the Turks are one of the healthiest and most powerful races of mankind. An official investigation reported that at least 300 criminal abortions took place in Constantinople monthly. Of how many cases do we know nothing? What reasons drive people to these crimes? Many of these kill not only the child in the mother's body, but also the unnatural mother herself."

If out of every 94 abortions in Paris the mother succumbed in 46 cases, how much greater must the percentage sacrificed be in Constantinople where only crude and barbaric methods are employed! The Mohammedan law is free of all blame in this matter, the Koran is quite clearly in opposition to such crimes, and it inflicts a penalty upon the woman who subscribes to such practices. It should be noted, however, that the population of Constantinople is only partly Mohammedan, the other part includes more Christians of various faiths and nationalities, as well as Jews. The wickedness is to be discovered just as frequently among all. The cause of this abnormality lies in the general condition of a lack of education, a crass ignorance. There is not here the over-refinement and the cultural bravado which appear as the reasons of like crimes in that wonderful novel of Zola, "Fecondite," but on the contrary: the lack of all culture and the lowest folly. One can imagine that Moslem women attempt to conserve their figures as long as possible as a result of fear of rivals and divorce. Among other nations, however, the crime usually takes place in order to prevent the discovery of marital faithlessness.

It is unbelievable with what lightmindedness, with what ease women bring this horrible thing upon themselves. They have recourse to these fearful pits of murder with less hesitation than going to a dentist. The deal is arranged cold-bloodedly with the doctor or the midwife. In many drug stores of Stambul or Pera one often sees a fetus displayed: it signifies that there is a doctor on the premises who practices this criminal trade. When the Society of Medicine once wished to call a doctor to account for such transactions, the good man did not even attempt to lie, and instead of defending himself, he boasted of his success and placed before the honorable association of doctors his discovery with which the operation could be performed simply, quickly, and harmlessly: this newly discovered instrument was an ordinary curling iron! The habitual lack of punishment had made the criminals bold. The Society, however, once wished to do its duty energetically. It denounced the incident to the government. That was in the year 1859. In the year 1873 Sr. Pardo affirms that the very same doctor had a greater practice than ever before, and he would be flooded with patients even today if he had not finally died.

It has already been said that the Moslem law prescribes a severe penalty for the woman who does away with her fruit. Omer Haleby comments extensively on the law. He thinks that prostitution of the idol worshiping people is the underlying cause and origin of the most condemned of all crimes, an abortion by force. The Prophet has expressly forbidden abortions; since he has forbidden man to kill, he at the same time forbade the killing of humans in the body of the mother, the murder of the child. For the word child must be deemed to include the embryo which is developing within the body of the mother.

337

The monstrous act of involuntary abortion is just like the cold premeditated murder of the angel which lives at the bottom of the womb and cries out at the moment of the intermingling of seed: "A drop, O master! a fruit!" Several scholars, continues Omer Haleby, consider the abortion rather as insanity than as a crime; but they had apparently forgotten that saying of the Prophet which Asmah, the daughter of Jesid, so often repeated: "Do not kill your children secretly in a manner which you cannot understand" . . . "Leave therefore," cries out Omer Haleby, "this practice of abortions to the descendants of the Romans, the heathens or the Christians!" One must unfortunately concede that there were many Moslem women who committed the crime for the sake of retaining "their breasts in a state of youthful hardness and original beauty" . . . "But do you forget that at the same time they were bringing about their own death, or at least severe disturbances of their organisms? That sterility is the mildest result of this crime? Others follow the bad advice of their lovers and husbands; in this case they need not worry about the judgment of the world, but can they avoid the judgment of God? . . . One once said: the performance of an abortion is less to be punished if it occurs in the first months of pregnancy. That is an enormous sophistry, for the incontestable word of the Prophet shows that there are in the drops of sperms themselves, which flows into the ovary after menstruation, life and organic intelligence; the ovum immediately becomes an embryo. . . . And has not the Prophet said, for the purpose of characterizing the great act which then takes place in the womb as the highest, and the crime which is committed by abortion as the lowest: "The mother who dies as a result of the pains of childbirth will be elevated to the rank of a martyr, and will effortlessly arrive in paradise"? . . . Flee, therefore, O believing women, from anything which may seduce you into committing an abortion. When one says: one of the traditions of the Prophet permits a woman to take medi-

338

cines to suppress her period; and when one says: it results from this that one may, in certain cases, bring about a premature birth through internal and external medicines, one places a false interpretation upon this tradition, an interpretation which is in direct conflict with the Koran and the laws of Islam. They place darkness in the position of light. The tradition just mentioned and the scholars of Islam who first transmitted it, really wished to say only that it was permitted for a woman voluntarily and with the consent of her husband or relatives to be given spices in order to prevent too great a flow of blood and a loss of health, as for example, through a hemorrhage."

In spite of all this, however, as I have said, the plague of criminal abortions flourished also among Moslem women; and it is contended, by Regla, that several women in the harem of the Sultan, called "the bloody midwives," are entrusted with this fearful practice.

The evil custom which is prevalent in Turkey for a woman who has given birth to two children to have recourse thereafter to abortions with the knowledge of her husband, partly to preserve her bodily beauty and partly to limit the number of her descendants, hold no sway in Persia, according to Dr. Polak; for, in the first place, it is very seldom that a Persian woman has more than two children in her life, and secondly, she takes great pride in possessing numerous descendants, who can serve her as support in her old age. If barrenness is looked upon as a misfortune by wives of all countries, it is truly the greatest misfortune in Persia; the barren one is almost always neglected by her husband, is ridiculed by the other women of the harem, and remains isolated and helpless in her old age.

# CHAPTER TWENTY-FIVE

# MIDWIVES

*Among ancient peoples—Heavenly midwives among the Chaldeans—The Goddess Mylitta—The cult of Astarte—Greek—Iranian—The moon as an assistant in birth—South Slavic birth goddesses—The Mandarin goddess Rucha—The Mother of God as an assistant in birth—The Jericho-Rose at birth—The history of midwives—Midwives among the Hebrews—Hellenish. Roman and Byzantine midwifery—Midwives in the Arabian era—Ignorance of the oriental midwives—Their bad reputation—Earlier position of birth help in Constantinople—Reforms under Sultan Abdul Medschid—The Viennese Dame Messani—Present conditions in Turkey—Names of midwives— Importance of midwives in Bagdad.*

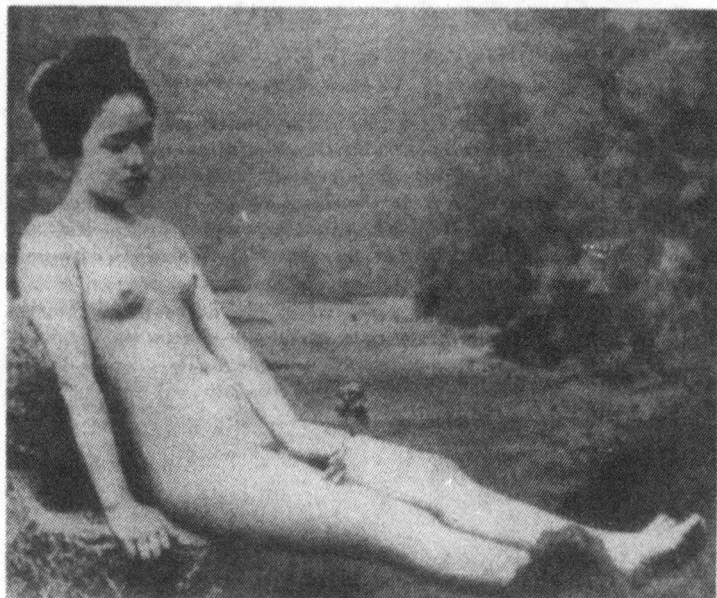

*Chosu Type Japanese*

The ancient peoples of the Orient assigned to various gods the roles of midwives. Among the Chaldeans the Goddess Thalat was the invisible assistant of those giving birth. Mylitta, the Goddess of fertility, the Assyrian-Babylonian Astarte, was simultaneously queen of the heavens and queen of the night, heavenly virgin and goddess of those who have conceived and are giving birth; religious prostitution took place in Babylon in her honor. The honoring of the Babylonian Astarte was borne from the Euphrates and the Tigris to Phoenicia, and it spread throughout all Syria; here also the cult was tied up with religious prostitution. The Phoenician Astarte, who gives birth to all, then came to the islands near Asia Minor and attained a great respect as Aphrodite. In Phrygia they honor Cybele, the allegorized earth. At the time of Solomon the cult of Aschera, which is identical with that of Astarte, was popular. The Ancient Arabs named the moon Goddess Al Jlahat of Herodot Alilath or Alytta the goddess of fertility and birth.

The idea of damp fertile fruitful earth and the fruitful and fertilizing moon was already bound up with the name of the Babylonian Astarte. In the descriptions of the Greeks this goddess is identified with their Aphrodite. The oldest goddess of birth among the Hellenes was Eileithyia, who was brought from the Hyperboreans to Delos and there served as the midwife of Leto. The representation of this goddess in the heavens was the moon, which caught the rays of the sun and fostered development and growth on earth; but the representation of this goddess on earth was the cow. Artemis was a later mythical goddess of birth in ancient Greece, while Hera was considered the goddess of marriage. Among the Iranian peoples of Asia, the ancient Persians, the Medes, and the Bactrians, the moon bore a relationship to sex in the religion of Zoroaster; it stood for birth. According to Herodot the Magyars invoke the moon as an effective power of heaven if they wish to evade interference with the normal course of birth or the effect of the spirits of

343

disease during labor. These moon goddesses, these heavenly assistants at birth, are called Anaitis, Anahita, Anaia, and Aine by the Persians, the Medes, the Cappadocians, and the Armenians. The goddess of the moon is the protector of those giving birth also among the Slavic folk.

Even today on the lower Euphrates and the Tigris the sect of Mandarins now living there honor a goddess Rucha, mother of the immense Ur, who assists women giving birth.

Among the Greek-Wallachians in Monastir the Mother of God is deemed the protector of birth. According to the opinion of Sajaktzis, she is here the successor of Hera, one of the protectors of birth among the ancients. As soon as signs of birth become evident, a little lamp is lighted before the picture of the Mother of God; it remains burning during the entire period of confinement. The midwife, the women of the family, and the neighbors wish: "Kali Eleuteria, good delivery, and may the Holy Virgin ease the birth for you!"

Besides her instruments, the midwife brings along the Jericho-Rose, which is called here, Cheri tis Panagias, hand of the Mother of God. It is a low full cabbage which was brought from the holy grave by pilgrims. The plant is so constituted that in a dried condition it rolls together into a fence-forming balloon, but after being made damp it again spreads itself out into a human hand. It is said in relation to this: it grows wherever the sacred Mary left the impression of her hand when she climbed alone in darkness to Golgotha. During the labor pains the suffering one wets her face and lips with water which has been sanctified by having Jericho-Rose dipped into it: *dia na eleutoroti m eukolia*, so that she might more easily survive the difficult hours. One finds this custom among all Greek families in the Orient. In Monastir the pregnant woman also held the Jericho-Rose in her hand, just as the women of ancient times held the sacred laurel of Apollo during delivery. In other respects the Jericho-Rose was honored in ancient times under the name of Glykiside.

The midwives among the Hebrews were a preferred class; one can see this in the 2nd Book of Moses, I, 21. The passage in the first Book of Moses, XXXV, 17, where the confinement of Rachel and the birth of Benjamin is related, can be taken as the first mention of midwives in the Holy Book. Following this comes the story of the two midwives, Sifra and Pua, of whom it is related in the 2nd Book of Moses, I, 15, how they cleverly and successfully circumvented the command of Pharaoh to kill all newborn Hebrew boys.

Freidreich believes that as early as the time of the confinement of Rachel the assistance at birth among the Hebrews had attained the level of a certain success. In any event, he adds, the rendering of assistance at birth dwindled merely to a trust in the self-help of nature, the comfort and admonitions of patience, turning to the best position for the purpose during the birth, taking the child, handling the umbilical cord, and rubbing the child with salt, as well as wrapping the child in swaddling clothes.

Ploss-Bartels, as well as Engelmann, have assembled all worthwhile knowledge on assistance at birth in ancient Hellas and Rome. We find there that the Roman and later the Byzantian midwifery developed under the influence of the Hellenes. Arabian doctors also derived a great part of their knowledge of help at birth from Greek sources. But after the fall of the Roman Empire, all knowledge and art sought a new home with the Arabs, and soon all this blossomed again among them, but midwifery remained a dead science; for the doctors did not care to have the practice requiring such important learning under their control and care. Midwifery did not lie in the hands of accomplished doctors, but was completely relinquished to midwives, who possessed a mere superficial knowledge. Doctors were called only in cases of absolute necessity. These,

345

however inexperienced in such cases, rarely brought help in these exceptional instances. With their powerful implements and instruments they had a deathly agonizing effect on the unhappy woman. If she survived her fright, she was sadly neglected or maltreated by the ineptness of the doctor, and the child rarely emerged from the body of its mother unmangled.

Hasselquist, in the previous century, has already related much of the ignorance of the oriental midwives. Titus Tobler, Robinson, Hantzscher, Quedenfeldt, and other travelers in the Orient, confirmed this judgment. Oppenheim, who lived for many years as a doctor in Asia Minor, censures not only the crass ignorance, but also the poor ethics of the midwives. In more recent times the Frenchman Eram made known his discoveries in the following sharp words: "The knowledge of these women is insufficient. Supervised midwives are found only in the cities. Most of them have a dishonorable life behind them. Besides their practice of midwifery they engage in a business of marriage brokerage. A proverb says: "Every woman who has begun with prostitution, ends up as a midwife."

Dr. Rementer Baurokordato has left us a time-honored report on the position of midwifery in Constantinople at the beginning of the nineteenth century: The midwives then constituted a separate class; their number was undetermined. They underwent no systematic training, but one passed along her knowledge to the other. Of the condition of the foetus, of the dimensions of the pelvis, particularly of anatomical-physiological facts they had either no idea at all or a false one.

Under Sultan Abdul Medschid the Viennese Dame Messani, an educated European midwife, founded a school for midwives. Since then the horrors of former times decreased, but they did not cease. To be sure, several doctors educated in the schools of Austria, Germany, France, England, and Italy attempted to establish themselves in the place of midwives, but their road was beset with difficulties.

346

Even as late as the year 1873 Dr. Pardo of Constantinople complained: "With the exception of a few righteous and truly educated women, the trade of midwives consists of disreputable ignorant women, who call themselves Mamy, or midwives, in order the better to undertake criminal abortions, and to be able to practice a business as marriage brokers. Such women stain the threshholds of respectable houses and by their mere presence dishonor the most righteous families. Those whose paths they ease in their misdeeds, they later lead on the road to crime and unhappiness and death. And all this transpires before the eyes of all people. There is no supervision. If one once transgresses a regulation of the authorities, she is no longer respected."

In many respects, therefore, the midwives of today in Turkey are on a low level. Unacquainted with the mechanism of the act of birth, they can do nothing in case of a hindrance to birth except to turn to superstitious methods and disused tortures. In many instances they call several wise women, and while these confer with one another on the proper method to accomplish their purpose, the mother and child are both lost. Only seldom do they decide to include in their intimate circle an educated graduate midwife. And in the neighborhood the midwives also enjoy an evil moral reputation. They are more concerned with building up for themselves a fertile business of making people sterile and performing abortive operations than with midwifery, and they are worthy of being placed at the side of those women whom Plinius has already described. The Thebanian Salpe and the modern Marseilles Sotira are their predecessors. There are, nevertheless, several famous rare exceptions. The midwife is called among the Turks: *Ebe Kade* or *Mamy*; among the Arabs: *Kabli, Kabla, or Gabla*, namely, she who takes, from *Kabul*, to take; she is often also called in Arabic: *Tebiba*, the female doctor; among the Persians she is called: *Kabli* or *Mamy*; among the Greeks: *Mamy, Maia,* or

347

*Agetria;* among the Greek-Wallachians: *Mamy* or *Mlampa;* among the Spaniards: *Mamy;* among the Bosnians: *Hadschika;* in Syria and Palestine: *Dye, Daye.* In general, she is designated as the wise woman, the understanding woman; wise woman—this expression has been adopted by all peoples of the earth for midwives; even the inhabitants of the Figi Islands say: *Alewa Wuku,* wise woman.

In all provinces which one can think of there are midwives: Arabians, Turks, Armenians, Greeks, Spaniards. The Persian midwives are usually widows. The Greek midwives use their own hands as instruments which they press deep into the vagina of the prospective mother. The assisting women in Palestine do likewise.

In Bagdad the Kalbi is the main personage at a birth. She is smiled at, entertained. While they bother least about the woman in labor herself, they pay all possible attentions to the midwife. As an honorarium she receives even from families in meagre circumstances at least 5, often even 10 pounds. She comes for months long, even years, to the house and exacts tribute at teething, at the first attempt to walk and the first attempt to speak of the child.

348

CHAPTER TWENTY-SIX

# CUSTOMS DURING PREGNANCY

*The growth of the fruit—The Bible and the Koran on the creation of human beings—Mosaic law for the protection of one who is pregnant—A practice of war—The killing of pregnant women—The Koran on pregnancy —Memory coins of the pregnancies of Sultanas—Pregnancy and coitus—Mohammed's advice—The diet of the Pregnant woman—The pomegranate— Albanian customs—Serbian superstitions—Mohammedan notions—Bosnian customs—Greek-Wallachian customs—The Palestinian Jews—Syrian—Pregnancy through baths—The mistake—Folk medicine.*

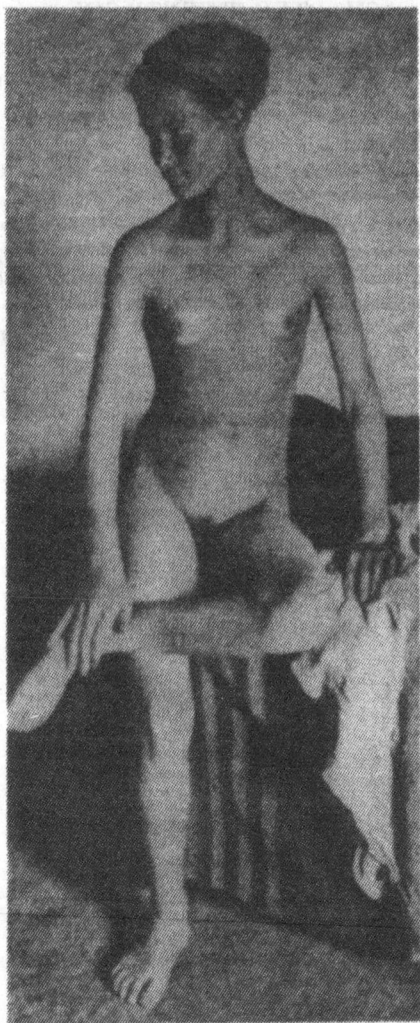

*Twelve-year-old Gypsy*

In the Old Testament the fruit or the fruit of the body is mentioned frequently, but nothing more is said of it than, "how the bones do grow in the womb of her that is with child," to use the words of Ecclesiastes, XI, 5.

In Psalms 139, it is said in verses 13-16: "For thou hast possessed my reins: thou hast covered me in my mother's womb. . . . My substance was not hid from thee, when I was made in secret, and curiously wrought in the lowest parts of the earth. Thine eyes did see my substance, yet being imperfect. . . ."

Similarly in the Book of Job, X, 8-11: "Thine hands have made me and fashioned me together round about; . . . Remember, I beseech thee, that thou hast made me as the clay; . . . Hast thou not poured me out as milk and curdled me like cheese? Thou hast clothed me with skin and flesh and hast fenced me with bones and sinews."

I show by the citation of the following passages of the Koran that Mohammed drew his picture of the creation of man only from the Old Testament, and it frequently says the same things.

Chapter IV, 95: "See, Allah lets the corn shoot up and the date kernel; he creates the living from the dead and the dead from the living."

The Moslems are always reminded that Allah created human beings and divided them into sexes.

Chapter 42, Verse 3: ". . . and among them were created man and woman . . ."

Chapter 78, Verse 8: ". . . and created you in pairs . . ."

XVI, 1: "God hath ordained you wives among yourselves, and of your wives hath granted you children and grandchildren."

IV, 1: "O man, fear your Lord who hath created you out of one man, and out of him created his wife, and from them two hath multiplied many men and women . . ."

Chapter 49, Verse 13: "O men, verily we have created you

351

of a male and a female; and we have distributed you into nations and tribes . . ."

All this concerns itself with the creation of the first human pair. But what does the Koran know of the manner in which man is now created, of the development of the foetus? No more than the Bible.

Chapter XIII, Verse 9, says: "God knoweth what every woman beareth in her womb, and what the wombs want or exceed of their due time, or number of young."

LIII, 33: ". . . He well knew you when he produced you out of the earth, and when ye were embryos in your mothers' wombs."

The 76th chapter of the Koran is entitled "Man". It is said here in the first and second verses: "Did not there pass over man a long space of time; during which he was a thing not worthy of remembrance?—namely, since his conception in his mother's body.

VI, 98: "It is he who hath produced you from one soul; and hath provided for you a sure receptacle and repository," in the womb of the mother.

XXXIX, 8: "He created you of one man, and afterwards out of him made his wife: . . . He formeth you in the wombs of your mothers, by several gradual formations, within three veils of darkness." Here the descriptions were more accurate and the body, womb, and placenta were indicated.

Now one knows where the fruit is found until it sees the light of day. But from what is the fruit derived? For this purpose the drops of seed are usually mentioned directly.

Chapter XXXVI, 77: "Doth not man know that we have created him of seed?"

In the XXXVth chapter, verse 12, however, the seed is represented as the second cause of conception. It is said here: "God created you first of the dust, and afterward of seed; and he hath made you man and wife."

352

Or Chapter XVIII, Verse 35: ". . . Dost thou not believe in Him who created thee of the dust, and afterward of seed; and then fashioned thee into a perfect man?"

LVI, 58-59: ". . . The seed which ye emit, do ye create the same, or are we the creators thereof?"

XVI, 4: "He hath created men of seed . . ."

LII, 45-47: ". . .. and he putteth to death, and giveth life: and that he createth the two sexes, the male and the female, of seed when it is emitted."

The 76th chapter mentions intercourse: "Verily we have created men of the mingled seed of both sexes . . ."

In another passage congealed blood is mentioned instead of seed.

XCVI, 1-2: ". . . who hath created man of congealed blood."

In another passage it is compared as in the Old Testament with the earth.

LV, 13: "He created men of dried clay like an earthen vessel."

XV, 28-29: "And remember when the Lord said unto the angels: Verily, I am about to create man of dried clay, of black mud, wrought into shape."

XV, 26: "We created man of dried clay, of black mud formed into shape."

Wherefrom comes the creating seed? The 88th chapter answers this in verses 5 and 6: "He is created of seed poured forth, issuing from the loins and the breastbones."

Chapter XXII: "O men, . . . consider that we first created you of the dust of the ground; afterwards, of seed; afterwards, of a little coagulated blood; afterwards, of a piece of flesh perfectly formed in part, and in part imperfectly formed . . . and we caused that which we please to rest in the wombs, until the appointed time of delivery."

XXIII: "We formerly created man in a finer sort of clay;

afterwards we placed him in the form of seed in a sure receptacle; afterwards we made the seed coagulated blood; and we formed the coagulated blood into a piece of flesh; then we formed the piece of flesh into bones; and we clothed these bones with flesh; then we produced the same by another creation"—namely, a man who consists of body and soul.

Subsequent passages of the Koran describe the giving of a soul and life to man through God's will and power:

XV, 29: ". . . when, therefore, I shall have completely formed him, and shall have breathed my spirit into him . . ."

XXXII, 5-8: "This is he who knows the present and the future; the mighty and the merciful. It is he who hath made everything which he hath created exceeding good; and first created man of clay, and afterwards made his posterity of an extract of despicable water; and then formed him into proper shape, and breathed of his spirit into him; and hath given you the senses of hearing and seeing, and hearts to understand.'

LXXXIII, 7-8: "He who has created you, breathed his spirit into you and formed you in the shape which most pleased him . . ."

LXIV, 2-3: "It is he who hath created you . . . and he hath fashioned you and given you beautiful forms."

XVI, 80: "God hath brought you forth from the wombs of your mothers; ye knew nothing, and he gave you the senses of hearing and seeing, and understandings . . ."

LXVII, 23: "It is he who brings, and endowed you with hearing, and sight, and understanding; . . ."

XC, 8-9: "Have we not made him two eyes, and a tongue, and two lips . . ."

LXXVI, 28: "We have created them and strengthened their joints; and when we please, we will substitute others like unto them, in their stead."

In the 2nd Book of Moses, XXI, 22-23, it is decreed for the protection of those who are with child: "If men strive, and hurt a woman with child, so that her fruit depart from her, and yet no mischief follow: he shall be surely punished according as the woman's husband will lay upon him; and he shall pay as the judges determine. And if any mischief follow, then thou shalt give life for life, eye for eye . . ."

In the Old Testament, Amos I, 13, 2nd Book of Kings, VIII, 12, Hosea XIV, 1, there are mentioned the gruesome practices of war, by which pregnant women were attacked.

A fearful superstition prevails even today among Bosnian thieves and robbers. They used to kill a woman in the seventh month of pregnancy, cut her open, and take the child from her womb, in order to cut in into long narrow strips. These were dried and used as candles when they wished to plunder a house. Then, so they believed, no home owner could awaken in that house where the thieves burnt such lights.

The Koran contains the following passages relative to pregnant women and pregnancy:

XIII, 9: "God knoweth what every female beareth in he womb; and what the wombs want or exceed . . ."

VII, 189-190: "It is he who hath created you from one person, and out of him produced his wife, that he might dwell with her; and when he had known her, she carried a light burden for a time, wherefore she walked easily therewith. But when it became more heavy, she called upon God their Lord, saying: If thou give us a child rightly shaped, we will surely be thankful."

The Koran commands in the 65th chapter that, if one divorces a wife, while she is in a state of pregnancy, one must provide for her that which is necessary until she is rid of her burden. "But as to those who are pregnant, their term shall be, until they be delivered of their burden."

The requirement of suspension of intercourse during pregnancy is quite firmly intrenched in the Orient. The Talmud had already said: "He who engages in intercourse after the

90th day after the beginning of pregnancy commits the same transgression as if he had disposed of a human life." Among the Javanese, who are known for the most part to be Moslems, as soon as the wife becomes pregnant, the marital right is suspended, and continence is practiced with religious care. Among the Persians, intercourse must cease after four months and ten days; coitus during this time is considered a capital crime, for they believe that the fruit of love is injured thereby.

Abu Naim reiterates the following words of the Prophet: "Give your pregnant women *olibanum* to eat; if the woman bears a male child in her body, that child will have a pure body; if the woman will give birth to a maiden, she' will have a round sensual backbone."

As in Europe, the opinion is prevalent in the entire Orient that a pregnant woman must eat everything which her heart desires. In many sections of Turkey she must not deny herself particularly those spices which appeal to her sense of smell. If she smells such spices and does not eat them immediately, there is danger that she may lose her child before its birth. The thought of the Syrians is not so horrible. If a pregnant woman among them does not eat everything which her heart desires, the child is not ruined as a result of this. It is merely born with a birthmark which resembles that spice of which the mother deprived herself during pregnancy.

Among nations of the past as well as many nations of the present, and also in the neighborhood of North Albania, the pomegranate is a symbol of fertility. But, if a woman who has eaten thereof in order to become fertile has really become pregnant, then she must no longer enjoy the pomegranate during the entire period of pregnancy. Among the ancient Greeks as well as among the North Albanians the pomegranate is not merely associated with sex and conception, but also with the fear of destruction and death. In the North Albanian region a pregnant woman must also observe the following: she must

356

bleach her hair at most three times during the entire period of pregnancy; and besides the pomegranates she must eat no snails.

According to Serbian superstition the pregnant woman must not kiss the cross, otherwise the child will be an epileptic; she must not step over a pitchfork, otherwise the child will be crippled; she must not eat hare meat, otherwise the child will squint; she must not step into the blood of a slaughtered pig, otherwise the child will have red specks in its face; she must not eat fish, otherwise the child will be dumb; she must not kiss a strange child, otherwise she will bring about an over-foetation; she must not permit a bad tooth to be pulled, otherwise the child will die immediately; and finally, she must be careful that no one makes a cut on the threshhold of her house, otherwise the child will come into the world with a harelip.

Mohammedan notions in Bosnia: If a pregnant woman meets a snake or a fox, her child will have happiness in life; if she meets a hare, it will degenerate morally and do evil to its neighbors. In order to prevent a still-birth, the Moslem woman in Bosnia takes a nail out of a horseshoe which had been taken off a dead horse. A smith fashions a ring out of this nail in the middle of the night, and the woman wears this until after the delivery. She then places the ring under the head of the new born child. In Bosnia a pregnant woman must not drink cold water, for that facilitates a miscarriage. If a Bosnian, Herzegowiner, or Serbian woman sees a grazing mare during her pregnancy, she fears that she may be pregnant for 11 months like a mare, and she leads a male foal to her and gives it a taste of salt over the threshhold of her house.

The Greek-Wallach woman in Monastir, as Dr. Sajaktzis relates, from the very first moment that she feels herself about to become a mother, observes an unceasing round of superstitious customs, some very painful, in order to provide a long life for her child. She neglects no dogma of religion, she unin-

357

terruptedly does good deeds, she wears all talismans which she deems useful, she wanders about the church with a sanctified candle, and lights a candle before the picture of the Mother of God, and offers on the altar a shirt, stockings, white linen, little pictures and figures, and—if she is well to do—she has the picture of the Mother of God gilded in whole or in part.

Among the Jews in Palestine, pregnant women measure the temple walls with a silk thread and then wind the thread around their hips; this protects them against damage to the being in their body. A similar purpose is fulfilled by a girdle which had been wound around a Torah in the synagogue. Other women hang about their neck a lock whose key has been thrown away.

Among the Christians in Syria a pregnant woman cannot be a godmother, for in such case a miscarriage or the death of the child is to be feared. If a fruit tree bears no fruit, Syrian superstition merely requires that a pregnant woman fasten a pebble to a branch of the barren tree, and the tree will bear fruit; besides making the tree fruitful, the woman brings about her own fruitfulness and this experiment prevents a miscarriage, so there can be found no woman who has not tried the effect of this method.

It is quite generally considered possible for a woman to become pregnant by bathing in water in which a man had been in shortly theretofore. That one believes in the possibility of this so-called accident in the entire Orient is frequently related. Professor Ebstein finds the first report of the accident in a passage in the first Book of Moses, XXX, 38: "And he set the rods which he had spilled before the flocks in the gutters and in the watering troughs when the flocks came to drink, that they should conceive when they came to drink. And the flocks conceived before the rods, and brought forth cattle ring-streaked, speckled, and spotted. "The work of Gerh. v. Welsen-

358

burg, "Mistakes of Women in the Past and Present," contains interesting reports on this remarkable theme.

According to superstitious customs there are now, more than ever, a number of folk remedies to relate: At the flow of blood during pregnancy one sticks a peeled lemon covered with a powder of burnt coffee into the suffering part. Internally the pregnant woman takes a mixture of cooked lemon peel with aloe, sweetened with white sugar. Among the Turks the body of the mother is bound tightly in the fifth or sixth month of pregnancy; this pressure on the body of the mother is maintained until the close of the bearing period, so that the child should not grow too large. In Smyrna and in other regions, blood letting of the pregnant woman is considered a preventative against lockjaw in the child.

If towards the end of pregnancy the womb sinks, then, in Constantinople and in other regions of Turkey, women in similar circumstances seize the pregnant woman by the ankles, lift her high, and shake her until they believe the womb has again returned to the proper position.

In conclusion, a curiosity: Bosnian women say of the womb, as Milena Mrazovic has related in the Proceedings in Ethnology 1896, 279-284, answer 51, it is a living being who drops out at birth and then returns to its normal position.

CHAPTER TWENTY-SEVEN

# DELIVERY

*Birth with pains!—Biblical references—Easy and difficult births—Hebrew women—Bosnian—Albanian—Montenegrin—Greek—Turkish, Persian, Kurdin, and Arabian—Opinions of Constantinople midwives—Concealment of the act of birth from men and strangers—Bosnian Graco-Wallavian customs—Greek—The hand of the Holy Virgin—Superstitious methods of easing birth—Serbian and Bosnian—Amulets—Turkish—Earth—Effective water —Crumbs from the Sultans' table—Syrian—Armenian—Persian—Enticing the child with sweets and play-things—Good deeds among the Spaniards— Folk remedies against weak pains—Old-Arabian methods—The burning of blood—Shaking the one giving birth—Massages—Sitting on stones—The position of the patient—Crouching—From the experience of my friend, Dr. Beck—In the lap of the midwife—The birth stool—Operations—Caesarian operations—What Dr. Gjòrjewitsch told me—A Turkish custom—A horrible practice of Jews from Beyruth—After the birth—The afterbirth—The naval cord.*

361

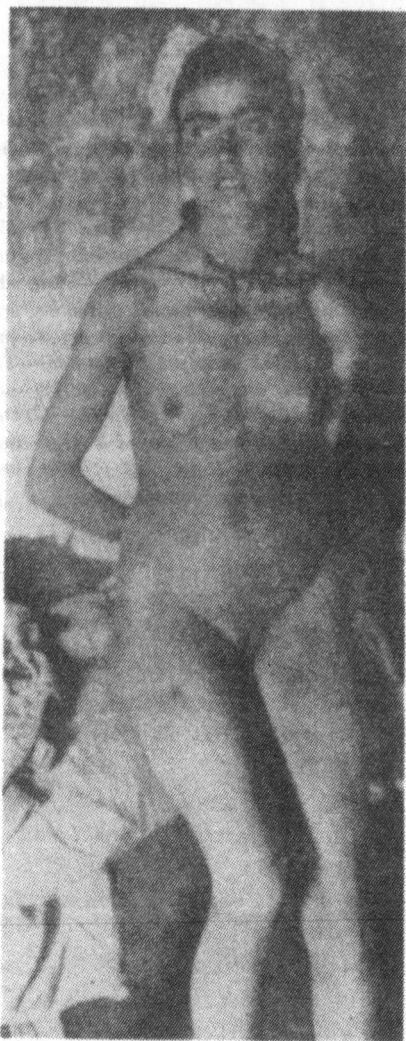

*Sixteen-year-old Gypsy*

In the first Book of Moses III, 16, it is said: ". . . I will greatly multiply thy sorrow and thy conception; in sorrow thou shalt bring forth children; . . ." Other passages describe this kind of pain. Psalm, 48, 6: "Fear took hold of them there, and pain, as of a woman in travail." Jeremiah VI, 24: ". . . our hands wax feeble: anguish hath taken hold of us, and pain, as of a woman in travail." Isaiah XIII, 8, says: ". . . pangs and sorrows shall take hold of them; they shall be in pain as a woman that travaileth. . . ." Jeremiah IV, 31, cries out: "For I have heard a voice as of a woman in travail, and the anguish as of her that bringeth forth her first child." In Hosea, XIII, 13, the difficulties which hinder the normal course are specified: "The sorrows of a travailing woman shall come upon him: he is an unwise son; for he should not stay long in the place of the breaking forth of children." In Isaiah XXXVII, 3, it is said: ". . . for the children are come to the birth, and there is not strength to bring forth." In such case they lose faith in the help of God, they lose faith in Jehovah who comforts them in Isaiah LXVI, 9: "Shall I bring to the birth, and not cause to bring forth?"

Hebrew women generally give birth easily. The Egyptian midwives said to Pharaoh: "The Hebrew women are not like the Egyptian, but powerful." They arrived at this conclusion from the fact that Hebrew women gave birth before the mid-wives had even come.

In Bosnia delivery is in general light. The help at birth consists there, as Milena Mrazovic relates, frequently merely in bringing the laboring woman to the house of labor. There she takes a mixture of oil and brandy as an internal medicine to ease the delivery.

Albanian women do not let pregnancy disturb them in their usual work, and they frequently deliver while at their work in the field. They then pack the new born child into their breast covering and hurry home in order to lie in bed, not because of comfort, but because of custom and because of a fear of being bewitched.

The Montenegrins also frequently deliver in the field or the forest, far from all help. As soon as they have come to themselves a little, they wrap the child in an apron or a head cloth. At the next well she draws water to wash the new born child. She then wanders home and lies in bed in order to adhere to the custom, rather than because of her real need of rest.

The Greek women in general have no long drawn out pains at childbirth.

Rigler reports from many experiences that Armenian and Turkish women in Constantinople frequently suffer from irregular births. In general, and in particular among the lower classes, birth seldom encounters any great obstacles, for the women are accustomed from childhood to sit on their knees or to crouch with knees outspread; because of their clothes and frequent baths.

In his narration of his journey to Palestine, Hasselquist remarked half a century ago: "The women here give birth easily, and one seldom hears of a woman who has had a difficult birth, and very rarely of one who has lost her life thereby. And this is particularly so of Turkish women." And Oppenheim, who studied the sanitary conditions in European and Asiatic Turkey in the first third of the nineteenth century, confirms the report of Hasselquist in the following words: "The confinements of women are not bound up with difficulties and complications as frequently as in civilized Europe. They take place so easily that the women are often surprised by them even before the midwife arrives." Morir says likewise of the Persians: "They are often already delivered before the midwife arrives, and among the lower classes they take care of it themselves." Chardin remarked: "The act of birth is a normal one among the Persians, because the body is not confined by corsets and the clothes are tied, not around the stomachs, but from the hip bones." Just as easily do the women of Kurdin give birth. One seldom hears an Arabian woman cry out.

The Constantinople midwives determine from the time which passes during the birth whether it is to be considered as regular or irregular; the quicker it passes, the better. They demand that the woman in labor bear down harder and harder. As an example of the ease with which births take place I need but mention the saying of a famous midwife to a parturient whose womb had just begun to open after three hours of pain: "Bear down, bear down a little! Has the child become a stone? By God, I have never in my life yet seen a birth take so long!"

Among Bosnian families the act of birth is kept as secret from the men of the house as possible. This desire prevails particularly in the country. When the woman begins to feel the pains, she banishes the men of all degrees of relationship.

The customs of the Graco-Wallavians in Monastir demand similar secrecy. Dr. George Sajaktzis has reported these customs of his homeland in his article already mentioned by me in the Chronicles of the Society of Folk-lore—IV. 1896, 134-148: As soon as the first signs of birth appear, a little lamp is lit before a picture of Mary and the midwife is secretly called. The secrecy, which is particularly for the benefit of the inhabitants of the house, is invoked so that the evil spirits may discover nothing and so that they may not interfere with the progress of the birth. The midwife likewise maintains silence, for she does not advise even her own family where she has been called. But if they believe that in spite of all precautions people who are not very familiar with the process have accidentally become aware of the impending delivery, they seek them out. If it is a woman, they lead her to the pregnant one and have her spray the pregnant woman with water which she has taken into her mouth. If it is a man whom one cannot yet lead to the laboring woman, they secretly take his shoe, pour some water into it, and let the water drip on her lips and breasts; if they cannot find one of his shoes, they take some possession of his, and leave it secretly with the laboring woman, as an assurance against evil.

When a birth is pending in a Greek house, the midwife opens all the locks, doors, chests, and coffers, for only then can the birth be an easy one. Whoever is in the room of the laboring woman must not leave until the excitement is over; also, no one from the outside is permitted into the room in the meantime. If the birth is difficult, the husband strikes his wife in the back with a shoe and says: "I permit you to be as you were." The Serbian husband also says these same words for the same purpose. The Greek woman also deems it useful, in order to make the birth easier, to strew certain plants in the rooms of the house; because of their handlike shape these plants are called: *cheri panagias,* the hand of the holy virgin. They also consider it necessary to have lamentations in the neighborhood of the laboring woman.

Among the Greeks the head of a hen is cut off at the moment that the child begins to come out of the body of the mother. The German Consul Roser, who made known this remarkable thing, thought that perhaps they considered this as an offer to Aeskulapius, to whom the hen was sacred.

When a Serbian woman feels her difficult hours approaching, she begins to observe all kinds of superstitious customs and formulas in order to assure a light birth. As before her marriage, she unties all the knots in her clothing. But now she also loosens all the knots and braids in her hair. Through her shirt front she throws an egg on the floor or a powder into the fire and she tears the shirt from top to bottom. Sometimes they tie a sack to her left side and give the woman water to drink therefrom. It is also necessary to thank her husband if she drinks water from his shoes. He carries her into the room and says: "I gave you your sorrow, and I will free you from it." And he blows three times into her mouth and she blows

366

three times into his. Or the husband takes a weapon and shoots it off over the body of his wife, so that he may hurry the movement of the child.

When the pains become stronger, the woman blows strongly into a horn or drinks water out of the mouth of her husband. Or she creeps between the legs of her husband while he strikes her with her wedding dress; also, if one beats her with what he has freed a frog from a snake, it will make the birth easier.

The Bosnian, Herzegowiner and other south Slavic women observe customs for easing the birth similar to those practiced by the Serbians: they loosen the knots in their clothes and the braids in their hair. They throw an egg from their bosom to the earth and tear the shirt from its breast lace to its lowest seam. Besides these, several other helpful remedies are known: above all one repeats a certain number of times the Lord's Prayer. One let herself be impregnated with the odor of the roasted peel of a sea onion. One cooks ten eggs in boiling water until they burst and then drinks the water. She also drinks water from her husband's hand or shoes, but it must be pure untouched water, during whose transportation from the well to the house the bearer said no word, water which must not have been drawn for any other purpose. If the birth is nevertheless drawn out, they strew nuts between the legs of the laboring woman so as to entice the child to play or to eat; or they seat the woman near an oven and let her hold an ax in the right hand and a spindle in the left, also to intrigue the child: if it is a boy the ax entices him; if it is a girl, the spindle lures her. They also place an egg on the nape of the woman's neck and let it roll down her back. Additional customs are: the stroking of the back of the body with the corners of sheets which women who have already given birth had wound about their bodies; a light stroke with a belt of a maiden, at the same time saying a special formula; the loosing of the braids of a maiden over the laboring woman.

367

If a Bosnian woman delivers with difficulty, she goes to a well, as Milena Mrazovic relates, fills a vessel with water, lets it drip out to the ground through a hole, and says: *"Prije diete palo, neg se voda iz posude izlila*, the child shall come sooner than the water from the pot."

At a difficult confinement the Bosnian Mohammedan woman takes in each hand the symbol of an amulet upon which the following formula is found in Turkish letters:

$$2 \quad 7 \quad 2$$
$$8 \quad 7 \quad 7$$
$$2 \quad 9 \quad 7$$

Another Moslem amulet which is tied to the back of the body of the woman in labor in order to ease the confinement, or which is placed in the four corners of the room, contains on paper an abstract of the first sentence of the 84th chapter of the Koran: "If the heaven breaks open listening to the call to duty of our Lord; and the earth opens up and brings forth that which is in it; and it empties itself listening to the call to duty of our Lord—then, O man, thou must also try to appease thine Lord whom thou must also meet."

If a Turkish woman finds herself in pains of birth, she has her husband open the doors of the *dschami* or mosque and engages in worthy deeds, gives presents to schools, dispenses alms, purchase a bird and grants it its freedom. Whenever possible the woman takes a drink of water from the sacred fountain at Mecca, that fountain which an angel showed to Hagar in the desert. A piece of candle which a pilgrim lit and brought home from the grave of Mohammed is also a good medicine.

For light pains one brings a tuft of earth coming from the holy land—they are to be had in the bazaar for this purpose—packs a little sack full of it, and ties it to the back of the woman in labor. Mohammedan women use earth which pilgrims bring from Mecca; Christians and Jews turn to the helpful earth from

Jerusalem. But women of all religions believe implicitly in the effectiveness of the remedy.

At times they also take earth as an internal medicine in a glass of water. The earth is most effective if it comes from the courthouse of a sacred place. Among Persian women earth is at times taken in the mouth during the last two months of pregnancy and dissolved gradually. To the most beloved earths there belong, according to Dr. Polak: two Hindoo kinds of *tabaschir, magnesiakalk,* particularly *tabaschir-kalami,* bamboo knots, and *tabischir-sadafi, gil-e-armeni,* Armenian bolus; *gil-e-dachistanti,* Caucasian bolus, and several other kinds of bolus; *padzeher-e-kaswini* or *padzeher maadeni,* earth from Kaswin, *halloisitor orawizit* from Mahalat, *a thonsilikat;* several animal excrements, particular *bezoar*—and bladder stones. Through practice the Persian women attain a fine taste for earths; they distinguish immediately between the different kinds and occasionally make tasty tid bits with it.

I am thankful to an official of the Sultan's kitchen for knowledge of a custom which seems to have arisen in recent years. Mohammedans, Christians, and Jews alike believe that the crumbs of bread which the *padischah* breaks off and drops possesses the power to ease the difficult hours of women. These bread crumbs are therefore carefully collected, wrapped in a cloth, and given to any persons who ask for them.

In Syria, in order to make confinement less difficult, they place a paper with the following inscription on the head of the women: "I have had my meal, and have given food to my donkey; it is the same to me if the judge's wife delivers, of if she never delivers, or if she never delivers in her whole life." They ascribe the good effect of their formula, which they expect to be certain, not to the sense of the words, but to the secret assembling of the letters.

If the confinement is difficult, the Syrian woman drinks water from the shoes of her husband—similar customs are to be found among the inhabitants of Syria and Palestine as among the south Slavic nations.

In the villages of Armenia on the Turkish-Persian border, it is customary to place a sable near the woman in labor and erect a row of puppets on the flat roof of the house, dressed as soldiers which are made to move by means of threads; also, as among the Serbians, a shot is fired from a flint iron over the woman in labor in order to drive away the devil.

In order to ease the birth for a Persian woman, they turn, as among the Turks, to the graciousness of Allah. They give presents to the mosques and have prayers said. They remember the poor and the sick and they give them alms. If the head of the child begins to appear, but it hesitates and presses itself back, the midwife begins—just as among the southern Slavs and the Bosnians—to entice the child by placing before the opening, playthings, sweets, and clothes, and winking to the child and saying: "Come, come!"

When the Spanish Jewess feels herself about to give birth, she prefaces the act above all with worthy deeds. At the beginning of the pains they hold before the woman—this takes place among the Jews in Europe as well—a dish of oil, so that she can see herself therein as in a mirror; they then send the oil to the synagogue. If the labor drags out for too long a time, or if they fear a bad result, they bury the headdress of the woman in labor in the grave of a dead relative, they read a page from the Torah in the room of the birth, they have the *Schofar* blown over the bed of the sufferer and they pay something to the synagogue so that womb may be opened.

Various folk remedies are in use as the wonder-remedies of superstition for weak pains. Of these a plaster in particular must be mentioned, which is used in Constantinople and contains according to Professor Rigler the following substances: *Gummi ammoniacum, Galbanum, myhr, olibanum, tutia prae-perata, minium,* dragon's blood and mother-of-pearl. Several

370

of these substances are also known in European medicine. Galbanum, for example, a strong, aromatic, turpentine-like smelling root, which comes from Persia, was previously prescribed internally in Europe for women's pains, and is now, as in Turkey, used in the preparation of plasters. Minium also serves in Europe as a constituent of plaster. The red dragon's blood root, which was once used as an internal medicine in the west just as Galbanum, is now employed only for tooth-powder. Finally, Olibanum, evergreen, and the myrrh related to evergreen are also well known in Europe. The myrrh which comes from Arabia serves especially as an internal balm for pains of the breathing organs, for catarrh of the stomach, externally as a tincture for healing badly cut wounds, and finally as an ingredient of a mouthwash and tooth powder. The Greeks use myrrh in the churches instead of evergreen. They paste this plaster on the back of the laboring woman.

Since the doctors in ancient Arabia had no or only rare opportunity to engage in practical assistance at birth, they usually commanded the helping women to employ numerous external means at difficult confinements. Ali ben Abbas advised: besides baths and oil massages, to have recourse to the smoke of mule's hoofs. Rhases and Abulkasem ordered: oil massages, warm baths, injections in the birth region and sneeze remedies. Rhases advised the midwives, in case of necessity, to open the ovary with their nails or with a small knife, which German doctors did in former times.

In Constantinople and in other regions mutton fat covered with honey or roasted onions is frequently placed on the womb in order to cause it to open.

The Bosnians place a warmed stone dipped in oil on the genitals or set a pot of warm water between the thighs of the woman in labor.

In general they consider blood letting necessary to ease the confinement. In Asia Minor they attempt to bring the child into the proper position by placing the woman on a bed sheet, the four corners of which are held by women who raise it and shake it. Or else the legs of the woman in labor are lifted and propelled to and fro on the ground. The laboring woman in ancient Greece was lifted by the doctors together with the whole bed and shaken. At times a powerful woman takes the woman in labor on her lap and massages her belly, at which the sufferer frequently assists by pressing down herself.

Just as the German doctors before the sixteenth century laid great stress on the stroking and pressing of the abdomen, so from then on and even to this day massaging is practiced in the orient as a means of easing childbirth. Many Arabian tribes have their own specialists for rubbing the abdomen and the thighs of the woman in labor in order to ease the pain. The massage of the outer portions continues throughout the entire birth. The midwife stretches the organ with her fingers and massages the genitals until the head of the child appears.

Other methods consist of constant shaking of the knees of the woman or the bending of the knee or the spraying of the abdomen with cold water. They also seat the woman on a hot stone or on a tub in which hay or straw has been cooked.

The French doctor Goguel was called into the tent of a sheik during his journey through Arabia in the year 1858 to lend his professional assistance at a confinement. As he later related in the Parisian Medical Gazette, he found the woman in labor sitting on two flat stones. At every pain she lifted herself into the air by a rope hanging from the middle beam of the tent, then to sink back again on the stones. Occasionally two helping women lifted the rope higher so that the woman in labor would be compelled to expend more energy. At the commencement of the pain they also lift the parturient on their shoulders and shake her as a miller shakes a sack of flour.

Among the Spaniards the pregnant woman is likewise well shaken so as to bring the child into the proper position; for this purpose she is wrapped tightly in a cover and then pushed about hither and yon. At a long drawn out birth the person functioning as midwife rubs the loin region of the sufferer and massages her abdomen. If the woman does not cry out strongly enough, they compel her to do so by pinching her. The pregnant woman must sometimes jump over steps in order to deliver more quickly, or she must seat herself on two stools which are suddenly pulled from under her.

Varied are the positions in which women in Turkey are delivered of children. According to the portrayals of Ploss-Bartels and Engelmann, who have reported these circumstances in detail, as I have not been able to do within the borders of my book—giving birth lying, the Spanish Jews; half lying or leaning and sitting, the Greeks, Turks, Cypriotins, Syrians, Arabians, and the women in Palestine; sitting, the women in Palestine and Arabia; squatting or crouching, the Arabians and Persians; finally, kneeling, the Persians, Armenians, and at times also the Greeks.

The Persians kneel on two stones. Or they crouch and support their knees and hands on three bricks which are raised at some distance from one another.

As Doctor Bernard Beck reported to me, the Arabs in Bagdad crouch on two flat stones, usually without any support, but at times they hold on to a rope. In other sections the Arabs give birth in a half lying position on a stool or in the lap of the midwife.

The Armenian woman usually kneels during delivery. The Turks give birth on the lap of the midwife or on a low chair, or they cower on the ground and support their hands on the wall. The peasant women in Palestine seat themselves on a pillow or crouch on stones. In the cities of Palestine, particularly in Jerusalem, as well as in Syria and in other sections of the Levant, the birth stool is well known. In Syria the woman often labors on a rocking chair. The woman in labor sat in the lap of her helper even in ancient Cypress.

The opinion of many authors that Hebrew women gave birth in the lap of another does not seem to Professor Ebstein to be very well supported. He says: In the first Book of Moses XXX, 3, Rachel asks of Jacob that he go in unto her maid Bilhah, "that she shall bear upon my knees." But in the 5th verse it is said casually: "And Bilhah conceived, and bare Jacob a son." It is not said that delivery takes place on the lap of another. Rachel's words are purely symbolic and must be taken to mean: "so that my lap may get children through her lap."

The birth stool which is at present used in China, Japan, Greece, and Egypt, as well as in Turkey, is said to have a distinguished history. It is supposed to have been known to the Hebrew women in ancient Palestine; according to other opinions they still await delivery crouching on two stones, just as the Arabian women of today.

Professor Ebstein thinks he can prove my several quotations from the Bible that the birth stool was in use among the Hebrews; he quotes the second Book of Moses I, 15, and Jeremiah, XXX, 6: ". . . wherefore do I see every man with his hands on his loins, as a woman in travail. . . ."

The birth stool is a large wooden stool with graded arms and a round hole in the seat. A semi-circular hole is more usual than the round one. So is the birth stool used in Syria; it is like a rocking chair with movable arms and allows the pregnant woman the possibility of getting her body into different positions. The seat is about two feet over the rollers and is cut in the form of a semi-circle so that it is possible for the embryo to make its exit. While the midwife supports the lower part of the body of the laboring woman, the upper part of her body is held in the lap of another helping woman sitting behind her. Every better *diyeh* or midwife in Syria has her own birth stool which she carries from house to house, like her Egyptian colleague.

My chief source of information, Dr. Beck, has frequently assisted at births during his sojourn of several years. He gave me the following reports: In a crouching position the woman in labor awaits the appearance of her child. She crouches on a hill of ashes on the floor, both feet rest on flat stones. She remains in this uncomfortable position uninterruptedly no matter how long the pains last. In the meantime, according to a custom in Bagdad, a band of musicians appears before the house in order to quit the woman's pain through noise and to greet the child with joy. The room of the laboring woman is also in a state of terrific uproar. All the neighbors and relatives have come in order to be present at the excitement. They eat, drink, prattle, and quarrel, smoke nargilleh and poison the atmosphere. If the delivery is normal, the new born being glides onto the heap of ashes and the woman is helped into a more comfortable position. But if the birth is a difficult one, then the *kabbi*, the midwife, dares unbelievable cruelty. She stands the woman on her head, and while two women hold her legs as far apart as possible without tearing them apart, the *kabbi* cuts the flesh in the middle with an ordinary, usually a rusty pair of shears, or even with a kitchen knife, unmercifully until the opening is large enough for the child to come out. If the patient bleeds to death as a result of this, they do not take much notice, for very little care is had for the welfare of the woman giving birth. On the other hand, it becomes very uncomfortable for the midwife if, during this barbaric operation, an arm or a leg of the child is cut off. The Bagdad women are accustomed to cruel treatment and so cases are not very frequent when they succumb at a confinement because of improper or negligent treatment.

Among the Bedouins the child is often caught in a sieve

375

while the helping women bear down on the abdomen of the mother.

Skillful operations and particularly the Caesarian operation are still very rarely performed. Dr. Wladan Gjorjewitsch, the former Serbian Minister President and the reformer of Serbian sanitary conditions, once told me of a clever operation which a Serbian woman from Pritschtina performed on herself: Plagued by three days of pain, she grasped a razor and performed a Caesarian operation on herself. A neighbor sewed the wound together. And mother and child survived. The law forbade Persian doctors and midwives to perform Caesarian operations after the death of the mother. In this way it happened that they killed a child which came out of the dead body of its mother; since the living could not be born from the dead, such a child could not be a creature of God, but only of the devil.

Ludwig August Frankl noticed among the Jews in Beyruth the gruesome manner in which a pregnant woman was buried: When the corpse was cleaned and the death clothes ready, the corpse watchers strained their eyes and ears to discover if the young life still existed in the dead one. If this was the case, they beat the body of the corpse until it became entirely quiet. For it was dishonorable to the dead one and her relatives if her body was opened; and it was a sin to bury the live one living.

When the birth has happily taken place, they anxiously await the coming of the afterbirth which is called in Turkish, Persian, and Arabic: *meschimeh*, while the Graeco-Wallavians call it "the little house of the child"; as soon as it makes its appearance, it is buried in the garden or thrown into flowing water, according to Macedonian custom. The same practice is prevalent in Bosnia.

If the afterbirth does not appear quickly, they employ the following remedy in Constantinople: They stitch the navel cord, draw a thread through the opening, and tie the navel cord fast to the ankles of the sufferer. They then give her brandy with pepper to drink; or they stick a finger deep into her throat in order to make her vomit; or they make her blow into a flask.

Similar practices are indulged in in other parts of Turkey in order to drive out the afterbirth.

The Bosnian Mohammedans are massaged or they blow into an empty flask.

The Greek women have their abdomen rubbed and pressed, and they stick a finger or even a braid into their mouth to make them vomit at the same time. Or they lift the delivered one several times high in the air and let her fall heavily.

In almost all of Turkey it is the practice not to separate the child from its mother immediately by cutting the navel cord, but to do it together with the afterbirth. Then the navel cord is cut with a knife or shears or another instrument, at times it is simply bitten through by the mother, the midwife, or another woman, after which the part of the navel cord left with the child is burnt with the flame of a candle and finally knotted. Among the Bosnian women the navel cord is not cut with shears, but usually with a knife; if shears are used, the next child will be a girl.

The Syrian women wait 20 to 40 minutes after the delivery for the appearance of the afterbirth. If this does not take place during the proper space of time, they cut the navel cord and put the woman to bed. In Jaffa the midwife tries to bring forth the afterbirth immediately after delivery. She presses on the navel with all her force until she accomplishes her purpose. In Jerusalem the midwife ties the navel cord with a thread to the feet of the patient. She then dips her finger in oil and drives it into the vagina in order to grasp the afterbirth and pull it out. After the afterbirth has appeared the midwife unties the navel cord. When she cuts through the latter, she leaves a remnant three fingers long with the child, wraps this remnant with cotton and thread and burns the end with the flame of a candle, so as to stop the bleeding of the cut navel. In Eriwan the navel cord is tied by the Armenian midwives immediately after birth with a woolen or silken thread and then cut with shears, without concern whether the afterbirth has come yet or not. The Persian women let the navel cord be pulled and torn by the helping women, until the afterbirth appears. The women of the Arab nomadic tribes, who, while on their roamings in the wilderness, are frequently left quite alone in their tents during their difficult hours, cut the navel cord themselves.

The navel cord holds an important position in the superstition of oriental peoples. Among the Graco-Wallavians the remnant of the dried up navel cord is carefully preserved by the mother, and particularly protected against dampness, for otherwise the child might suffer bodily pain. After several years it is brought forth and shown to the child so that he might succeed in everything which he undertakes. They say of a man of many affairs: "He has seen his navel." The mother avoids, however, showing the navel remnant of her child to other children. The midwives in Syria are careful not to cut the navel cord of the child too short; this precaution assures the child of a beautiful voice. If it is a girl, they add another precaution for this purpose: they strew on the lips of the little one, dust which has been taken from under the hinge of the door to the birth chamber. The navel remnant must be salted—they say finally; if this does not take place the child will have a bad odor emanating from its mouth.

CHAPTER TWENTY-EIGHT

# CONFINEMENT

*First treatment of the woman after delivery—Constantinople customs—What Dr. Beck reported to me from Bagdad—Syrian diet of the woman in child-bed—Jaffa—Palestine—The 40 days—Graco-Wallavian customs—Fear of demons—Uncleanness of the woman in child-bed—Hebrew—Ancient Greek; —Modern Greek—Superstitious notions—The woman in child-bed and the kitchen—The woman in child-bed and coitus—Moroccan customs—Protection of the woman in child-bed from evil charms—Albanian method of protection—Laws and prohibitions with respect to women in child-bed and the new-born—The white nymphs among the Graco-Wallachians—The fire near the woman in child-bed—Jewish customs from Palestine—Syrian— Writings on visits to women in child-bed—Prohibition of the lending of fire, salt, and bread.*

*A Veddah Girl—Fifteen Years Old*

In Constantinople the midwife usually works on the body of the woman after delivery in the following manner so that the parts which have suffered during delivery should return to their former position: she presses on the abdomen, she raises the hands of the sufferer high in the air, and pushes her about, and then binds her abdomen and also her head tightly with cloths.

As Doctor Beck has told me, the women in Bagdad must swallow a huge portion of shelled nuts, almonds, pistachios, and Indian roots immediately after delivery. They call this: *Hatter kuwet el rasfad*, namely: for strengthening the point of the heart. Surprisingly enough, this strange strengthening of the point of the heart does not harm all women in child-bed.

On the first and second day in Syria they give the woman in child-bed mutton broth or chicken soup; for the next six days only inflaming drinks and cinnamon tea. Not until the ninth day does she receive real nourishment, at first in small quantities and then in ever greater portions. Wherever the home remedies are themselves of no avail, superstition must again render assistance. If a woman endures great pain in the abdomen after her delivery, the Syrians place the shoe of her husband under her pillow without her noticing it, and the pains immediately cease.

In Jaffa, immediately after delivery the woman receives a glass of brandy; at times, before, a glass of olive oil. In Jerusalem she gets brandy with muscat nuts or wine with olive oil, and after three or four hours tea or chicken soup, sometimes chocolate. For forty days she never drinks fresh water, but only concoctions of orange blossoms.

During the first three days the Persian woman in child-bed eats only vegetables in butter and sugar.

In Palestine the midwife binds a wide girdle about the body of the patient. The first two hours after the birth they let the woman sit upright in her bed so that the blood shall not come to her, as they express themselves in Palestine. Just as the deliveries are usually very easy, so the conditions of the sick ones are often bad afterwards. In particular, the bleeding is so strong that it frequently brings about death. The midwife accompanies the woman in child-bed to her first bath in order to return the genitals to their proper condition. There the woman is laid on the ground, and the midwife rubs her abdomen with all her strength.

For forty days the woman in child-bed is considered a patient; but she is not one in all places. Among the south Slavic peasants one rarely finds one who remains in bed for more than two or three days. It has even been noticed that a Bosnian woman of the soil who had given birth at night, stood barefoot on the next day at the brook chopping ice. The fellah mother goes about her domestic business two or three days after delivery.

The Turkish and Arabian women in Bagdad leave their bed on the third day. Only among the rich people is the woman favored with a longer period for recuperation.

Dr. Sajaktzis reports on the customs among the Graco-Wallavians in Monastir: After the birth, about nine o'clock in the evening, everybody except the closest associates of the house must leave. They lock the door, burn incense with which they fumigate the mother and child on this as well as the next 39 days, so that evil, the shadows, or the bad spirits shall not harm them.

The Hebrews considered the woman in child-bed as unclean. In the 3rd Book of Moses, XII, 2, it is said: "If a woman have conceived seed, and borne a man child, then she shall be unclean seven days; according to the days of the separation shall she be unclean. . . . And she shall then continue in the blood of her purifying three and thirty days; she shall touch no hallowed thing nor come into the sanctuary, until the day of her purifying be fulfilled. But if she bear a maid child, then she shall be unclean two weeks, as in her separation: and

382

shall continue in the blood of her purifying three score and six days. And when the days of her purifying are fulfilled, for a son, or for a daughter, she shall bring a lamb of the first year for a burnt offering, and a young pigeon, or a turtledove, for a sin offering, unto the door of the tabernacle of the congregation, unto the priest: Who shall offer it before the Lord, and make an atonement for her; and she shall be cleansed from the issue of her blood." On the 40th day the ritual of a bath complete the cleansing.

In ancient Athens the woman in child-bed was not permitted to go out before the 40th day; she was forbidden to enter the temple or to undertake any sacred enterprise. After the forty days a feast took place, called: *tesserakostos.* She then took a bath, the cleansing bath, and became clean again.

According to Sajaktzas, the Graco-Wallavians have adopted all of these customs from the ancients. The woman in child-bed, the new-born child, and all of the women who have come in contact with them are considered unclean. All of those who have touched the woman in child-bed must not cook before they have become clean. This takes place in Monastir in the following manner: The servant of the Almighty comes, fumigates all who are with the woman in child-bed, as well as the woman herself and the new-born child, sanctifies a flask of water closed with basilicum leaves, and says various prayers. All those present wet their faces with holy water and spray it on the woman in child-bed and the child. The more superstitious among the women, as well as the midwife, go home immediately after the delivery and change their clothes, which they also used to do after touching a dead person. Even the house in which the birth took place is considered unclean; it is fumigated and sprayed with holy water; they burn incense in the house every evening until the 40th day after the birth. On the 40th day all the furniture is washed or sprayed with holy water.

During the first forty days after the delivery the Greek woman must not go into the church. Near the house of a woman in child-bed every talisman loses its power. On the 40th day the woman takes a cleansing bath and devotes herself to thanksgiving in the church. Here also ancient Greek customs have remained almost entirely unchanged. Among the Albanians the woman is considered unclean for 40 days, and for that period she must neither cook nor bake.

The Bedouin woman remains in the house for only one week, sometimes less, but never more. She is, however, considered unclean for 40 days, and before she can again be considered as a clean person, she must also wash all of her clothes.

The Egyptian woman in Cairo is considered unclean for 40 days, and then she takes a cleansing bath. In the rest of Egypt the period of the uncleanness of the woman in child-bed is of various duration.

The Turkish woman is considered unclean for 40 days, as well as the Armenian and the Spanish.

The Moroccan Arab woman becomes a hermit for a full two years. Her husband may nevertheless approach her as soon as she has menstruated for the third time after her confinement.

The superstition that the woman in child-bed easily attracts evil charms is prevalent among all the peoples of the orient. They therefore cover the woman in child-bed all over with amulets, they seek through magic sayings and magic remedies to protect her room from spirits of disease, from the evil eye, and from envy and revenge. They usually do not leave the young mother and the new-born child alone.

The Armenian woman never remains alone in her room during the first six weeks after her delivery, from fear of the devil.

During the first 40 days among the Albanians, as Hahn reports, neither the child nor the woman in child-bed must leave the house, and at night not even the room where the birth took place. This occurs not from reasons of health, but from fear of bewitchment. In order to protect one's self from bewitchment during these 40 days, a fire must be maintained carefully in the house during the entire six weeks, and neither a splinter nor a piece of coal must be given away; whoever comes into the house at night must jump over a flaming torch at the door; neither dancing nor singing must take place in the house during the forty days.

Throughout the first seven nights the neighbors make a very great noise in front of the house in order to prevent the woman in child-bed and the child from falling asleep, for they fear that evil spirits might be able to harm them during their sleep.

According to the stories of Dr. Sajaktzis, among the Graco-Wallavians in Monastir, a third person, who has been baptised, must linger around the woman in child-bed and the child until the seventh day after the birth. After the christening of the child this third person is no longer required; but the mother must remain with the child until the 40th day. If she is compelled to go out, she leaves a housemaid with the child for company. All this is done for protection against the machinations of both apparent and invisible spirits, which pursue the mother and the child until the end of nursing time or until baptism. At night the mother must not go out for any reason; she must never sit under the eaves of a roof, for the white-clad, flower decorated nymphs might appear, the nymphs which are smilingly called: "the white ones, the wise ones, and the friendly ones" and who are believed to be virgins of exquisite beauty. They come from cold gusts of wind, from the peaks of mountains, they tarry under the eaves of roofs, under trees, in brooks; or like the Klodones and Mimmalones of ancient Macedonia, they storm with tympans, they dance invisibly, they do evil through a lusty blow, they choke in their arms that unhappy mortal who crosses their path.

In case a woman in child-bed goes out at night in spite of the prohibition and is stricken by the white ones and succumbs to a severe sickness, her mother goes at midnight—"when even the water sleeps"—to the house well, to the eaves, to the fountain in the garden, to the lake in the field, in short, to all quiet waters, and cries "the white ones, the wise ones, the friendly ones, the most beautiful," appealing with song to the nymphs to return the invalid to her cheaply held health, for the poor woman is baptised and a good Christian. In order to appease the spirits, the supplicant spreads honey on the home of the spirits. At times the nymphs accede to the supplications; sometimes, however, they also strike the pleading mother.

In order to protect the woman in child-bed and the child from the "white ones," their clothes and their wash must never be permitted to remain under a strange heaven. When the child is taken for baptism, they offer instead of the child, a *kopanos* or clothes mallet, cleverly constructed and hidden under a cover, so that the evil spirits might be warded off.

Among the Jews in Palestine a watch is set at the bed of a woman in child-bed for the entire first week; day and night women sit near her, and in a nearby room men read holy books uninterruptedly. They consider it most dangerous to leave the woman alone for even a moment. For forty days a lamp burns in the room of the woman in child-bed in order to protect the mother and child from the approach of evil spirits. The Christians and Moslems in Palestine protect their women in child-bed from the evil eye and other bad things, hanging on the mother and child all kinds up superstitious tokens. The most effective, but also the rarest, is a gold coin from Venetian times which they call the amulet of *Maschchas* or *Muschchas*. They consider a woman in child-bed most susceptible to evil influences and severe sicknesses and they say of her: "For forty days her grave stands open." They must say nothing harmful of her or before her.

Innumerable are the Syrian superstitious notions and customs which are associated with the woman in child-bed. I mention here from Eijub Abela only the following: He who goes from a house in which someone has died to the house of a woman in child-bed without resting or urinating in between brings death to that woman, according to a general wide-spread notion of the people; it is forbidden to sew in the room of a woman in child-bed, for that causes the death of the new-born child; no newlywed must come to the woman in child-bed, or else the latter loses her milk; two women in child-bed must not talk to each other, else the first to open her mouth loses her child. Also among the Jews in Palestine two women in child-bed must not visit each other during the first month after the birth; the unobservance of this prohibition is most dangerous, particularly if the mother is holding the child in her arms at such a visit. The woman in child-bed must not look into a mirror, else she will squint; the latter happens to anyone who looks at himself in a mirror after the sun goes down.

Grimm relates the customs in the mountains in the Kingdom of Saxony: No fire, no salt, no bread must be lent from the house of a woman in child-bed. Among the Graeco-Wallachians in Monastir, neither bread nor wine must be taken from the room of a woman in child-bed before the 40th day after the birth of the child, lest the happiness of the house which these things symbolize disappear; likewise, until the 40th day a burning light must neither be brought into the room of the woman in child-bed nor taken out, for the demons might harm the mother's milk through the light. The Jews in Palestine say: During the first week nothing must be loaned from

the room of the woman in child-bed; least of all must one permit fire to be taken therefrom. In Syria no fire must be given
to a neighbor from the house of the woman in child-bed until
the navel of the child is completely healed; otherwise the
new-born child will be pursued by misfortune or disease.

CHAPTER TWENTY-NINE

# MOTHER'S MILK AND WET-NURSES

*Duration of nursing—Bewitching the milk—Graco-Wallavian customs—Al
banian customs—Persian customs—Nursing is the duty of the mother—
Paid wet-nurses—Reverence of wet-nurses among the Turks—History—
Weaning the child—Market for women's milk.*

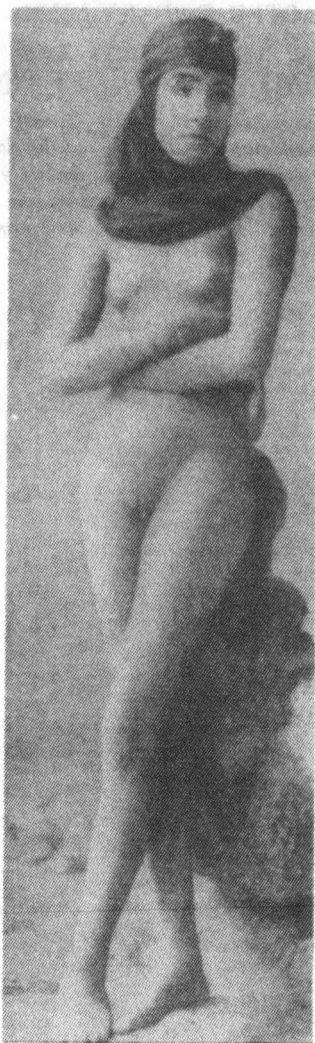

*Fellah Girl*

If one wishes to say a friendly word to a woman in child-bed in Palestine about her appearance, one must not forget, as Dame Lydia Einszler relates, to add numerous wish formulas, so that the praise may not be accompanied by evil results. If this is not done the woman in child-bed is in danger of acquiring a bad breast and losing her milk. Out of fear of bewitchment and envy, the mother 'keeps the child hidden from curious eyes during the first time that it rests at her breast and while it is drinking. In order not to deprive the young mother of her right to milk, they do not call the thing by its proper name. One does not ask the woman in child-bed: "Have you much milk?" but: "*Kif dirtik?* how is your flow?" And the young mother answers: "*Fi barake,* it is there for nursing." Even if a third person speaks of a woman in child-bed and her milk, he adopts the same precaution. They say: "*Dirratha kanije,* her flow streams." Or: "*Dirratha chafife,* her flow is light."

Among the Graco-Wallavians in Monastir, as Dr. Sajaktsiz reports, the child receives camomile tea as its first nourishment; then it comes to its mother's breast. While it is nursing for the first time, the mother holds a flask of wine in her right hand as a symbol of happiness, while another woman holds a sieve containing a loaf of bread over the head of the woman in child-bed. On the third day they bake two twisted buns of wheat, a smaller one for the child and a larger one for the mother, "for demanding the milk." If no milk appears in a week, then an old woman wets the bun of the mother in three fountains at dawn, while she says no word, so that the nymphs who bathe in the fountains might not know that she is there and would not harm her. The mother eats this wheat bun, so that her milk should flow, as the water from the fountains. They hang the smaller wheat bun about the hips of the child until the 40th day; then they throw it in flowing water, "so that the child shall stop crying." In order to assure herself of milk, the woman in child-bed must also fetch water herself from the house-well on an early morning, wash herself with it, wet her breasts with the tips of her fingers, and intone: "As your water, so may my milk flow." Finally Sajaktzis relates the strange custom of the "milk withdrawal": If a woman in child-bed has no milk, but a neighbor has more than enough, the former does the following: She takes two breads under her arms and a flask of water in her right hand. She then slinks secretly before sunrise to a tree in the court where she can see the window of her neighbor. When she sees the neighbor quieting her child, precisely at sunrise, she raises the flask in the air three times, murmurs an oath, and in three gulps with the water drinks down all the milk of her neighbor, who is now left as empty as the flask! Until the 40th day a mother must nurse no child other than her own; only in the rarest case of necessity is a child given a strange breast. According to Hahn the following customs also exist in Albania: Immediately after the delivery, the woman sends a container of pure water to the priest or to the *imam* for consecration. After this is done, they bring the water back to the house of the woman in child-bed, and all of those who served as midwives or were present at the birth wash their hands with a portion of the sacred water; the container with the remainder is placed near the bed. All who come to visit during the following days dip their fingers into the consecrated water and spray the mother and the child with several drops, at the same time wishing the child good health and the mother rich milk. The children in Albania are weaned towards the end of their second year of life. Towards the end of the time when they are still nursing at the breast of their mother, they are, however, already fed with substantial foods which the nurse in the ancient Greek manner chews piece by piece before the child and feeds it from her mouth. In order to strengthen the nursling they frequently let it drink wine. The Jews in Syria believe that if the back-bone of a flying fish is fastened to the neck or head of a woman in child-bed, then the milk of the mother's breast must flow more rich. In Constantinople, as soon as she can leave the child-bed and the room, the mother usually takes a warm bath; there they place cataplasms of beans and onions on her breasts and back, and this is supposed to afford the separation of the milk.

It is generally believed in the orient: If a mother who approaches a child drinks cold water, the nursling is in danger of being ill with diarrhoea. In order to avoid the foregoing sickness, it is necessary to do the following: one must throw a needle into a glass of warm water and take it out several hours later, the mother must then drink some of the water and wet the forehead of the child with the rest, among the Moslems in the form of a half moon, among the Jews in the form of a star, among the Christians in the forms of a cross, and finally one must make a small present to the mosque, the synagogue, or the church, and everything will immediately become good.

In the African Tripolis the nurses believe: that their milk becomes poisoned if a *dschardun*, a small harmless lizard jumps over their breasts. This notion is particularly noteworthy for the reason that among many nations, the lizard, like the snake, is brought into a relationship with women. In Polynesian mythology the lizard is considered a sacred animal, and the legends tell of women who have given birth to lizards. Among the Port-Lincoln tribe in southern Australia it is said that a lizard has separated man from his wife. Frazer also knows of a Greek story according to which a princess during puberty did not permit herself to remain in the sunlight, lest she be transformed into a lizard. Even in modern Europe similar ideas are prevalent. Ellis repeats a tale of Reys: it is believed in Portugal that women are easily bitten by lizards during menstruation; to protect themselves against this they wear tight fitting clothes.

As long as the child receives its mother's milk and during its first year, the mothers or nurses of the Hebrews were directed, according to Psalm 121, 6, to employ the greatest care in nursing, never to leave their bosom uncovered, to leave the child naked neither by day nor by night, not to let it go barefoot nor bareheaded, not to bring it in a place where the sun would overdry it, nor place it in the moonlight on a damp evening, neither to take it from the bath early in the morning nor to bathe it often.

The so-called milk grotto at Bethlehem, to which the holy virgin was brought the night before her flight to Egypt, has a great reputation among nursing mothers and nurses whose flow of milk threatens to run dry. The white kind of earth, *bolus*, from which the designation of the grotto is taken, according to the legend is said to have originated thus: When the Virgin Mary took the Christ child to her breast, several drops of milk fell to the ground, whereupon the latter immediately acquired the appearance of milk white dust. Out of the earth of the milk grotto there are prepared small round cakes, to which is ascribed the soul of the sacred place. Dissolved in water and taken as an internal medicine, these pastilles are said to bring back the flow of the milk which has run dry.

Among the Hebrews nursing is considered as one of the first duties of the mother. In the First Book of Moses, XLIX, 25, the "blessing of the breasts" are glorified; in Hosea, IX, 14, the "dry breasts" are bemoaned. In Lamentations, IV, 3, the reproach is intoned: "Even the sea monsters draw out the breast, they give suck to their young ones: the daughter of my people is become cruel, like the ostriches in the wilderness. The tongue of the suckling child cleaveth to the roof of his mouth for thirst."

As one of the most fearful accompaniments of the "earthquake at the time of the last hours" the Koran prophesies in

394

the XXII chapter which is entitled "The Pilgrimage": "On the day wherein ye shall see it, every woman who giveth suck shall forget the infant which she suckleth, and every female that is with young shall cast forth her burden."

Good examples are frequently mentioned in the Bible. In the first Book of Samuel, I, 21, it is said: "And the man Elkanah, and all his house went up to offer unto the Lord the yearly sacrifice, and his vow. But Hannah went not up; for she said unto her husband, I will not go up until the child be weaned." In the first Book of Moses, XXI, 8, it is reported: "And she said, Who would have said unto Abraham, that Sarah should have given suck? for I have borne him a son in his old age. And the child grew and was weaned."

The fellahs in Palestine say of a powerful boy among them: "*Raso malan min halim ummo*, his head is full of his mother's milk"; or: "*Hu schab an min halim ummo*, he has drunken himself full of his mother's milk." If a child is not strong, they believe the reason is that he did not drink his fill of his mother's milk. Only when the mother dies do they give the child over to a wet-nurse; until such a one is found the orphaned infant is nursed by one or more of the neighbors of the house. In rare instances it happens that they nurse the child with goat's milk.

The Imam el Haremeim ascribed his constant ill health to the remainder of the milk left by a strange wet-nurse who nursed him as an infant during the illness of his mother. His father saw this and immediately stood the child on its head to make him return the milk he had taken, but several drops remained, and from this resulted all of his suffering, so contended this wise man.

Usually a wet-nurse is taken only if the mother is not in a position to nurse the child herself. In spite of the fact that nursing was considered one of the most important duties of a mother among the Hebrews, paid wet-nurses were not unknown even among them. In the first Book of Moses, XXIV, 59, and XXXV, 8, Deborah, the nurse of Rebecca is mentioned; Deborah later remained with Rebecca, enjoyed great honor, and when she died she was buried on the outskirts of Bethel under an oak which has since been called the mournful oak. Wet-nurses were later popular, particularly in the families of the kings. In the second Book of Kings, XI, 2, it is related: "But Jehosheba the daughter of King Joram, sister of Ahaziah, took Joash the son of Ahaziah, and stole him from among the king's sons which were slain; and they hid him, even him and his nurse, in the bed chamber from Athaliah so that he was not slain."

In the Koran II it is said: "And if ye have a mind to provide a nurse for your children, it shall be no crime in you, in case ye fully pay what ye offer her, according to that which is just."

Koran 65 says: "And if ye be put to a difficulty herein, and another woman shall suckle the child for him, let him who hath plenty expend in proportion out of that which God hath given him."

Sometimes the desire of the mother to preserve the beauty of her bosom is the reason for giving the child to a nurse. The nurses of Constantinople all come from the Archipelagoes, from the small Greek island. Formerly the island Tino furnished most of the nurses for the Turkish capitol; necessity now compels them to be recruited from Naxos, Samos, Chios, and even from Crete. During the shorter or longer sea journey, the nurses usually retain their milk through young dogs.

Among the Greeks the wet-nurse is called: *bagia, bysastria, trofos,* and *paramana* or *paramanna.* The last designation, which means mother duty and developer, is most common in Constantinople.

In Turkish houses the wet-nurse enjoys the highest respect for the rest of her life. If the mother dies, the nurse—Turkish: *Sut ana*, milk mother—is the first person in the house of the son or daughter. In the Sultan's palace, after the death of the *walide*, the mother of the Sultan, the nurse is elevated to *walide* and becomes the most respected of all the women in the imperial harem.

In Persia, during the first two days, the child receives no food but a little butter; from the third day on it is nursed for two full years by its mother, in exceptional cases by a wet-nurse. In very rare cases, if the mother is sick and incapable of nursing, the new-born child is nourished for several days on cow or goat milk; they have no conception, however, of true artificial nursing of children in Persia. If the child is weak, or if his parents are worried over his development, it frequently happens that he is not weaned until the end of his third year. Dr. Polak often had occasion to see children at the mother's breast, at the same time holding a huge piece of melon in their hands and in turn enjoying milk or melon.

As nurses they prefer the Nomad women of the land. The fledgeling often acquires a great affection for the nurse who suckled him, takes her into his house in her old age, and considers her as a second mother. Marriages between two persons who were suckled by the same nurse are forbidden by law.

Nurses at times played a significant political role in the court of the Osman Sultan. Sultan Mustafa I named Mustafa Pascha from Lefke as Grandvizier in the year 1622 only because Mustafa's wife was the nurse of the Sultan.

Nursing of children is not of the same duration all over Turkey; among several nations it is only from one to two years, among others five and even six years.

Among the ancient Hebrews the child was also frequently nursed by its mother for several years.

The Koran says in the II chapter: "Mothers, after they

are divorced, shall give suck unto their children two full years, to him who desireth the time of giving suck to be complete; and the father shall be obliged to maintain them in the meantime, according to that which shall be reasonable. No person shall be obliged beyond his ability. A mother shall not be compelled to what is unreasonable on account of her child nor the father on account of his child. And the heir of the father shall be obliged to do in like manner. But if they choose to wean the child before the end of two years, by common consent and on mutual consideration, it shall be no crime in them."

Ploss-Bartels maintain that the Armenian women in Eriwan, the Levantine, the Frankish, the Slavic, and the Greek women nurse their children from one to two years; the Turkish women, the Persian, and in some regions the Arabian keep their children at the mother's breast for about two years; the Armenian women in general, the women in Syria, and in part, also the women in Palestine nurse their children from two to three years as the Koran and the great Arabian doctor Avicenna have directed; in rare instances it happens that children of five and six years are not compeltely weaned, as at times among the fellahs in Palestine, where they believe that those children are the strongest who longest enjoyed their mothers' milk. Soon, however, the child becomes accustomed to eating bread and frequently his stomach is overfilled with other heavy foods. As a result of this, in the villages of Palestine, one often sees a child of three and even five or six years with a piece of bread in his hand, running to his mother to ask for *massa*, a gulp. It is particularly customary for widows to nurse their youngest child for the longest possible time, because they think that that will be especially good for his health.

Among the Serbs nursing lasts until the fourth or fifth year of the child. Usually the mother nurses the child until she again becomes pregnant. If a Serbian mother wishes to wean her child, she seats herself on the threshhold of her room and takes the infant to her breast for the last time. She thereupon places him on the ground, gives him a light stroke, puts a piece of bread in his hand, and says: "This shall be your nourishment; go forth calf, among the cattle!" According to the Serbian thought, a child who has once been weaned must never again be held to the breast, else he acquires bad eyes. If a woman, even for a short time, nurses a strange child together with her own, these two children cannot, according to Serbian custom, marry each other, but they are thought of as brothers or sisters.

If a Serbian woman gives birth to a second child while the first is still being nursed, the first one must immediately be weaned, even if the second one is born dead. For a child must not drink two kinds of milk, else it runs the danger, according to Serbian superstition, of becoming a sorcerer or a witch.

According to Syrian superstitions, the *moment* that a child is weaned is important not merely for his physical well being, but is also significant for his character. In order to protect his character from being ruined, they adopt the following method: In the evening they place a container with food on the steps and leave it there all night. The next morning, the first morning after the weaning, they put the child's shirt on on the wrong side and then they take the container from its retreat and give the child his first nourishment not coming from the breast.

On the day of the weaning of the infant, there took place among the ancient Hebrews feasts of sacrifice and especial festivities within the family circle. In the first Book of Moses, XXI, 8, it is told: "And Abraham made a great feast the same day that Isaac was weaned." In the first Book of Samuel, I, 24, the sacrifices which were given for such reasons are mentioned.

From the passage in Isaiah, VII, 14: "Behold, a virgin

shall conceive and bear a son. . . . Butter and honey shall he eat. . . ." Professor Ebstein deduces that even at that time substitutes for mother's milk were employed in bringing up children. Today one can find such substitutes in all city pharmacies in Turkey.

Convalescents and persons weakened by disease seek in Persia, through the use of women's milk, *schire dachter*, daughter-milk, to recover their lost power, and to be sure, in many cases, as Polak reports, with undeniably favorable results. At the straw market at Teheran one can often see Nomad women selling milk from their full breasts to sick ones.

Just as in these cases the women's milk creates a new life for those who are dying, so the southern Slavs believe that through terrible magic the women's milk may bring about death: if anyone spills the milk of two sisters at a definite time into a grave, a pestilence will come over the land. More delicate is the story of the southern Slavs which tells of a young woman who, as she was about to be built into a wall as a tree-offer, asked the builder to leave merely enough room for her to be able to offer her breast to her child. Numerous Bulgarian and Bosnian variations exist of this touching story of mother love: On the old mountain of Tesany in Bosnia there is a place where, according to the belief of the people, even today the milk bubbles forth from the breasts of the young woman Gojkovica who was walled in as a tree-offer; Moslem women journey here if their milk has run dry, and scrape cement and dust from the wall; this taken in food restores them to a richness of milk.

Finally, a custom is worth mentioning which is current among the Armenians and Maronites in Libanon: The mothers do not take their children to their breasts to nurse them, but they kneel down to the cradle and bend down with their breasts over the child, a staff over the cradle serving them as a support for the armpit.

CHAPTER THIRTY

# THE CHILD

*The happiness hood—The hood as a love charm among the Serbs—White
and hoods—Dalmatinian superstitions—Graco-Wallavian notions—Bosnian
and Syrian—First handling of the new-born child—Rubbing with salt—
Air and sun baths in Palestine—Blood-letting—First bath of the new-
born child in Monastir—Medicine and superstition—Blacking the face to
scare off the spirits—Earrings—Protection coins—Preventatives against sickness—Albanian and Serbian methods—Persian customs—Syrian customs—
Kisses prohibited—Cradle-superstition—Children's diseases—Their prevention and cure—Baths—Clothes of the children—The children's wetting—
A cause of epilepsy—The teeth—The schooling—Protection against premature death of children—Customs which affect an only child.*

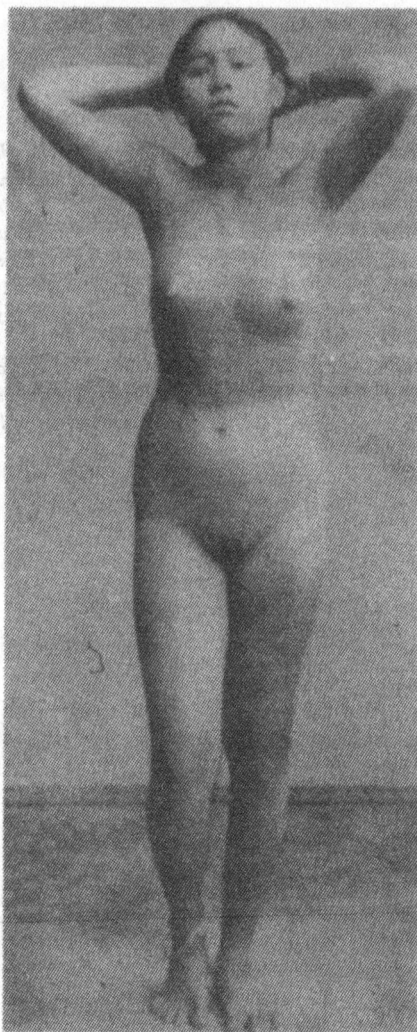

*Javanese—Mixed Type*

Among the Serbs a child which is born with a hood is called: *widowit;* the hood itself is called: *koschuljiza,* lucky shirt. They differentiate there between white and black (really, red) shirts. A lucky human is born with a white shirt. The black shirt, *crvena koschuljiza,* means that the child will become a sorcerer if it is a boy, and a witch if it is a girl. If the misfortune can be discovered in time, it can never happen. So says Krauss according to Vis Vuletitsch.

A Serbian maiden who is born with a hood, always carries it with her. It is particularly effective in matters of love. If a virgin falls in love with a young man, and he remains cool towards her, she need merely touch a naked part of his body, his face, his neck, or his hands, with the wonder-hood, and flaming love will spring from the boy of ice towards the possessor of the amulet. Also according to Dalmatinian superstition people born with white hoods are considered as children of happiness. In this case the hood is always carried on the body as an amulet. But if the hood is reddish, then it can easily become a witch's hood: a child born with a red hood is in danger, as the Serbians also believe, of becoming a sorcerer or a witch.

The Graco-Wallavians in Monastir call a child born with a hood, according to Dr. Sajaktzsi: *me tychi,* favored by fortune. The shirt is loosened by the midwife and pasted to a sheet of paper to dry. Since the wise woman loves to retain this much sought for piece so that she can produce it again at another birth, so the mother is careful that it shall not be mislaid; she takes it to her and keeps it under her pillow until *sarantismos,* that is until the woman in child-bed receives the blessing of the church. The precious piece is then brought to the church and it remains lying on the altar for 40 days. After it is thus sanctified, they wait until an official, a judge, or any person of standing, comes to visit in the place, and at this happy moment they place the shirt under a stone on the road or under a bridge so that the high person must cross over it.

One then makes it certain and protects it. Now it is forever effective. If an unjustly accused man wears a small piece as a talisman, he need have no anxiety over the success of his defense. During the trial at the speech of the complainant, he lets his arm hang loosely, and this demeanor of the possessor of the talisman deprives his opponent of his power and weakens his arguments. If the accused speaks in his own defense, he presses his arm to himself and through contact with the talisman he becomes wise and his arguments triumph. They often also carry the shirt under the arm or in the right shoe; in the latter case they must do with the foot as with the arm. The wanderer carries his shirt with him, and every enemy who crosses his path is blinded.

Among the Bosnian they cut the skin under the shoulder of a child born with a hood and place the lucky hood on the fresh wound so that it shall grow together. Such a child is forever protected against bewitchment.

In Syria they say of a child who came into the world with a lucky hood: it was born under a good star. At times the lucky skin is dried and worn as an amulet, not by the child itself, however, but by its father.

The most that one can say of their superstitious customs is that they are not useful, but they are also not harmful.

The entire body of the new-born child is almost always sprayed with salt and cinnamon by the oriental midwives. The worst is done, as Dr. Beck relates, by the Arabian Kabli in Bagdad; instead of pouring a mild powder on the small being who has just first seen the world, they always use *spidschad sykajun*, cinnabar and white lead. The most frequent results are quicksilver poisoning and lead colic.

Among the fellahs in Palestine the child is not washed after its birth but rubbed with finely powdered salt. This practice which is engaged in for several weeks is said to strengthen and harden the child. Not infrequently does this result in severe injury, such as loss of sight. But he who survives such treatment grows powerful and accustoms himself to a rough life. This manner of handling the new-born child is very old. In Ezekiel, XVI, 4, 6, 9, one finds the following description; " . . . in the day thou wast born thy navel was not cut, neither wast thou washed in water to supple thee; thou wast not salted at all, nor swaddled at all. . . . And when I passed by thee, and saw thee polluted in thine own blood. . . .Then washed I thee with water, yea, I thoroughly washed away thy blood from thee, and I anointed thee with oil." The healing of children's diseases is attempted to be effected by superstitious means or left entirely to nature. If a child scratches himself, he is sprayed with water containing a dissolved red powder; this powder is called *zerakon* and is said to be cinnabar. Among the Bedouins in Palestine, so Pastor Klein reports, the father carries the new-born child naked into the open, and lays it down where it is exposed to the hot rays of the sun for two or three hours. This is done to strengthen the child's eyes.

In Constantinople, at the slightest convulsion of the new-born child, his spine is tapped. The treatment which is the portion of the new-born child among the Graco-Wallavians in Monastir is, according to the reports of Dr. Sajaktzis, the following: The midwife pours some warm water and a handful of slat into a bucket, often also a few drops of wine, and bathes the child in this. The mother and the women looking on throw several coins of gold and silver into the bath, as a symbol that the child also in later life might travel a road strewn with gold. The coins and the other things naturally belong to the midwife. If the vessel in which the water for washing the child is cooked is uncovered, then the child will suffer with eye trouble. After the bath the midwife dresses the child in a little shirt, a little coat, and swaddling clothes: *hypo-*

*kamisso, anteraki* and *polopana;* she covers his head with a hood, wraps him in a large napkin, binds him with three ells of cord or *fasskia,* places him in a satin coverlet, attaches it to the hips with a cloth, and puts the child to bed in his own bed which is next to his mother's.

If·the child sleeps, the midwife finally wishes the mother luck in the following words: *Na ssass sisse,* may it remain with you, or: *Kalorrisika,* may you be happy; *me tus goneis,* may it become large. To the women present she says: *Na ssass eine gyrismena,* may it now be your turn! Then the midwife washes her hands, the other women do the same, and then enjoy glyco, sweets and coffee. On leaving they say to the woman in child-bed again: "May it remain with you!" And: "With a full breast and a full arm"—meaning: with the child— "shall you arise!" The first napkin and the first shirt for the child are presented with great festivity. On the evening before Green Thursday, if this holiday happens to fall about the time when the child is expected, the relatives of the prospective mother assemble in her house; all night long the wool is washed, dried, ironed, knitted—until in the morning, the first napkin, called *kolopanon,* is finished. Two weeks before the birth they take sheets from three strange houses and bring them near an innocent maiden who still has her parents; she must sit on a stone in the court from morning to night, under the guidance of an experienced woman, and begin and finish a shirt for the expected being.

Immediately after its first wrapping, the child is taken by an old woman and carried into a locked neighboring chamber, where she holds it in her arms throughout the first night, so that in no circumstance might it touch the ground and become bewitched by evil spirits. They also blacken the face of the child in order to scare away evil spirits. The right ear-lobe of the child, whether it is a boy or a girl, is pierced before its first drink and decorated with a silver or a gold earring, which it wears uninterruptedly for its first year. This earring has long before been provided: on Green Thursday they seek three families where the children are named Constantine, Helene, or Marie, and from each they take a gold or silver coin; these are brought to a goldsmith who fashions from them an earring.

It frequently happens that they take the new-born child to a woman who is known to possess an inherited ancient silver coin, which is called *Penezi*, so that she may scratch a cross with this coin between the eyebrows of the child.

In North Albania the mother of the woman in child-bed has the right to wrap the child. During the first weeks she takes care of this business indefatigably. Before the child is wrapped for the first time, they place on his bare belly for one moment a sickle with which straw has been shortly before cut. This action protects the small being from stomachaches.

Among the Serbians the mother prevents the new-born child from suffering with stomach pains by taking a little hay from the bed of the child on the first morning after its birth and holding it between her teeth.

The children are tightly wrapped all over. They place whole balls of cloth between their feet for reasons of cleanliness, their arms are pressed to their body and wrapped up. In Bagdad they free the arms of the children after a lapse of six weeks; in other places the term is varied.

Wrapped tightly hand and foot, the child in Persia is placed in a cradle, *gewahreh*, usually in a hanging one, because the latter swings more easily and the mother can remain away for a longer period of time. In order to induce sleep, they frequently give him *schaerbete chasch, syrupus diacodii*; in his second year he is given various fruits, and in poorer families rice.

Without end are the Syrian customs assembled by Eijub Abela which affect the child; sometimes the same are current

407

in other regions, and are even widespread in Europe. So this one: To cover a child's bed or to rock it when the child is not in it has a bad effect on the health of the child. In Syria especially they believe that the child can get pains of the back, if a child is left alone in his bed. The least that can be done for his protection against the evil one is to place a housemaid near his bed. The generally known prohibition in Europe of kissing a sleeping child is also intrenched among all nations of the Orient, among Christians, Moslems and Jews. It is most strictly observed by the Syrians.

Other superstitious Syrian notions are: When a new-born child is placed into its cradle for the first time, one must make a lusty noise so that the child shall become accustomed to the loud noises on earth and not be easily frightened. Since a girl does not become hairy, she is streaked with the blood of a bat immediately after birth. The first excrement of the child is preserved with particular care. It is wrapped in a sheet and placed under the mat near the threshhold of the door which leads to the room of the mother. Here it remains for three days, so that all visitors may step on it. That is a good method of protecting the health of the child. If they let the children cry much, they acquire black eyes; elsewhere they believe that it is good for the lungs, for the voice. If a child is put to bed with its stockings on, according to the opinion of the Christian Syrian, it gets scrofula. In order to cure this, the mother takes a silk thread, goes to the church, there makes a knot at every gospel, hurries home, and ties the silk thread about the arm of the child.

Another superstition of the Syrians known elsewhere is this: One must not step over a child lying on the ground, or the latter is in danger of ceasing to grow. If a person does this inadvertently, the threatening evil can be paralyzed if he immediately steps back over the child. According to a Syrian belief, one also prevents growth if he kisses the feet of a small child.

In order to free a child from drivel, the Syrians believe it is good to let the child be kissed by a negro.

A child is never bathed on Sunday or on Friday; on Sunday particularly among the Christians, on Friday, among the Moslems. If this is done the child gets convulsions. In order to make the convulsions disappear, two methods are preferred above all: rubbing with hydrogen sulphide and starch-flour.

If children or adults take a bath on the day of fasting if they are Christians, or during *Ramasan* if they are Moslems, they become subject to fearful skin diseases. Children's wash must not be hung up in the moonlight, or the child will be sick with diarrhoea.

If a child wears gold coins on his cap, he must remove these from the cap over night; if this is not done, the health of the child will suffer.

In order to cure a grown child of wetting himself at night, the women in Syria give him a roasted mouse to eat, concealing its identity. Among the Christians of Levantin, it is considered bad for a child to urinate on ashes. If this misfortune happens, then they must promptly draw a cross on his forehead with the ashes. If this is not done immediately, the child becomes an epileptic. If a child has become an epileptic through such neglect, a cross is impressed on his forehead with indigo. If the disease nevertheless continues, then the child must be given another name. If this is also of no avail, then the child is incurable, but no one can reproach his parents for not doing everything possible for his cure.

The orientals feed children who teethe with difficulty a hare's brain. When the child gets his first tooth, great joy prevails all over. Characteristic is the cry of joy with which the fellahs in Palestine greet this velepoment: "*Tela sino, chabbi lehubz anno*, his tooth is out, put the bread into the house!"

If the child teethe with difficulty, they call the midwife and she burns the skin underneath the tongue of the child several times with a glowing needle; if this does not help, her knowledge is at an end, and they must leave further developments to Allah. If the child is afflicted with inflammation of the brain as a result of difficult teething, they draw a glowing needle several times across his head.

The following practice was to be found among the ancient Arabs: If the milk tooth of the child fell out, the father of the child took the tooth between his thumb and index finger, held it toward his son and said: "Give me a better one for this." This practice which is said to guarantee growth and painlessness, goes back to very ancient sun worship.

The Moslems in Syria place a child who has not learned to walk after the lapse of the usual time is put into a basket. This is carried through the streets by two larger children, accompanied by innumerable boys and girls, and the entire small company sing: "Give the cripple something so that he may learn to walk. His little teeth have appeared; may it be as well with his feet!" This procession is most effective if it takes place on Friday at midday.

If the children of a woman die in Serbia or in Bosnia, a superstition directs them to have recourse to the magic of *Kojoj Gataju* without the knowledge of the mother. One of her friends obtains a horseshoe from a dead horse and gives it to a smith. In the middle of the night he must fashion out of this a slave ring or an arm band; during this work he must be entirely naked, "as he was born to his mother." If the woman afflicted with this misfortune receives an arm band created under such circumstances and always wears it on her right arm, she will never again lose a child.

Another Serbian method: The mother cuts off a reed and pours wine into it. She then places the reed near 9 cakes of wheat flour and an old knife into a linen bag and sews this together. With this packet she wades in flowing water, and while she carries the bag under her left arm, someone must pray on the bank and call upon all that is holy. She thereupon lets the bag fall and strides out of the water placing both feet in a vessel which stands on the bank; from this her husband lifts her and carries her on his back to the house.

In order to prevent premature death of the child, Moslem women in Bosnia make him a shirt out of rags which have been cut from the shirts of nine widows.

If a new-born child is the only one of his parents, he is drawn through an iron ring or brought in contact with an iron tripod, so that his bones may become strong as iron.

CHAPTER THIRTY-ONE

# BOYS AND GIRLS

*Demand for girls among the Kurds—Preference of boys over girls among
all other oriental nations—Will it be a boy or a girl?—Oriental pre-deter-
mination of sex—Retention by the pregnant woman—Its significance—The
significance of the raven's croaking and the hen's cry—Sayings—Desire for
boys—Bosnian method—Serbian superstition—The Old Testament on boys
and girls—Opinion of the Jews in the middle ages—Superstition of present-
day Jews in Syria—Elijah the boy bringer—Syrian customs—Arabian customs—The simple Turkish method—Birth feasts at the Osman Sultan's court
—Difference in festivities for princes and princesses—Historic exceptions—
The Koran on the superiority of man over woman—The daughter of
Allah— Murder of daughters among the heathen Arabs—The Koran on the
birth of Jesus.*

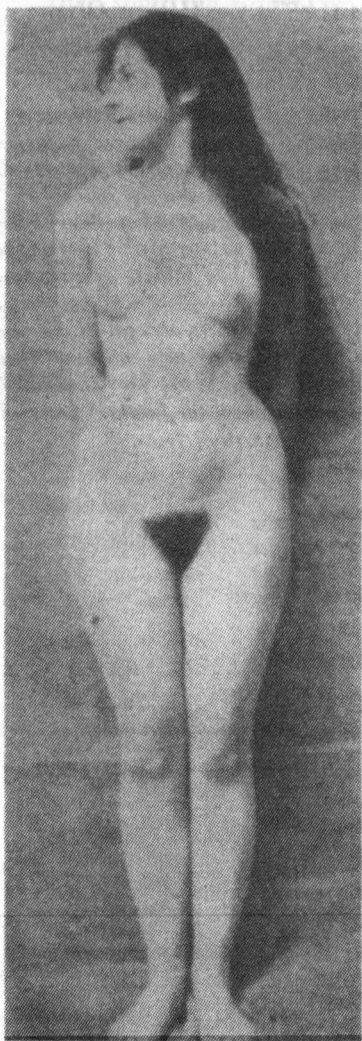

*Nineteen-year-old Roumanians*

In the Orient practically only the Kurds prefer girls to boys. The heads of the tribe purchase for their harems only maidens of their people and pay a great price for them. They prefer not to take the daughters of a strange people as wives, but usually as slaves; to honor them by marriage is deemed a terrible mesalliance. The demand for Kurden maidens is therefore great, and a greedy father is only too happy to be able to profit by this. Elsewhere, however, boys are quite generally desired.

Will it be a boy or a girl? This is the most important question which can be heard in a house which expects to be blessed by a new arrival. There are many specialists who claim to be able to tell by unfathomable signs what the sex of the child will be, and if they once guess correctly, they are thereafter always believed. Above all, the women pay careful attention to their dreams. These attentions bring in their train an unending group of actions and practices.

In Macedonia the Serbian and Bulgarian women gather from the kind of dreams they have during their pregnancy whether the expected child will be a boy or a girl. For example, if a pregnant woman dreams that a stone fell out of a ring or is broken off, then she is certain she will have a boy, but at the same time she receives the horrifying conviction that the boy will die immediately after birth.

In Albania the pregnant women know that they must expect a boy if a raven croaks near the house, or a cock crows out of turn at night. If, however, the owl hoots, then a girl will be born. In no event do they look forward to a girl with joy. They see death forecast in the same signs which indicate the birth of a girl. If there is no pregnant woman in the house, the hooting of an owl sitting on the roof signifies a premature death.

Among the Albanese and the Greeks the birth of a girl is deemed a misfortune for which the curses of a neighbor are to be thanked. They thereafter seek to protect themselves through all kinds of counter magic against the magic power of rivals or envious ones. The Graco-Wallavian women say: "Man is born with a cross on his head; we women, however, are poor Evas." Or: "Man comes into the world with a golden bag around his neck." If a boy is born among the Graco-Wallavians in Monastir, the midwife cries out: "Oh, a girl!" This is done so that the envy of the evil spirits may not be brought to bear upon the new-born child through great joy. After the first bath of the boy, his brothers and sisters hurry to their relatives and inform them: "A girl has been born!" Then they tell the truth. But if the new-born child is a girl, the midwife makes a hole in its earlobes immediately after the first bath and before it is placed on its mother's breast. If a girl is born after a girl, and not after a boy, the Graco-Wallavian women comfort the mother and say: "There is no harm done, may it live; each one has his fate; the parents are still alive, so the next one will be a boy!"

The Bosnian woman knows at her wedding the apportionment of her male or female descendants; if she puts on her wedding clothes "from a nail" she will have boys; if she wishes to give birth to girls, she dresses herself "from the polster", that is, she does not take her clothes from a nail but first lays them on the pillow of her bed. When the bride approaches the house of the bridegroom, there is placed into her hands a boy, whom she turns around three times, kisses and presents with something. In this manner she assures herself of a fruitful marriage and of the birth of boys. If a woman has brought only girls into the world and desires a boy, according to a south Slavic notion, she must wrap the lucky shirt—or the after-birth—of the first born girl in a shirt which her husband has already worn, and bury it; then the next child will be a boy.

According to Serbian superstition, a sty on the eye of a pregnant woman is considered a sign of whether she should ex-

pect a boy or a girl; if the sty is on the under lid, it means
that a girl will be born; on the upper lid, the birth of a boy.

Among the Jews boys were always more welcome than girls.
Psalm 127, 3, says: "Lo, children are a heritage of the Lord;
and the fruit of the womb is his reward." In the third Book of
Moses, XII, 2, there is portrayed in a drastic manner the difference between the birth of a boy and a girl. It says here: "If a
woman have conceived seed, and borne a man child, then she
shall be unclean seven days; . . . and she shall then continue in
the blood of her purifying three and thirty days; . . . But if
she bear a maid child, then she shall be unclean two weeks, . . .
and she shall continue in the blood of her purifying threescore
and six days."

The Jewish women in the early middle ages said that if the
house worm which was kept in the sleeping chamber fell on the
bed: The woman of the house is pregnant and will give birth
to a boy. The religious condemned such beliefs as heathen.

The present-day Jews in Syria are convinced that a boy
will be born if the dogs assemble in front of the house of the
woman in labor and bark. The Syrian Jews believe that the
dogs bark as soon as they see the Prophet Elijah, who remains
invisible to humans; the dogs rejoice with him, remembering
the huge meal which the Prophet made for their forefathers
through the killing of the priests of Baal. Humans, however,
consider the Prophet Elijah as the protector of every woman
who gives birth to boys.

Among the Syrians, just as among the other nations of the
Orient, they begin to train the young people even at the wedding for life to grant them boys: Old women at the wedding
discussion, relates Eijub Abela, give the newlyweds olives to
eat—that is an excellent method of empowering them to create
boys. When the woman becomes pregnant, she observes all
kinds of superstitious customs so that she might not be dis-
appointed in her hope to give birth to boys. It seems to her

as a good sign—as a sign that she will bring life to a boy—if she inadvertently takes a false step. If a small girl, who cannot yet talk, grasps a broom before the eyes of her pregnant mother and acts as if she wishes to sweep the room, then the mother knows that the next child will also be a girl. If this is the case, then the woman in child-bed eats much fish so that at least in the future she may give birth to sons.

The most passionate wish of the inhabitant of an Arabian village in Palestine is a numerous male progeny. At the birth of a boy, all the relatives, friends, and neighbors come and congratulate him with the words: "*Mubarak ma adschak,* be blessed for what you have acquired!" If the child is a girl, no notice of her birth is taken.

According to a Dalmatinian song from Ragusa, it is quite simple for a Turk to assure himself of the birth of a son. "The Turk," it says there, "beats his wife on the abdomen, hoping that she will bear him a son, and says: "O thou bitch, bear me a son!"

At the Sultan's court, usually only the birth of princes is brought to the public notice. The oriental historians speak of festivities in honor of the birth of a princess only as extraordinary, rare events.

The birth of a prince is always celebrated with special festivities if his mother was also the favorite. So says the historian of Sultan Mohammed IV: "The seven-day illumination which was ordered on account of the birth of the Prince Mustafa was even a greater happiness for the Sultan since the mother of the prince was the new favorite Sultana Chasseki." The Sultan later comforted himself over the loss of the battle of Chocim with the birth of his second son, Achmed, and ordered illumination for three days in the entire kingdom.

The historian reports an incident which transpired at about that time in the capital as something unheard of before: it concerned a cradle set with precious stones which the Sultana favorite presented to her sister-in-law, the wife of Kaimakam-paecha Redscheb, at her delivery of a female child; such a present and such disturbance over the birth of a girl, the daughter of a Vizier, had never been heard of before.

Under Sultan Mustafa III, the birth of the Princess Hebe-tullah, the first child of the Sultan, was celebrated with the extraordinary seven-day illumination, usually reserved for the birth of a prince. A month before the birth the prominent men of the guilds and the markets were instructed to keep themselves in readiness for an extraordinary decoration and illumination of the city. The whole city, therefore, swam in joy and a flood of light; poetry, laughter, and enthusiasm reigned. On the seventh day, in the name of the Vizier, the minister of the interior brought a golden cradle, set with precious stones. If Mustafa III celebrated the birth of a daughter to such an extent, it is not surprising that at the birth of the crown prince Selimhe he directed that the city be illuminated for seven nights and the sea for three nights with a flood of light. Captives from the Bango were given their freedom, among them several Catholic Armenians. The mother of the prince was a Georgian slave. Their joy was tempered by the death of the first-born daughter, Hebetullah, who had been engaged while yet in her cradle.

In several passages the Koran takes no notice of man's supremacy over woman. Chapter IV, 36: "Unto the men shall be given a portion of what they shall have gained, and to the women shall be given a portion of what they shall have gained."

IV, 38: "We have appointed unto every one kindred, to inherit part of what their parents and relations shall leave at their death." The Koran frequently objects sharply to any failure to give a woman her just due; so in VI, 140: "That which is in the bellies of these cattle is allowed to our males to eat, and is forbidden to our wives: but if it prove abortive, then they are both partakers thereof."

But contrary to all that goes before, Mohammed himself, in another passage, quite openly indicates a superiority of man over woman; chapter IV: "A male shall have as much as the share of two females. . . ." For: "Men are given more than women because Allah created man before woman, and because man pays for woman with his money."

An oriental tradition records the creation of the first human in the following manner: Adam was among the angels. Like all inhabitants of paradise he was sexless; in himself, in the power of his development he found all the happiness that he desired. Adam was therefore a hermaphrodite. He fertilized himself, and so Eve came from Adam. Adam himself was the fruit of a similar act of his creator.

The Koran is in every respect opposed to this fairy tale. In the second chapter, entitled "The Cow," it says: "There are some who say, God bringeth up children. This is far from truth!" In Chapter XVI, entitled "The Bee," the Koran says: "They attribute daughters unto God (far be it from him)."

The ancient Arabs considered the angels as daughters of God. They themselves wished to beget only sons. The birth of a daughter was thought of as a great misfortune, and they often killed these immediately after birth. There is a passage in the XVI Chapter of the Koran with relation to this: ". . . but unto themselves children of the sex which they desire. And when any of them is told the news of the birth of a female, his face becometh black and he is deeply afflicted; he hideth himself from the people because of the ill tidings which have been told him; considering within himself whether he shall keep it with disgrace or whether he shall bury it in the dust. Do they not make an ill-judgment?"

Koran, Chapter 43: "But when one of them hath the news brought of the birth of a child of that sex (namely, a girl), which they attribute unto the Merciful, as his similitude, his face becometh black, and he is oppressed with sorrow."

VI, 138: "... their companions have induced many of the idolators to slay their children ..."

VI, 141: "They are utterly lost who have slain their children foolishly, without knowledge; ..."

Koran, 43rd Chapter: "Do they therefore attribute unto God female issue, which are brought up among ornaments, and are contentious without cause? And do they make the angels, who are the servants of the Merciful, females? Were they present at their creation? Their testimony shall be written down, and they shall be examined concerning the same on the day of judgment. ... They have no knowledge herein: they only utter a vain lie. Have we given them a book of revelations before this; and do they keep the same in their custody? But they say, Verily, we found our fathers practising a religion; and we are guided in their footsteps."

LII, 39; LIII, 19-24: "Hath God daughters, and have ye sons?"—"Have ye male children, and God female? This, therefore, is an unjust partition. ..." "Verily they who believe not in the life to come give unto the angels a female appellation."

VI, 100-101: "Yet have they set up the genii as partners with God, although he created them: and they have falsely attributed unto him sons and daughters, without knowledge. Praise be unto him; and far be it from him which they attribute unto him! He is the maker of heaven and earth: how should he have an issue since he hath no consort?"

XXXVII, 149-157; XLIII, 14: "Have we created the angels of the female sex? and were they witnesses thereof? Do they not say of their own false invention, God hath begotten issue? and are they not really liars? Hath he chosen daughters preferably to sons?"

LXXII, 3: "He hath taken no wife, nor hath he begotten any issue."

VII: "Will they associate with him false gods which create nothing, but are themselves created; and can neither give them assistance nor help themselves."

XXXI, 12: "And remember when Lokman said unto his son, as he admonished him: Oh my son, give not a partner unto God; for polytheism is a great impiety."

CXII: "Say, God is one God; the eternal God: he begetteth not, neither is he begotten: and there is not any one like unto him."

X, 69-70: "They say, God hath begotten children; . . . ye have no demonstrative proof of this. Do ye speak of God that which ye know not? Say, Verily they who imagine a lie concerning God shall not prosper."

IX, 30: "The Jews say, Ezra is the son of God: and the Christians say, Christ is the Son of God. This is their saying in their mouths; they imitate the sayings of those who were unbelievers in former times. May God resist them. How they are infatuated!"

It is interesting to note that which is written in the Koran, XIX, 16-36, with reference to the birth of Jesus: "And remember in the book of the Koran the story of Mary; when she retired from her family to a place towards the east, and took a veil to conceal herself from them; and we sent our spirit Gabriel to her, and he appeared unto her in the shape of a perfect man. She said, I fly for refuge unto the merciful God, that he may defend me from thee: if thou fearest him, thou wilt not approach me. He answered, Verily I am the messenger of thy Lord, and am sent to give thee a holy son. She said, How shall I have a son, seeing a man hath not touched me, and I am no harlot? Gabriel replied, So shall it be: thy Lord saith, This is easy with me; and we will perform it, that we may ordain him for a sign unto men, and a mercy from us: for it is a thing which is decreed. Wherefore, she conceived him; and she retired aside with him in her womb to a distant place;

and the pains of child-birth came upon her near the trunk of a palm-tree. She said, Would to God I had died before this, and had become a thing forgotten, and lost in oblivion. And he who was beneath her called to her saying, Be not grieved; now hath God provided a rivulet under thee; and do thou shake the body of the palm-tree, and it shall let fall ripe grapes upon thee ready gathered. And eat, and drink, and calm thy mind. Moreover, if thou see any man, and he question thee, say, Verily I have vowed a fast unto the Merciful: wherefore I will by no means speak to a man this day. So she brought the child to her people, carrying him in her arms. And they said unto her, O Mary, now hast thou done a strange thing: O sister of Aaron, thy father was not a bad man, neither was thy mother a harlot. But she made signs unto the child to answer them; and they said, How shall we speak to him, who is an infant in the cradle? Whereupon the child said, Verily I am the servant of God; he hath given me the book of the gospel, and hath appointed me a prophet. And he hath made me blessed, wheresoever I shall be; and hath commanded me to observe prayer, and to give alms, so long as I shall live; and he hath made me dutiful towards my mother, and hath not made me proud or unhappy. And peace be on me the day whereon I was born, and the day whereon I shall die, and the day whereon I shall be raised to life. This was Jesus, the son of Mary; the Word of truth concerning whom they doubt. It is not meet for God, that he should have any son; God forbid! When he decreeth a thing, he only saith unto it, Be; and it is."

CHAPTER THIRTY-TWO

# MISCARRIAGES AND THE NAMING
# OF CHILDREN

*The Old Testament on monstrosities—Anxiety of orientals over monstros-*
*ities—Humans with tails—Known instances of such people—Albanian and*
*Wallavian opinions on the causes of deformities—Miscarriages in Crete—*
*From my notebook—Strange miscarriages in Constantinople and in Cavadar*
*—A Biblical story of many fingers—Means of strengthening weak children—*
*Bringing back to life apparently dead children—Protection of the new-*
*born child from evil spirits—Good names for the bad ones—Terrible names*
*for children—The giving of names among the Turks—Arabian names—The*
*unhappy name, Mustafa.*

425

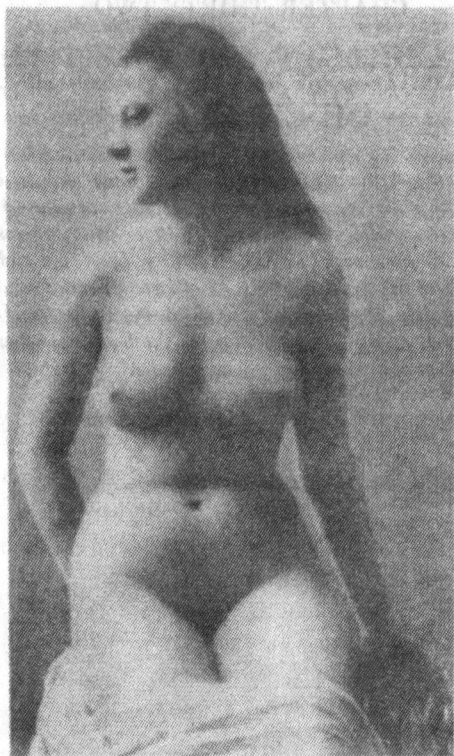

*Eighteen-year-old Czech*

Speaking of monstrosities, it is said in the 3rd Book of Moses, XXI, 17: "Speak unto Aaron, saying, Whosoever he be of thy seed in their generations that hath any blemish, let him not approach to offer the bread of his God. For whatsoever man he be that hath a blemish, he shall not approach: a blind mand, or a lame, or he that hath a flat nose, or anything super-fluous, or a man that is brokenfooted, or brokenhanded, or crookbacked, or a dwarf, or that hath a blemish in his eye, or be scurvy, or scabbed, or hath his stones broken . . ."

Considering the superstitious character of the orientals, it is self-evident that they must see something to be anxious over in the freaks of nature. The Albanese have a horrible fear of monstrosities and attribute to them all possible evil powers; they also believe that many spirits take the shape of deformed people. The female monster *Sukjennesa*, dog's eye, of their legends has four eyes: two in front and two behind. A child who is born with hairy pads on his shoulders is a *Drangoj*, a spirit in human form; it can fly or at least jump. On stormy night the infant flies out of the house of his parents and fights with demons. Only the mother must see the malformation on the boy of her child; if a stranger notices it, the power of the child, and his very life, vanishes.

In South Albania, Greece and Asia Minor they believe in the existence of humans with tails; humans with goats' tails and humans with little horses' tails. Sometimes they are recognized by other characteristics. They are exceptionally strong, built stockily and with heavy footsteps. Hahn, who first mentioned this, remarked: there is more to this than merely the legend of a people. Meckel related more ancient instances of this kind in his "Handbook of Pathological Anatomy," appearing in 1812. In more recent times similar reports have been made by Forster, Gerlach, Neumayer, Ornstein, and Bartels. Gerlach wrote an account of a foetus 77 millimeters long with a hairy tail-like growth. Doctor Ornstein, chief physician of the Greek army, made known the most interesting case in the year 1879 at a meeting of the Berlin Anthropology Association: In July, 1879, a 26-year-old Greek by the name of Nickolaus Agos, born in Livadia, was presented to him; this man had a five-centimeter-long tail hanging behind him.

The Graco-Wallavians in Monastir say of irregularly developed children or monsters: they bear a token of God. As fantastic-superstitious cases they offer: The wrath of God, the curse on a family, severe crimes which followed conception at a forbidden time.

Crete seems to be a land of horrible monstrosities, apparently corroborating the opinion of those philologists who derive the word cretin or idiot from Crete. Of the numerous cases which I noted, I wish to relate here but a few of the most noteworthy: In March, 1895, a Greek woman in Kanea gave birth to a child with two tongues, six fingers on each hand, and six toes on each foot, as was then reported in the Turkish records. The child died after several weeks. A shorter existence was the fate of a being that was born in July, 1895, in the village Sozurokefali Pedias on the island Crete to an insane Greek maiden; this body had the body of a human boy, but with the head, the feet, and the teeth of a dog. The monster was born alive, but it lived for only a few minutes. About May 15, 1895, in Constantinople, a Turkish woman gave birth to a child with two heads; the two-headed child lived for about ten weeks and died on July 22nd. The newspaper "Le Progres de Salonique" contained the following item in its issue of May 18, 1900: Several days ago a Turkish woman in Cavadar gave birth to two dead children; the twins were joined together at the hips, having a body with two heads, four arms, and four feet; just like the famous Siamese twins.

According to the belief of Professor Ebstein, the oldest example of superfluous fingers is reported in literature in that passage in the second Book of Samuel, XXI, 15-22, where

David's contest against the four giants of Gath is related. One of the four giants had six fingers on each hand and six toes on each foot.

For still-births and weak children they employ the following remedy: In Constantinople they stick the beak of a living hen into the rectum of children dead at birth, and hold the hen fast there. The convulsions and efforts of the hen to free her beak are supposed to awaken life in the child. If the child is merely unconscious, they must roast the placenta on a coal fire before cutting the navel cord; they believe that the child must be brought to life through the resulting smoke.

Among the Graco-Wallavians, if they notice that the child is born weak, or that it is a still-birth, they bring it to the church for baptism immediately after the bath, so that the child may not die as a heathen or Ebraiopulo, as a Jewish child; if it dies before baptism, then it is buried apart from baptised people, without benefit of clergy.

The first care of the parents in all places is to protect the new-born child against bad demons. An indispensable amulet is a piece of the navel cord which the child wears on his cap at least as long as he is kept at the mother's breast. When a Wallavian woman presses her new-born child to her breast for the first time after her delivery, she must say loudly, in order to protect it from all evil: "May a stone fall in the throat of the evil spirit!" But in Monastir they say euphemistically: "That comes from a good one!" if a child is ill through the wickedness of an evil spirit.

I have already mentioned several similar euphemisms. Since they are afraid to use the true names of witches and spirits of disease, they give them false descriptions and names. For a witch the Balkan Slavs say: *Mora* or *Krstatscha*, one designated with a cross, or *Rodulja*, the horned one.

According to Hahn the North Albanese call the hobgoblins, who signify only evil, and bring disease and death to all

429

upon whom their gaze falls, nothing less than: *Stojzowale*, which means propagator of the choir, that is, the choir which sings hymns of praise to God. This religious designation is supposed to put the hobgoblins in a friendly mood. When one speaks of them, he disguises his meaning for the same reason with the wish: may God increase them like grass and leaves! In South Albania, likewise, they give the demons antonymical names. They call them: *Fatmire*, the happy ones; *Nus e Mallpet*, brides of the mountain.

In times of pestilence the Serbs do not mention the name *Kuga*, but say: *Kuma*, godmother. It is considered sinful, even dangerous, to enunciate the name of death, *Smrt*, they say simply: *Bolestschiza*, the disease; or: the beloved disease; or also, *Kuma*, godmother.

If one inadvertently lets fall the word *Jejina* before children, he must immediately pull on the ears of the children to prevent the development of paralysis. Lilith, who according to Jewish superstition, is dangerous for women in child-bed and children, has the nickname: "The beautiful." In Damascus the Moslems call the lepers: "the gentlemen"; but the Christians say "the brothers".

The Bedouins never call a dangerous snake anything but "maiden". The ape, whom the Bedouins believe to be one who brings illness, is nevertheless called "the bearer of happiness". They carefully give the devil merely the title: "furious beard". If one is disposed to ward off and pacify evil spirits through the use of friendly appellations, he may also endeavor, conversely, to scare them off by giving the new-born child a horrifying name; in this manner they believe they can frighten the demons of disease from the new-born children.

I have related similar Caucasian customs in my book, "Between Kaspi and Pontus". But one also finds these customs among the Russians, the Tong Chinese, and the Siamese, as well as in many sections of Europe.

The ceremony of the giving of the name among the Turks can take place according to law at any time within the first 40 days after the birth. But it is customary for this to happen on the very day of the birth during the first three hours. It is not necessary for the *Imam* to be present. The father of the child, in his capacity as head of the family, has the right to give the child any name which pleases him; the mother is not asked for her opinion. In the cities it is customary for the *Imam* to be called; but here also it is not obligatory. The giving of the name is very simple. The person giving the name approaches the right ear of the child and says the *Esann*: "Great God! Great God! Great God! Great God! I show you that there is no God but God. I show you that Mohammed is the Prophet of God! Come to prayer! Come to prayer! Come into the temple of healing! Great God! Great God! There is no God but God!" Then he bends over to the left ear of the child and says the *Ilkameth*: that is, he repeats the *Esann* until he comes to the words, "come into the temple of healing" and then adds: "See, everything is ready for prayer!" He then gives the child the name: "Your name is ——." And the ceremony is over.

The word *Ibn*, which appears in Moslem names, means son, and if it is prefixed to a name it means: "the son of". So, for example, Hassan Ibn-Mehmed: Hassan, the son of Mehmed. Among respectable and important families, as *The Journey to Nolde* has already related, the name of a particularly prominent man is adopted as the family name. So, for example, in spite of the fact that the father of the Emir of Hail was called Abdallah, the Emir was not called Ibn-Abdallah, but Ibn-Raschid, after another famous ancestor. Besides this, the prefix is often dropped for the head of an important house and used only for the younger members of the family. So: Ibn-Raschid, Ibn-Haddal, are simply the equivalent for: "The Raschide", "the Haddal". These examples of Nolde are of special significance, for they speak in Europe of the Emir Ibn Raschid since the tenth year without having any idea that he was the second or third bearer of that name in distant Arabia.

A name distinguished in Osman history through its sorrowful fame is Mustafa, of which Hammer reports in the fourth volume of his history of the Osman Kingdom.

Sultan Mustafa, the third of that name, the son of Achmed III, was born in an unlucky year of the Osman kingdom, and his name, Mustafa, had been unlucky in Osman history from the beginning of the kingdom. The first prince of that name, the son of Bajesid, was lost in the battle of Angora in which his father was taken prisoner by Timur, without ever being heard from again, unless he was the Mustafa who arose in Europe as the dangerous successor to the throne of Mohammed I and Murad II, and who was then beseiged in the battle of Ulubad and hanged on a steeple in Adrianople.

Another Mustafa, Boreludsche Mustafa, was the leader of the great Dervish resolution in Asia Minor; he was crucified, while his adherents were cut to pieces before his eyes. Mustafa, the thirteen-year-old brother of Murad II, also an heir to the throne, just as were the three previous ones, was betrayed by the cupbearer Elias and hanged on a fig tree before Nicaa. Mustafa, the son of Mohammed II, the general and governor of Karaman, died prematurely, poisoned at the behest of his father. Mustafa, the son of Suleimus, a lover of knowledge and poetry, succumbed to the intrigue of the Sultana Roxelane and her son-in-law, Rustem Pascha, at Eregli; he was suffocated in the presence of his father. The most hopeful of the nineteen sons of Murad III was a Mustafa, whose poetic mourning at the death of his father presaged his own. After the disposal of eight heirs to the throne by the name of Mustafa, one by that name finally became Sultan, and he was deposed and thrown into the dungeon at Kafig. Mustafa, the second Sultan of that name, deserter at the field of battle at Zenta, subscriber to the worst peace treaty of the Osman kingdom, namely, that of Karlowicz, and was dethroned through revolution. After these ten unfortunate Mustafas, the third Sultan of that name arose as a twenty-six-year-old ruler of the Osman throne; he is the only one of that name who lost neither throne nor life violently, but he did not understand how to conduct either one properly.

## CHAPTER THIRTY-THREE

# CIRCUMCISION

*Mosaic writings—Opinions of Maimonides—The Turk Omer Haleby on circumcision among the Moslems—Circumcision not a purely religious act— Difference between the Jewish and the Moslem interpretation—Circumcision not compulsory for renegades—Circumcision and sex life—Curious observation of Omer Haleby—The ceremonies—Time of circumcision—The operation for grown persons—From the practice of my friend, Dr. Beck—Circumcision in Persia—Circumcision and wedding called "high-time"—Circumcision feasts at the Osman court—Circumcision of Christian boys in honor of the Moslem belief—Circumcision of orphans as a good deed.*

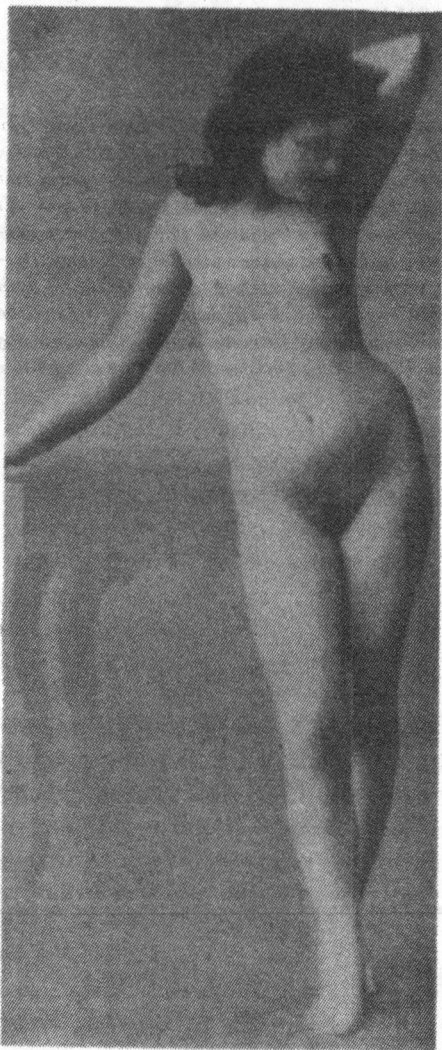

*Fifteen-year-old Greek*

In the first Book of Moses, XVIII, 11-14, it is decreed: "And ye shall circumcise the flesh of your foreskin; and it shall be a token of the covenant betwixt me and you. And he that is eight days old shall be circumcised among you, every man child in your generations, he that is born in the house or bought with money of any stranger, which is not of thy seed. . . . And the uncircumcised man child whose flesh of his foreskin is not circumcised, that soul shall be cut off from his people; he hath broken my covenant."

Following this passage, circumcision was instituted among the Hebrews of Abraham in the year 2107 since Adam, as a sign of the covenant. There is a diversity of opinion on whether circumcision was first practiced by Abraham, or whether Abraham adopted it from other nations. Other writers have said enough about circumcision among the Hebrews. I mention only several things from which parallels must be drawn to Moslem circumcision. Maimonides was of the opinion that circumcision was instituted for the prevention of abuse of the sexual urge. The Turk, Omer Haleby, also considered circumcision mainly from the sexual point of view. On the command, "on the eighth day the foreskin must be circumcised," Rabbi Jacob commented in the following manner: The circumcision could also be performed later, if the child is sick on the eighth day after its birth; likewise if an adult is taken into the covenant and is sick on the eighth day. A sick child must not be circumcised until he is completely well. Seven days are counted from the day of his return to health, and on the eighth, circumcision takes place. A child whose body is yellow and red must not be circumcised. Circumcision is always dispensed with if it is feared that it may be dangerous to the life of the child. If two sons of a family die as a result of circumcision, then the third must not be circumcised.

It is worthy of note that at the present time the law of

437

circumcision is no longer observed by many Jewish families in Europe.

Omer Haleby defines the act of circumcision among the Moslems so that it appears to be quite different from that among the Hebrews; it is no sign of a covenant; Christians converted to Islam are not compelled to have themselves circumcised. "Many believe," says Omer Haleby, "that circumcision is a purely religious act commanded by the Prophet. That is an error. Among the Hebrews circumcision was a sign of their belief. But they were not the first to do that. Before them, circumcision was prevalent among many Asiatic nations, where it happened, no because of religion, but for hygienic and social reasons. The Jews borrowed this operation from the Egyptians, and created from it, in the form of an unquenchable sign of their belief, a truly national baptism, the most significant religious act of Judaism. When Mohammed proclaimed the good message of Islam, circumcision existed according to the manner of the Israelites or according to other methods among almost all nations. Only the Christians and the Sabaers were exceptions. The disciples of John the Baptist were included, and they are among the circumcised today; but circumcision is not treated as a sign of baptism among them, but is merely a general rule of hygiene and a sign of their Hebrew origin. The same holds true for the Abyssinian Christians. Mohammed recognized the hygienic and social effects of circumcision and permitted the operation to be performed upon all true believers, but without making it an absolute religious duty. It is therefore improper to see a religious dogma in the circumcision of the foreskin among Moslems, which reminds one of the Jewish ceremony. For us circumcision is not a kind of baptism, nor a strengthening of our belief; it is an act the practice of which can be dispensed with in case it becomes apparent that life may be in danger as a result of it, or in case of a natural obstacle."

These, according to Omer Haleby, are the "principles". In general circumcision, which may be performed by any public barber, is prescribed for all good Moslems as a lawful, hygienic, and if they wish to observe the religious laws, as a religious practice. One can, repeats Omer Haleby, be a true Moslem according to the laws of Islam, although uncircumcised; but circumcision brings so much good with it that every good Moslem should have his children circumcised. The good which is primarily derived therefrom is moral; circumcision is, as for example among the Jews, a suggestive sign, a symbol of an entire religious or political unit. This sign, indicated on that organ which bears a direct relation to the brain, is desired particularly for the purposes of suggestion. Under the suggestion of such a sign, all those circumcised feel as one race, which has the same general intellectual and physical characteristics. Thus, circumcision is a political and social act; a sign that those joined therein live in the same belief, according to the same principles. In this manner generations follow generations, maintaining the same ideas, the same laws, the same attributes, the good as well as the bad. This atavistic law explains in truth the perpetuation of the Jewish character in spite of all disruptions and misfortunes which the children of Israel have undergone to this day.

The influence of circumcision among the Moslems is, however, different in a moral as well as in a suggestive connection. It is true that there exists in it for Islam also a suggestive power which draws all Moslems together. But this suggestion is not the same as among the Jews. It has only little influence on the different characters and the physiological types which are found among the many different nations of Islam. Among the Moslem it is somewhat similar to what it is among the Abyssinians and the Coptic Christians, among the disciples of John the Baptist and the Sabaers, who have also adopted circumcision, without being considered as having any absolute re-

439

ligious significance. It is neither a baptism, nor a symbol of belief, it can neither hinder the spread of Islam among all other nations, nor can it foster progress of the race. Its primary significances is hygienic. And by hygienic, our friend Omer Haleby means the following, to which we immediately take exception: "The removal of the foreskin protects the child from rubbing his penis to remove the residue which remains on the gland after urinating, in other words, to prevent the stimulation of an unconscious urge for onanism. Furthermore, through the performance of this operation, the development of the *dkor,* the sex organ, is facilitated, and its power is increased. And when the youngster attains the age when dawn brings with it the desire for sexual enjoyment, his circumcised organ is fully developed and powerful, and it permits him to practice coitus with no fear for his health and with great pleasure for the woman whose sex organ is touched by a thoroughly hard, sweet and complete *dkor.* If a man has intercourse with a woman who is sick, he runs less danger of catching the disease than one who is not circumcised; and if he does become sick, he can more easily be cured. Circumcision is for us, therefore, a virile power against onanism when we are children, and against ithyphallic immoralities when we are adults. For the foregoing reason circumcise your sons—but do not force the operation on new converts to Islam!"

The ceremony of circumcision can take place during the first 40 days after birth at the same time as the giving of the name or separately. But the time is not definitely fixed by law. Usually the operation is performed on children between their ninth and thirteenth year. Dr. Beck told me that in the interior of the kingdom the operation is postponed until the young men are called for military service; at one time in Damascus Dr. Beck circumcised a whole company, which came from Kurdistan. The soldiers did not suffer this ceremony

440

without loud complaints, which is certainly not a simple one for adults.

In Persia, as Dr. Polak reports, circumcision takes place about the third or fourth year; it is considered there, quite in contrast to the opinions of the Turk, Omer Haleby, as the most important act at conversion to Islam. The operation is performed by forcing the head of the penis into a split tube and having the barber, *dalak*, cut off the foreskin in the middle with a razor. The blood flow is stopped by use of a styptic powder; the application of water is strictly forbidden. Of course, the ceremony is accompanied by many festivities, gifts are dispensed to the army, guests are invited and showered with sweets, the patient receives a new dress; in general, however, they do not display as much pomp as in other Moslem countries.

According to the language custom of the Arabs, the Persians and the Turks, as Hammer declares, not only the wedding of a maiden, but also the circumcision of a boy is conducted under the name of "high-time"; according to the concept of the east, the wedding feast is given only for the bride and not for the groom, who as a boy received compensation in the form of the feast of the circumcision for the pain he suffered thereby, while the wedding festivities are now given as compensation for the pain of the maiden and to dry her tears.

The circumcision feasts at the Osman court were always ostentatious, according to the reports of Hammer. When Murad I left Brussa in order to extend his conquests to Europe, he first, in the year 1387, celebrated the circumcision feasts of his three sons, Bajesid, Jacob, and Saudschi with the invitation of many guests, and the dispensation of presents and clothes of honor to the shahs and dervishes. When Sultan Mohammed, in the year 1457, was compelled to withdraw in disgrace from Bagdad and turn back to Adrianople, he was urged to eradicate the sad impression of his position with his people through feasts and splendor. He therefore ordered the circumcision feasts of his two sons, Bajesid and Mustafa, one of whom resided at Amasia, the other at Magnesia. These were invited to Adrianople with their households; at the same time circulars were sent all over the kingdom calling together those learned in the law and those valiant in war, the judges and the poets. Tents were set up on an island near Adrianople, and among them a throne was erected for the festive assemblage of the Sultan. On the second day the shahs and fakirs were treated in a royal manner after the Sultan had entertained them with spiritual conversation; on the third day there took place the contests with weapons, horse races, and bow-and-arrow contests; and the victors were given royal prizes; on the fourth day, the last of the circumcision feast, money was distributed among the people. All the nobles brought presents for the Sultan.

In the year 1491, Sultan Bajesid II came back to Constantinople only for the purpose of celebrating the double feast of the circumcision of his grandson and the wedding of his daughter. Sultan Suleimus followed the example of the conqueror Mohammed. With the idea of falsifying the reasons for his retreat from Vienna, Suleimus ordered a feast to be given at Constantinople, the splendor of which had never before been equalled. The circumcision of his sons furnished the opportunity for this. Besides the usual invitations to the officials and great men of the kingdom, one was also extended this time to the Doge of Venedigin Order to bring him to the circumcision feast of the four princes as a friend and neighbor. The latter excused himself, however, on the ground of his age and the distance of the journey, but he was represented by a most unusual messenger, bearing gifts for all.

At noon on the 27th of June, 1530, reports Hammer's history, accompanied by his entire household, Suleimus went to the hippodrome, at whose northern side, near Mehterchane, the place where the orchestra was quartered, there arose a splendid throne, covered with rick silks, decorated with many different

442

kinds of draperies, and surrounded by many tents. For fifteen days jubilation reigned, contests of various kinds and descriptions were conducted, presents were given and honors bestowed. On the fifteenth day the great banquet of the Sultan took place.

Circumcision, which according to the example of Abraham was made the duty of every Moslem, is still today celebrated in the Sultan's court midst great festivities; but it is no longer an affair of state as formerly, and the time is past when the Sultan had to give the appearance of inviting the Doges and the Emperors in person to the circumcision feasts of the princes, and when the foreign powers *nolens volens* had to send costly presents as inevitable tributes.

In closing I must not forget to mention that circumcision among the Osmans often gave them an opportunity to show their acquired magnanimity, especially towards opponents and enemies. The Grandvizier Ali, the son of the doctor, so it is reported, in his last will and testament, particularly expressed the wish that both of his minor sons, whose circumcision feasts he had been unable to celebrate himself, be circumcised at the first opportunity. The Grandvizier Raghib took upon himself the duty to further this good work of Islam. At the circumcision of his own sons, Hasanbey and Suleimusbey, the sons of the son of the doctor, the son of the deceased Kiaja Dervish, and the executed Grandvizier Silihdar Ali, were circumcised at the same time.

# HIGHWAYS
# OF PROGRESS

BY
JAMES J. HILL

Books for Business
New York - Hong Kong

# Highways of Progress

by
James J. Hill

ISBN 0-89499-025-X

Copyright © 2001 by Books for Business

Reprinted from the 1910 edition

Books for Business
New York - Hong Kong
http://www.businessbooksinternational.com

# CONTENTS

# INTRODUCTION

NATIONS, like men, are travellers. Each one of them moves, through history, toward what we call progress and a new life or toward decay and death. As it is the first concern of every man to know that he is achieving something, advancing in material wealth, industrial power, intellectual strength and moral purpose, so it is vital to a nation to know that its years are milestones along the way of progress.

About this conviction centre much of our public thought, most of our public discussion, nearly all of our public action. The methods suggested or adopted may be mistaken; may, and indeed often do, lead in the wrong direction. But the aspiration is true and it is constant. It searches always among policies, devices, inventions and systems for the few broad ways that lead to a real advance all along the line. This is the ancient method of natural selection, by which men and nations have improved upon their own past.

Down to within a century this study of ways and means dealt almost wholly with abstractions. It sought to establish certain general principles and universal laws which, once put into words, would be as final for social activity as the rules of arithmetic are for the solving of its problems. These made up the science of the old political economy. But the application of a system of unchanging laws to those variable quantities, man and society, proved unworkable; and orthodox political economy fell into a deeper disrepute than it deserved.

This has been followed by a period of almost pure empiricism in our economic thought and conduct. Each incident, each danger and each need has been isolated, enlarged and studied alone, with little regard to the organic relation between the different interests in the life of man, and the general laws that unify them. The result is conflict, confusion, failure and waste of material and mental forces. Many thoughtful people, including some of those who should be instructors and leaders of the public, have fallen victims to the purely imaginative theories of socialism; theories which, if they could be literally applied, would destroy the vitality of society as an organic thing and establish a tyranny so universal and so minute as to make both the industrial and the social life of man intolerable. There is great need of a broader understanding of the relation of one interest to another in the social life of man; of their interdependence as well as their separate values; of the community as an economic whole.

The physical sciences have added to knowledge by applying the particular fact to the general law as explanation or corrective, and the general law to the particular fact for purposes of classification and new generalization. By this same combination of the abstract and the concrete, the general and the particular, they have thrown new light on the material world and its laws within a century. It seems to be time to apply their method to economic facts and changes.

The present volume is, within the limits set by its range of subjects, an effort in that direction. In it I have discussed those matters with which study and experience have made me best acquainted, and endeavoured both to fit laws to facts and to combine facts so that their laws may be made plain. Just such a combination of the inductive and the deductive methods every successful man makes every day of his life. It is, indeed, the main secret of his success. It should, therefore, make clear what are some of the things that we must seek and what some of those that we must avoid. This volume does not attempt to cover the immense field; but simply, as a collection of studies in applied economics, to erect here and there, along the road the nation travels, certain sign-boards where the ways diverge and mark them, "Highways of Progress." The effort may not be successful, but it is at least sincere.

The first chapter indicates the scope and outline of the work. It consists of an address delivered in 1906 before the Agricultural Society of Minnesota. This was published nearly a score of times by individuals, institutions and societies in this and other countries, and has been translated into several languages. It was the first to announce the doctrine of Conservation as a whole, and not an incident of some one occupation; and it sought through this to fix the nation's attention upon the necessary re-adjustment of industry with reference to our greatest asset, the soil. The eager interest with which the discussion thus opened up was received and taken up by the public, and by the President of the United States, was proof of the need for it and its timeliness. Because of its part in the development of a more practical industrial ideal, and because the other chapters follow out in detail the lines of its argument, this has been republished unchanged.

The last chapter, also, is published substantially as delivered before the Conference of Governors that met at the White House, Washington, in the latter part of 1907. Looking backward over the field of conservation, as the opening chapter looks forward, it is given as a fitting conclusion to the volume.

The intermediate chapters, some of which appeared in recent numbers of *The World's Work*, deal with conclusions of fact reached by the method just stated. Many of their ideas and expressions may be found in addresses made or articles published by me during the last ten years. But they are here arranged for the first time around their logical central thoughts; here first connected with all the lines of statistical fact that substantiate them; here first set in that relation of parts to a whole which gives to the book its title, *Highways of Progress*. If it shall help to make that way plain, the labour that has gone to its preparation will be well repaid.

SAINT PAUL,                     JAMES J. HILL.
    May 1, 1910.

HIGHWAYS OF PROGRESS

# HIGHWAYS OF PROGRESS

## CHAPTER I

### The Nation's Future

THE highest conception of a nation is that of a trustee for posterity. The savage is content with wresting from nature the simple necessaries of life. But the modern idea of duty is conservation of the old and modelling of the new in order that posterity may have a fairer dwelling place and thus transmit the onward impulse. The ideal of the prudent, loving, careful head of every family is the true ideal for a nation of rational men. The people of the United States, as far as any perhaps, have meant to follow this pattern. It is worth while to consider how far they have been successful and where they have failed.

The average man is often more interested in speculative theories than in his plain duty toward himself and his neighbour. The average state is filled with visions of its place in the procession of the years, while it overlooks the running account of daily expenses. Problems we have found and trifled with, in confusing number and variety; but the problem of the future material condition of our country, of an inventory of its assets and liabilities, of the inevitable demands upon its resources and the careful adjustments by which alone they may be preserved, has thus far been a subject for little more than a passing thought. National security calls for a just accounting of the business affairs of this great nation.

Let us try to cast our minds twenty or twenty-five years ahead and see what will then be our condition. The main elements of this problem, which above all others should command our attention, are three: Possibilities of population, actual and possible natural resources, and possibilities of productive application of one to the other. As the prudent man, about settling himself in life, sums up his possessions, his opportunities for earning income and the demands upon him of a family to be fairly cared for and left in a position to begin the world at least as advantageously as he did himself, so the people of the United States should know with reasonable exactness just where we must stand half a century from now.

The population index has the simplicity of ascertained vital statistics. Subtracting from the total population of the country as returned by each census since 1880 the immigration for the decennial period, the ratio of increase for the first decade is slightly over, and for the second decade slightly under fifteen per cent. So careful an observer as Leroy Beaulieu gives the natural increase of our population as fifteen and two-tenths per thousand per year. It is fair, therefore, to reckon the increase by the excess of births over deaths at fifteen per cent. on the average, for each decade. The additions by immigration are more variable. It is highly probable, however, that the incoming tide will increase. Only in periods of severe depression has immigration fallen much below the half-million mark for the last twenty-five years. In good or fairly good times it has gone greatly above. In the two years before 1905 it exceeded 800,000 annually, while for 1905 and for 1906 it exceeded 1,000,000. It is a conservative estimate, therefore, to add 750,000 a year for increase of population from this source, or 7,500,000 for each decade. Computed on this basis, the population of the United States in the near future will show these totals:

| Population in 1910 | . . . . . . . | 95,248,895 |
| Population in 1920 | . . . . . . . | 117,036,229 |
| Population in 1930 | . . . . . . . | 142,091,663 |
| Population in 1940 | . . . . . . . | 170,905,412 |
| Population in 1950 | . . . . . . . | 204,041,223 |

These figures announce the magnitude of our problem. It is not even a problem of to-morrow, but of to-day. Within forty-four years we shall have to meet the wants of more than two hundred million people. In less than twenty years from this moment the United States will have 130,000,000 people. Where are these people, not of some dim, distant age, but of the generation now growing to manhood, to be employed and how supported? When the searchlight is thus suddenly turned on, we recognize not a mere speculation, but the grim face of that spectre which confronts the unemployed, tramping hateful streets in hope of food and shelter.

We cannot adapt our conditions to our future by restricting the growth of population. The natural increase by birth will continue. We may not, did we wish it, interfere with the immigration movement, except perhaps to enforce a more careful scrutiny of the moral and industrial fitness of these newcomers. Notwithstanding the addition of more than a million people a year from abroad, nearly all of them men and women who must work for a living, labour outside of the cities was never as scarce or wages as high as at the present time. Immigration lingers in the great centres and adds to the difficulties attending employment.

The farms stretch out their hands in vain. Railroads have to get labourers for building extensions at the highest market price, and find a large percentage of those whom they employ mere hoboes who desert as soon as they have succeeded in getting transportation from one part of the country to another. Farmers besiege the employment agencies in vain, and offer the lazy tramp a sum for a day's work in the field unheard of in any other country in the world. The situation grows more embarrassing yearly. Hours of labour are being reduced in some of the states for farm as well as shop hands. Men are scarcer as the movement of population to the cities grows more pronounced. A considerable portion of any crop more than usually abundant is either reduced in quality or altogether lost by reason of the impossibility of getting labour to handle it properly. Discouraged small farmers sell their land to larger proprietors who can profitably substitute machinery for men.

The country needs more workers on the soil. Not to turn the stranger away, but to direct him to the farm instead of the city; not to watch with fear a possible increase of the birth rate, but to use every means to keep the boys on the farm and to send youth from the city to swell the depleted ranks of agricultural industry — this is the necessary task of a well-advised political economy and an intelligent patriotism.

The United States has been able easily to take care of its great increase of population in the past because it had a vast area of unoccupied land. This was the main asset in its natural inheritance. Within practically the last half of the last century the whole country from the Mississippi River to the Rocky Mountains was occupied. No pressure of population could make itself severely felt when it might be turned loose in such an empire. In those fifty years there were added 547,640,932 acres to the agricultural area, an increase of nearly two hundred per cent., and the increase in the actually improved acreage was nearly three hundred per cent. This is cut off from the list of our resources. Within the last six years there have been transferred from public to private ownership more than 100,000,000 acres of Government land, an area twice the size of the State of Minnesota. The entire area of surveyed and unappropriated land within the United States is only two and a half times that amount.

At the present rate, therefore, every acre of public land would disappear within the next fifteen years. But as a large percentage of the lands included in this estimate are wholly or partially unfit for tillage, it is literally true to say that our arable public lands have almost disappeared. And where are our children to find standing room, and the tens of millions of the future a place for wholesome industry? This is an intensely practical question. It is immediate. For within twenty years we must house and employ in some fashion fifty millions of additional population; and by the middle of this century, at a time when the child now born will be in the prime of life, there will be approximately two and a half times as many people in the United States as there are to-day.

No nation in history was ever confronted with a sterner question than this certain prospect sets before us. What are we to do with our brother, whose keeper we are? How are we to provide our own children with shelter and their daily bread?

Rational consideration of our potential resources and of available future employment for this great multitude must, of course, proceed together. Labour must have material to work upon; and labour and material must also be so conjoined that the sum total shall be an increase of product equal to the advancing demands upon it, while at the same time our natural resources shall not be exhausted. Only thus can the future be made safe. Only thus can the people of the years to come be saved from retrogression. We come back to the big, fundamental things; to raw materials, and supply and demand, and the severe utilities without which no nation, great or small, can long keep poverty and distress or even death at bay.

"Of all the sinful wasters of man's inheritance in the earth — and all are in this regard sinners — the very worst are the people of America." These are the words of a great scientific authority, the late Professor Shaler, of Harvard University. This nation of presumably busy and serious men has originated many wasteful and extravagant policies; nay, worse, it prides itself upon some of the very records of consumption which establish the astonishing fact of national destruction and waste that cannot be repaired. The mighty wealth of this continent was adequate, with ordinarily provident handling, for an indefinite increase of the demands upon it. The inheritors of this wealth have already so far dissipated it that some prudent care of the residue cannot be postponed without certain disaster.

The summation of actual resources of national wealth is a comparatively short and simple process. Passing over the atmospheric elements that minister indirectly to the national economy, there are just four sources from which mankind must draw all natural wealth. Of these the sea does not supply more than two or three per cent. of man's food. It may therefore be dropped from the calculation, as it cannot be made much more largely contributory to human support. The forest, once a rich heritage, is rapidly disappearing. Its product is valuable not for food, but for shelter and as an accessory in the production of wealth. Its fate is interesting here rather in the role of an example. For we have done already with our forests what we are doing just as successfully with the remainder of our natural capital. Except for the areas on the Pacific Coast, the forest as a source of wealth is rapidly disappearing. Within twenty years, perhaps, we shall have nowhere east of the Rocky Mountains a timber product worth recording; and must then begin in earnest the slow process of reforesting.

What is less clearly perceived is that we are wasting in the same fashion other resources which no repentance and no ingenuity can restore or replenish. The exhaustion of the greatest of these, the land, will be spoken of later. Our mineral wealth, however, stands on another plane. What is taken from the mine can never be replaced. Through all eternity, so far as we can see, the consumption of mineral wealth stored in the ground must be a finality. The possible gross product is mathematically limited. The adaptation of this to future uses should be a matter of infinitely greater anxiety than the present balance sheet of a business concern. Yet the singular fact is that, among a people supposedly grounded in the rudiments of political economy, the progressive exhaustion of this precious resource is everywhere heralded as a triumph of enterprise and a gauge of national prosperity. The nation publishes periodically the record of its scattering of assets never to be regained; and waits, with a smile of complacence, for general congratulation.

The two great resources of the under earth, economically speaking, that are indispensable to human comfort and growth, are coal and iron. Our inheritance of these was princely. The most wonderful achievement of this age is the incredible activity with which we are exhausting them. The coal areas and measures of the United States are describable only in somewhat general terms. But the fact of the future is not doubtful. No dependable authority gives more than a century of life to our main available coal supply. It will not all be gone by that time, but the remainder will have to be obtained from deposits of low grade or at great depths, or from points remote from where it is most needed. It will be poor in quality, or high in price, or both, so that its economic employment on existing terms will be very difficult. A generous estimate of competent geologists for the life of the better coal measures of Europe as a whole is less than one hundred years. The output of the United States is now more than 350,000,000 tons annually. It doubled within the decade from 1895. It amounts to between forty and fifty per cent. of the world's entire supply. The estimated life of the Pennsylvania anthracite fields, whose narrow area has permitted closer approximation, is put at little more than fifty years. The larger supply of soft coal has to answer a demand many times as great.

It is certainly a moderate statement to say that, by the middle of the present century, when our population will have reached the two hundred million mark, our best and most convenient coal will have been so far consumed that the remainder can only be applied to present uses at an enhanced cost which would probably compel the entire rearrangement of industries and revolutionize the common lot and common life. This is not a mere possibility, but a probability which our country must face.

The prospect of the iron interest is even more threatening and more sure. Our available iron deposits have been carefully catalogued. All the fields of national importance have been known for at least twenty years. Within that time their boundaries and probable capacity have been estimated, and the whole country has been prospected. The most reasonable computation of scientific authority affirms that existing production cannot be maintained for fifty years, assuming that all the available iron ore known to us is mined. In fact, the period of free supply is likely to be much shorter.

In 1870 the United States produced a little more than 3,000,000 tons of iron ore. It increased by about one hundred and fifty per cent. for each decade to 1890. As late as 1895 it was a trifle short of 16,000,000 tons. In 1902 and 1903 it was, in round numbers, 35,000,000 tons, and in 1905 it rose to about 42,000,000 tons. At this rate, as all the trade statistics indicate, and as our present policy and growth in population require, it will soon reach 50,000,000 tons. By every possible means we are stimulating consumption; especially by a tariff that places a bounty on the exhaustion of the home supply of both coal and iron, thus prohibiting recourse to outside supplies and compelling the exhaustion of our own reserve.

The main iron deposits in this country are those of the Lake Superior region. These furnish nearly or quite three-quarters of the entire product of the United States. Deprived of these, our output would shrink to a beggarly ten million tons or so a year. And these deposits are not veins of unknown depth and richness, but pockets of ascertainable volume. There is within reach possibly 1,500,000,000 tons of merchantable iron ore in the deposits of Minnesota, Wisconsin and Michigan. This will keep our industry going, supposing consumption to remain stationary, for thirty or forty years. In the year 1950, so far as our own resources are concerned, will approach an ironless age. For a population of 200,000,000 people, our home supply of iron will have retreated almost to the company of the precious metals.

There is no substitute whose production and preparation for practical use is not far more expensive. Not merely our manufacturing industries, but our whole complex industrial life, so intimately built upon cheap iron and coal, will feel the strain and must suffer realignment. The peril is not one of remote geologic time, but of this generation, And where is there a sign of preparation for it? Where, amidst our

statistical arrays and the flourish of trumpets with
which the rise of our manufactured product is always
announced, do we hear so much as a whisper of care
about the needs of the time marching so swiftly upon
us? Instead of apprehension and diligent forethought
for the future, the nation is engaged in policies of
detail and opportunism.

If any man think this prophecy of danger fantastic,
let him glance at Great Britain. That nation was
not so extravagant as we, because it did not compel
the instant exhaustion of its resources by a tariff
prohibiting such imports, and because its surplus
population could and did scatter over the globe. But
it has concentrated effort upon the secondary form
of industry — manufacturing; at the sacrifice of the
primary — the tillage of the soil. Its iron supply is
now nearly exhausted. It must import much of the
crude material or close its furnaces and mills. Its
coal is being drawn from the deeper levels. The
added cost pinches the market and makes trade smaller
both in volume and in profits.

The process of constriction has only begun. None
are advertising it, only few understand it. But already
there is the cry of want and suffering from every street
in England. From a million to a million and a half
of men are huddling together in her cities, uttering that
most pathetic and most awful ultimatum, "Damn
your charity, give us work." And this is only the
beginning of that industrial readjustment which the
unwise application of industry and the destruction

of natural resources must force everywhere. He who doubts may easily convince himself by an honest investigation of the facts, that this is no sensational prediction, but something as established and inevitable as an eclipse or the return of the seasons. The most amazing feature of our situation, indeed, is its vast and compelling simplicity.

Every people is thus reduced, in the final appraisal of its estate, to reliance upon the soil. This is the sole asset that does not perish, because it contains within itself, if not abused, the possibility of infinite renewal. All the life that exists upon this planet, all the development of man from his lowest to his highest qualities, rest as firmly and as unreservedly upon the capacities of the soil as do his feet upon the ground beneath him. The soil alone is capable of self-renewal, through the wasting of the rocks, through the agency of plant life, through its chemical reactions with the liquids and gases within and about it. A self-perpetuating race must rely upon some self-perpetuating means of support. Our one resource, therefore, looking at humanity as something more than the creature of a day, is the productivity of the soil. And since that, too, may be raised to a high power or lowered to the point of disappearing value, it is of first consequence to consider how the people of the United States have dealt with this, their greatest safeguard and their choicest dower.

This is pre-eminently and primarily an agricultural country. Its soil has been treated as have been its forest and mineral resources. Only because the earth is more long-suffering, only because its exhaustion is difficult and occupies a long period, have we escaped the peril that looms so large in other quarters. The reckless distribution of the land; its division among all the greedy who chose to ask for it; the appropriation of large areas for grazing purposes, have absorbed much of the national heritage. Only one-half of the land in private ownership is now tilled. That tillage does not produce one-half of what the land might be made to yield, without losing an atom of its fertility. Yet the waste of our treasure has proceeded so far that the actual value of the soil for productive purposes has already deteriorated more than it should have done in five centuries of use. There is, except in isolated and individual cases, little approaching intensive agriculture in the United States. There is only the annual skimming of the rich cream; the exhaustion of virgin fertility; the extraction from the earth, by the most rapid process, of its productive powers; the deterioration of life's sole maintenance. And all this with that army of another hundred million people marching in plain sight toward us, and expecting and demanding that they shall be fed.

From 1860 to 1900 is a far cry. In that time our population leaped from 31,000,000 to 76,000,000. In that time a vast area of wilderness was put beneath the plough. Yet in those same years the area of improved land in the North Atlantic States remained stationary. It is now steadily on the decrease. In the South Atlantic States, while the inclosed area is larger, the farming area has decreased by more than 2,000,000 acres.

The test of values is still more indicative. Every farm properly cared for should be worth more money for each year of its life. The increase of population and demand, the growth of cities and markets, and the development of diversified farming with density of settlement should insure a large increment. Even where large quantities of new and fertile land are opened, these influences, together with the lowest cost of transportation in the world, should make the growth of values steady. Within the twenty years between 1880 and 1900 the aggregate value of farm lands and improvements, including buildings, declined in every one of the New England and Middle States except Massachusetts. The total decrease in values, for these ten states, of the first asset of a civilized people is more than $300,000,000. Nor is the attempted explanation by the census bureau of this shrinkage either adequate or convincing. Even the great and fertile State of Ohio, in the Middle West, showed a decline of more than $60,000,000. This change in the section of oldest cultivation under modern conditions is significant. It is not singular. The soil of the South is moving on the same decline, though the fact is less obvious in the total change of agricultural conditions since the Civil War. On the new lands of the West, where once the wheat yield was from twenty to thirty bushels per acre, it is now from twelve to eighteen. Frankly, and without shame, this is attributed to "the wearing out" of the soil, as if the earth were a garment that must be destroyed by the wearing.

If the earth, the mother of humanity, is to "wear out," what is to become of the race? The fact is that soils, properly treated, maintain their productiveness indefinitely under cultivation. The further fact is that, with the disappearance of pestilence and the discontinuance of war that belong to the future, all contributing to the growth of population, the productive capacity of the soil must be sustained at its highest point or the world suffer want.

The life-sustaining power of the soil is lowered in two ways: First, by physical destruction, through the carrying away of the earth to the sea; and, second, chemically, by the withdrawal of the elements required for plant life. The waste from the former cause is very great. It accounts for sterility in the older, which are also the more hilly, portions of the cultivated country. It may be easily checked or prevented. The agriculture of Japan, which is of the highest type, preserves a mountain farm intact by terracing and careful modulation of its level. Professor Shaler says that a field lying at an angle of twenty degrees can be totally destroyed in a hundred plowings. Throughout the South this process of denudation has proceeded far and is going forward rapidly. He estimates from personal observation that in the State of Kentucky, where cultivation is hardly more than a century old, one-tenth of the arable soil has been destroyed, and that a considerable portion of this cannot be restored by any application of industry and care.

More serious and even more universal and speedy is the process of deliberate soil exhaustion. New England once supported a population of farmers whose shot was heard around the world. Professor Carver, of Harvard, after a tour of five hundred and fifty miles on horseback in 1905, records his conclusion that "agriculture as an independent industry, able in itself to maintain a community, does not exist in the hilly parts of New England." It is not many years since the favoured wheat-producing areas of the American Northwest gave a yield of from twenty-five bushels per acre upwards. Now an average of twelve to fifteen is accepted as satisfactory. Under the stress of need, by intelligent cultivation, many of the lands of Great Britain, cropped for a thousand years, are made to bear thirty bushels to the acre. The rich, deep soil of our own country, drawn upon for a few decades, produces about twelve. The same ratio holds good of other cereals and of every product of the field. The sea islands that once grew the most famous cotton staple in the world are virtually abandoned.

The people have neglected the preservation of the soil. They take away all and give nothing back. Thorough fertilization of the land has no place in the general work on the American farm. Average American agriculture means the extraction from nature of the greatest immediate return at the lowest possible outlay of labour or money, with sublime disregard of consequences. Except at scattered experiment stations and in isolated instances there is little done in the United States toward farm economies. Scientific adaption of soil to product, intelligent rotation of crops, diversification of industry, intensive farming — constitute the rare exception and not the rule.

Only two states in the Union show an average total value of farm products in excess of $30 per acre of improved land. The figure for Illinois in 1900 was $12.48; for North Carolina, $10.72; for Minnesota, $8.74. By proper cultivation these returns could easily be doubled and still leave the soil's resources unimpaired. The doubling of all products of the farm would add to the wealth of this country from $6,000,000,000 to $8,000,000,000 every year, according to the crop yield of the season and the range of market prices.

Therefore, and this is the focal point of the whole matter, the country is approaching the inevitable advent of a population of 150,000,000 or 200,000,000, within the lifetime of those now grown to man's estate, with a potential food supply that falls as the draft upon it advances. How are these people to be fed?

The foreign trade of the United States has been made an object of more or less solicitude and self-gratulation. What we do is to export in immense volumes two great classes of commodities. One contains raw materials, the products of the upper and the under earth. It includes, adding articles like flour, provisions and refined oil, which are but one degree removed from the raw state, changed in form for economy of transportation, three-fourths of our entire exports of domestic commodities. The treasury of our future is being despoiled to swell the rapidly growing riches of the day. The remaining thirty per cent. or less, which is all that can properly be classed as products of manufacture, is this stored treasure in another form. Exports of domestic manufactures, construing the term with proper strictness, constitute a trifle more than twenty per cent. of the total.

This pitiful showing in the markets of the world where our people might find occupation, where a larger proportion of them must find it in the future if all are to survive or remain, a showing that not even the endeavours of boasters can improve, is the inevitable consequence of a policy more destructive than that of the spendthrift. Lest the conditions of life should be made too favourable for this people, its home markets are surrendered, bound rigidly by law, to the comparatively small number who control domestic supplies of raw material for manufacture. At the same time the cost of production effectually prevents the securing of any considerable or permanent control in the markets of the outer world, where alone our millions of to-morrow could find outlet for this form of their activity.

The single intelligent advance on practical lines made by public authority within the last quarter of a century is the reclamation law. Initiated and paid for by a few western railway companies, it provides for a real addition to the sources of food supply and the opportunity for employment. But it is only a light breeze blowing in the face of a cyclone. If every project contemplated as feasible were executed, and if all were completed instantly by the rub of a magic lamp, some 60,000,000 acres would be added to the arable national domain. And if only forty acres of this were assigned to each family, it would supply the needs of the actual addition to population, by natural increase and by immigration, for less than three years.

Professor Shaler, in a survey of world conditions from the broadest scientific point of view, looking at man and his storehouse in the large, at supply and exhaustion, says, in "Man and the Earth": "This attitude of men as regards the future of the material value of the earth notably contrasts with what they hold to the moral and political future of their kind. A large part of their thought and endeavour goes to that group of problems, but practically none at all to the immediate questions that relate to the material foundations on which all the higher development of the life of their kind has to rest." Man may win, beyond peradventure man will win, from the silent willingness of nature, from her sternness and her clemency, from her outpouring and her withholding, the utmost of his aspiration. But the highway to the perfect condition must be fashioned from the common clod under his feet. And for every error and omission he must pay the uttermost farthing. It is not so much, at this point, a question whether it is to be our people or another who win to higher ideals of life, of government and of conduct, as it is whether they are to escape the shock of an awakening that must leave them face to face with the old struggle for existence, with weakened moral fibre and submerged in profound discouragement. Certain it is that the time has come for setting our household in order, and creating a serious study of national activity and economy according to a truer insight and a more rational mood.

The first step is to realize our dependence upon the cultivation of the soil. To this end all that has been said thus far is contributory. The next will be to concentrate popular interest and invention and hope upon that neglected occupation. We are still clinging to the skirts of a civilization born of great cities. We at this very moment use a slang which calls the stupid man a "farmer." Genius has shunned the farm and expended itself upon mechanical appliances and commerce and the manifold activities whose favourable reactions filter back but slowly to the plot of ground on which stands solidly the real master of himself and of his destiny. If we comprehend our problem aright, all this will change; and a larger comprehension of agriculture as our main resource and our most dignified and independent occupation, will for the future direct to their just aim, in the improvement of methods and the increase of yield, the wisdom and the science and the willing labour of the millions who thus may transmit to posterity an unimpaired inheritance.

Agriculture, in the most intelligent meaning of the

term, is something almost unknown in the United States. We have a light scratching of the soil and a gathering of all that it can be made to yield by the most rapidly exhaustive methods. Except in isolated instances, on small tracts here and there, farmed by people sometimes regarded as cranks, and at some experiment stations, there is no attempt to deal with the soil scientifically, generously or even fairly. In manufacture we have come to consider small economies so carefully that the difference of a fraction of a cent, the utilization in a by-product of something formerly consigned to the scrap heap, makes the difference between a profit and bankruptcy. In farming we are satisfied with a small yield at the expense of the most rapid soil deterioration. We are satisfied with a national average annual product of $11.38 per acre at the cost of a diminishing annual return from the same fields, when we might just as well secure from two to three times that sum. Here is a draft which we may draw upon the future and know that it will not be dishonoured. Here is the occupation in which the millions of the future may find a happy and contented lot.

When we have added to the national export trade half a billion dollars per annum, the country rings with our rejoicings and we demand the plaudits of the world. If a process for extracting metallic wealth from rocks were to be discovered to-morrow, such as to assure the country an added volume of a billion dollars in wealth every year, the nation would talk of nothing else. Yet these things would be but a trifle when compared with the possibilities of agricultural development in the United States. The official estimated value of all farm products of the country in 1905 was $6,415,000,000. Discount this for high prices and generally favourable conditions by twenty per cent. and over $5,000,000,000 remain. It is also officially recorded that of the appropriated farm area of the United States a little less than one-half is under cultivation. Utilize the other half and, without any change whatever in methods, the output would be practically doubled. Change methods only a little, not to high-class intensive farming, but to an agriculture as far advanced as that of those other countries which have made most progress, and without any addition whatever to the existing culti-vated farm area, the product per acre would be doubled. We should be able, by directing surplus population to the land, and by the adoption of a system of culture in full operation elsewhere, greatly to increase this minimum present yield of $5,000,000,000 per annum of farm products. That is, we may add $10,000,000,000 or $15,000,000,000 every year to the national wealth if we so choose. And this is but a beginning.

It will be well, in defence of a prospect so promis-ing, to glance at the achievements of other peoples upon whom necessity has already imposed wisdom. It is, perhaps, not as generally known as it should be that Great Britain, with a soil and climate far inferior to our own for wheat growing, produces more than double the quantity that we do per acre. The average for the United States in 1899 was twelve and three-tenths bushels per acre. In 1904 it was twelve and five-tenths. That is about the figure for a long series of years. More than half a century ago the average yield in England had risen above twenty-six bushels to the acre. In the latter part of the eighteenth century agriculture had reached almost its lowest estate in the United Kingdom. Men who saw then as we should see now the paramount importance of its restoration devoted themselves to its advancement. Arthur Young made the most complete study of local conditions ever attempted. Statesmen were interested and men of science enlisted. A board of agriculture was created in 1793. Sir Humphry Davy delivered before it in 1812 a series of remarkable lectures on scientific agri-culture. Landed proprietors took up the cry, interest was evoked everywhere, new theories were put into practice almost as rapidly as the commons were inclosed, and between 1770 and 1850 there was an immense rise in production, in labourers' wages and in rents. Although agriculture in England has suffered in the last twenty-five years, by the opening of new land in America and the cheapening of the world's transporta-tion, it has profited by further advances in knowledge. To-day a yield of thirty bushels of wheat per acre is about the average for the country. In Minnesota, with her fresh soil and unrivalled product, an average of fourteen bushels is looked upon with satisfaction. The average of Great Britain, applied to the acreage

in this country, that now gives us something over
600,000,000 bushels of wheat in a fair year, would
increase our product to over 1,500,000,000 bushels.

There are more instructive studies in national efficiency than this. The German Empire has nearly
60,000,000 people compressed within a little more
than 200,000 square miles of territory. She has not
tied her fortunes to a single interest. Her manufacturing industries are thrusting themselves into the
markets of every country. How to meet German
competition is to-day the study of every intelligent
leader of industry and every cabinet on the Continent
of Europe. It will be found that a large share of her
world-wide success is due to symmetrical national
development. Agricultural industry has not been
slighted. Behold a contrast that throws light upon
the idle hosts of England's unemployed, marching
despondently through streets whose shop windows
are crowded with wares of German make. Between
1875 and 1900 in Great Britain 2,691,428 acres which
were under cereals, and 755,255 acres which were under
green crops, went out of cultivation. In Germany
during the same period the cultivated area grew from
22,840,950 to 23,971,573 hectares, an increase of five
per cent.; and the area given over to grass shrank
one-third. While her foreign trade was making the
great leap from $1,800,000,000 to $2,650,000,000, the
yield of her cultivated fields per hectare made the
following advances, measured in kilogrammes: Wheat,
from 1,670 to 1,970; rye, from 1,490 to 1,650; barley,

from 1,480 to 1,950; oats, from 1,070 to 1,840; and hay, from 2,230 to 4,450. The wages of agricultural labourers rose about twenty-five per cent. between 1873 and 1892, and have advanced another twenty-five per cent. since then. This is the work of intelligence, of a complete appreciation of the national problem as a whole, of universally practical and technical education and of infinite patience. To agriculture as well as to other occupations will apply the conclusion reached by Professor Dewar after a study of German industry and progress as a whole: "The really appalling thing is not that the Germans have seized upon a dozen industries, but that the German population has reached a point of general training and specialized equipment and possesses a weapon of precision which gives her an enormous initial advantage."

For half a century Japan has been studying and assimilating the best to be found in the world. Japan is a world's university for instruction in the art of agriculture. Her national greatness is not merely built upon that, it grows out of that as the grain itself springs from the soil. Of her 45,000,000 people, 30,000,000 are farmers. The whole body is supported by a cultivated area of but 19,000 square miles. Every foot of soil is utilized; the farmer is a specialist. For twenty-five centuries this nation has turned to tillage as the basic industry of life. Her progress is in the right direction; growth, like that of the tree, from the ground up. The message of the victorious guns of Japan is a reminder of the fixed order and proportion in a healthy national development of industry. No nation that does not throw its intensest interest and expend the bulk of its force upon the cultivation of the soil can become or remain permanently great.

In France a careful system of agriculture took root earlier than in Great Britain, and from it has been wrought a far stronger fabric of national prosperity. France is to-day the banker nation of Europe. Any sound loan can be placed in Paris on short notice. In 1871 impoverished France was compelled to pay $1,000,000,000 to the conquering Germans. Thirty years afterward France had $500,000,000 seeking for investment. To-day her national debt of $6,000,000,000 is practically all held at home, and her holdings of foreign securities are not far from $15,000,000,000. She controls the purse strings of Europe; and Russia and Germany are guided in their foreign policies, are urged into or restrained from war, not so much by the pleasure of emperor, king or kaiser as by the decision of the world-financiers of France. The funds for this international financing are obtained largely from the savings of the industrious and frugal small farmers of France.

Within the first fifty years of the nineteenth century agricultural improvement alone doubled the wealth of the country. Landed estates sell to-day for from three to four times as much as they brought at the time of the Revolution. The valley of the Loire is one great garden. Every foot of soil has been studied and devoted to the growing of what will produce the largest return. Although one-third of the area of the country is classified as uncultivable, the tilled portion yields food enough for one hundred and seventy inhabitants per square mile. Kropotkin says, in his remarkable study of agricultural methods: "Some thirty years ago the French considered a crop quite good when it yielded twenty-two bushels to the acre; but with the same soil the present requirement is at least thirty-three bushels; while in the best soils the crop is good only when it yields from forty-three to forty-eight bushels, and occasionally the product is as much as fifty-five bushels to the acre." From limited areas on experimental farms under special care as high as eighty bushels per acre have been obtained. But, taking cultivation as we find it for the country as a whole, the French now draw from the soil more than five times as much wealth as they did a century and a half ago.

This is the result merely of the common agricultural industry of France. The strength of the nation, its endurance of political changes, its economic place and its persistence as a wealth creator are due primarily to the fact that it is a nation of small farmers, pursuing what in this country would be called intensive, but what is really diversified farming.

It is to Belgium and the island of Jersey that we must look if we would see the supreme achievement of careful farm industry exercised under conditions not specially favourable. The agriculture of these countries represents a fair average of what the people of any other might do, with equal patience, intelligence and industry. Originally the soil of Belgium as a whole was not highly favourable to cultivation. Yet Belgium produces now, after allowing for all imports of food products, and exclusive of exports of the same, enough home-grown food to supply the wants of four hundred and ninety inhabitants to the square mile. This is in addition to the large manufacturing industries of the country, and offers a fair model and measure of what might be done under ordinary conditions with the earth by man in any part of the world not cursed by sterility.

These figures, which in reality supply the answer to our problem, convict the American farmer of carelessness and want of knowledge, and the economic and political leaders of the people of unfaithfulness to their trust. To restore and maintain the fertility of the soil, to assure food and occupation for a greater population than may be expected in a long future, we have but to study the experience of older peoples and to follow lessons written plainly in the history of the world's agriculture.

There are three essentials in any agriculture worthy of the name. The first is rotation of crops. Our low average yield is due to the too-prevalent system of raising the same crop indefinitely on the same land, until it has been worn out or so reduced that the owner is in danger of poverty. The yield of a given area may be increased and its productive powers preserved from exhaustion merely by the restorative variety of change, which seems to be a law of all living things.

Some interesting facts have been brought out by the work of the Minnesota State Agricultural School. With only ordinary fertilization, and with such farm culture as could be applied to large areas, the average yield of wheat on the plots under experiment for seven years was 26.4 bushels per acre; of oats, 67.2 bushels; of corn, 42.8 bushels; and of hay, the average for five years was 3.91 tons per acre. This was accomplished merely by using a system of five-year rotation; the land being treated in this order: corn, wheat, meadow, pasture, oats. The figures given are nearly double the average yield from the farms of the state. There is, therefore, no exaggeration in the statement that our farm production could be made two-fold what it is by the mere application of more careful methods without any intensive cultivation whatever.

If the lands of the state were cultivated according to a seven-year system of rotation — grain, grain, grass, pasture, grain, oats, grain — without fertilizers, it is estimated on good authority that the same amount of grain would be gathered during the four seasons in which it appears in this regular order as is now obtained from cropping grain every year. That is to say, the farmer would obtain at the end of seven years exactly the same amount of grain that he now takes as the entire product of his fields; while in addition he would have the whole amount of other crops and of stock for which the three seasons of vacation from grain growing would furnish opportunity. He would, while preserving the fertility of his acres and guarding against soil deterioration, add three-sevenths to the volume of his material profits. Such is the promise of the simplest of all improvements in method.

This is but the beginning of agricultural possibilities. Calling in the aid of the second method of increasing yield and preserving soil productivity, which is a more liberal use of fertilizing material, such as is possible where farms are of small size and cattle are kept, there is abundant evidence of the extraordinary results that may be obtained. Illustrations may be found in every part of the country where individual small farmers have had the intelligence to put the system into effect. A recent report of the Department of Agriculture cites the case of a farm in Pennsylvania which was so exhausted as to be incapable of production. This little tract of fifteen acres, devoted strictly to dairying and treated each year with every particle of the natural fertilizers thus obtained, produces a revenue of about $3,000, or $200 per acre, annually. There is no secret in the process, just as there is no uncertainty in the result. And by a combination of judicious crop rotation, which admits and requires diversification of farm industry, with careful fertilizing, the estimate of a doubled money value for the yield of the present farm area of the United States would be found under the mark.

The third factor in improvement, better tillage, is most interesting of all because it opens up unmeasured possibilities. We no more know what is the maximum food-bearing capacity of the earth or of any small portion of its surface than we do the rate at which people may be able to travel a century from now. But what has been done is sufficiently startling. It has been seen that a population of 45,000,000 people in Japan is supported on 19,000 cultivated square miles, aided by the food products obtained from the sea. This is because cultivation in Japan is truly intensive; that is, it is no longer even highly developed farming, but market gardening. As we approach that science, the actual creation of soils for growing purposes, the shelter of plants from frost and unfavourable elements, and the treatment of grains and vegetables by separate planting and individual nurture, all limitations upon earth's bounty appear to recede afar.

From two and seven-tenths acres in the suburbs of Paris there have been grown in a single season 250,000 pounds of vegetables. A market gardener of Paris declares that all the food, animal and vegetable, required for the 3,500,000 people of two great departments could be grown, by methods already in use, on the 3,250 square miles of gardens surrounding the city. Thus, while it appears that in Belgium a population of approximately five hundred persons to the square mile can subsist on the products of farm industry alone, this figure, by high intensive culture, such as becomes possible and profitable where population is extremely dense, might be more than doubled.

In one district of East Flanders a population of 30,000 peasants obtains its food from 37,000 acres of ground, at the same time raising thousands of beasts and exporting considerable produce. The farmers of the island of Jersey, by no means a paradise for the agriculturist, manage to obtain an annual agricultural product valued at about $250 from each acre of their land. In Germany they have produced thirty tons of potatoes to the acre. The same has been done in Minnesota; and might become the rule rather than the exception. The Japanese obtain their yields of rice, from twenty to thirty-two bushels per acre in poor provinces and sixty to sixty-seven bushels on the best land, by separate planting. After the plant has been started in a bed it is taken up individually and transferred to the field by hand.

Interesting experiments have been made in the United States with wheat. If the best seed be selected and planted, and a vigourous young plant be grown, four inches distant from its nearest neighbour, it is possible, with the most prolific varieties and the utmost care, to produce as high as one thousand five hundred grains of wheat from a single grain. A yield of one hundred grains would be a practical minimum. This would give one hundred bushels of crop for every bushel of seed; a multiplication now deemed incredible. By this method from sixty-two to ninety bushels of wheat to the acre have actually been obtained. The objection to the amount of labour required may be answered by the query whether it would be more difficult to grow ten acres after this fashion than a quarter section in the old way. And the food demand of a population growing by millions is soon to force such questions to the front. Even if the soil produces only the thirty bushels of wheat to the acre which Great Britain can raise, a square mile would grow nineteen thousand two hundred bushels. If five hundred persons were living on a square mile, it would allot to each one of them thirty-eight and four-tenths bushels as a supply. Distribute this in terms of any measured food ration and it will not be inadequate.

It may be affirmed with perfect confidence, as a conclusion of this brief investigation of soil preservation and development, that the possibilities of agriculture make it difficult to set any specific limit to the population that could sustain life on the produce of a given area. This, however, presupposes cultivation as carefully studied and applied as are the details of manufacturing processes or the manipulations of a chemical laboratory. Such must be the ultimate goal of American industry. And although the American farmer need not yet become a market gardener, it is time to make a beginning of better methods.

From the review given of actual accomplishment in treatment of the soil, from the promise of this most dependable asset, something may be asserted with confidence of our own future. It can be shown that an average of two persons or more may be supported on every acre of tillable land, by the highest form of intensive farming. But dismissing this as unnecessary, it has been shown that a people like those of Belgium to-day, not an Oriental race accustomed to a standard of living and of labour inapplicable to us, not living in virtual serfdom like the peasants of Russia, but an industrious, fairly intelligent and exceedingly comfortable agricultural community, can raise from the soil food enough for the needs of four hundred and ninety persons to the square mile.

Adopting provisionally that ratio as a point of departure, though the actual ratio of area to population gives a figure considerably higher even than this, the 414,498,487 acres of improved farm lands in the United States on the date of the last official report, an area materially enlarged by the present time, would support in comfort 317,350,405 people; enabling them at the same time to raise considerable food for export and to engage in necessary manufacturing employments. Applying the same ratio to the entire acreage of farm lands within the United States, both improved and unimproved, which was at the same date 838,591,774, the population indicated as able to live with comfort and prosperity on the actually existing agricultural area of this country, under an intelligent system and a fairly competent but by no means highly scientific method of culture, rises to 642,046,823.

The conclusion is that, if not another acre were to be redeemed from the wilderness, if the soil were treated kindly and intelligently, if industry were distributed duly and popular attention were concentrated upon the best possible utilization of the one unfailing national resource, there would be produced all necessary food for the wants of, in round numbers, 650,000,000 people. But this means such study and labour to raise production to its highest terms as have entered scarcely at all as yet into the American comprehension.

Failing to understand the needs of the hour or to appreciate the moral to which they point, what fortune must await us? Within twenty years 125,000,000 people, and before the middle of the century over 200,000,000 people, must find room and food and employment within the United States. Where are they to live? What are they to do? By that time our mineral resources will have been so nearly exhausted that the industries built on them must fall into a minor place. By that time it is apparent that our dream of a conquest of world markets will be a burst bubble. Mr. Harold Bolce has demonstrated that the peoples of the Orient, the hundreds of millions of Japan and China, with their imitative quality, their proved ability to operate modern machinery and to create it in their workshops after once using it, their enormous supply of coal and iron, their limitless cheap labour and their patience like that of Fate, are prepared to control the markets of the future. They must control as against a policy which has established in manufacturing business domestic conditions making production so expensive an affair that we could not hope to meet the mechanic of Germany on even terms and must retire before the despised Chinaman.

It is a mathematical fact that within twenty years under present conditions our wheat crop will not be sufficient for home consumption and seed, without leaving a bushel for export. Will these coming millions go into the factories? But where can we then expect to sell shop products in a world competition, and who will furnish the payrolls? All industry stops when these are not forthcoming. That is the deadwall before which England stands dismayed. The shops are there, the workingmen are there clamouring for employment, but capital can find no profit in the enterprises, nobody offers to advance money for the payrolls of unprofitable business, and a top-heavy industry surely falls.

Let us be warned in time. On every side there is menace if our national activity be not reorganized on the basis of old-fashioned common sense. The safety valve for older peoples has been found in emigration. Their relief has contributed to our danger. The United States cannot follow their example. It is against the genius of our people; and besides, the circle of the northern hemisphere is closed. At home the problem must be worked out; and its terms have been clearly stated.

The conclusion reached points out and emphasizes a national duty so imminent and so imperative that it should take precedence of all else. Our foe is one that has overthrown civilizations as proud, as prosperous and far more strongly fortified than our own. Nothing can stop the onward march of nature's laws or close the iron jaws of her necessities when they open to crush their victims. Either we shall understand our situation and make such provision as her benignancy affords to meet it, or we shall meet conditions of overcrowding and artificial standards and food and employment inadequate to the national needs, and so be in danger of destroying the stately temple once reared with the highest hopes that ever animated humanity. Which is it to be?

If we are to walk safely in the way of wisdom, there is much to be done. It is time to begin. There must be, first, a return to conservative and economic methods; a readjustment of national ideas such as to place agriculture, and its claims to the best intelligence and the highest skill that the country affords, in the very forefront. There must be a national revolt against the worship of manufacture and trade as the only forms of progressive activity, and the false notion that wealth built upon these at the sacrifice of the fundamental form of wealth production can endure. A clear recognition on the part of the whole people, from the highest down to the lowest, that the tillage of the soil is the natural and most desirable occupation for man, to which every other is subsidiary and to which all else must in the end yield, is the first requisite. Then there will be a check administered to the city movement that lowered the percentage of agricultural labour to the whole body of persons engaged in gainful occupations in the United States from forty-four and three-tenths in 1880 to thirty-seven and seven-tenths in 1890 and to thirty-five and seven-tenths in 1900. With public interest firmly fixed upon the future, the country, in mere self-preservation, must give serious attention to the practical occupation of restoring agriculture to its due position in the nation.

The Government should establish a small model farm on its own land in every rural congressional district, later perhaps in every county in the agricultural states. Let the Department of Agriculture show exactly what can be done on a small tract of land by proper cultivation, moderate fertilizing and due rotation of crops. The sight of the fields and their contrast with others, the knowledge of yields secured and profits possible, would be worth more than all the pamphlets poured out from the government printing office in years. The Government ought not to hesitate before the comparatively small expense and labour involved in such a practical encouragement of what is the most important industry of our present and the stay and promise of our future. Disseminate knowledge of farming as it should and must be, instead of maintaining the pitiful bribe of a few free seeds. Declare everywhere, from the executive chamber, from the editorial office, from the platform, and, above all, from every college class-room and from every little school-house in the land, the new crusade. Let the zeal for discovery, for experiment, for scientific advancement that has made the last century one of multiplied wonders focus itself upon the problems of the oldest of sciences and arts; the corner stone of all civilization — the improvement of tillage and making grow two grains where only one grew before. Only thus may a multiplying population secure its permanent maintenance. Only thus may the struggle for existence that has power to either curse or bless be brought to any other termination than the peace of death.

I have not drawn upon fancy for a single detail of this picture. This growing increase of population, its rise to over 200,000,000 before 1950, the approaching exhaustion of much of our mineral wealth, the vanishing of our public domain, the deterioration or our soil, the terrible need which these must bring, the strain on institutions and the stress of industrial perplexity or decline are as certain as the passage of the years. I have given the facts, drawn from authentic sources, and in every case under rather than over stated. Let them be examined, criticised, compared with official records. For this is not a controversy about theories, but a plain statement of natural facts in the light of nature's laws. Then let the statesmen, the writers and the thoughtful workers of to-day say if they are not true. If true, what are we to do? Where, save in a concentration of national effort upon that first and last resource of man ever since he left Eden, is there a sure escape and a safe relief? Let the leaders of men give their answer.

The situation is not at all hopeless or even desperate if the nation turns to its task with appreciation, with wisdom and with courage. The saving qualities of the American people are intelligence, adaptability and patriotism. Given a situation, simple or complex, demanding sacrifice or promising reward, they are quick to comprehend it and to mobilize their forces for its mastery. If they turn with comprehension of their situation manfully to the most vital work of the present, our children's fortunes may be made secure. Instead of a world filled with human beings struggling against advancing necessity, instead of the grim choice between the slow but sure decline to an ever-lowering scale of comfort, there appears a beautiful conformity to nature's order and the blessing of service to her law. This country may easily become the happiest and most favoured portion of the earth, the sure refuge and defence of the destitute and oppressed, because of its mighty heritage of that one resource which may increase and be replenished as the ages roll by. This is not the conception of a new Arcadia or a return of the golden age. Industry will sufficiently diversify itself, once the order of it is rescued from a false appreciation and restored to that found on nature's roll of honour.

In the last census year the value of agricultural products was less than $5,000,000,000. But the farm products of that year devoted to manufacturing uses were valued at $2,679,000,000; the product of the industries using these materials was $4,720,000,000; and in these industries, capitalized at over $4,000,000,000, there were 2,154,000 persons employed. A profitable husbandry is the very fountain from which all other occupations flow and by which they are nourished in strength. A symmetrical development of industry is by no means the least important reward of a readjustment of industrial occupations and interests in harmony with their real relation to man and his active life upon this planet. Not lessened but enhanced and greatly varied industry in the end will follow the rearrangement and restoration of industrial values.

Now as ever, to the nation and race as to the individual, nature, the unrelenting task-mistress of the centuries, holds out in one hand her horn of plenty and in the other her scourge. This country has brought itself within reach of the thong, while grasping at the satisfaction of present appetite and forgetting the primal relation between the earth and man. The pathway to prosperity is still open. The divinity of the earthly life at heart is kind. Under her rule there is work and abundant reward for all, but these must be won in her designated way and in none other. Her pointing finger, that has never varied since man came upon the earth, shows the old and only way to safety and honour. Upon the readiness with which this is understood, the sober dignity with which a whole nation rises to the winning of its broad and permanent prosperity, will depend the individual well-being of millions of this and many generations. Largely by the result will posterity, our fit and righteous judge, determine whether what issues from the crucible of this twentieth century is a bit of worthless dross to be cast aside or a drop of golden metal to shine forever upon the rosary of the years.

# CHAPTER II

## Agriculture and the National Life

LAND without population is a wilderness, and population without land is a mob. The United States has many social, political and economic questions, some old, some new, to settle in the near future; but none so fundamental as the true relation of the land to the national life. The first act in the progress of any civilization is to provide homes for those who desire to sit under their own vine and fig tree.

A prosperous agricultural interest is to a nation what good digestion is to a man. The farm is the basis of all industry. The soil is the only resource that renews itself continually after having produced value. I do not wish to belittle the importance of manufacture or its relative value in general growth. But for many years this country has made the mistake of unduly assisting manufacture, commerce and other activities that centre in cities, at the expense of the farm. The result is a neglected system of agriculture and the decline of the farming interest. But all these other activities are founded upon the agricultural growth of the nation and must continue to depend upon it. Every manufacturer, every merchant, every business man, every good citizen is deeply interested in maintaining the growth and development of our agricultural resources.

It is strange that almost all countries, including our own, should, until taught by approaching misfortune, fail to realize the primary and indispensable place of agriculture in sound national development. Probably, as both industry and society grow more complex, we lose sight of their plain connection with the soil, just as some of the most baffling diseases with which modern medical science has to deal originate in violations of the simplest and most ancient laws of health. At any rate, it is but recently that there has been revived somewhat in this country a sense of the dependence of all progress, of national prosperity and individual existence upon the land and its proper care. We do not even yet feel the force of this old law as we should and must. Some other peoples, equally intelligent, appear to have almost lost sight of it, although accepting it heartily in earlier ages, when there were fewer great interests to distract attention and confuse judgment.

One hundred and fifty years ago Dr. Samuel Johnson, one of the closest observers and most philosophic thinkers of the English race up to his time, wrote these words:

"Of nations, as of individuals, the first blessing is independence. Neither the man nor the people can be happy to whom any human power can deny the necessaries or conveniences of life. There is no way of living without the need of foreign assistance but by the product of our own land, improved by our own labour. Every other source of plenty is perishable or casual."

Comparing other leading national interests with this, he said:

"Trade and manufactures must be confessed often to enrich countries . . . but trade and manufactures, however profitable, must yield to the cultivation of lands in usefulness and dignity. . . . Mines are generally considered as the great source of wealth, and superficial observers have thought the provision of great quantities of precious metals the first national happiness. But Europe has long seen, with wonder and contempt, the poverty of Spain, who thought herself exempted from the labour of tilling the ground, by the conquest of Peru, with its veins of silver. Time, however, has taught even this obstinate and haughty nation that without agriculture they may, indeed, be the transmitters of money, but can never be the possessors. . . . Agriculture alone can support us without the help of others, in certain plenty and genuine dignity. Whatever we buy from without, the sellers may refuse; whatever we sell, manufactured by art, the purchasers may reject; but while our ground is covered with corn and cattle, we can want nothing; and if imagination should grow sick of native plenty, and call for delicacies or embellishments from other countries, there is nothing which corn and cattle will not purchase. . . . This, therefore, is the great art, which every government ought to protect, every proprietor of lands to practise, and every inquirer into nature to improve."

These are great truths set in great words. If Dr. Johnson could revisit his country to-day, he would find his argument vindicated and his vision justified by an alignment of industries so uneven and a balance so poorly maintained that business in the streets of her cities is impeded by processions of gaunt men shouting in wretched concert, "We want work! We want work!" He would find her legislators trying to alleviate symptoms by socialistic nostrums, instead of striking at the disease itself. He would find even her industrial supremacy in many directions, once based upon the prosperity of the small farmer, passing away or jeopardized. In the west of England, which was a great centre of broadcloth manufacturing and of the weaving of other woollen goods, their output is less than a quarter of what it was twenty-five years ago. Germany is taking the cutlery trade of Sheffield. The German people, who have cared jealously for their farming industry at the same time when they were learning economy and efficiency in all other forms of production, to-day lead the world, or any period in its history, in scientific industrial intelligence and systematic management.

In view of such contrasts it is most important that our own country should realize the situation and take thought for its own future. When the United States shall have from 150,000,000 to 200,000,000 people, they must be employed; they must earn a living. How will their occupations and products stand in relation to one another? Will there be mutual internal support, or mutual destruction and decay? Who will employ these millions? Who will buy the goods they produce? In what shape will they be to meet the competition that England faces to-day? Hosts of idle men in Great Britain ask for the opportunity to win bread by work, and there is nothing for them but the dole of charity. We must avoid for all time that extremity.

With our magnificent areas and the relative sparseness of our population as compared with the more densely peopled countries of the Old World, the time of economic trial should be a long way off for us. With greater wisdom than we have exercised in the past it may never come. But we must preserve jealously the right and the possibility of free access to the soil, out of which grow not only all those things that make happy the heart of man and comfort his body, but those virtues by which only a nation can endure, and those influences that strengthen the soul. This is the safe-guard not only of national wealth but of national character. The fertile fields of this country are its real gold mines, from which it will gather a richer yield than the deposits of Alaska or South Africa or any other land can furnish. These are the true national inheritance. We must treasure what is left of them. Ever since the first settlements at Jamestown and Plymouth Rock, the United States has had an unlimited domain where men might find homes. Now it is all fairly occupied. Fifty-two years ago, a hundred miles from Chicago there was an unoccupied prairie. Now the land from the Mississippi Valley to the Pacific is opened up and populated, and the wave of emigration is turning back and filling the places that were passed over.

For the first time in the history of this country thousands of farmers from states like Iowa, Kansas, Missouri, Michigan, Wisconsin and Minnesota are seeking homes in the Canadian Northwest, owing to the cheap lands offered there and the difficulty of securing such lands in the United States. Toward saving a supply for the future something is now being done. We are at least saving at the spigot, though we have not quit wasting at the bung. While we are spending great sums to transform worthless lands into orchards and gardens by the work of the reclamation service, we still retain as to other areas the land laws under which for many years the great heritage of the people has been passing so largely into unworthy hands.

For the sake of our national future, for the sake of the coming millions who will be helpless unless each can be furnished with a piece of tillable land as a defense against misfortune, we should see that the speculative abuses which these laws have fostered are brought to an end. It should not be possible to obtain public land of any kind anywhere in the United States henceforth except after complying with all the terms of the homestead law. I cannot urge too strongly upon every man who wishes his country well and who desires all to be prosperous in order that he may prosper with them, the importance and growing necessity of taking such care of our public domain as shall preserve the remnant of it for the use of generations yet unborn.

Such close and careful cultivation as will yield the highest profit per acre can best be given to land when it is cultivated in comparatively small farms. The greater the number of prosperous farmers, the greater will be the prosperity of every business man. It takes more labour to earn the same profit from a tract too large to be tilled thoroughly. Ten farmers, each cultivating from forty to one hundred and sixty acres at the outside, with the most approved methods, supplemented where necessary by irrigation, can each earn a profit equal to that taken from two or three times the same area by slovenly tillage. Ten farmers instead of one increase the aggregate volume of trade with the merchants of the community and add in the same ratio to the general prosperity.

Following unconsciously this law, many of the bonanza wheat farms of earlier days have been or are being broken up into smaller holdings. It is certain that in every state farm lands will ultimately be divided and subdivided until each farmer has only so much as will yield him an ample reward for his labour and enable him to support his family in comfort. Our agriculture will take a place midway between the miniature garden-farm of Japan and the vast estates of countries that still support a landed gentry. It is far better that it should be so. The farm life of the future will have many advantages — some of them already beginning to be realized — over the isolation of an earlier day; because the multiplication of smaller farms has begun to bring good roads, schools, near neighbours, farm telephones, churches, libraries, improved mail facilities and a social environment which is impossible where farms are so big that homes are far removed from one another.

Including Alaska, this country has about the same area as Europe. It has a little more than one-fifth as much population. With a trifle over 5 per cent. of the population of the world, we are producing 43 per cent. of the world's supply of wheat, corn and oats. We raise over 70 per cent. of the world's cotton. All political economy that is not mere empty theory rests upon the ratio of population to land area, the abundance and value of the products of the soil, and the proper balance and inter-relation of different industries. We have been busy as a nation helping the so-called industrial interests of the country — in fact, everybody except the man on the farm.

But when we have as many people to the square mile as Europe has now, we will know the economic troubles of Europe. Our task will be to increase correspondingly the volume of the earth's product. When we get down to business and take stock of those national affairs in which we are vitally concerned as workers and home-builders, as citizens and as fathers of the children who are to make our future, we find that the main thing is the utilization and conservation of the soil and the resources drawn from it. This interest must more and more take precedence of all others. The man must be encouraged to go to the farm. The man on the farm must be considered first in all our policies, because he is the keystone of the national arch. When he has produced the share of natural wealth that corresponds to his best effort, he must be able to find a purchaser at prices that will enable him to live in comfort and enjoy at least a moderate degree of prosperity. This has been the final test of every country and every civilization; and it will no more change than the seasons are likely to reverse the order of their succession.

History makes all this a twice-told tale. As far back as we know anything about civilization, the cultivation of the soil has been the first and most important industry in any thriving state. It always will be. Herodotus, the very father of history itself, tells the story of the human race in the valley of the Euphrates. He says that with poor cultivation those who tilled the soil there got a yield of fifty fold, with fair cultivation one hundred fold, and with good cultivation two hundred fold. That was the garden of the world in its day. Its great cities, Babylon and Nineveh, where are they? Piles of desert sand mark where they stood. In place of the millions that overran the world there are a few wandering Arabs feeding some half-starved sheep and goats. The Promised Land — the Land of Canaan itself — to which the Children of Israel were brought up from Egypt, what is it now? A land overflowing with milk and honey?

To-day it has neither milk nor honey. It is a barren waste of desert, peopled by scattered robber bands. A provision of Providence fertilized the soil of the valley of the Nile by overflowing it every year. From the earliest records that history gives, Egypt has been a land of remarkable crops; and to-day the land thus fertilized by overflow is yielding more abundantly than ever.

It is made clear by every process of logic and by the proof of historic fact that the wealth of a nation, the character of its people, the quality and permanence of its institutions are all dependent upon a sound and sufficient agricultural foundation. Not armies or navies or commerce or diversity of manufacture or anything other than the farm is the anchor which will hold through the storms of time that sweep all else away.

Our agricultural population will compare favourably with any in the world; but it must be taught to honour its occupation and to make that occupation worthy of honour.

Elsewhere I deal with the substitution of new methods of tillage for old, by which the average crop return of the country might be doubled, and over eight billion dollars be added annually to the nation's wealth. As they learn how this may be done, the farmers of the nation will realize more fully the dignity, the independence and the comfort of their calling. Their children will understand that the farm is not a prison from which they should escape at the first opportunity, recalling its surroundings only with aversion or contempt, but the real bulwark of liberty and the home of happiness. There can be no greater aid toward the maintenance of a prosperous, free and enlightened nation than the inculcation of the precept, "Keep the children on the farm."

In 1790 only about 3.4 per cent. of the American people lived in towns. At the time of the Civil War the percentage had risen to 16. In 1900 more than 31 per cent. of our population was urban. The census of 1870 was the first to group the population of ten years old and upward in great divisions according to occupation. The drift away from the land became pronounced in 1880. Since then the process has been continuous and the results cumulative. The percentage engaged in agricultural pursuits of the whole number of persons ten years old and upward engaged in gainful occupations in this country is as follows by decades:

| | |
|------|------|
| 1870 | 47.36 |
| 1880 | 44.3 |
| 1890 | 37.7 |
| 1900 | 35.7 |

From all the states, East and West alike, comes the complaint that the children will not stay on the farm, and that other labour cannot be enticed there except by high wages for a few weeks in summer. It is quite probable that the new census will show this farm population reduced to 30 per cent. of the whole. Certainly it does not exceed one-third. And, unless this tendency is counteracted, no one can now predict to what inconsiderable fraction it may one day decline. Totals of farm products expressed in dollars and those expressed in bushels or pounds tell quite different stories. We maintain the financial showing because new and fertile land is still being opened, while at the same time older lands are abandoned or deteriorate. The possibility of this disappears with the appropriation of most of our available unoccupied land. The further fact is that we are now and have been for more than a generation, in spite of our boasted progress, in the grip of a revolution that has preceded declining wealth and falling institutions wherever it appeared since history began.

If, in a population of 100,000,000 people, which we shall have shortly, 45 per cent. are engaged in agriculture, then 45,000,000 people are calling upon the labour of 55,000,000 for clothing, professional service, commercial help, tools and furniture and all the smaller comforts and luxuries. If, instead, the agricultural percentage is reduced to 30, only 30,000,000 people instead of 45,000,000 people make such demands, while 70,000,000 instead of 55,000,000 compete in supplying them. A stationary or declining product, a soil becoming annually less productive, a revolt against the life of the farm and a consequent rise in wages amounting, since 1895, to 55.6 per cent. for ordinary day labour on the farm without board and 61.3 per cent. with board, compel such a rise of prices as bears ruinously upon town and country alike.

Our real concern is not so much to save the home market from the inroads of the foreigner as to keep it from destruction by an enlarged city life and a neglected country life, a crowded artisan population clamouring for food and a foreign demand for the product of their wages limited to fields where the competition of all the world must be met and overcome.

Civilization is mostly the story of the triumph of the human stomach in its struggle for food sufficient for the work of physical and mental evolution. Events and epochs that puzzled the historians of the past are explained by a study of common human experience. An economic cycle runs through all the affairs of men from the earliest times. There is a period of foundation laying, in which agriculture is the accepted resource of the state and national strength is built upon it. Then the demand for an enlarged life stimulates the manufacturing and the commercial interests, and there ensues a period of great prosperity, which sees the rise of great fortunes, the relative decline of the food supply, the introduction of luxury, the growth of indolence and a universal increase in prices. Never yet has this enhanced cost of living, when due to agricultural decline and inability to supply national needs, failed to end in national disaster. Professor Ferrero, in his story of the Greatness and Decline of Rome, after describing the agricultural depression of Italy, the ruin of her peasantry and the distress of all classes that followed, attributes it "simply to the increased cost of living." This, rather than imperial ambition or race decay, is the key by which history unlocks the secrets of the past.

This country has from the beginning established and maintained a common school system on the sound principle that education is essential to a right discharge of the duties of citizenship. Another element must be introduced into the educational system. To direct the minds of the young to work upon the land as an honourable and desirable career, and to prepare them for work when they return there by suitable instruction, is to promote good citizenship and national security. To raise the productivity of our soil 50 per cent. would be an increase greater in value than the entire volume of our foreign trade. These results can be brought about only by a general understanding and practice of agriculture as modern science and experiment work explain it; by such instruction as we now give in our technical schools and institutes for the trades. Any one who has studied the growth and decline of nations and would read our own industrial future must be convinced that instruction in farm economy and management should become an indispensable part of the educational work of this country.

In addition to all that those of our schools where farming is taught are doing, and all that ought to be done, there should be speedier and more direct work for the immediate improvement of the agricultural interest. The older generation, and those of the new who have not been adequately taught, should have abundant object lessons.

If I could have my way I should build a couple of warships a year less. Perhaps one would do. I would take that $5,000,000 or $6,000,000 a year and start at least one thousand agricultural schools in the United States at $5,000 a year each, in the shape of model farms. This model farm would be simply a tract of land conforming in size, soil treatment, crop selection and rotation and methods of cultivation to modern agricultural methods. Its purpose would be to furnish to all its neighbourhood a working model for common instruction. Cultivating, perhaps, from forty to sixty acres, it could exhibit on that area the advantages of thorough tillage which the small farm makes possible; of seed specially chosen and tested by experiment at agricultural college farms; of proper fertilization, stock raising, alternation of crops and the whole scientific and improved system of cultivation, seeding, harvesting and marketing. The farmers of a county could see, must see, as they passed its borders how their daily labours might bring increased and improved results. The example could not fail to impress itself upon an industry becoming each year more conscious of its defects and its needs. As fast as it was followed, it would improve farm conditions, make this a form of enterprise more attractive to the young and the intelligent, and add enormously to the volume of farm products which constitutes our enduring national wealth.

The experiment would cost but a fraction of the amount sometimes given freely for more questionable purposes. It would require a small amount of land, all told, to place a model farm in every agricultural county in the United States. There should be a trained man to each farm of, say, eighty acres; and a general superintendent, a thoroughly trained agriculturist, to manage three of four counties and visit the different farms. All such farms in a state might be put under the general supervision of the agricultural college in that state, as a part of its experimental work. Results reached by this arrangement would have the conclusiveness of a demonstration in science. Every crop that could be or ought to be raised should be experimented with, not at some distant spot seldom visited, but right at home on the farm. I would bring the model farm into every agricultural county; and if any farmer was in doubt, he could visit it, see with his own eyes, and find out what he ought to have done and what he could do next time. It would do for the farming population what the technical school does for the intending artisan, and the schools of special training for those who enter the professions. Side by side with the common school it would work for intelligence, for progress, for the welfare of the country in a moral as well as a material aspect.

Perhaps even this is not all that should be done; and perhaps we need to move even more quickly and effectively. Formerly the decreased productivity of our older lands, due to poor cultivation, was more than made good by large yields from the immense acreage of new land continually being brought under the plough. This cannot be true in the future. If the average yield per acre of old land continues to fall as it has in the past, the total national product will soon begin to decline. The additional demand of a constantly increasing population, added to this deficit, compels us to consider at once the only practical remedy — the raising of the product of the land per acre by methods already broadly outlined and to be considered in more detail in the following chapters.

We cannot wait for the work of the agricultural colleges; because the emergency is one not for the next generation, but for this. Instruction in improved methods should be carried to the farmer, just as he is, upon his own farm. The state might profitably employ a considerable number of men educated in practical agriculture; supply them with seed selected for quality; send them out to the farms and have each farmer put in a few acres, under the direction of its agents, sowing and tilling these according to their instructions. The great increase in both the quantity and the quality of the yield would be a convincing education.

When we set out to educate the children in the public schools, we do not establish one or two large ones in each state and expect them to go there. The farmer is almost as numerous, as much in need of instruction and as unable to leave home in search of it or to absorb it through literary channels as the child. If all the graduates of all the Agricultural Colleges were sent out as missionaries to the farm, there would not be enough of them to do the work. But it is the sort of work in which every state should engage without delay.

What has to be taught is not abstruse. While highly scientific farming can furnish employment for the best intelligence, instruction in a few simple subjects will enable the ordinary farmer to double his product. He needs to be taught how to prepare a field properly for the seed; how to select and where to get the seed that will yield the best return; how to cultivate each crop; how to combine stock raising with tillage; and how to rotate his crops and preserve unimpaired the richness of his soil. On his own farm, with the material and the object lesson before him, under instruction that comes with public authority and sanction, he will be a pupil apt to learn. It is on a par with the importance of the public school. We have not yet made a beginning; but every other interest and every other item of proposed legislation might well wait until we do.

National wealth and all the activities concerned in its production and distribution depend, we see, upon the soil. So do the political fortunes of nations. In 1889 seventy years after Great Britain started on her era of expansion, one of the oldest banking houses in Great Britain failed. Who came to her aid? France, after paying a thousand millions war indemnity to Germany, came to the relief of Great Britain; and to-day if any power in Europe thinks of engaging in war, it first sounds carefully the opinion and disposi-

tion of the bankers of France.    Again it is interesting
to refer to a judgment a century and a half old.    In
the paper before referred to, Dr. Johnson makes this
shrewd comparison between France and Spain:

"It is well known to those who have examined the
state of other countries that the vineyards of France
are more than equivalent to the mines (gold and silver)
of America.  .  .  .    The advantage is indeed always
rising on the side of France, who will certainly have
wines when Spain by a thousand natural or accidental
causes may want silver."

Spain is to-day a beggar among the nations.    To
the fruit of the vine France has added a thousand
other products of her fertile fields and gardens; but
still her main reliance is upon agricultural wealth.    It
has made her the great creditor nation of the world.
Comparative history points to agriculture and its
varied fortunes as a powerful producing cause in the
rise and fall of nations.

Professor Ferrero, scanning the history of more
than twenty-five hundred years with the eye of the
philosopher, determined to extract from this vast
store of facts, according to the modern scientific method,
some fixed principle in the affairs of men, announces
this conclusion: "The only durable conquests, even
in ages of barbarism, are conquests made by the
plow."    If this was true of the rude ages when men
lived for the sword, and the tiller of the earth was
either a slave or a still more wretched peasant, it is
far truer to-day when civilization has built her impos-

ing fabric upon the expected bounty of the earth. We must maintain, protect and extend these conquests by which the race has won its way. It is not, as in the old mythology, Atlas whom we see groaning beneath the weight of the world upon his shoulders, but the homelier and humbler figure of the cultivator of the soil. It is for each of us, in every capacity, public and private, to do what in us lies to enlighten, reinvigorate and sustain this common benefactor of our kind.

# CHAPTER III

## FARM METHODS — OLD AND NEW

IT IS in order now to consider more in detail just what constitutes a system of tillage scientific in its methods and satisfactory in its results; to set forth how far and why we have fallen short of attaining it in the past, and what the failures and successes of ourselves and others have to teach us for the future.

We have begun to realize only recently that farming is to a great extent an exact science. The man no longer deserves the name of farmer who conceives of his industry as a scratching of the earth, a hit-or-miss scattering of seed and a harvesting of such yield as soil and weather may permit. That is not farming, but a game of chance. After an army has been raised and before it can enter upon any campaign, the first consideration is to provide its food. If that is a failure, the bravest and best-organized force will melt away in a week. Our national supply of food, in like manner, is fundamental to the organization of our social life and to the progress of all our industries.

It is as well assured as any future event can be that the population of the United States will be 200,000,000 by about the middle of the present century, or in less than fifty years. It may come a few years later or a few years earlier, according to circumstances, for good times lift both the immigration total and the domestic birth rate, while depression decreases both, but this is immaterial. Millions of persons now living will see the 200,000,000 people here; and the first question is, How are they to be fed ? There will be many grave problems accompanying such human growth, but we may for the time being dismiss all the others until we have considered the primary one of the bare maintenance of life. The food problem itself has numerous collateral issues, but for the sake of simplicity we may here consider only the matter of bread. Where and how are we to obtain loaves enough to feed these coming millions ?

The average yearly consumption of wheat per capita varies considerably with seasons and prices, but it rises steadily with our constantly advancing standard of comfort. Of late it has been either slightly under or slightly over seven bushels for bread and seed. Suppose that it is six and one-half bushels per capita, which is certainly within the mark. It will then require, unless we are to fall to a lower scale of living, a total product of 1,300,000,000 bushels of wheat for our bread supply, if we did not export any. From 1880 to 1906 inclusive, our crop averaged 521,738,000 bushels annually. Twice only before 1909 have we exceeded 700,000,000 bushels. It is fair to say that 650,000,000 bushels is our present average capacity. Of course, with an increasing population may come a somewhat increased total production, though it will not advance as rapidly as many suppose. We grew 504,185,470 bushels in 1882, when our population was a little over 52,000,000, and 634,087,000 bushels in 1907, twenty-five years later. The increase in wheat yield during these years, when much of the new land of the West was being brought under cultivation, was a little over 25 per cent., while population increased 33,000,000, or over 63 per cent. Obviously, bread supply and demand will not keep pace through the working of any law of nature.

Moreover, possible increase of wheat production by increasing acreage is limited. We have no longer a great area of free public lands. Some wheat will be grown on reclaimed arid land, though this is mostly devoted to the raising of fruit and fodder plants. Some lands will be drained, and there are a few acres of public land left on which wheat may be raised. But a denser population makes new demands upon the soil; and it is more likely on the whole that wheat acreage will be reduced, to raise all the other food supplies consumed by 200,000,000 people, than that it will be enlarged. Nothing but a material rise in price could accomplish this; and we may, perhaps, assume that a steady and certain price of one dollar or one dollar and a half per bushel would raise, with better work on the farm, our total annual wheat product to 900,000,000 bushels, which would be 50 per cent. more than the present average. This is the extreme limit of probability. The country could do no more, with present methods of culture, unless it took land just as necessary for other purposes and devoted it to wheat raising. We are left, practically, with a shortage of 400,000,000 bushels in our wheat supply, even if we consume every grain we raise. This amount we should have to procure from some other source. Where are we to get it, and how is it to be paid for?

Where in the world is there a surplus of 400,000,000 bushels? We ourselves furnished the great surplus in the past. Canada is now rapidly approaching us, and so is Argentina. But with the present rate of immigration into the Canadian Northwest, and with a rapid increase of population throughout the Dominion, it will not be long before they need 100,000,000 bushels for their own use. They may be able to sell 150,000,000 or even 200,000,000 bushels, and they are close to our markets, but all they could give would not furnish us the 400,000,000 bushels we must have. Manchuria will eventually produce much wheat, but its development will probably no more than supply, if it does not fall below, the increasing demand of China and Japan. Russia and Argentina and Australia together are scarcely keeping up with the world's present necessities. Wheat bread and high civilization go together; and as labour conditions everywhere improve, more and more people who once lived on black bread or rice will want the white loaf. A supply to meet the coming new demand is nowhere in sight.

Because of these facts I have said many times in different articles and addresses for years past that wheat must advance; and that a price of over rather than under one dollar per bushel might be expected hereafter. Market quotations verify the prediction. Without any artificial support, cash wheat in New York reached $1.50 early in June, 1909. The latest statistics completely confirm the view that the condition which the country faces is permanent. Lest the comparison already made, covering two years a quarter of a century apart, should not have selected representative years, take two five-year periods instead. This will give a fair measure of the average producing capacity of our wheat acreage and its insufficiency for growing demands. The average wheat crop of the United States during the five years 1880–84 was 463,973,317. For the five years 1904–08 it was 655,865,795 bushels. The increase is 41 per cent. But the population of the United States was 50,155,783 in 1880, and the official estimate for 1908 is 87,189,392, an increase of 74 per cent. Home demand has grown 80 per cent. faster than supply.

The same rapid transition appears in the records of our exports of breadstuffs. A wheat crop of 700,000,000 bushels is unusual. Allowing six and a half bushels per capita for home consumption and seed, this leaves a surplus of 115,000,000 bushels as a practical maximum. Our average exports of wheat and wheat flour, reckoning four and one-half bushels to the barrel, were 149,572,716 bushels for the five years 1880–84, and 113,146,896 bushels for the years 1905–09. For the former period the average amount retained for home consumption was 301,598,927 bushels; for the years 1904-1908 it was 542,180,037. The decrease in exports for the quarter-century is 24 per cent., and the increase in the amount held for our own needs is 80 per cent. These figures coincide with and confirm one another They lend probability to the suggestion that in another ten years the United States may have become a wheat importing nation.

The price of wheat has responded, naturally and inevitably, to these price-making conditions. As long as we have a large surplus for export, the price will be determined by the figure at which this can be disposed of abroad; will be fixed in the markets of the world by the adjustment of the world's supply and demand. So prices in all the markets of this country in the past have varied with the cable quotations from Liverpool. But the moment our surplus disappears or becomes inconsiderable, our own requirements will have more influence upon prices, which will be made more and more in our own markets. We can see the change toward this, just as we can see the decline of exports and the increase in home consumption. In May, 1909, wheat that had been shipped from Kansas City to Chicago and sold there was re-sold and shipped back to Kansas City at an advanced price. In the same month wheat was taken out of storage in New York City, shipped by steamer to Galveston and sent by rail to supply the immediate needs of mills in the wheat belt.

When the speculative element in recent wheat prices

is allowed for, there remains a considerable margin of permanent advance. The collapse of all artificial support leaves this unchanged. The same economic forces which have been at work for the last twenty-five years are still operative. They confirm the advice given to farmers during that time and throw new light upon markets and prices. The improvement of farm methods will henceforth feel both the goad of our growing necessities and the stimulus of prices kept permanently higher by conditions so inseparably connected with the future growth of the United States that no probable change in world conditions could alter them.

With this strong light of fact upon the subject, if it be granted now that the additional 400,000,000 bushels of wheat which will be required to feed the country a little later on will be supplied from some now undetermined source, wherewith shall the bill be paid? It is not a rash statement that if we have to step into the markets of the world and buy 400,000,000 bushels, we should have to pay $1.50 per bushel and perhaps more. Where is the money to come from? In the year ending June 30, 1908, we exported wheat and wheat flour to the value, in round numbers, of $164,000,000. That will be cut off. So we must find over $700,000,000 in all to pay our bread bill. That is one-third of the value of our entire exports in the year 1908.

We cannot provide for this vast annual payment by increasing exports. Already the products of the soil, the minerals and oils taken from the earth, and such raw materials as leather and lumber, drawn immediately from the earth's products, constitute two-thirds of all our exports. Our whole export of manufactured goods other than products of the farm amounted to $480,000,000 in 1907. For 1909, the value of our total exports classified as foodstuffs, either crude or partly or wholly manufactured, and food animals, amounted to $438,000,000. We imported of the same classifications nearly $329,000,000. The idea that we feed the world is being corrected; and unless we can increase the agricultural population and their product, the question of a source of food supply at home will soon supersede the question of a market abroad. For the most part we are only artificial competitors in the outside markets of the world, and would have to withdraw from the foreign field if we were obliged to depend solely upon our own industrial merits. Our factories could not keep open and pay the current scale of wages if they received for their total product the prices now charged the foreign purchaser. We shall never be able to make a much better showing than we do now in international commerce. We shall be fortunate, rather, if we hold our own. The soil alone renews itself, endures patiently, and is capable of yielding increasing rewards to industry as agriculture conforms more closely to the principles that science and experience have established. The products of the earth and the population of the earth may increase together, if we are wise, so that the one will support the other. And this is the sole escape from the melancholy conclusion to which Malthus was forced long ago because, in his time, the possibilities of modern soil culture were not understood.

But our need is more urgent than has yet been made apparent. I have said that improvement in agriculture could not afford to wait upon the slow work of the agricultural colleges and the rise of a new generation. We must make haste. Let us look a little more in detail at the twenty-five years between 1882 and 1907 and some impressive facts will appear. The net increase in wheat acreage in that time was 8,143,806 acres and in production 129,901,530 bushels. This rise was wholly due to the opening of new Western lands, without which both acreage and production would have declined heavily. The wheat acreage of three rich, representative agricultural states in the older section of the country compares as follows:

| STATES | ACRES IN 1882 | ACRES IN 1907 |
|---|---|---|
| New York . . . . . . | 772,400 | 416,000 |
| Ohio . . . . . . . | 2,876,000 | 1,882,000 |
| Michigan . . . . . . | 1,985,000 | 878,000 |

On the other hand there were enormous additions of the new and fertile land in the West and Southwest. The following table of wheat acreage in more recently occupied territory shows how we have been able to add 130,000,000 bushels to our product, while old

lands were being withdrawn from wheat growing and
the yield per acre of the best lands was falling:

| STATES | ACRES IN 1882 | ACRES IN 1907 |
|---|---|---|
| Minnesota . . . . . . | 2,547,000 | 5,200,000 |
| North and South Dakota . . | 720,000 | 8,413,000 |
| Montana . . . . . . . | 42,812 | 139,000 |
| Washington . . . . . . | 148,000 | 1,349,000 |
| Kansas . . . . . . . | 1,573,000 | 5,959,000 |
| Nebraska . . . . . . | 1,657,000 | 2,535,000 |
| Oklahoma . . . . . . | | 959,000 |
| Total . . . . . . . | 6,687,812 | 24,554,000 |

It is clear that we cannot make up in the future for
either decreasing acreage or declining productivity as
we have in the past. And there will be a big gap to
fill. The total wheat product of the three older states
selected to illustrate our farm tendency — New York,
Ohio and Michigan — was 87,914,200 bushels in 1882
and 50,605,000 bushels in 1907. If we estimate the
future falling off in our wheat supply from similar
causes at half a bushel per acre per annum, and apply
this to an acreage of 45,000,000 it gives an annual
deficit of 22,500,000 bushels. But we are also adding
to our population about 2,000,000 each year by immigration and natural increase, and these must be fed.
At six and a half bushels per capita — the low average
already used — they would consume 13,000,000 bushels.
We must, therefore, provide from some source
for an annual deficit of more than 35,000,000 bushels.

The startling feature of this changed aspect of demand and supply is that it is immediate. We have to provide for a contingency not distant from us by nearly a generation, but already present. The food condition presses upon us now. The shortage has begun. Witness the great fall in wheat exports and the rise of prices. For the first nine months of the fiscal year, ending June 30, 1909, our export of wheat and flour combined was but 103,251,200 bushels. Such is the size of the national surplus in a fair crop year. It must shrink more than 100,000,000 bushels for each three years hereafter. Obviously it is time to quit speculating about what may occur even twenty or thirty years hence, and begin to take thought for the morrow. As far as our food supply is concerned, right now the lean years have begun.

I have stated the national problem in terms of wheat for the sake of clearness; its solution admits of similar statement. The average wheat yield per acre in the United States in 1907 was 14 bushels. The average for the last ten years is 13.88. That is, in 1907 it required 45,211,000 acres to produce the 634,087,000 bushels that we raised. It is a disgraceful record.

About a century ago this was the average production per acre of Great Britain. After the appointment of a Royal Commission and a campaign for better methods of cultivation begun over a hundred years ago, the fields of the United Kingdom to-day, tilled for a thousand years, in a climate whose excessive moisture is unfavourable to the wheat grower, yield over 32 bushels of wheat per acre. Germany, an agricultural country almost from the time of Tacitus, produces 27.6 bushels per acre. Suppose that the United States produced 28 bushels, or double its showing in 1907. That would be nothing extraordinary in view of what European countries have done with inferior soils and less favourable climates. It would have added 634,000,000 bushels to our product in 1908.

Here we perceive an answer to the question that the future asks. Here we see how the 200,000,000 people of about the year 1950 are to be fed. Here we see where the money will come from for our national support. It must be earned by and paid to the farmers of this country. But this implies a kind of agriculture differing greatly from that which now prevails.

The disease of bad farming, from which this country suffers, is a chronic complaint. The following is an extract from a letter written by Washington to Alexander Hamilton:

"It must be obvious to every man, who considers the agriculture of this country (even in the most improved parts of it), and compares the produce of our lands with those of other countries, no way superior to them in natural fertility, how miserably defective we are in the management of them; and that if we do not fall on a better mode of treating them, how ruinous it will prove to the landed interests. Ages will not produce a systematic change without public attention and encouragement; but a few years more of increased sterility will drive the inhabitants of the Atlantic States westwardly for support; whereas if they were taught how to improve the old, instead of going in pursuit of new and productive soils, they would make those acres which now yield them scarcely anything turn out beneficial to themselves."

Washington's foreboding has been justified.

A recent bulletin of the Federal Department of Agriculture says:

"Wheat was produced quite successfully in central New York for something like forty years. During the latter part of that period the yields began to decline, and at the end of another twenty years they were so low that exclusive wheat growing became unprofitable. Ohio, Indiana, Illinois and Iowa have each in turn repeated the history of New York. The soils of these states were productive in the beginning, and it required forty, fifty or sixty years for the single crop system to materially reduce the yields."

Good farms in the Mohawk Valley in New York State forty years ago were worth from $100 to $150 per acre; now many are sold at from $25 to $30. This is not because wheat has become cheap, for it is dear, not entirely because of Western competition, but because there is neither good cultivation nor enough cultivators. The younger generation throngs the cities; and the land, rented by its owners to tenants careless of everything but immediate profits, is abused and robbed of its fertility. In New York State 20,000 farms are for sale. The southern central portion shows a progressive loss of population. Professor Tarr, of Cornell University, in an article pub-

lished during 1909, says: "I have driven much over
the country roads of this section, and have been aston-
ished at the evidence of general decline in the farming
industry, especially in the hilly sections. Abandoned
houses in all stages of decay abound, and in some
cases the forest is encroaching on the pasture." Schuyler
County had 3,815 less population in 1895 than in 1860,
Tioga County 2,000 less and Yates 992 less.

If anybody imagines that this process of exhaustion
and abandonment or transfer to other uses is peculiar to
the East, let him look at Iowa, whose average wheat crop
in the five years 1883–87 was 29,682,560 bushels, and in
the five years 1904–08 was 9,976,488 bushels. In 1908 it
was 8,068,000. The following table of the wheat production of the forty counties of northern Illinois by decades
tells the story more forcibly than words could express it:

| YEAR | BUSHELS |
|------|---------|
| 1870 . . . . . | 10,476,011 |
| 1880 . . . . . | 7,122,963 |
| 1890 . . . . . | 5,073,070 |
| 1900 . . . . . | 637,450 |

Instead of preserving the fertility of their lands, our
farmers have gone in search of new soils to be skinned,
robbed and abandoned as soon as the old showed
signs of exhaustion. Now that they have reached
the jumping-off place, and there is no longer any
"West" to move on to, what have they left behind?

The average yield of wheat in New York State as recently as 1898 was 21.2 bushels per acre; in 1907 it

was 17.3. But for considerable tracts in the state which have been carefully farmed from an early date, the general average would be much lower. In the same short time the average crop in Indiana has fallen from 15.6 bushels per acre to 14.4; in Minnesota from 15.8 to 13; in North Dakota from 14.4 to 10; in Oklahoma from 14.9 to 9; and in the entire United States from 15.3 to 14. We cannot feed our future population with our present methods. We must improve; and years of scientific investigation and practical experience have demonstrated how it may be done.

There is scarcely a limit, at least none has yet been reached by the most intensive cultivation, to the value which an acre of ground may be made to produce. Right methods of farming, without which no agricultural country such as this is can hope to remain prosperous, or even to escape eventual poverty, are not complicated and are within reach of the most modest means. They include a study of soils and seeds, so as to adapt the one to the other; a diversification of industry, including the cultivation of different crops and the raising of live stock; a careful rotation of crops, so that the land will not be worn out by successive years of single cropping; intelligent fertilizing, by this system of rotation, by cultivating leguminous plants and, above all, by the economy and use of every particle of fertilizing material from stock, barns and yards; a careful selection of grain used for seed; and, first of all perhaps in importance, the substitution of the small farm, thoroughly tilled, for the large farm, with its weeds, its neglected corners, its abused soil and its thin product. This will make room for the new population whose added product will help to restore our place as an exporter of foodstuffs. The fruit farmer, the truck farmer, every cultivator of the soil who has specialized his work, has learned the value of these simple principles. The problem is, how to impress it upon the thirty million or more persons who live on the land and till it.

The modern agricultural method is both a money-maker and a labour-saver. The cost of rent and production for continuous wheat cropping averages $7.50 per acre. When, therefore, the farmer obtains, as so many in the Northwest do, a yield of eight or ten bushels per acre, it just about meets, at average farm prices, the cost of production; leaving him either nothing at all for his year's toil, or else a margin of debt.

For the same amount of labour, covering the same time, but intelligently applied to a smaller area, he might easily produce by improved methods twenty bushels to the acre, leaving him a profit of over $12 per acre. The not unreasonable yield of twenty-eight bushels would net him $20, which is 10 per cent. on a valuation of $200 per acre for his land.

This gigantic waste, applying the same measure to the production of the entire country, is going on every year. If it can be stopped, the saving would pay for building a Panama canal every year; it would, in two years, more than pay the estimated expense of improving every available waterway in the United

States; it would save more money for the farmer than the railroads could if they carried all his grain to market free of charge. Let us set these simple principles of the new method out again in order.

*First* — The farmer must cultivate no more land than he can till thoroughly. With less labour he will get more results. Official statistics show that the net profit from one crop of twenty bushels of wheat to the acre is as great as that from two of sixteen, after original cost of production has been paid.

*Second* — There must be rotation of crops. Ten years of single cropping will pretty nearly wear out any but the richest soil. A proper three- or five-year rotation of crops actually enriches the land.

*Third* — There must be soil renovation by fertilizing; and the best fertilizer is that provided by nature herself — barnyard manure.

Every farmer can and should keep some cattle, sheep and hogs on his place. It is not in the nature of things that a man on a wheat farm, working four or four and a half months a year, can make as good a living for himself and family, or that he will be as happy over it as if he worked a reasonable portion of the whole twelve months; as if he fed some cattle; as if all his time were employed. The farmer and his land cannot prosper until stock raising becomes an inseparable part of agriculture The natural increase of animals, the butter and milk, the stock sent to market — all add materially to the income of the farm. Still more important is the fact that of all forage fed to live stock at least one-third in cash value remains on the land in the form of manure that soon restores worn-out soil to fertility and keeps good land from deteriorating. By this system the farm may be made and kept a source of perpetual wealth.

Without difficulty, following approved agricultural methods, the wheat average of the United States can be raised from 13.88 bushels per acre for the ten-year period stated to the 28 bushels produced by the inferior soil of Germany, the 19.8 of France of the 32.2 of the United Kingdom, to say nothing of the immensely greater yields than this of all varieties of farm products in Belgium and the Netherlands, on the Island of Jersey, and wherever intensive farming has been followed. Reports from the experimental farms of the agricultural college in Montana show that crops are obtained by summer fallowing from two to four times as great as by continuous cropping  The value of farm lands will rise in proportion to the increase of the values produced. The total value of farm property with improvements in the United States, given by the census of 1900, shows, when divided by the whole number of acres in farms, an average value of a little over $20 per acre; when divided by the number of improved acres only, the average value is a trifle over $40. It would be a simple matter to raise the market value of farm property the country over to $100 an acre by a system of careful, intelligent, diversified farming.

Other peoples have been quicker to learn this than we.  Denmark has an area of less than 16,000 square miles, a little less than one-fifth that of Minnesota, and a population in 1906 of 2,605,268. Only 80 per cent. of her area is productive, and her population is 167 per square mile. Yet in 1906 she sent abroad over $80,000,000 worth of her home product of provisions and eggs. Great Britain bought from her that year butter to the amount of $48,000,000 and bacon worth over $21,000,000. It is interesting in this connection to note that, though her population is so dense, there were in 1905 but 754 men and 69 women in her penitentiaries.

The Netherlands has a still more closely compacted population of 5,672,237 on an area of 12,648 square miles, or 448 per square mile. The advantage of this is that it forces smaller holdings and a more thorough tillage. The average wheat yield in the Netherlands is 34.18 bushels as against our 14; she produces an average of 53.1 bushels of oats per acre, where we are satisfied with 23.7 bushels in 1907 and an average of less than 30 bushels for the preceding ten years; her farmers gather 232 bushels of potatoes from every acre so planted, while in this country, with soil capable of fabulous yields, we averaged 95.4 bushels in 1907 and a trifle less than 96 bushels for a six-year period ending with 1907. The difference between 95 bushels and 230 bushels at 50 cents a bushel, is $67.50 per acre.

The value of our annual farm product is now over eight billion dollars. It might easily be doubled. When the forests are all cut down and the mines are nothing but empty holes in the ground, the farm lands of the country will remain capable of renewing their bounty forever. But they must have proper treatment. To provide this, as a matter of self-interest and national safety, is the most imperative present duty of our people. Indolence, bad farming methods, greed and the idea that it needs no brains to run a farm have prevented agriculture from taking its true place in the national life and multiplying the value of both the soil and its product. They should not be proof longer against the progress of new ideas. The armed fleets of an enemy approaching our harbours would be no more alarming than the relentless advance of a day when we shall have neither sufficient food nor the means to purchase it for our population. The farmers of the nation must save it in the future, just as they built its greatness in the past.

The man who assumes to be the farmer's friend or hold his interests dear will constitute himself a missionary of the new dispensation. It is an act of patriotic service to the country. It is a contribution to the welfare of all humanity. It will strengthen the pillars of a government that must otherwise be endangered by some popular upheaval when the land can no longer sustain the population that its bosom bears. Here lies the true secret of our anxious interest in agricultural methods; because, in the long run, they mean life or death to future millions; who are no strangers or invaders, but our own children's children, and who will pass judgment upon us according to what we have made of the world in which their lot is to be cast.

# CHAPTER IV

## Reciprocity with Canada

THE development of any people is affected profoundly by the character, resources and disposition of its neighbours. England's insularity struck the note of all her great policies, at home and abroad, for centuries. Both France and Germany have histories vastly different from what they would have been but for propinquity working upon jealousy, rivalry and ill-will. The United States has had from the beginning only two neighbours to consider. Since the episode of Maximilian, our interest in Mexico has been scarcely more than a friendly observation of growth along lines so different, in the main, from our own that the question of conflicting interests could scarcely arise. On the north has arisen a Confederation so closely akin to us in all respects, so remarkable in recent expansion and promise, so well worth taking note of either as a helper or a competitor in American continental development, that the question of our trade relations with Dominion of Canada is one of the most practical issues of the day.

These relations were, in the first period, slight and unfriendly, owing to hostile feelings carried over from our wars with Great Britain, and to disputes over rights in sea fisheries, almost the only point where the two interests touched; in the second period there was a gradual drawing together, due to such uniformity of development, politically and materially, that it was easily expressed in the adoption of trade reciprocity; in the third period there was a growing indifference on our part, in response to Canada's desire for a practical zollverein, our attitude being determined partly by a totally inadequate comprehension of the resources and future of the Dominion and partly by the tightening bonds of a protective system determined upon universal sway; the fourth period, which includes the present, is marked by great progress in our neighbour of the north. What, in the light of business fact and of economic law, should be our trade policy as far as Canada is concerned ? For geographical position makes of that a separate and independent question; and by our answer to it will the fortunes of a continent be in no slight degree determined.

The interests of these two peoples are as similar as the territories which they occupy. Place a pair of dividers with one leg on Chicago and the other at Key West, swing the latter to the northwest, and it will not reach the limit of good agricultural land. Nature knows no artifical boundaries. "Classing the United States and Canada together," says Mr. Edward Atkinson, "occupying nearly the whole continent, it may be observed that the English-speaking people of this vast domain will constitute the only great nation producing a large excess of every kind of food that is essential for the support of life." Here are to be found also the largest known deposits of nearly all the useful metals, much precious ore, the greatest existing body of valuable and accessible timber and other natural resources. No parallel of latitude marks where one form of wealth ends. The great central plain of North America is a physical unit. The characteristic and imposing feature of the interior of this continent is its material integrity. The two countries have identical languages, customs, usages of trade and agencies for development. In all that relates to their progress there is a natural oneness and necessary harmony as obvious as the unbroken extent of land that stretches north to the limit of settlement.

As they began history together, the settlement at Quebec and that at Jamestown being separated by but a single year, so have the struggles of their childhood been mellowed into respect and regard by years and adult understanding. And never, save after the rending of an empire by civil dissension, were there two peoples with distinct and hostile commercial systems yet possessing experience so similar in all that enters into nationhood. In each have been gathered human materials from every race and country, and out of the furnace where the fierce currents of free institutions run to and fro there arises a homogeneous race. Probably 50 per cent. of the population lately pouring into Western Canada, and the bulk of capital newly invested there, have come from the United States.

On this side of the line reside 1,200,000 persons born in Canada. Each people is eager for an opportunity to enter the markets of the other. Despite tariff walls erected by both, traffic between them increases continually. Ontario gets her coal from Pennsylvania, and New England would naturally get hers, if not prohibited by the tariff, from Nova Scotia. Geography, ethnology, commercial interest and all the great, silent forces are drawing us closer all the time.

What has this sturdy young neighbour of the north to put into a partnership? Her area is over 3,700,000 square miles, about the same as our own. She has more than twice the population of the American Colonies at the time of the Revolution. But all instrumentalities of progress are now so great that her development is like that of the United States in the twenty-five years following the close of the Civil War. Her population has doubled in the forty years since confederation. That of the Northwest Provinces has doubled in the last five years. Her timbered area is four times greater than that of the United States. In 1846 she had but sixteen miles of railroad; in 1908 she had 22,966 miles. The capitalization of these lines runs above a billion and a half of dollars. Upon her splendid canal system she has spent upward of $100,000,000. Her local water transportation extends unbroken from the Straits of Belle Isle to Port Arthur and Fort William on Lake Superior, more than 2,200 miles. She may soon construct a ship canal from Georgian Bay, by way of Lake Nipissing, with continuous deep-channel navigation to Montreal, which will reduce the distance 300 miles. It will make Fort William 800 miles nearer Liverpool than New York is. By this route it will cost little more to deliver grain at Montreal or Quebec than it now costs to Buffalo. The total water-borne traffic of the Dominion for 1907 was 20,543,639 tons. Her mercantile marine, nearly equal to that of Japan, is the fourth largest in the world.

Statistics of commerce bear similar witness to progress. Our trade with Canada is exceeded in volume only by that with Germany and Great Britain. In 1907 the aggregate imports and exports of the United States in trade with the Dominion were, in round numbers, $260,000,000. We think it worth while to negotiate reciprocity treaties — which the Senate quietly pigeonholes — with France; but our business with France in the fiscal year 1909 fell short of that with Canada by more than $25,000,000. We are spending some four or five hundred million dollars possibly on the Panama Canal, one object of which is to increase trade with the west coast of South America. Our trade with all the countries on both coasts of South America in 1908 was only a little over $200,000,000. With all Asia we did, jn 1907, but $50,000,000 more than with Canada. The increase of Canada's foreign trade is interesting to this country in more than one relation. First, as has been shown, it makes her one of our best customers. Second, it is a measure of national growth that reminds us of our own earlier experiences. The total imports into the

Dominion in 1897 were valued at $111,294,021 and in 1907 at $345,271,690. Her total exports in the former year were $134,003,123, and in the latter, $226,512,063. This is a growth of 133 per cent. in the ten years. Her total foreign trade in 1909 was over $640,000,000. It is most interesting, in the third place, to note how calmly but irresistibly natural laws and the advantage of favourable markets sweep away the barriers which the petty policies of legislators erect. In spite of hostile tariffs in both countries, directed especially against each other; in spite of the large market offered by Great Britain for the raw products of Canada; in spite of political connection and the offer of preferential advantages to British goods in Canadian markets, Americo-Canadian commercial intercourse has prospered and grows at the expense of other countries.

From 1898 to 1906 Canadian imports from Great Britain increased from $32,043,461 to $69,183,915, or over $37,000,000. During the same time her imports from the United States increased from $74,824,923 to $168,798,376, or $93,973,453, according to her official statistics. In these years the exports of Canadian products to the United States increased over $49,000,000 and those to England less than $34,400,000. In 1895 her dutiable imports from the United States exceeded in value those from the United Kingdom by $2,500,000; in 1909 the difference in our favour was nearly $43,500,000. Her imports of articles on the free list from the United States were nearly $74,500,000 greater than those from the United Kingdom. The value of goods reaching Canada in bond from United States ports in 1906 amounted to $25,936,120, while the merchandise received in transit from Canada in 1908 at the Atlantic seaports of the United States and thence shipped to foreign countries was valued at $25,300,790. These figures are striking. Each country has built up its foreign trade by heroic efforts and continued national encouragement. In each there has been provided an ample system of internal transportation, and each has ocean ports possessing every required advantage for the receipt and shipment of commodities entering into international commerce. Yet, to an extent aggregating an appreciable portion of their entire foreign trade, each finds it convenient to use the ports, the railroad systems and the canals of the other. There can scarcely be a more forcible commentary upon the policy of mutual exclusion.

The development of our neighbour in other respects has kept pace with the increase of her population, her transportation facilities, her agricultural wealth and her trading interest. The capital of her chartered banks is nearly $100,000,000 and their combined assets but little short of a billion dollars. The value of her field crops in 1908 was $432,534,000, and of her mineral products more than $87,000,000. Stimulated by both tariffs and bounties, the output of her factories in 1901 was valued at $481,000,000. By 1906 its estimated value was over $700,000,000. Figures such as these give to the Dominion her just

confidence in the future. She will not go to any partner empty-handed.

That commerce must eventually move unrestrained
between these two peoples is self-evident. Trade will
go her own way, even though she must walk in leg-irons.
Why not strike them off now and let her move freely,
instead of paying the penalties of delay? There is
not one valid argument in favour of the system that
makes our international boundary bristle with custom
houses, and forces every dollar of trade between them
to show its passport and pay its entrance fee. There
is not one sound objection, on the side of either Canada
or the United States, to unrestricted intercourse.
Whatever men may think of the policy of protection
as a general principle, it has no meaning and no excuse
for being as applied by either of these countries against
the other. The assumption of some fixed variation
in the wage level is nonsense. Men are free to come
and go; and New England depends at this moment
for her labour largely upon her French Canadian
population. Wages do vary, just as they vary between
New York and Colorado; but their average under
similar conditions is the same in the two countries.

The true commercial relation between Canada and the
United States is indicated by every fact in their commercial history. It is suggested by that common intellectual
inheritance which has made the most scholarly mind
in Canada, Goldwin Smith, as much at home perhaps
in New York as in Toronto; and impelled one of the
really great historians of our own country, Francis

Parkman, to devote his life and genius to the story of the founding of Canada. It is taught by their parallel development, and by the mingling of their commerce. The most natural, the most rational, the most highly profitable commercial relation between two peoples so situated and so dowered is absolute freedom of trade. The first step toward that must be the establishment of a trade reciprocity in natural products as generous as public opinion will approve.

If either reciprocity or free trade could injure any interest, it must be the manufacturers or the farmers of one country or the other. But not only the logic of the situation but the plain facts of the case prove that no one of these four parties could suffer harm; that all, on the contrary, would benefit by the removal of restrictions that each is at times forced to evade or nullify in its own interest. The manufacturer of Canada, standing behind his bounty and his tariff, has no need to fear the powerful combinations in the United States that require similar entrenchments. Not one of these great concerns controls production in its own country. Right here the small manufacturer competes successfully with his greater rival. Anywhere on American soil the cost of carrying the manufactured article to market is sufficient handicap upon the distant as compared with the home producer. Indeed, the policy now followed by many large American concerns, of throwing their surplus upon the outside market at prices scarcely above the cost of production, a policy that could not be applied to Canada if the two countries were one uniform trade field, is now a greater disadvantage to Canada than her tariff can remedy. Any similar fear on the part of our manufacturing interest is fictitious and assumed. The grown man does not fear the infant's blow.

A few years ago there was not a smelter on Canadian soil west of the Rocky Mountains. To-day there are eight in British Columbia, and these are largely occupied with the reduction of American ores. Our manufacturers have as much reason to dread Canadian competition as Pennsylvania has to cry for protection against North Dakota. Canadian manufacturers would be no more endangered than is Montana by the competition of Ohio. Iowa, first of the states of the Union in the value of agricultural products, has risen to seventeenth place in manufacture, with a gross product of over $164,000,000 in 1900, without a tariff against New England. It is clear enough to people mentally honest with themselves that if there were no duty on any natural product of either country when entering the other, not a wheel would stop, not a man be thrown out of employment in either. But the business of each would feel the stimulus of enlarged markets. It is as certain a case of reciprocal advantage as can be found in the whole history of trade; which rests upon the axiom, sometimes forgotten or purposely ignored, that both parties to an exchange of commodities may be gainers by the transaction.

The agricultural interest in both countries would benefit by freedom of markets. Our cities afford a market for everything that the Canadian farmer can furnish. His breadstuffs, cattle and meat supplies, butter, cheese, eggs and wool would reach new consumers. In 1906 Canada exported to the United States 3,831,988 bushels of wheat, valued at $2,981,608 according to her official statistics. This is an average price of 77 cents per bushel. In the same year the United States exported 34,973,291 bushels of wheat, valued at $28,757,517, or an average price of 82 cents per bushel, according to her official statistics. The average price of No. 2 red winter wheat that year in the New York market was 86½ cents per bushel. This difference is not always the same, nor does it exist at all times; but it is true that the price on the American side is usually from three to five cents greater than on the Canadian. Would this prospective gain to the Canadian farmer involve a corresponding loss to the farmer of the United States? Not at all. The time has now arrived when the home demand for many of the products of the soil is greater than he can supply. Again, taking wheat as an illustration, so great is our need of the grain of Canada that we have been obliged to cut a sluiceway through tariff restrictions and invent a milling-in-bond system, by which wheat may come over the line, be converted into flour and then exported free of duty. Opposition to that arrangement or any attempt to destroy it is an appeal to ignorance. The existing custom is in the interest of the farmers of both countries, just as a still larger measure of liberty would be. It is the surplus of each country's grain, which must be marketed elsewhere, that fixes the price. The same cable that announces a price change to New York carries it to Minneapolis and to Winnipeg, and these markets vary in harmony with the relation of each to the world distribution of grain. As a matter of fact, every bushel of wheat that is converted into flour aids to maintain wheat prices by reducing the "visible supply"; that world accumulation of stocks according to whose volume prices steadily rise or fall. It has been shown in a preceding chapter that our annual consumption of wheat in the near future will be 1,300,000,000 bushels. Whatever part of the deficit thus created Northwestern Canada can supply should be free to flow untaxed to the consumer.

Has Canada anything to fear from the most liberal reciprocity? Her former growth under such a policy, the ability of her manufacturers and their large supplies of raw material, the magnitude of the market expansion assured by an addition of over eighty-seven million customers, all declare that the period of such trade emancipation would be the most splendid in her remarkable history. Has the United States anything to fear from competition on the north? Few men in this country are better qualified to answer this question than Mr. D. M. Parry, formerly President of the American Manufacturers' Association. Mr. Parry says: "The Canadian trade is more important than all the commerce anticipated for the Panama Canal, and yet our tariff policy in respect to Canada could hardly be worse had it been dictated by a foreign enemy. . . . .

As for the tariff on raw materials, why should this country be so anxious to exhaust its mineral wealth and denude its forests that it should bar these products from other countries?" A big lumber manufacturer of Saginaw, Michigan, representative of an industry once most hostile to reciprocity, writes these words in the Annals of the American Academy for the Advancement of Political and Social Science: "As a manufacturer, as an employer of labour, and as one who has been in the lumber business all his life, and is now engaged in it, as an owner of forests and timber lands and sawmills, I cannot see wherein the government of the United States is not making a great mistake in maintaining this tariff upon rough lumber, taxing our home industries for their raw material and offering a premium for the destruction of our present forest area."

After all, the most conclusive argument for reciprocity with Canada always has been and must be the experience of our own states. Had it not been prohibited by the federal constitution, each state of the Union would speedily have levied a duty on all commerce crossing its boundaries. Even with the enlightenment of our own past about us, it is probable that, if this prohibition were removed, not many years would pass without some such restrictive legislation by certain of the states. Yet all acknowledge at this moment that one great factor in the development of the United States has been the commercial elimination of state lines. Unrestricted trade between the states has aided all of them. The force of this argument as applied to distant nations is broken by differences of race, custom, standards of living, wages and other elements in cost of production. But it applies with full force to this contiguous territory north of us, so nearly allied to us in natural conditions, in institutions and in every condition by which material growth is determined. Canada is merely a portion of our own Western country, cut off from us by the accidents of original occupation and subsequent diplomatic agreement. The proof that it would benefit both her and us to draw closer the commercial tie is written in the history of the soil on which we live.

In this country the policy of reciprocity with Canada has won its way to favour over all opposition. New England wants it, the tier of important states facing the Canadian boundary and the Great Lakes favours it, the Middle West believes in and asks for it. It has been too long considered only as a boon for us to grant and Canada to ask. If that was true thirty years ago, it is not true to-day. Canada no longer comes as a suppliant and can never again be so dealt with. Her interest is no greater and no less than ours, her position as independent. Every turn of the tariff screw by the United States merely exasperates Canada, and hardens her determination to achieve industrial independence even if it should have to be purchased at the cost of industrial isolation. Both peoples should put away selfish greed and selfish fear, and join in the creation of a great zone wherein trade as well as men may be free. From this country, as the older, larger and more developed community, and the one whose past attitude has been marked by greater indifference, the invitation should come now for the adoption of a system of reciprocity that means not only international friendliness, solidarity and mutual support, but also large trade expansion and financial gain for both parties concerned.

The tide of time sweeps all nations into a closer concordance, willing or unwilling, of governmental policies. The world grows smaller in the separateness of its people and greater in its possibilities of united action every day. Moving in the sunlight of such an era, the two peoples whom ties of blood and capacity for self-government and material achievement have knit so closely should oppose a nobler manhood and a larger statesmanship to the policy of estrangement and jealousy that has been permitted to guide their fortunes in the past. The beginning of all reform or progress in public policies under a republic is the creation of an intelligent public opinion. Already our own people are ready, many of them eager to be convinced. There is most need of strong and intelligent leadership, to force and keep before the public as a living issue this question of more generous trade relations with Canada, and all that such a measure would mean to us. It would enhance the greatness and the wealth of the United States by the addition, in all but the political relation, to our working body of a population of some seven million people, as industrious, moral and sturdily bent upon progress as any in the world. It would mix to the finest temper and unite in due proportion those elements of world traffic whose fusing and blending are going on before the eyes of this generation. It would read a new moral into the lessons of history by proving the ability of the English-speaking races to combine in essentials, however they might differ in details, for the work in the world that has been allotted to them as their share and the price of their leadership. Nor could it fail to foster, in slower and more permanent ways, the growth of that sentiment of human kinship, moving toward a unity of human effort and aim and sympathy, which seems to be among the ultimate purposes and last events of the life of man upon this earth.